William D. Killen

History of Congregations of the Presbyterian Church in Ireland

and biographical notices of eminent Presbyterian ministers and laymen, with the

signification of names of places

William D. Killen

History of Congregations of the Presbyterian Church in Ireland
and biographical notices of eminent Presbyterian ministers and laymen, with the signification of names of places

ISBN/EAN: 9783337324384

Printed in Europe, USA, Canada, Australia, Japan

Cover: Foto ©ninafisch / pixelio.de

More available books at **www.hansebooks.com**

HISTORY

OF

CONGREGATIONS

OF THE

PRESBYTERIAN CHURCH IN IRELAND

AND

BIOGRAPHICAL NOTICES

OF EMINENT

PRESBYTERIAN MINISTERS AND LAYMEN.

WITH INTRODUCTION AND NOTES
BY THE
REV. W. D. KILLEN, D.D.,
PROFESSOR OF ECCLESIASTICAL HISTORY,
GENERAL ASSEMBLY'S COLLEGE, BELFAST.

ILLUSTRATED WITH PORTRAITS OF
THE REV. HENRY COOKE, D.D., LL.D.; REV. J. S. REID, D.D.;
AND REV. W. D. KILLEN, D.D.

WITH THE SIGNIFICATION OF NAMES OF PLACES.

BELFAST: JAMES CLEELAND.
EDINBURGH: JAMES GEMMELL.
1886.

BELFAST:
PRINTED BY HUGH ADAIR, ARTHUR STREET.

CONTENTS.

INTRODUCTION, ... 1—9

HISTORY OF CONGREGATIONS.

	Page		Page
Aghadowey	11	Ballymena 2nd or High Kirk,	40
Ahoghill 1st ...	12	Ballymena, West Church,	41
Anaghlone 1st ...	13	Ballymena, Wellington St.,	42
Anaghlone 2nd ...	13	Ballymoate, ...	43-247
Anahilt	14	Ballymoney 1st, ...	43
Antrim 1st	15	Ballynahinch 1st, ...	45
Ardglass	18	Ballynahinch—Spa ...	229
Ardstraw 1st ...	19	Ballynure, ...	46
Armagh 1st	20	Ballyrashane 1st, ...	48
Armagh 3rd	22	Ballyroney, ...	49
Armoy	22	Ballyshannon, ...	50
Athlone	23	Ballywalter 1st, ...	50
Aughnacloy	23	Ballywalter 2nd, ...	51
		Ballywillan, ...	52
Badoney	24	Balteagh, ...	53
Bailieborough 1st ...	25	Banagher, ...	53
Ballacolla	26	Banbridge 1st, ...	54
Ballina	245	Bangor 1st, ...	55
Ballinderry	27	Bangor 2nd, ...	56
Ballindreat	28	Ballymacarrett 1st ...	57
Ballinglen	246	Belfast—Donegall Street	57
Ballybay 1st	29	Belfast—Fisherwick Place	58
Ballybay 2nd ...	30	Belfast—Fitzroy Avenue	59
Ballycarry	30	Belfast—May Street ...	60
Ballycastle	32	Belfast—Rosemary Street	61
Ballyclare	32	Belfast—Townsend Street	64
Ballyeaston 1st, ...	33	Belfast—York Street ...	65
Ballygawley, ...	34	Belturbet	66
Ballygowan, ...	35	Benburb	66
Ballygrainey, ...	35	Billy or Bushmills ...	68
Ballyjamesduff, ...	36	Boardmills	69
Ballykelly, ...	37	Boveva	69
Ballylennon, ...	38	Boyle	248
Ballymena 1st, ...	39	Brigh	70

	Page		Page
Broughshane 1st	70	Dervock	111
Buckna	72	Donaghadee 1st	111
Burt	73	Donaghadee 2nd	113
Bushmills or Billy	68	Donagheady 1st	113
		Donagheady 2nd	114
Cairncastle	74	Donegal	114
Carlan	75	Donegall Street	57
Carlingford	76	Donegore 1st	115
Carlow	77	Donoughmore, Co. Down	117
Carndonagh	78	Donoughmore, Co. Donegal	118
Carnmoney	78	Douglass	119
Carntall or Clogher	89	Downpatrick	119
Carrickfergus 1st	80	Drogheda	120
Castlebar,	248	Dromara 1st	121
Castleblayney	84	Dromore 1st	122
Castledawson	85	Dromore West,	250
Castlederg 1st	86	Drum 1st	123
Castlereagh	87	Drumachose	124
Cavan	87	Drumbanagher 1st	125
Cavanaleck	88	Drumbo	126
Clare	89	Drumlough	127
Clogher	249	Drumquin	127
Clogher or Carntall	89	Dublin—Mary's Abbey	128
Clonmel	90	Dublin—Usher's Quay	130
Clontibret 1st	91	Dunboe	132
Clough, Co. Antrim	92	Dundalk	132
Clough, Co. Down	93	Dundonald	134
Clougherney	94	Dundrod	135
Coagh	94	Dunean	135
Coleraine 1st	95	Dunfanaghy	136
Coleraine 2nd	97	Dungannon 1st	137
Comber 1st	97	Dunluce	138
Comber 2nd	99	Dunmurry	139
Conlig	99		
Connor	99	Enniskillen	140
Convoy	102	Ervey	142
Cookstown 1st	103		
Cootehill	104	Fahan	143
Corboy and Tully	104	Fannet	144
Cork—Trinity Church	106	Faughanvale	144
Corlea	106	Fintona	145
Creggan	107	Finvoy	146
Creevelea	249	Fisherwick Place,	58
Croaghmore	108	Fitzroy Avenue,	59
Crumlin	108		
Cullybackey	109	Galway	146
Cumber, Co. Derry	109	Garvagh 1st	147
Cushenduu	110	Glastry	148

vii.

	Page		Page
Glenarm	149	Maghera	188
Glendermot 1st	151	Magherafelt 1st	190
Glendermot 2nd	152	Magherally	191
Glennan	153	Magilligan	192
Glenwherry	154	Maguiresbridge	192
Grange	155	Malin	192
Greyabbey	156	Markethill 1st	193
Groomsport	158	May Street,	60
		Milford	194
High Kirk or 2nd Ballymena	40	Millisle	194
Hillsborough	158	Minterburn	195
Hilltown	159	Moira	196
Hollymount	250	Monaghan 1st	198
Holywood 1st	159	Moneymore 1st	198
		Monreagh,	200
Inch	161	Mountmellick	201
Islandmagee 1st	161	Mountjoy	203
		Mourne	203
Keady 1st	163	Moville	204
Keady 2nd	163	Mullingar	205
Killala,	251	Mary's Abbey	128
Killead	164		
Killeshandra	165	Newport	252
Killeter	166	Newry 1st	206
Killinchy	167	Newtownards 1st	207
Killyleagh 1st	168	Newtownards 2nd	208
Kilmore	169	Newtowncrommelin	209
Kilraughts 1st	170	Newtownhamilton	210
Kilrea 1st	171	Newtownstewart 1st	210
Kingstown	173		
Kirkcubbin	173	Omagh 1st	211
Knowhead	174	Omagh 2nd	211
		Ormond Quay	130
Larne 1st	174	Orritor	212
Letterkenny 1st	176		
Limavady 2nd	176	Pettigo	212
Limerick	177	Portadown 1st	213
Lisburn 1st	178	Portaferry	214
Lislooney	180	Portglenone 1st	217
Lissara	181	Portrush	217
Londonderry 1st	181		
Londonderry 3rd	184	Ramelton 1st	220
Longford	184	Ramoan	221
Loughbrickland	184	Randalstown 1st	221
Loughgall	185	Raphoe 1st	224
Lurgan 1st	186	Rathfriland 1st	225
		Ray 1st	225
Macosquin	187	Richhill	227

	Page		Page
Rosemary Street	61	Tobermore	236
Rutland Square	128	Townsend Street	64
Saintfield 1st	227	Trinity	106
Scriggan	228	Tullamore	237
Sion and Urney	240	Tully and Corboy	104
Sligo	252	Tullylish	239
Spa—Ballynahinch	229	Turlough	253
Stewartstown 1st	230	Urney and Sion	240
St. Johnstone	230	Usher's Quay	130
Stonebridge	231	Wellington Street	42
Strabane 1st	232	Westport	254
Stranorlar 1st	233	West Church	41
Tandragee	234	York Street	65
Templepatrick	235		

BIOGRAPHICAL NOTICES.

	Page
The Fathers of the Irish Presbyterian Church	256
Walter Travers	257
Rev. Samuel Hanna, D.D.	258
Rev. James Seaton Reid, D.D.	260
Rev. James Carlile, D.D.	262
Rev. John Edgar, D.D., L.L.D.	263
Rev. James Morgan, D.D.	264
Rev. Henry Cooke, D.D., LL.D.	266
William Kirk, Esq.	271
John Getty, Esq.	272
James Kennedy, Esq., J.P.	273
William M'Comb, Esq.	274
Rev. William M'Clure,	276
S. Hamilton Rowan, Esq.	276
William Todd, Esq.	278
Miss Hamilton	279
John Sinclair, Esq.	279
Rev. John Thomson	280
Rev. Henry Jackson Dobbin, D.D.	283
John Young, Esq.	284

Signification of Names of Places	288

INTRODUCTION.

THE greater part of the information contained in the work now presented to the public, was collected by the Rev. J. S. Reid, D.D., before his appointment as Professor of Ecclesiastical and Civil History in the University of Glasgow. For the twenty years preceding, his attention had been specially directed to the rise and progress of the Presbyterian Church in Ireland; and he had enjoyed special facilities for becoming acquainted with its condition. He had travelled through most parts of our Northern Province; had gathered up the traditions of the Presbyterian inhabitants; had carefully examined the manuscript records of the Synod of Ulster; and had noted down, in a little volume which he usually carried about with him, every important fact or date which helped to guide him in his investigations. Shortly after his decease, I undertook, at the request of his executors, to complete his unfinished History; and this manuscript book was put into my hands to assist me in the work. I found that it contained a brief account of the congregations of the Synod of Ulster, arranged in alphabetical order; and as, for many reasons, it appeared very undesirable that the rare knowledge it supplied should be lost to the public, I suggested to the proprietor of M'Comb's PRESBYTERIAN ALMANAC that he should permit me to introduce some extracts from it, year after year, into his well-known annual. He adopted the advice; and thus it has been that for upwards of thirty years past these notices have been continued in that publication. They are now collected together; and, with not a few additions, are to be found in the present volume.

To many readers the following pages,—consisting, to a great extent, of dates and names,—may have a rather uninviting aspect; but, to thousands and tens of thousands in this and other lands, they cannot be altogether without interest. The inscription on a tombstone generally furnishes very scanty information relating to the dead; and yet, at the distance of a century or more, it is perused with avidity by heirs or descendants. The departed ministers of the Presbyterian Church in Ireland have multitudes of living representatives scattered all over the world; and, to these, this work will supply some statistical details relating to their ancestors which they must seek for in vain elsewhere. Nor to readers of another class can it be altogether devoid of value. It incidentally throws light on the state of society at different periods during the last two hundred and seventy years; and illustrates in various ways the progress of the country.

The Presbyterian Church in Ireland has had a somewhat strange and eventful history. It was planted in Ulster early in the seventeenth century by immigrants from Scotland, who hoped to have here a greater amount of religious freedom than they were permitted to enjoy at home. For a time their pastors were suffered to exercise their ministry without disturbance; and a signal blessing rested on their labours: but the hand of High Church intolerance was soon put forth to interfere with their operations; they were ejected from the parish churches in which they had heretofore officiated; and were otherwise exposed to grievous persecution. The Black Oath—pledging them to obey all the royal commands—no matter how wicked or unreasonable—was next required from all the Scotch settlers; and when they refused to comply with this unrighteous demand, they were fined and imprisoned. But He who can bring light out of darkness overruled these oppressive measures for their good. The Presbyterian ministers and people, thus driven out of the country, escaped to a large extent the Irish massacre of 1641, in which so many thousands of the Protestant inhabitants perished. A Scottish army soon afterwards arrived in the north to quell the insurrection of the Romanists; and, under its auspices, on the 10th of June, 1642, the first Irish Presbytery was constituted at Carrickfergus. Congregations were established almost immediately afterwards in various parts of Down and Antrim; and, ever since, the Presbyterian Church has maintained a firm footing in the Province of Ulster. The Solemn League and Covenant—adopted in 1643 by the English Parliament and the Assembly of Divines at Westminster—

was entered into with enthusiasm by the Scottish settlers in Ireland; and at the same time a considerable number of the Episcopal clergy in the north joined the Presbyterian standard. Presbyterianism was now rapidly developed in the country; fresh immigrants arrived from Scotland and England; and the Reformed faith spread its influence to the utmost bounds of the Northern Province.

On the accession of Oliver Cromwell to supreme power, the Presbyterian ministers in Ireland were involved in trouble; for they gave deadly offence to the Republicans by protesting against the execution of Charles I., and by refusing to take the Engagement binding them to the support of the new government. When, however, the Protector saw that they were men not disposed to create political disturbance, and bent mainly on the spiritual enlightenment of the people, he changed his policy, and gave them considerable encouragement. Presbyterianism meanwhile made steady progress for several years, so that, at the period of the Restoration, its adherents in Ulster were computed to amount to one hundred thousand. But dark days now awaited it. The ministers were exposed to a fresh proscription when the Protestant bishops, who had meanwhile been in exile, were restored to power.

During the twenty-eight years intervening between the Restoration and the Revolution, the Irish Presbyterian Church was almost uninterruptedly in the furnace. Its ministers were often obliged to preach to their people under cover of the darkness of the night; they were again and again thrown into confinement; they celebrated their ordinations in places of concealment; and, if they ventured to dispense the Lord's Supper, they were liable, on conviction in each case, to a fine of one hundred pounds. Strange as it may appear, they obtained, during this dreary interval, their first grant of *Regium Donum*. It was given in 1672, and amounted only to £600 per annum. It seems to have been due, as much to the fears, as to the gratitude of Charles II. He knew, indeed, that the Presbyterians had contributed efficiently to bring about the Restoration; and he admitted the hardship of their being obliged to suffer, first for him, and then under him; but, had he not dreaded the machinations of the disaffected Cromwellians who were still in Ireland, and had he not expected that the grant would help to keep the Presbyterians from joining with these exasperated enemies, it may be doubted whether he ever would have thought of bestowing on them the Royal Bounty. It was paid very irregularly; and, when his brother, James II., succeeded to the throne, it ceased altogether.

The Revolution of 1688 was like life from the dead to the Irish Presbyterians. They hailed with delight the arrival of their Dutch Deliverer in England; and, mainly through their instrumentality, the city of Derry brought its memorable siege to a triumphant termination. The new monarch was well aware that they were almost the only reliable friends he had in this country; and, a few days before the battle of the Boyne, he testified his appreciation of their support by bestowing on their ministers a grant of £1,200 per annum. But, notwithstanding this token of royal favour, they were still left to struggle under various legal disabilities. The members of the Irish Legislature were, with a very few exceptions, High Churchmen; and even the influence of the King could not induce them to concede to their non-conforming fellow-subjects the indulgence of an Act of Toleration. The war of the Revolution had well-nigh depopulated not a few districts of the country; many farms in Ulster had become vacant; and Scotchmen, tempted by the prospect of cheap rents and a fertile soil, had, in a few years, vastly augmented the Presbyterian population. Prelacy had just at this time been overthrown in North Britain; and its friends began to entertain fears that it was destined to share a similar fate in this country. Hence it was that Presbyterianism was viewed with so much jealousy in high places throughout the whole reign of William III. The Episcopal clergy felt very uncomfortable as they contemplated its progress. As a body they stood low in ministerial character; many of them had continued to pray publicly for the success of James II. until they found that they could no longer with safety proclaim their attachment to his dynasty; they had little of the zeal, and they could not emulate the ability of the ministers of the Presbyterian Church; and they resisted most vehemently every attempt to improve the political position of their dreaded rivals.

When the grave closed on King William, the Irish Presbyterians were made to feel that they had lost a friend. He had been unable to induce the Irish Parliament to relieve them from the pressure of the penal laws; but, when they were harassed for non-conformity, he had kindly interposed, and quashed the prosecution. They experienced very different treatment in the reign of Queen Anne. Their disabilities were then increased; and had it not been for the rather unexpected death of that weak-minded Princess, they would have been deprived of almost the last vestige of religious freedom. The Test Act, passed soon after she ascended the throne, excluded them from all offices of trust and emolument under the Crown, whether civil or military; and by this most nefarious piece of legislation, some of the very men who had so nobly defended Derry were driven out of the corporation of the Maiden City, and marked with a brand of social degradation. Before the close of her reign the doors of some of their meeting-houses were nailed up, and the *Regium Donum* withdrawn. On the accession of George I. the grant was restored; and soon afterwards a considerable addition was made to it. In 1719 they at length obtained an Act of Toleration; but at this time their numbers began to be much thinned by emigration. Many of the leases given, on very moderate terms, about the close of the wars of the Revolution, then expired; and the farmers, discouraged by the demand of doubled or tripled rents, crossed the Atlantic in large numbers, and settled in the Western world. It is said that in 1729 six thousand Irish—almost all of whom were Presbyterians—removed there. Before the middle of the century twelve thousand persons of the same class arrived *annually* on the Western shores. When we consider that this emigration has been going on constantly, and sometimes to a far greater extent, for upwards of one hundred and fifty years, we may well wonder that Irish Presbyterianism holds its present position in the national census. It has been computed that its children now in the great Western Republic amount to about two millions. Had it not been for this prodigious drain of emigration, Presbyterians would at this day constitute an overwhelming majority of our Irish Protestant population.

In the reign of George I. a calamity of a far more serious character sadly weakened the Irish Presbyterian Church. At that time some of its leading ministers began to plead for relief from subscription to its recognised creed—the Westminster Confession of Faith. They did not openly attack its doctrines—though they were suspected of a leaning to a more lax theology—but they maintained that all such formularies were unauthorised as tests of orthodoxy; and they argued with so much plausibility that they secured the adherence of a number of the more influential laity. The controversy, which was carried on for several years with much bitterness, terminated in 1726 in a separation. The majority, forming by far the greater portion of the Synod of Ulster, persisted in requiring subscription to the Westminster Confession from candidates for the ministry; and the minority, who were known as *Non-Subscribers*, formed themselves into what was called the Presbytery of Antrim. This schism greatly impaired the strength and reputation of the whole Presbyterian body. Several members of the Synod of Ulster, who did not join with the Separatists, were understood to sympathise with them; and from this period till the end of the century a section of its ministers, designated the New Light party, and preaching a diluted Arminianism, if not something worse, occupied not a few of its pulpits, and controlled its deliberations. The Synod thus lost much of its prestige as an evangelical denomination.

When the controversy between the Subscribers and Non-Subscribers was agitating the North of Ireland, the Church of Scotland was disturbed by disputes relative to ecclesiastical patronage. In the end the Erskines and a few other ministers withdrew from its pale; and in 1739 formed a new organization, which assumed the name of the Associate Presbytery. The Seceding preachers soon found their way into Ireland; and as the more pious portion of the Presbyterian laity in this country had little confidence in the New Light ministers, these new evangelists were cordially received here, and quickly succeeded in collecting congregations. The first Irish Seceding minister was ordained at Lyle Hill, near Templepatrick, in the County of Antrim, on the 9th of July, 1746. Within fifteen years afterwards no less than three Seceding Presbyteries were constituted in the North of Ireland; and in 1784 their ministers received from Government an endowment of £500 per annum. In the forty-six years, between 1746 and 1792, they erected in the north forty-six congregations and ordained forty-six ministers. In the next seventeen years they increased still more rapidly, for in 1809 their pastors amounted to ninety-one, having been nearly doubled during this short interval.

The last twenty-five years of the eighteenth century witnessed the rapid advance of the Irish Presbyterians in political importance. When the settlers in North America set up the standard of independence, so many troops were sent there that most parts of Ireland were left almost destitute of military protection; and when France declared on the side of the revolted colonies, her ships of war appeared in the British Seas and threatened a descent on the coasts of Ulster. The people in Down, Antrim, and other counties, obliged, in consequence, to take measures for their own defence, formed military organizations in their respective districts, and accustomed themselves to martial exercises. These Volunteers soon combined; appeared together in thousands at reviews; and presented the appearance of a large and well-equipped army. At their great meetings they discussed the politics of the day, passed resolutions, adopted petitions to the legislature, and proclaimed their determination to exert their united strength in struggling for the removal of existing grievances. As the Presbyterians in the north constituted the bulk of the Volunteers, they wielded for the time being a preponderating influence; and Government soon saw the expediency of lending a favourable ear to their representations. Thus it was that several disabilities under which they had long laboured were quickly removed. In 1780 the Test Act was repealed. In 1782 an Act was passed declaring the validity of all marriages celebrated among Presbyterians by ministers of their own denomination; and in the same year another Act permitted Seceders to swear by lifting up the right hand, instead of kissing the book. Other favours soon followed. In 1784 one thousand pounds per annum were added to the *Regium Donum* of the Synod of Ulster; and in 1792 an additional augmentation of £5,000 per annum was granted.

Whilst the ministers and people of the Synod of Ulster were obtaining relief from their political disabilities, they were otherwise exhibiting few indications of improvement. For the twenty years preceding 1789 not one new congregation was erected; and much the same state of things continued for the twenty years following. Little regard was paid to the sanctification of the Lord's Day; intemperance abounded; family worship was neglected; error in various forms raised its head; and infidelity made not a few proselytes. But the awful scenes connected with the rebellion of 1798 helped to awaken a sleeping Church. From that date we may trace the development of a more religious spirit among both ministers and people. Evangelical preachers appeared in greater numbers; decayed meeting-houses began to be repaired or rebuilt; increased attention was given to the education of candidates for the sacred office; and arrangements were made for the more faithful administration of ecclesiastical discipline. At length the New Light party in the Synod found themselves so encircled by a network of regulations for the conservation of orthodoxy, that they saw they must be prepared either to leave the body or to submit to certain extinction. In 1829 they accordingly withdrew from it, constituted themselves into a new society, and adopted the title of *Remonstrants*. Their separation prepared the way for a junction between the Ulster Synod and the Seceders. The union was consummated in 1840, when the ministers and people thus incorporated assumed the designation of "The General Assembly of the Presbyterian Church in Ireland." The Synod of Ulster contributed 292 congregations to the United Church, and the Seceding Synod gave 141—thus making up a total of 433. Since that period the congregations have continued to increase; and at present (1886) they amount to 553.

In the early part of this century a new arrangement was made in reference to the *Regium Donum*. It had before been generally distributed, share and share alike, among the ministers, so that, as their numbers multiplied, the portion of each diminished. With all the augmentations made since the days of William III., the share of each recipient of the Synod of Ulster in 1800 little exceeded £30 per annum. But shortly after the Union between Great Britain and Ireland the grant was increased to considerably above £14,000 per annum, and the ministers were divided into three classes—the first class receiving £100 per annum, the second £75, and the third £50. In 1809 the Seceders also obtained an enlarged grant of Royal Bounty, and the recipients were arranged in three divisions: but they were dealt with according to a lower rate of payment—the first class receiving £70 per annum, the second £50, and the third £40. In 1838 this system of classification was abandoned; and Government agreed, on certain conditions, to grant £75 per annum, late Irish currency, to every minister connected with the Synod of Ulster and the Secession Synod. This endowment added very considerably to the amount paid out of the Imperial Treasury; but it was exceedingly satisfactory to the two Synods, as the unequal payments under the rule of classification had ever since the time of its introduction been the subject of complaint and remonstrance. The money was annually voted by Parliament, and the erection of every new congregation involved an enlargement of the allowance. In 1868, when the grant was about to be discontinued, the portion of it paid to the ministers of the General Assembly had grown to about £37,000 per annum.

In March, 1868, Mr. Gladstone moved, in his place in Parliament, a series of resolutions to the effect that the Irish Protestant Episcopal Establishment should cease—that the endowment of the Roman Catholic College of Maynooth should be discontinued—and that the *Regium Donum* should be withdrawn—full compensation being made for the life interests of the existing beneficiaries. These resolutions were adopted by a large majority of the Commons, and a Bill—known as the Suspensory Bill—was introduced to legalise them; but though the proposal was readily adopted by the Lower House of Legislation, it was negatived by the Lords. A dissolution of Parliament followed. Mr. Gladstone was sustained in the new house by an increased majority of supporters—and in the end the Disestablishment Bill became the law of the land.

The period of Disestablishment was an anxious time with all interested in the prosperity of the Presbyterian Church of Ireland. Some feared that it could not well survive the crisis of the withdrawal of the *Regium Donum*. But its doctrines and polity are very dear to thousands and tens of thousands of those connected with its communion; and it soon appeared that its friends were prepared to meet the emergency. With very few exceptions its ministers commuted their life incomes in the interest of the Church; and in this way a capital fund of upwards of £580,000 was at once created. A Sustentation Fund—now amounting to about £25,000 per annum—was also commenced; and thus, notwithstanding the depression of the mercantile and agricultural interests for some years past, the ministerial income has not suffered. At a great public meeting, held in Linen Hall Street Church, Belfast, on the 29th of September, 1869, John Lytle, Esq., J.P., in the chair, the representatives of the laity pledged themselves to do their utmost to raise a Sustentation Fund of not less than £30,000 per annum, with a view to make up the income of all participators in the Sustentation Fund and their successors to at least £100 per annum independent of congregational payments. The Sustentation Fund has not yet received the support of a considerable section of the Presbyterian laity: and the unfavourable circumstances of farmers and traders have hitherto interfered with the accomplishment of these good intentions; but it is to be hoped that in a short time the sum aimed at by the Belfast meeting will be fully realised.

The manuscript volume—most parts of which have been transferred to the following pages—was left behind him by the writer in a state evidently not designed for publication; and it is quite possible that the critical reader may be able to detect some slight errors in dates or the spelling of names; but Dr. Reid was remarkable for the accuracy with which he noted down all things of historical value; and I believe that if any mistakes have been committed, they will be found to be but few and unimportant. It may be that some of them are to be attributed, rather to the editor, than the author. The ministerial succession in the several congregations are brought down to the present time; and as upwards of thirty years have now passed away since the last entry was made in Dr. Reid's book, I must be held accountable for these recent additions. In all such cases I have taken the dates and names from the Minutes of the General Assembly.

Appended to the history of congregations, it has been thought desirable to supply the readers of this volume with a few brief notices of distinguished ministers and laymen who have adorned the Irish Presbyterian Church during the present century. Some other articles of an historical character have also been subjoined.

W. D. KILLEN.

Yours ever,

W. D. Killen

Professor of Ecclesiastical History,
Assembly's College, Belfast.

HISTORY OF CONGREGATIONS.

AGHADOWEY.

The first minister was the Rev. Thomas Boyd. He was deposed in 1661 for non-conformity, and in 1662 was ordered to be tried by the House of Lords; but, notwithstanding, he still continued to minister to the people. We find him in this charge in 1671-2. He retired to Derry at the period of the troubles, and remained in the city during all the time of the siege. He died in this charge in 1699. He was succeeded by the Rev. James M'Gregor, who was ordained here June 25th, 1701. About 1720, Mr. M'Gregor resigned the charge of the congregation, and went to America. He was succeeded by the Rev. John Elder, who was ordained here by the Presbytery of Coleraine, May 7th, 1723. In 1726, Mr. Elder joined the Non-Subscribing Presbytery of Antrim, and a new erection was in consequence attempted, but without success. Mr. Elder died on the 24th of September, 1779, in the 87th year of his age. He had previously become infirm; and, on his resignation of the congregation, it reverted to the Synod, and the Rev. Samuel Hamilton was ordained here June 8th, 1773. Mr. Hamilton died July 18th, 1788. The next minister was the Rev. Archibald Fullerton, who was ordained on the second Tuesday of December, 1790. He died January 1st, 1813, and left a large family. One of his sons, the late George Fullerton, M.D., rose to distinction in the Australian colonies, and when a Representative Government was granted to Queensland, he was appointed a member of the Legislative Council or Upper Chamber. Shortly before his death—which happened only a few years ago—he gave a donation of £2,000 to Magee College, Derry. His father was succeeded as minister of Aghadoey by the Rev. John Brown, who was ordained on the 11th of December, 1813. In 1820, Mr. Brown appeared before the public as an author. His sermon on "The importance of learning to Society and the Christian Ministry," then issued from the press. In 1832 he was chosen Moderator of the Synod of Ulster, and about that time commenced an agitation for an equalization of the *Regium Donum*, which eventually proved successful. In 1839 he received the degree of D.D. from the University of Edinburgh. Dr. Brown wrote numerous letters in the newspapers, and published several tracts and sermons. In 1844 he was unanimously chosen Moderator of the General Assembly. He was never married, and lived to an advanced age. In 1872 he retired from the active duties of the ministry, and died on the 27th of March, 1873. He was succeeded by Mr. Alexander Wallace, who was ordained to the pastoral charge on the 6th of May, 1873. His ministry was very short, as he died on the 14th of July, 1874. He was succeeded by the Rev. James B. Huston, formerly minister of 1st Randalstown, who was installed here on the 22nd of December, 1874.

AHOGHILL 1st.

The first minister we find here was John Shaw, who was ordained in May, 1658. He was deposed by the bishop in the year 1661, but continued privately to officiate among his people. In February, 1674, Adam Strehorn, commissioner to the presbytery, reported that "though the charge be great and vast, yet the quota to the minister is small, being considerably short of £30 per annum, and that even of it there are arrears due." Mr. Shaw died in 1674-5, and his successor, M. Haltridge, was ordained here on March 8th, 1676. A visitation was held here in 1790, when it appeared "that the arrears due to Mr. Haltridge were £177, that all was desperate but about £12, and that they could only secure £21 for the next year." He continued in this charge till his death, which occurred October 20th, 1705. His successor was Thomas Shaw, ordained here December 20th, 1710. He became a member of the Non-Subscribing Presbytery of Antrim in 1726, in whose communion he died in October, 1731. In 1732 the congregation applied to the Synod of Ulster, stating that they were about 200 families, and wished to be joined to the Presbytery of Route. The request was granted, and supplies were ordered. Their next minister was Mr. John Semple, ordained here June 1st, 1736. The same year the

Synod ordered a collection through all their churches to aid the people of Ahoghill in erecting their meeting-house. In 1749 Mr. Semple was removed to Anahilt, and was succeeded here by Mr. James Ker, formerly minister at Pettigo, who was installed here in the beginning of 1753. He died in this charge September 18th, 1757. The next minister was Mr. James Cuming, ordained here October 14th, 1760. He was grand-uncle to Professor Gibson of Belfast. Becoming infirm, Mr. Joseph Howard was ordained his assistant and successor June 20th, 1808. Mr. Cuming died March 3rd, 1809, leaving a widow, but no family. Mr. Howard died on the 2nd of May, 1810. The next minister was Mr. George M'Clelland, ordained December 24th, 1810. Mr. M'Clelland having retired from the discharge of the active duties of his congregation, Mr. David Adams was ordained his assistant and successor on the 8th of June, 1841. Mr. M'Clelland died on the 15th of February, 1850. Mr. Adams died on the 6th of March, 1880, and was succeeded by Mr. William Colquhoun, who was ordained here on the 18th of January, 1881.

ANAGHLONE 1st.

This congregation was established by the Seceders about the beginning of this century. Its first minister was Mr. David M'Kee. His ministry was of great length, extending to sixty-six years. Mr. M'Kee died on the 12th of January, 1867, and was succeeded by Mr. John Waddell, who was ordained here on the 31st December, 1867. Mr. Waddell, on his removal to Belfast, demitted this charge on the 4th of April, 1876, and was succeeded by Mr. David T. Mackey, who was ordained here on the 24th of October of the same year.

ANAGHLONE 2nd.

In 1819 certain inhabitants of the Parish of Anaghlone, who had hitherto adhered to the congregation of Loughbrickland, applied to the Synod of Ulster to be erected into a separate charge. Leave was granted to them to build a meeting-house, and the Presbytery of Dromore was appointed to supply them with preaching as they should see cause. In 1820 they were erected into a congregation, and their first minister was Mr. Samuel Crawford, who was ordained here on the 21st of June, 1821. He resigned this charge on the

22nd of August, 1822, and removed to a congregation in Leeds, England. After much altercation and frequent appeals to the Synod, Mr. Alexander Orr was ordained here on August 5th, 1824, by a Committee of the Synod of Ulster. In 1827 this congregation was annexed to the Presbytery of Armagh. On the 11th of September, 1838, Mr. Orr resigned the charge of this congregation, and removed to Ballyhemlin, under the care of the Remonstrant Synod. He was succeeded by Mr. William Dobbin, who was ordained here by the Presbytery of Dromore on the 19th of June, 1839.

ANAHILT.

THIS congregation was sometimes called Hillsborough. We find Mr. John M'Broom settled here before the Revolution. He died in 1682, as appears from the tomb-stone still to be seen in Anahilt graveyard. It is there stated that his ministry was of twenty years duration. Some disputes about the boundaries of the congregation and that of Lisburn arose in 1696. In those days people were required to go to the meeting-house of the district, and not to another at a greater distance, even though they greatly preferred the distant minister. In 1697 perambulators were appointed by the Synod of Ulster to settle these disputes between Anahilt and Lisburn about boundaries; but in 1698 we find the people of Blaris supplicating the Synod of Ulster to be rejoined to Lisburn, "finding by experience their annexation to Hillsborough (as it was then called) to be extremely inconvenient." The next minister, after Mr. M'Broom, of whom we have any account in this charge was Mr. James Ramsay, who had previously supplied Maghera, and who appears to have been ordained here shortly after the Revolution. He was present at the Synod in June, 1694. He died February 24th, 1708. The next minister was Mr. Charles Seaton, who was ordained here December 9th, 1708. He died in this charge August 27th, 1737. He was succeeded by Mr. Samuel Simms, who was ordained here June 18th, 1739. He removed to Tullylish in November, 1746, and was succeeded by Mr. John Semple, formerly minister of Ahoghill, who was installed here by the Presbytery of Dromore on the 7th of June, 1749. Mr. Semple took an active part in the controversy with the Seceders, then beginning to establish congregations, and published a pamphlet, which obtained extensive circulation, entitled "The Survey Impartially Examined," in answer to another pamphlet entitled "A Brief Survey." He died in this charge March 24th, 1758. The next minister was Mr. Robert M'Clure, who was ordained here on the 29th of April, 1760. Becoming infirm, Mr. William Wright was ordained his assistant and successor on the 24th of June, 1802. Mr. M'Clure died May 11th, 1823, leaving a family. Mr. Wright, commonly called Dr. Wright, becoming infirm, Mr. Thomas Greer, son of the minister of Dunboe, was ordained assistant and successor on the 17th of January, 1839. Mr. Wright died August 20th, 1844, in the 73rd year of his age.

ANTRIM 1st.

THE first minister here was John Ridge, an Englishman, who had been admitted to the order of deacon on the 8th of March, 1611, by the Bishop of Oxford, and was instituted to the vicarage of Antrim, July 7th, 1619, on the presentation of Arthur Lord Chichester. He was deposed August 12th, 1636, by Leslie, Bishop of Down and Connor, and flying to Scotland, died shortly after at Irvine. In April, 1642, John Livingston spent six weeks at Antrim, entertained by Sir John Clotworthy, and held the communion there. They gave him a call, but he would not accept it. Archibald Ferguson was ordained here by the Presbytery about 1645. In 1646 he was Moderator of the Presbytery of Antrim, and presided at the ordination of Kennedy, at Templepatrick. He was imprisoned by Venables in Carrickfergus in June, 1650, and summoned to Dublin in 1653. He died the following year. He was succeeded by James Cunningham, son of Mr. Cunningham, of Holywood, who died, as his tomb-stone relates, minister of Antrim, October 2nd, 1670. In July, 1671, they called Thomas Gowan, formerly minister of Glasslough, who appears to have been engaged in supplying Connor from 1667. The following reasons were drawn up in April, 1672, in favour of his removal and settlement at Antrim :—1. The parish of Antrim being more considerable than Glasslough. 2. The unhealthfulness of his body in his former place. 3. His usefulness in philosophy, and the accommodation in Antrim for his scholars. 4. The great difficulty of planting Antrim in the person of another with consent of all parties. These reasons prevailed, and his relation to Glasslough was formally loosed in August, 1672. Shortly after we find him complaining to the Presbytery of want of a preaching-house. It may be here noticed that the celebrated John Howe came to Antrim in May, 1671, as chaplain to Lord Massereene, that he assisted the Presbytery, and joined with them in their proceedings, and that he continued here till 1676, when he removed to London. When in Antrim he often preached in the parish church. In February, 1673, Mr. Gowan also had liberty offered him to preach there, through the influence of Lord Massereene, and the propriety of his accepting the offer was discussed at the subsequent meeting in March in these terms:—" A case being propounded by Mr. Thomas Gowan concerning an offer of liberty to him to preach in the church, the question was put whether, if Mr. Gowan should embrace this liberty, so that the people who own him be not ensnared to countenance the liturgy, or to profane the Sabbath by attending at the church door when it is reading, and withal, so that a considerable number of the people do not absent themselves from the public ordinances in the congregation; whether, these cautions being observed, the brethren will take offence at his practice?" It was answered to this query, "That the brethren would not take offence." But in June the people of Muckamore complained of this arrangement, and the Presbytery met at Antrim in July to consider the business more fully, but did not come to any positive decision. They concluded, however, by stating " that, upon the whole matter, if it were not for their great respect for Lord Massereene and his family, they would be clear to advise Mr. Gowan to withdraw altogether from using the church." In consequence of this, Lord Massereene wrote to the Presbytery, in September, that he hoped to get all grievances and difficulties removed. In April, 1674, John White, elder, reports that they pay £40 per annum stipend, and that the cause of the quota being so small was owing to its falling on the town, and little on the country. Mr. Gowan died in August, 1683, leaving a widow. In August, 1684, they called Jo. Abernethy, but he having another call from Moneymore, accepted it in preference to Antrim. In October, 1685, they succeeded in obtaining Mr. John Anderson, who was removed from Glenarm, and who continued with them till April, 1688, when he returned to his former congregation in Scotland—a liberty which he had reserved for himself when he settled at Glenarm and Antrim. In July following they called Mr. William Adair, minister of

Ballyeaston, but, the troubles soon coming on, this intended arrangement was interrupted. In May, 1690, the Presbytery recommended to them Neil Grey, of Clogher, but the congregation did not relish it, because they thought his voice was too low. They then presented their call to Mr. Adair, and the Synod—the first that met in the North after the Revolution—in September, 1690, countenanced them in it, and in November he was removed thither, the congregation promising him £48 per annum. Mr. Adair died February 14th, 1699. This same year they called Mr. James Kirkpatrick, afterwards of Belfast, but he had previously a call from Templepatrick. They at length succeeded in obtaining Mr. John Abernethy, son of Mr. Abernethy, of Coleraine, who was ordained here August 18th, 1703. In 1711 he had a call to Derry, but the Synod would not permit him to remove. In his time the Subscription controversy occurred. Mr. Abernethy was one of the leaders of the Non-subscribers; and, in consequence, a schism took place in his congregation. In 1726 those dissatisfied with his proceedings were erected into a new congregation by the Synod of Ulster. In 1727 the Synod granted them assistance to build their meetinghouse. In 1728 their commissioners, Robert Rainey and David White, acknowledged the assistance they had received from several congregations. In 1729 they called Mr. Hemphill, minister of Castleblayney, but the Synod would not permit him to remove. They then supplicated for supply of probationers, which was granted, the congregation promising thirty shillings each month, with entertainment for man and horse. Their first minister was Mr. William Holmes, a licentiate of the Strabane Presbytery, who was ordained here by the Presbytery of Templepatrick, September 7th, 1730. In 1731 he had a controversy with Mr. Duchal, the minister of the Non-subscribing congregation. He died in this charge May 1st, 1750. He was succeeded by Mr. John Rankin, who was settled here October 16, 1751. Mr. Rankin died in this charge in 1789. He was succeeded by Mr. Alexander Montgomery, ordained here May 31st, 1791. He was suspended by the Presbytery in 1806 for two Lord's days for celebrating marriages irregularly. Becoming infirm, Mr. Robert Magill was ordained his assistant and successor June 20th, 1820. Mr. Montgomery died October 19th, 1820, leaving a widow and family; and Mr. Magill died on the 19th of February, 1839. He was succeeded by Mr. Charles

B

Morrison, who was ordained here March 24th, 1840. Mr. Morrison demitted this charge on the 6th of September, 1859, and was succeeded by Mr. George Magill, minister of Lylehill, who was installed here on the 20th of December, 1859. Mr. Magill, having accepted a call from Cork, resigned the charge of this congregation on the 1st of May, 1867, and was succeeded by Mr. Thomas West, who was ordained here on the 20th of November of the same year.

ARDGLASS.

ARDGLASS, though now but a small place of little consequence, chiefly known in connection with the herring fishery, was, four or five hundred years ago, the second trading town on the eastern coast of Ulster. Carrickfergus then held the first rank. Presbyterianism never seems to have obtained any very broad footing in the neighbourhood of Ardglass. In 1697 the Synod of Ulster ordered that Ballee, Down, and Drumca or Clough, should be formed into two congregations. Ballee is only two or three miles distant from Ardglass; and in August, 1701, William Smith was ordained by the Presbytery of Down as minister of Ballee. He died in this charge in July, 1747. He was succeeded by Mr. Robert Smith, probably his son, who was ordained here by the Presbytery of Killileagh on the 3rd October, 1750. He died June 15th, 1787, having obtained as his assistant and successor Mr. James Patterson, who was ordained here October 28th, 1782. He died in this charge on May 7th, 1798, leaving a widow and family. The next minister was Mr. Josiah Ker, who was ordained here March 18th, 1799. He resigned this charge in August 26, 1809; and was afterwards suspended for immoral conduct. The next minister was Mr. David White, who was ordained here August 27, 1811. The Arian controversy soon afterwards commenced in the Synod of Ulster; and in 1829 the Unitarians withdrew. Mr. White adhered to the separatists; and, in consequence, the orthodox party were left for several years without a ministry. At length, about 1841, chiefly through the exertions of the late Dr. James Seaton Reid, then Professor of Church History for the General Assembly, and the late Captain Rowan, of Downpatrick, a congregation was organised at Ardglass; and, on the 31st of May, 1842, the Rev. Joseph Burns was ordained the pastor. The congregation had then no place of worship, and the ordination took place in one of the outbuildings connected with Ardglass House. Mr. Burns resigned the pastoral charge on the 13th of August, 1844—having accepted a call from the congregation of Whitehaven, England. On the 28th of March, 1845, Mr. Thomas Macafee was ordained to the charge.

ARDSTRAW 1ST.

THE first minister was Mr. William Moorcroft. The second minister of this congregation appears to have been Mr. Adam White. He had been settled in Fannet in 1654, where he was deposed in 1661, and with three others was imprisoned by Leslie, bishop of Raphoe, for six years. He resigned Fannet in 1672, and removed to Ardstraw, which was vacant in 1671—probably after the death of Mr. William Moorcroft, its first minister. In 1688 Mr. White fled to Scotland, whence by letters he demitted the charge to the Presbytery of Lagan in January, 1692, and afterwards settled at Billey, near Dunluce. Their next minister was Samuel Holyday or Haliday. He had been minister of Omagh, and retired to Scotland at the Revolution. On his return, Omagh congregation declared its inability to support him; and, ministers being then scarce, in November, 1692, he had calls from Donagheady, Urney, and Ardstraw. The two former offered £30 per annum, to provide a farm for him, and build the necessary accommodation; Ardstraw offered £27 per annum, with 27 barrels of corn, and to advance half a year's salary to defray his charges in removing his family from Scotland. He accepted Ardstraw, and was installed here in December, 1692. He was the father of Dr. Haliday, minister of the 1st Congregation of Belfast, so famous in connection with the Subscription controversy. He died in February, 1724; but previously, in March, 1718, Mr. Isaac Taylor had been ordained here as his assistant and successor. In May, 1729, Mr. Taylor conformed to the Established Church. In 1731 the people called Mr. John Holmes, of Donegall, but the Synod opposed his removal. The next minister was Mr. Andrew Welsh, ordained here August 22nd, 1733. In 1736 an application was made to Synod by a discontented party for a new settlement, but the Synod refused to interfere. Disputes, however, continued; and the Synod, in 1741, sanctioned a new erection at Clady, and put it under the care of the Presbytery of Letterkenny. Mr. Welsh died May 15th, 1781, leaving a widow and children. In October, 1779, Mr. Robert Clarke was ordained here as assistant and successor to Mr. Welsh. Mr. Clarke becoming infirm, Mr. Matthew Clarke was ordained his assistant and successor September 21st, 1820. Mr. R. Clarke died December 3rd, 1821, leaving neither widow nor family. On the 21st February, 1861, Mr. Leslie A. Lyle was ordained assistant and successor to Mr. M. Clarke. Mr. M. Clarke died on the 28th of December, 1875.

ARMAGH 1ST.

PRESBYTERIANISM was first introduced into Armagh after the great rebellion of 1641. From "Goodall's Memoirs" it appears that Mr. Hope Sherrid, who was minister here in 1661, was deposed with his brethren by Bramhall. Worship was, however, continued in a private manner. We have no account of this congregation till we find Archibald Hamilton, son of James Hamilton, of Ballywalter, loosed from his charge in Benburb, in May, 1673, and thereafter settled in Armagh. At the time of the troubles in 1688, he retired to Scotland, and afterwards in 1692, at his own request, the Synod dissolved his connection with this congregation. He was then settled as minister at Killinchy. In 1694 the people of Armagh applied for Mr. Hutchison, minister of Downpatrick, and soon after, for the return of Mr. Hamilton; but the Synod declined to accede to either of these applications. In 1697 they called Francis Iredell, minister of Donegore, but he declined their offer; and in the end of the same year they obtained John Hutchison, formerly minister of Downpatrick, and son of Alexander Hutchison, minister of Saintfield. The second son of this minister of Armagh was the celebrated Dr. Francis Hutchison, Professor of Moral Philosophy in the University of Glasgow. Mr. Hutchison died on the 10th of February, 1729. In 1731 the congregation applied for the removal of James Bond (ancestor of Captain Bond, of Farra, County Longford), who was then minister of Longford; but the Synod would not sanction this translation. Mr. John Maxwell, son of the minister of Omagh, was ordained here March 15th, 1732. Mr. Maxwell, who had much influence during his time in the Synod of Ulster, died on the

13th of December, 1763. In December, 1764, the famous William Campbell, D.D., was installed his successor. Dr. Campbell had been minister of Antrim where he was ordained in 1759. He was an excellent scholar and a vigorous writer. He attracted much attention by a controversy in which he was engaged with the Bishop of Cloyne. In 1772 it was reported to Synod that Arthur Graham, Esq., had bequeathed £130 for the use of the ministers of Armagh, which sum, with additional subscriptions, was laid out in building a manse on a tenement which had been granted for lives renewable for ever, in December, 1768. In 1730 a large tenement was taken for three lives from Mr. Maxwell, afterwards Lord Farnham, on part of which the meeting-house stood and also the manse; the rest was given up to John Johnston, Esq., for valuable consideration. The manse was built during the ministry of Dr. Campbell. This gentleman removed from Armagh to Clonmel in 1789 and died there November 17th, 1805. His successor in Armagh was Mr. William Henry, formerly minister of Stewartstown, who was installed here July 14th, 1791, but in May, 1795, he was suspended *sine die*. He was succeeded by Mr. Thomas Cuming, father of Dr. Cuming, of Armagh, and uncle of Professor Gibson, of Belfast. Mr. Cuming, who had formerly been minister of 1st Dromore, was installed here January 9th, 1796, and died August 19th, 1816. He was for many years the clerk of the Synod of Ulster, and was brother-in-law of the celebrated Dr. Black, of Derry. The next minister was Samuel Eccles, who was ordained here June 16th, 1817, and who died February 21st, 1823. After a protracted vacancy, Mr. P. S. Henry (son of the minister of Randalstown), was ordained here December 7th, 1826. On the 2nd of February, 1846, Mr. Henry, afterwards D.D., resigned the charge of 1st Armagh, in consequence of his appointment as President of Queen's College, Belfast; and on the 17th of April, 1846, Mr. Alexander Fleming was installed as his successor. On the 17th of November, 1851, Mr. Fleming died; and was succeeded by Mr. John Hall, who was installed on the 30th of January, 1852. On the 17th of August, 1858, Mr. Hall, now D.D., of New York, resigned the pastoral charge, and removed to Dublin; and on the 27th of June, 1859, Mr. Jackson Smyth, now D.D., was installed as his successor.

ARMAGH 3RD.

THIS congregation was erected by the Presbytery of Armagh in connection with the Synod of Ulster in November, 1837. The first minister was Mr. John Richard M'Alister, formerly minister of Ballygrainey, who was installed here on the 13th of June, 1838. Mr. M'Alister died on the 27th of June, 1871, and was succeeded by Mr. T. B. Meharry, formerly minister of Moy. Mr. Meharry was installed as minister of 3rd Armagh on the 9th of October, 1871. On the 2nd of March, 1875, Mr. Meharry resigned the charge of this congregation, having accepted a call from the congregation of Trinity Church, Newcastle-on-Tyne; and on the 30th of June, 1875, Mr. John Elliott, formerly minister of Donoughmore, County Down, was installed as the pastor.

ARMOY.

THIS congregation was erected in 1768 by the Presbytery of Route. The Synod of that year disapproved of the erection, but permitted the Presbytery, if they saw cause, to supply the place till next meeting. In 1769 the people sent John Neal and Hugh Fulton as commissioners to the Synod, and the Synod appointed a committee of its members to meet at Ballywillan and determine the propriety of the erection. The erection was thus sanctioned; and the first minister was Mr. Hugh M'Clelland, who was ordained here June 10th, 1771. He died in this charge in October, 1813, leaving a widow and family. He was succeeded by Mr. Jackson Graham, who was ordained here August 15th, 1814. Becoming infirm, Mr. John M'Dermott was ordained his assistant on the 24th of February, 1869. Mr. Graham died on the 9th of January, 1880. Mr. M'Dermott resigned the pastoral charge on the 7th of October, 1873, on his removal to Strabane; and, on the 22nd of July, 1874, Mr. William J. Thomson was ordained here. On the 15th of October, 1879, Mr. Thomson resigned the charge, having accepted a call from the Free Church congregation of Bridgeton, Glasgow; and, on the 18th of August, 1880, Mr. John Milliken was ordained as minister of this congregation.

ATHLONE.

In 1704 Major Thomas Handock supplicated the Synod of Ulster to send supplies of preaching to Athlone. On this occasion it appeared that it had already been visited by Presbyterian preachers. As an encouragement to a minister to settle among them, the people offered £30 per annum and a farm of twenty-five acres free, and free accommodation to the minister so long as he remained unmarried. They did not, however, succeed in obtaining a minister until 1708, when Mr. Samuel Dunlop was ordained here by the Presbytery of Monaghan on the 29th of April of that year. His support was but scanty, and in 1722 he resigned the charge because of insufficient maintenance. For a long time Athlone remained without any stated Presbyterian ministry; but in 1836 the congregation was revived, and the Rev. E. H. Allen, formerly minister of Hilltown, was installed here on the 29th of March, 1837. Mr. Allen died on the 18th of July, 1849; and on the 25th of March, 1851, the Rev. James Mawhinney was installed as minister here. On his appointment as an army chaplain, Mr. Mawhinney resigned this charge on the 3rd of April, 1861; and was succeeded by the Rev. S. E. Brown, who was installed here on the 18th of June, 1861. Mr. Brown resigned this charge on the 5th of November, 1878, having accepted a call from the congregation of Clough, in the County of Antrim. He was succeeded by Mr. Robert Watson, who was ordained here on the 5th of August, 1879.

AUGHNACLOY.

The first minister was Mr. Baptist Boyd, who was ordained here some time before the year 1697. He died in this charge November 25th, 1749. He was succeeded by Hugh Mulligan, formerly minister of Bailieborough, who was installed here October 13th, 1757. He died January 1st, 1786. The next minister was Mr. James Davison, who was ordained here by the Presbytery of Clogher to the joint charges of Aughnacloy and Ballygawley July 10th, 1787. He was suspended for two months in June and July, 1811, and finally resigned this joint charge on the 19th of August, 1811. He was succeeded by Mr. John Anderson, who was ordained to the same charge

June 23rd, 1812. Mr. Davison died February 3rd, 1813, leaving a widow and family; and Mr. Anderson died May 15th, 1829, leaving a widow. At Mr. Anderson's death, Ballygawley was separated from Aughnacloy, and each became a separate congregation. Mr. John Henderson was then chosen to the pastoral charge of Aughnacloy, and was ordained here on the 8th of October, 1830. On the 11th of May, 1842, Mr. Henderson demitted the care of the congregation, and on the 14th of February, 1843, the Rev. William M'Ilwain was ordained to the pastoral charge.

BADONEY.

THE first notice we have of this congregation is in connection with the ordination of Mr. Alexander M'Cracken, who was set apart to this charge on the 26th of July, 1710. He appears to have been educated at the University of Glasgow, where, as we learn from the college registry, Alexander M'Cracken, *Scoto Hybernus* matriculated on the 27th of February, 1702. Mr. M'Cracken was minister of Badoney upwards of thirty years. He died in September, 1743, and was succeeded by Mr. Hugh M'Cracken, probably his son, who was ordained here June 4th, 1751. He at length demitted this charge, and resided at Carrickfergus, within the bounds of the Presbytery of Templepatrick, where he conducted himself imprudently, and in 1775 he was deposed by the Synod for irregular marriages. In 1768 we find Mr. Joseph Coulter minister of this congregation. Mr. Coulter died in 1789. He was succeeded by Mr. William Dunlop, who was ordained here March 15th, 1790. In 1798 he removed to Strabane, and was succeeded by Mr. Charles Hemphill, who was ordained here February 21st, 1799. Mr. Hemphill becoming infirm, the Rev. Thomas Johnston was ordained as his assistant on the 15th of June, 1843. Mr. Hemphill died on the 13th of January, 1844. Mr. Johnston died on the 1st of September, 1875; and on the 19th of January following, Mr. John Boyd was ordained here. On the 26th of November, 1880, Mr. Boyd resigned the pastoral charge, having accepted a call from the congregation of Portaferry; and on the 31st of May, 1881, Mr. Jackson M'Fadden was installed here.

BAILIEBOROUGH 1st.

THE first minister of this congregation of whom we have any account was Mr. David Simm, who was ordained here by the Presbytery of Monaghan March 25th, 1714. In 1724 he had a call to Carlow, and the Synod of Ulster permitted him to remove. He was succeeded by Mr. Wilson, who was ordained here December 20th, 1726, after which he was joined to the Presbytery of Dublin. In 1732 the people stated to the Synod that they were able to pay him but £12 per annum. He died in this charge November 11th, 1735. He was succeeded by Mr. Hugh Mulligan, who was ordained here July 27th, 1742. He removed to Aughnacloy in October, 1757. The next minister was Mr. Alexander M'Kee, formerly minister of Drum, who removed here May 4th, 1761, and died the 13th of the same month. He was succeeded by Mr. Jo. Mathewson, who was ordained here by the Presbytery of Cootehill February 10th, 1762. He resigned this charge October 3rd, 1780. He was succeeded by Mr. Robert Montgomery, who was ordained here by the Presbytery of Monaghan June 5th, 1781. He died January 1st, 1803, leaving a widow and family. The next minister was Mr. John Kelso, who was ordained here February 7th, 1804. He died March 23rd, 1810, leaving neither widow nor family, and was succeeded by Mr. Patrick White, who was ordained here August 28th, 1810. In 1819 the minister, session, and congregation applied to the Synod of Ulster for their support in defending their title to a farm set apart for the benefit of the pastor, upwards of one hundred years before, by the proprietor, Mr. Hamilton, of Bailieborough. The Synod agreed, and the suit was gained. The farm thus secured is, perhaps, the most valuable glebe belonging to any congregation connected with the Presbyterian Church in Ireland; and Mr. White gained great credit for the integrity and zeal with which he contended for the conservation of the property. Mr. White died on the 17th of January, 1862, and on the 13th of March following, his son, the Rev. Patrick White, who had been minister of Donoughmore, was invested with the pastoral charge. On the 7th of October, 1873, Mr. Patrick White, having received a call from a congregation in Liverpool, resigned this charge; and Mr. Thomas R. White was installed as pastor.

BALLACOLLA.

AFTER the famine of 1847-50, a few Scotchmen took farms from Lord De Vesci near Abbeyleix, and Lord Castletown near Rathdowney. These families were occasionally visited by Rev. H. M'Manus, of Mountmellick, but no attempt was made to organize a congregation for some time. A lady has the credit of doing that. The young wife of Mr. Jonathan Millie, Abbeyleix, a Scotchwoman, feeling the want of the simple form of Presbyterian worship, to which she had always been accustomed, and seeing if the two little colonies of Presbyterians, only a few miles separated, could be united by meeting to worship at a central point, there was the nucleus of a substantial congregation. She visited each, and obtained their adherence to her plan. She and her husband afterwards waited on the late James Gibson, Q.C., the chairman of Queen's County, when on his Sessions Circuit, who entered heartily into the plan, and by his wise counsel the matter was brought to a successful issue. Messrs. Millie and Purves attended the next meeting of Dublin Presbytery with a memorial for organization. The Presbytery, after due inquiry, granted the request, and formed them into a congregation on 7th April, 1858. The courthouse of Ballacolla was applied for and granted to hold public worship on every Sabbath until a church would be erected; and supplies were sent. No Presbyterian family resided at the small village of Ballacolla, but it was a central point for the members to meet. Three acres of land at a nominal rent, with lease for 999 years, was obtained close to the village from Richard Caldbeck, Esq., J.P. A substantial church was erected, and opened, free of debt, by Rev. H. Cooke, D.D., LL.D., Belfast, on 22nd March, 1860, and the week after, on 27th March, Mr. Alexander Milligan, a licentiate of Newry Presbytery, was ordained the first minister of this charge, Rev. J. Elliott, of Armagh, taking part. The Rev. John Hall, D.D., then of Dublin, gave the charge on the interesting occasion. It was upwards of two years after this when the manse was built and ready for the minister to occupy. It was gratifying to all that when finished both church and manse were free of debt, showing the liberality with which the people contributed; they were aided also by a grant from the Church and Manse Fund. The strong Presbyterianism of Mrs. Millie was shown in the blue cloth, with blue trimmings, she put on the pulpit. A member of the Purves family presented a superbly-bound pulpit bible and psalm book. As all the members of Ballacolla congregation live at a distance from the church, and ride or drive to worship, they were greatly inconvenienced for accommodation for their horses in the village till Mr. George Purves, the secretary, aided by other members of the congregation, built stables sufficient for them all, and handed over the building, a free gift, to the congregation. A call from the congregation of Corlea, Bailieborough, came to Mr. Milligan, which he accepted, and resigned the pastorate of Ballacolla on 7th March, 1882. The congregation next called Mr. Alexander Mogee, a licentiate of Route Presbytery, who was ordained here on 7th August, 1882.

BALLINDERRY.

The first settlement in this neighbourhood was at Glenavy. In February, 1672, the Presbytery of Antrim, considering the need the people had of preaching, sent one of their number to examine what encouragement there was for the settlement of a minister. In April of that year, Robert Scott and John Johnson appeared as commissioners at the Presbytery, and they were recommended to make arrangements for building a meeting-house and manse. In August the people obtained a hearing of Mr. Archibald Young, a probationer; and they presented him with a call in the September following, promising to give him £30 per annum, and to provide him with a house and garden. He proceeded with his second trials; but, in May, 1673, he had a call to Downpatrick, which the Presbytery permitted him to accept, and he removed there in June. In September of the same year the people presented a call to Mr. Matthew Haltridge, which he accepted; and, in February, 1674, their commissioner, John Ferguson, promised for his support £25 per annum, with a sufficiency of turf and a manse. With the exception of a visit to Cork in June and July, he continued to supply the congregation till December, when, the people having failed in their promises to him, the Presbytery freed him from the charge of this place. He was afterwards settled at Ahoghill; and Glenavy was thus again left vacant. In January, 1683, we find Mr. David Airth settled in this parish, having been ordained here some time in the interval between 1675 and that date. His support being small and badly paid, he is declared transportable in August, 1685; and, in June, 1694, he removed to a charge in Scotland. The congregation was now long vacant. The next minister, Mr. John Riddel, was ordained by the Presbytery of Belfast on the 12th of March, 1701. In 1712 he was prosecuted as a non-juror. In 1713 the congregation of Ballinderry, as it at present exists, was formed—part from Glenavy and some from Moira—whilst the greater part of Glenavy was incorporated into a later erection at Crumlin. The commissioners from Ballinderry to the Synod were Arthur Maxwell, Esq., a great benefactor of the Irish Presbyterian Church; Dr. Ferguson, and Thomas Beatty. Their first minister, after their separation, was Mr. John Hasty, who was ordained here June 11th, 1724. He died in this charge on the 6th of April, 1743. Their next minister was Mr. Clotworthy Dobbin, ordained here February 5th, 1746, but in the following year he was removed to Ballynure. He was succeeded by Mr. William Rowan, who was ordained here by the Presbytery of Bangor on the 30th of October, 1751. In 1783 he demitted his charge, and was succeeded by Mr. Robert Carlisle, who was ordained by the Presbytery of Belfast in September, 1784. In May, 1794, on account of indisposition, the Presbytery disannexed him from this charge, and Mr. William Whitlaw was ordained his successor on the first Tuesday of August, 1794. Mr. Whitlaw becoming infirm, Mr. John Shaw was ordained his assistant and successor on the 6th of February, 1826. Mr. Shaw resigned his charge here in 1831, and removed to Ballynahinch. The next assistant to Mr. Whitlaw was Mr. Henry Leebody, who was ordained here by the Presbytery of Belfast on the 17th of April, 1833. Mr. Whitlaw died January 11th, 1836. Mr. Leebody having become infirm, Mr. James Meeke was ordained his assistant and successor on the 24th of May, 1877. Mr. Leebody died in May, 1879.

BALLINDREAT.

THIS congregation was formerly known by the name of Lifford. Its first minister appears to have been Mr. William Traill. He came from Scotland as a probationer in 1671, and was secretly ordained here the next year. Being much persecuted, he fled to Scotland about 1682. His successor was Mr. John Rowat. Mr. Rowat was in Derry during the memorable siege. He died January 4th, 1694. He was succeeded by Mr. James Pringle, who was ordained here on the 27th November, 1695. He demitted this charge in July, 1699, and removed to Moywater (now Killala), in Mayo. The next minister was Mr. John Ball, who was ordained here September 25th, 1706. He died in this charge August 22nd, 1739. The next minister was Mr. John Marshall, who was ordained here by the Presbytery of Letterkenny, July 27th, 1743. He died in this charge in the first week of May, 1795, leaving a family. After much disputing, the people obtained for their minister, Mr. James Houston, who was ordained here on the 10th of July, 1799. About this time a species of theological institute had been established at Strabane, conducted by the Rev. William Crawford, D.D., the minister of that place, and Mr. Houston was one of the students educated in that seminary. Becoming infirm, Mr. William M'Crea was ordained as assistant and successor to Mr. Houston by the Presbytery of Raphoe, on the 20th of June, 1838. Mr. Houston died November 27th, 1839. On the 31st of January, 1871, Mr. M'Crea was suspended from the office of the ministry; and on the 18th of December, 1872, Mr. James M'Farland Guy was ordained to the pastoral charge of this congregation.

BALLYBAY 1st.

The first minister of this congregation of whom we have any account was Mr. Humphrey Thompson, who seems to have been ordained here about 1698. He died in this charge April 7th, 1744. The next minister was Mr. Alexander Wadsworth, who was ordained as assistant and successor to Mr. Thompson January 19th, 1744. Mr. Wadsworth died, after a short ministry, on the 31st of March, 1747, and was succeeded by Mr. James Jackson, who was ordained February 21st, 1750. He demitted the charge through bodily indisposition in May, 1781, and died in September, 1792, leaving a widow and family. He was succeeded by Mr. John Arnold, who was ordained here December 18th, 1782. Mr. Arnold removed to America in 1797. After great disputes, Mr. James Morell was ordained here August 6th, 1799. He died in this charge on the 31st of August, 1831, leaving a widow and family. Of his sons, two are now ministers of the Assembly, the Rev. John Morell of Second Ballybay and the Rev. Charles L. Morell (now D.D.) of Dungannon, one of the ex-Moderators of the Assembly. After the death of Mr. James Morell, the congregation divided into two parts. Over First Ballybay, Mr. William Gibson (afterwards D.D. and Professor of Christian Ethics in the Assembly's College, Belfast), was ordained on the 1st of January, 1834. On the 29th of October, 1840, he resigned the charge, having received a call to Rosemary Street Congregation, Belfast. He was succeeded in Ballybay by Mr. Joseph Crawford, who was ordained here on the 23rd of August, 1842. Mr. Crawford resigned the charge on the 5th November, 1844, and was succeeded by Mr. John Moran, who was ordained on the 24th of March, 1846, and who, on the 27th of the following October, resigned the charge, having received a call from 1st Newry. He was succeeded by Mr. John Gordon Smith, who was ordained here on the 28th of September, 1847.

BALLYBAY 2ND.

This congregation was established upwards of forty years ago. After the death of Mr. James Morell, who died, minister of Ballybay, on the 31st of August, 1831, a division took place among the people. A new place of worship was erected near the town of Ballybay, and Mr. John Harris Morell, son of the former minister, was ordained to the pastoral charge of 2nd Ballybay on the 2nd of January, 1834. Mr. Morell has obtained leave to resign.

BALLYCARRY.

This congregation was formerly better known by the name of Broadisland. It is confessedly one of the oldest, perhaps the very oldest, of the Irish Presbyterian congregations. Its first minister, Mr. Edward Brice, had been minister of Drymen, in Stirlingshire, whence he was obliged to fly to Ireland to escape the severities of Spotswood, a Scotch prelate, notorious as a persecutor. Mr. Brice settled in Broadisland about 1611, under the sanction of his countryman Echlin, Bishop of Down and Connor. He preached in the parish church, and enjoyed the tithes, though he came under no engagement to use the Liturgy or conform to the discipline of the Episcopal Church. In 1634 the Calvinistic Confession, adopted in 1615 by the Reformed Church of Ireland, was set aside, and a series of canons requiring strict conformity was adopted. Mr. Brice was some time afterwards assailed for non-conformity, and a sentence of deposition was pronounced on him, but he died before the sentence could be carried into effect. All Presbyterian ministers were now driven out of the country, and multitudes of the laity fled to Scotland to escape the imposition of the Black Oath. But they were thus providentially taken away from the evil to come; for whilst a considerable number of the Episcopal clergy perished in the Irish massacre of 1641, not a single Presbyterian minister suffered any injury, for they had all before been obliged to take refuge in Scotland. In 1645 Mr. Robert Cunningham, son of Mr. Cunningham, of Holywood, was ordained in Ballycarry. In June, 1673, a complaint was made to the Presbytery that the people were paying no rent for the building which they used as a place of worship, whereupon they agreed to pay the arrears demanded, and to commence the erection of a meeting-house for themselves. In April, 1674, the state of their congregational accounts was reported to the Presbytery, from which it appeared that they had been making very little provision for the support of the minister. About that time the first grant of *Regium Donum* was made to the Irish Presbyterian ministers, and, probably, many of the people imagined that they did not require to supplement it. At the same meeting Matthew Logan and George Straight appeared as commissioners from the congregation, and informed the Presbytery that "they were laying down a way for securing their minister £30 per annum for the future." In May, 1688, Mr. Haltridge, of Islandmagee, was appointed to inquire into the state of Mr. Cunningham's maintenance; and in June it is reported that the "Laird of Duntreath" wrote to Mr. Henry, of Carrickfergus, showing "that the people are now very poor; but that, if trading come in, he will be as active as may be in stirring up the people; and, as for himself, he promises to do what he did for Mr. Pitcairn in Ballymena." Mr. Cunningham continued in this charge till his death in 1698. Mr. James Cobham was the next minister. He was ordained here about 1700. He died in this charge February 23rd, 1759. He was succeeded by Mr. John Bankhead, who was ordained here August 16th, 1763. Becoming infirm, Mr. William Glendy was ordained as his assistant and successor on the 30th July, 1812. In 1829 Mr. Glendy, who avowed himself an Arian, seceded from the Synod of Ulster, with a portion of the congregation. The people adhering to the Synod gave a call to Mr. John Stuart, who was ordained to this charge by the Presbytery of Templepatrick on the 3rd of April, 1832. Mr. Bankhead—who was the father of Dr. Bankhead, the celebrated physician, in whose arms the famous Lord Londonderry expired—died July 5th, 1833, after having been in this charge seventy years all but forty-two days. Mr. Stuart died on the 6th of February, 1880; and was succeeded by Mr. John Dickson, who was ordained here on the 27th of July, 1880.

BALLYCASTLE.

THE Presbyterians of the town of Ballycastle, in the County of Antrim, formerly worshipped at Ramoan. They were at length erected into a separate congregation by the Presbytery of Route in the beginning of the year 1827. Their first minister was Mr. Samuel Lyle, who was ordained here on the 4th of March, 1829. At the meeting of Assembly in 1866, Mr. Lyle obtained leave for the congregation to choose an assistant and successor, and on the 19th of June, 1867, Mr. George M'Farland was ordained there by the Presbytery of Route. Mr. Lyle died on the 26th of August, 1868. Mr. M'Farland, on his appointment as Mission Secretary to the General Assembly, in June, 1882, resigned the pastoral charge, and was succeeded by Mr. John Jackson, formerly minister of Cloughwater, who was installed here on the 26th of October of the same year.

BALLYCLARE.

THE first minister of this congregation of whom we have any account was Mr. Gilbert Simpson, who was ordained here August 9th, 1655. He was here in 1662. The next minister was Mr. Robert Patton. He was here in 1671, and probably for a considerable time before. We find him going on a visit to Scotland, with the leave of the Presbytery, in July, 1674, and returning in the November following. In June, 1675, John M'Cully and John Wilson appeared as commissioners at the Presbytery, "acknowledging great deficiency in the paying of their minister; and proposing that if the meeting would condescend to remove the able unwilling party of the parish from any particular inspection of their minister, their able willing party would augment their several proportions, and endeavour to maintain him." The Presbytery, however, would not agree to the proposal. Mr. Patton, in conjunction with Mr. Gowan, of Antrim, was sent to Dublin in 1679 to satisfy Government that the Presbyterians in the North did not approve of the proceedings of the Scotch Covenanters, then just defeated at Bothwell Bridge. But, about this time, the famous Willie Gilliland, who was at the battle of Bothwell Bridge, had taken refuge in Glenwherry, and was hunted from place to place by the troopers stationed at Carrickfergus. Mr. Patton died shortly after his return from Dublin. His successor was Thomas Tuft, who was ordained here on December 7th, 1681. He died in December, 1713. He had previously become infirm; and Mr. Thomas Wilson, a licentiate of the Presbytery of Kircaldy, was ordained here as his assistant and successor on the 27th of February, 1711. In 1725 Mr. Wilson joined the Presbytery of Antrim. He was degraded in 1757. Among his successors, who were connected with the Presbytery of Antrim, were Mr. Futt Marshall, who was ordained in 1785, and who died in 1813. He was succeeded by Mr. Heron, who was ordained here on the 21st December, 1813. The next minister was Mr. John Hall, who was ordained here on the 5th September, 1839. Meanwhile, a number of people in the place still adhered to Orthodoxy. In February, 1856, a memorial from certain inhabitants of Ballyclare and its vicinity, praying to be erected into a congregation, was presented to the Presbytery of Carrickfergus; and the General Assembly of the same year granted this request. On the 5th of March, 1857, Mr. Robert M'Cully was ordained to the pastoral charge. On the 2nd of May, 1865, Mr. M'Cully resigned, on his designation as a missionary to Australia; and on the 8th March, 1866, Mr. Ebenezer M. Legate was ordained as minister.

BALLYEASTON 1st.

THIS congregation at first formed a part of Ballyclare. In August, 1672, the people of Glenwherry applied for privileges to the Presbytery, and they were then advised to join themselves to some neighbouring congregation. In the following month they annexed themselves to Ballyclare, and Mr. Paton, the minister of that place, took charge of them.

c

In the interval between 1676 and 1681, Ballyeaston was erected into a separate congregation, and the first stated minister was Mr. William Adair, son of Patrick Adair of Belfast. Mr. Adair was ordained here December 7th, 1681. In November, 1690, the Synod removed him to Antrim. The next minister was Stafford Pettigrew, who was ordained January 11th, 1699. Shortly after his ordination he was tried for a violation of the Seventh Commandment, but unanimously acquitted. He died March 28th, 1718, aged forty-four years. The next minister was Timothy White, who was ordained here by the Presbytery of Antrim August 8th, 1723. In 1749 he was removed to Loughbrickland. The next minister was William Montgomery, ordained here July 27th, 1758. His settlement was preceded by much disputing, but he was an eminently peaceful and worthy minister. He died April 24th, 1809, aged seventy-nine years, leaving a widow and family. On his demise, there was again much disputing with respect to a successor, and at length Mr. S. H. Elder, son of the Rev. James Elder, of Finvoy, was ordained June 22nd, 1813. Mr. Elder died February 21st, 1821. The next minister was William J. Raphael, ordained here September 25th, 1821. Mr. Raphael died on the 5th of August, 1865, and was succeeded by Mr. William Young, who was ordained here on the 30th of March, 1866. On receiving a call from Manchester, Mr. Young resigned this charge on the 29th of May, 1877; and was succeeded by Mr. William John M'Cracken, who was installed here on the 17th of April, 1878.

BALLYGAWLEY.

In 1829 this congregation was divided from Aughnacloy, with which it had been formerly connected as a joint charge. The first minister was Mr. David Cochrane, who was ordained by the Presbytery of Clogher on the 30th of November, 1830. On the 15th of May, 1837, he was suspended for intemperance. Soon afterwards, that is, on the 1st of August, 1837, he resigned all connection with the congregation and presbytery. He was succeeded by the Rev. W. Freeland, formerly minister of Kingstown, who was installed here on the 16th of April, 1838. Dr. Freeland resigned the charge of this congregation on the 8th of July, 1841; and on the 18th of October, 1842, Mr. John Steel Dickson was ordained to the pastoral charge.

Mr. Dickson resigned this charge on the 1st of March, 1844, on his removal to Ballysillan; and on the 24th of September, 1844, Mr. William Ferguson was ordained to it. Mr. Ferguson died on the 9th of December, 1859; and on the 27th of March, 1860, Mr. John M'Bride was ordained as minister of this congregation. Mr. M'Bride's health soon gave way; and in July, 1862, the Assembly granted leave to his congregation to choose an assistant and successor. Mr. M'Bride died on the 23rd of June, 1863; and on the 26th of January, 1864, Mr. William Ross Hamilton was ordained to this charge. Dr. Hamilton resigned the charge of the congregation on the 18th of March, 1872, on his removal to Galway; and on the 28th of May of the same year the Rev. David Gordon Smyth was installed minister here.

BALLYGOWAN.

This congregation was erected by the Presbytery of Belfast in 1837. Its first minister was Mr. John Gamble, who was ordained here on the 23rd of August, 1838. Mr. Gamble died on the 8th of January, 1854, and was succeeded by Mr. Thomas Shaw Woods, who was ordained here on the 28th of September of the same year.

BALLYGRAINEY.

This congregation was erected by the Presbytery of Bangor in 1837. Its first minister was Mr. J. R. M'Alister, who was ordained here on the 20th of February, 1838. He resigned this charge on the 20th of May, 1838, and removed to Armagh. He was succeeded by Mr. Samuel Blair, who was ordained here on the 29th of November of the same year. On the 31st of December, 1844, Mr. Blair resigned the charge, having accepted a call from the congregation of Sorbie in the Free Church of Scotland; and was succeeded by Mr. Samuel Megaw, who was ordained here on the 19th of August, 1845. On the 2nd of April, 1861, Mr. Megaw was degraded for immorality; and was succeeded by Mr. William Clarke, who was ordained here on the 3rd of September, 1861. On the 29th of June, 1876, Mr. Clarke resigned this charge, having accepted a call from the congregation of Burt; and was succeeded by Mr. S. W. Morrison, who was ordained here on the 28th of March, 1877.

BALLYJAMESDUFF.

It is believed that Mr. Nathaniel Glasgow, who had been ordained to go to America in 1719, was installed here by the Presbytery of Monaghan on the 3rd February, 1721. He resigned his congregation and removed to Fintona in 1732. The place of worship is said to have been originally at Oldcastle, where Mr. James Hamilton was installed by the Presbytery of Monaghan on the 15th of May, 1733. He had previously been minister of Killyshandra. He died here in August, 1756. In 1757 Lord Farnham wrote to the Synod on behalf of the congregation.* Some time afterwards Mr. William Sprot was installed here. The installation took place on the 16th of May, 1759. He died on the 20th of April, 1789, leaving a widow and family. The next minister was Mr. Samuel Kennedy, who was ordained here by the Presbytery of Monaghan on the 4th of March, 1790. Becoming infirm, Mr. John King was ordained as his assistant and successor on the 3rd of May, 1826. In 1833 Mr. King resigned this charge, and removed to the newly-erected congregation of Bellasis. He was succeeded by Mr. Hutchinson Perry, who was ordained here as assistant and successor to Mr. Kennedy on the 8th of October, 1834. On the 6th of November, 1836, Mr. Perry resigned this charge and removed to Raws, near Castlefin. He was succeeded by Mr. Hugh Robert Gilchrist, who was ordained here on the 17th of May, 1837. In June, 1837, Mr. Gilchrist resigned the charge, and emigrated to Australia. He was succeeded by Mr. Hugh Pollock, who was ordained here on the 6th of December, 1837. In the month of December, 1838, he was suspended by the Presbytery of Cavan; and by the Synod of Ulster in 1839 he was disannexed from the congregation. He afterwards went to America. The next minister was Mr. William Hamilton, formerly of Killeter, who was installed here on the 24th of December, 1839. He resigned the charge on the 6th of April, 1840, and removed to Edenderry. He was succeeded by Mr. John Ritchie, who was ordained here on the 30th of September, 1840, as the *sixth* assistant and successor to Mr. Kennedy. Mr. Kennedy died on the 12th of June, 1842. Mr. Ritchie died on the 10th of March, 1855.

* The Farnham family have long exhibited a kindly feeling to the Irish Presbyterian Church. The late Lord Farnham, at the time of Disestablishment in 1870, was very bountiful to it.

He was succeeded by Mr. William Hogg, who was installed here on the 30th of May, 1856. Mr. Hogg, having been appointed a missionary to New Zealand, resigned this charge on the 21st of July, 1863. On the 11th of the following December Mr. Robert H. Clarke was invested with the pastoral charge. Mr. Clarke died on the 20th of February, 1883; and was succeeded by Mr. Robert H. Boyd, who was ordained here on the 1st of August, 1884.

BALLYKELLY.

THE earliest minister of whom we have any notice here was Mr. William Crooks. He appears to have been ordained in this congregation about 1665. He was in Derry during the siege, and afterwards returned to Ballykelly, where he continued till his death, in 1699. The next minister was Mr. John Stirling, who was ordained in 1701. Mr. Stirling died in this charge January 21st, 1752, and was succeeded by Mr. John Haslett, ordained here by the Presbytery of Derry, April 21st, 1752. He left his congregation about the year 1757, and settled at Bandon, in the south of the kingdom. He was succeeded here by Mr. John Nelson, who was ordained October 5th, 1762. Mr. Nelson appears to have been at heart a Unitarian; but he contrived for a time so to gloss over his creed that it could not be well detected, acting upon the principle of Erasmus, " to think with the wise and speak with the vulgar." But his wisdom only proved to be Jesuitism, and the people of Ballykelly soon found that his preaching was quite unprofitable. The Synod of Ulster at the time was in a very lukewarm condition, and gave them little encouragement when they remonstrated against the doctrine of their minister; so that they were obliged to take up the matter earnestly themselves, and they quickly made the place too hot for their false shepherd. Mr. Nelson was accordingly obliged to demit the charge in the year 1765, and soon afterwards published a pamphlet, in which he appeared in his true colours. He was succeeded by Mr. Benjamin M'Dowel (afterwards (D.D.), one of the most eminent ministers ever connected with the Presbyterian Church in Ireland. Mr. M'Dowel was ordained here on the 2nd of September, 1766. In July, 1778, he was removed to Mary's Abbey, Dublin. The congregation was now annexed to the Presbytery of Route, and Mr. Robert Rentoul, formerly minister of Lurgan, was installed here October 3rd, 1779. Becoming infirm, on the 22nd of December, 1822, the people gave a unanimous call to Mr. Richard Dill, formerly minister of Drumachose; but the Presbytery of Route refusing to sustain it, the Synod of Ulster, in 1823, removed the congregation at their own request to the Presbytery of Derry, and Mr. Dill was installed October 9th, 1823. Mr. Rentoul died November 1st, 1824, leaving a widow and family. During Mr. Dill's ministry the present large and excellent church was erected at Ballykelly, at the expense of the Fishmongers' Company—an act commemorated in an inscription on an elegant marble tablet, placed in a conspicuous position behind the pulpit. The erection of Ballykelly Meeting-house, gave an impulse to the cause of ecclesiastical architecture among the Presbyterians of the North of Ireland. Mr. Dill died 17th Dec., 1854, and was succeeded by Mr. Thomas Y. Killen, formerly minister of 3rd Ramelton, who was installed here by a commission of the Assembly, March 31st, 1857. Receiving a call from Duncairn, Belfast, Mr. Killen (now D.D.) resigned this charge on the 27th of January, 1862, and was succeeded by Mr. William Charles Robinson, formerly of Ramelton, who was installed here on the 27th of March, 1862.

BALLYLENNON.

BALLYLENNON is halfway between Raphoe and St. Johnston. The people of the district, most of whom are Presbyterians, had long felt the inconvenience of being so remote from a house of worship—being about three Irish miles distant from either of the places just mentioned. Nearly sixty years ago they began to think of obtaining more accessible church accommodation; but there were adherents of the Secession Synod as well as of the Synod of Ulster in the locality; and the rivalry of these two bodies created considerable difficulty. The Seceders, however, first occupied the ground; and in October, 1829, Mr. John Lecky was ordained here as minister of the Secession Church. A house of worship was soon erected; but, not long afterwards, another made its appearance in its immediate neighbourhood on the opposite side of the road, built by the adherents of the Synod of Ulster. On the 10th of February, 1835, Mr. George Hanson was ordained to the pastoral charge of the second congregation.

Messrs. Lecky and Hanson both reached old age; and, in the course of nature, both required assistance in the performance of their pastoral functions. Meanwhile the Secession Synod and the Synod of Ulster were united in the General Assembly, and the two congregations, which had all along been comparatively weak, very wisely resolved on incorporation. At this time Mr. Lecky had a son in the ministry; the people of both congregations had known him from his childhood; but he was now settled at Armaghbrague. They agreed, however, to give him a call to his native place; and on the 5th of December, 1878, Mr. Alexander G. Lecky was installed as pastor of the united congregation of Ballylennon. Mr. John Lecky died towards the close of 1885.

BALLYMENA 1st.

The first pastor who ministered to the Presbyterians of Ballymena was the Rev. Geo. Dunbar, minister of Ayr, in Scotland. Banished from that kingdom for his attachment to the cause of Presbyterianism, he took the charge of this congregation about 1627, but removed to Larne a few years after. He was subsequently deposed by Lesly, Bishop of Down and Connor, in 1636, when he returned to Scotland, and became minister of Calder, where he died in 1638. From his removal till after the rebellion of 1641 no Presbyterian minister had liberty to officiate here. The first minister who was statedly ordained by a Presbytery to this charge was the Rev. David Buttle, ordained in 1645; he was imprisoned for his loyalty by the Republican authorities in 1650, but soon after released; he was deposed by Jeremy Taylor, Bishop of Down and Connor, in 1661, for refusing to conform to Prelacy, but continued to minister privately to this people till his death about the year 1665. He was succeeded by the Rev. Adam Getty, ordained about 1666, who died in 1675. The Rev. Jas. Pitcairn, licensed by the Presbytery of St. Andrews, in Scotland, was ordained to this charge in 1676, but he returned to Scotland in 1687, and having accepted a parish there, he demitted his charge of this congregation in 1689. The Rev. Joshua Fisher, previously minister of Minterburn, near Armagh, was installed here in 1689, and was removed by the Synod to the congregation of Donoughmore, in Donegall, in 1694, where he died in 1696. The Rev. Thos. Leech, ordained here in the month of April, 1698, died September 10th, 1738. The Rev. John Brown ordained as assistant and successor to Mr. Leech, September 21st, 1737, died June 5th, 1771. The Rev. John Lindsay ordained as assistant and successor to Mr. Brown, May 28th, 1771, died May 17th, 1795. The Rev. Wm. Hamilton, ordained June 21st, 1796, died January 15th, 1811. The Rev. William Wauhope, ordained June 23rd, 1812. died January 20th, 1837. The Rev. Henry Jackson Dobbin (afterwards D.D.), previously minister of Hillsborough, was installed here June 20th, 1837. Dr. Dobbin died on the 15th of April, 1853, and was succeeded by Mr. Samuel M. Dill (afterwards D.D.), who was installed here on the 27th of September, 1853. On his appointment as Professor of Theology in Magee College, Dr. Dill resigned this charge on the 9th of October 1865 ; and was succeeded by Mr. William Park, who was ordained here on the 25th September, 1866. On receiving a call from Rosemary Street Church, Belfast, Mr. Park resigned this charge on the 29th of July, 1873 ; and was succeeded by Mr. S. M. Dill who was installed as pastor on the 7th of May, 1874. On receiving a call from Ayrshire Mr. Dill resigned this charge on the 19th of April, 1881; and was succeeded by Mr. George Hanson, who was ordained here on the 4th of October, 1881.

THE HIGH KIRK, OR BALLYMENA 2ND.

THIS congregation originated in connection with the Secession Church in June, 1798. There were two congregations ministered to by the one pastor. One of these churches was known as the Moor Meeting House, parish of Kirkinriola, some two miles from Ballymena; the other was erected in the neighbourhood of Broughshane, in the Braid district. The first minister was a Mr. Carmichael. After him there seems to have been an interruption in the ministry. He was succeeded by a Mr. Wilson. In the year 1819 the Rev. William Campbell, A.M., a licentiate of the Donegal Presbytery, was ordained pastor. He continued to preach alternately in the two places of worship for three years, when the service at Broughshane was discontinued. On the 14th May, 1823, workmen commenced to take down the old church in the parish of Kirkinriola; a new site was selected in High Street, Ballymena, and on this a church and manse were erected. The church was opened for public worship on the

4th April, 1824, by the Rev. William Carr, Belfast. This being the second Presbyterian church erected in Ballymena, it was afterwards known as such. From the year 1840 it was connected with the Ahoghill Presbytery, but the General Assembly in 1875 transferred it to the Ballymena Presbytery. It is licensed for marriages as the High Kirk, Ballymena. Mr. Campbell died on the 26th of January, 1872; and on the 26th of March of the same year Mr. David M'Meekin, a licentiate of the Ballymena Presbytery, was ordained to the pastoral charge, and the congregation has much improved under him. When opened for worship in 1824 the eldership consisted of Messrs. John Gregg, George Dugan, Andrew Thompson, John Eaton, Nathaniel Grant, Robert Smyth, and Matthew Montgomery. With the exception of Robert Smyth these are all long since dead. The elders at present in office are Messrs. Matthew Eaton, William R. Thompson, John Thompson, Samuel Millar, William Erwin, Thomas Eaton, Quintin O'Hara, and James King.

BALLYMENA WEST CHURCH.

LITTLE more than fifty years ago, there was only one Presbyterian Congregation in Ballymena. About two miles from the town, towards the north-west, there was, as already stated, a small meeting-house connected with the Secession Church, which stood upon a piece of naked moorland, but was frequented by few worshippers. As the town was increasing, the difficulty of obtaining accommodation in its only Presbyterian Church was more and more felt: and it occurred to the seceding minister that he would considerably improve his position could he remove into it what was then commonly known as *the Moor Meeting-house*. Having procured a site and obtained subscriptions from sundry of the town's people and others, he successfully accomplished this object: and thus it was that what is now the Second Presbyterian Church was erected in Ballymena. But the Secession Church was not very popular in that locality: and many who wanted church accommodation did not care to connect themselves with the transplanted building. About 1827 a number of persons of this description, associated with others, signed a memorial addressed to the Presbytery praying for the erection of a new congregation in connection with the Synod of Ulster. This petition did not meet with much encouragement from some members of the court to which it was presented: and one venerable minister pleaded that, according to an old Synodical law, no new meeting-house could be built within *two miles* of another already in existence! But the Rev. Robert Stewart, of Broughshane, who was then a leader in the Presbytery, and who was well aware of the want of another place of worship, easily removed this difficulty: and in due time leave was granted for the building of a new meeting-house. Though the edifice, which thus originated in Wellington Street, was considerably more capacious than the old Presbyterian Church, it was soon found to be not more than sufficient to meet the demands of the applicants for pews. On the 6th of April, 1830, the Rev. Alexander Patterson, who had previously been minister of Clontibret, was installed as the first pastor. Mr. Patterson laboured here with much acceptance and diligence for seventeen years : but early in the Summer of 1847 he fell a victim, in the prime of life, to fever caught in the discharge of his professional duty. He was succeeded by the Rev. James M'Keown, a young minister of much ability who was ordained here on the 14th of March, 1848. Mr. M'Keown commenced his pastoral career most auspiciously : but he had occupied his position somewhat less than two years when he too fell a victim to fever. He died on the 8th January, 1850. He was succeeded by the Rev. Samuel J. Moore, who had formerly been minister of Donoughmore, and who was installed here on the 24th September, 1850. A few years ago the congregation resolved on the erection of a new Church ; many contributed most liberally to the object ; and in due time what is now known as the West Church was opened for worship. Mr. Moore died on the 8th of April, 1876 ; and was succeeded by Mr. Edward F. Simpson, formerly minister of Lislooney, who was installed here on the 3rd of October, 1876.

BALLYMENA, WELLINGTON STREET.

A NUMBER of the people hitherto connected with the 3rd congregation declined to remove to West Church ; and those who thus adhered to the former building in Wellington Street were recognised by the Assembly as a congregation. On the 31st of March, 1863, the Rev. William Macloy was ordained as their minister. Thus Ballymena which in 1820 had only one Presbyterian Church, has now no less than four, three of which are each much more capacious than the solitary edifice then in existence. Mr. M'Cloy resigned this charge on the 9th of August, 1881, on his acceptance of a call from a Free Church in Paisley; and was succeeded by Mr. William John M'Caughan, who was ordained here on the 1st of January, 1884. Mr. M'Caughan, on receiving a call to Mount Pottinger Church, Belfast, resigned this charge about the close of 1885.

BALLYMOATE.

This congregation appears to have been erected in 1759. It then consisted of fifteen families. It became a part of Sligo congregation about 1760. In 1822 the people applied to the Synod of Ulster to be erected into a separate charge; but the consideration of the subject was deferred in consequence of the non-attendance of Commissioners, and the absence of Mr. Scott the minister of Sligo and Ballymoate. The application was granted in the following year. Mr. Jacob Scott then resigned the charge of Sligo, and was appointed to labour exclusively in Ballymoate. In 1828 Mr. Scott was deposed from the ministry. The congregation was then put under the care of a committee of Synod, and Mr. James Fleming was ordained here on the 22nd of January, 1829. Mr. Fleming died on the 8th of May, 1850, and on the 9th of October of the same year, Mr. John Dewart was ordained to the pastoral charge and also as missionary to the surrounding district. At the Assembly of 1885, Mr. Dewart obtained leave for his congregation to choose an assistant and successor.

BALLYMONEY 1st.

The first minister here was Mr. Ker. His settlement was opposed by Mr. Stewart, of Ballintoy, who had some interest here. Mr. Ker was supported by the majority of the people; but Mr. Stewart appealed to the Parliamentary Commissioners, and they referred the case to the Presbytery. He was ultimately settled about the end of the year 1646. In April, 1649, Mr. Ker refused to join in the Presbytery's protest against the murder of Charles I., and took part with the Republicans and Independents. He was in consequence suspended by the Presbytery for some time; but upon owning his errors, he was afterwards restored. At the Restoration in 1660, he was deposed by Jeremy Taylor, bishop of Down and Connor. He now passed over to Scotland where he died not long after. Ballymoney was without a minister in 1671. It was supplied for a time by David Houston; but he was suspended by the Presbytery in 1672 for irregular and insubordinate conduct.* This suspension caused a great division in the congregation, part adhering to Houston, and part to the Presbytery. We hear nothing farther of Ballymoney for some time. It was again vacant in 1688. In April, 1692, the people applied to the Synod of Ulster for advice about a minister, David Boyd and Robert Love being their commissioners. In 1693, the Synod transferred Mr. Hugh Kirkpatrick from Lurgan to this congregation; but he being in Scotland, where he had fled at the Revolution, did not come over to his new charge till 1695. Mr. Kirkpatrick was Moderator of Synod in 1699. He was father to the Rev. Dr. James Kirkpatrick, afterwards of Belfast, the author of "Presbyterian Loyalty." Mr. Hugh Kirkpatrick died in April, 1712. In 1714, the Sub-Synod of Derry divided this congregation, deeming it too large for one minister, taking from it 20 quarter-lands, of which 14 were annexed to Kilraughts, and 6 to Derrykihan, or Dervock. Of this dismemberment the people complained to the Synod in 1715, and stated their willingness rather to support two ministers than have their congregation divided. It was accordingly declared a collegiate charge, and appointed to pay £35 and 10 bolls of oats yearly to each minister, and to provide convenient farms: but, on failing to give security for this, the order of the Derry Sub-Synod was to take effect. On reconsidering the matter, the people gave up the idea of becoming a collegiate charge, and consequently lost the 20 quarter-lands. They then obtained as minister Mr. Robert M'Bride, son of the Rev. Mr. M'Bride, of Belfast, the author of "A Sample of Jet Black Prelatic Calumny." Mr. M'Bride was ordained here on the 26th September, 1716. He died September 2nd, 1759, aged 73. In 1753, having become infirm, Messrs. John Thompson and Gabriel Todd, as commissioners from the congregation, supplicated the Synod to grant them supplies with a view to obtaining an assistant to Mr. M'Bride. They now obtained

* Mr. Houston held the principles of the Cameronians; and was a somewhat turbulent and unsteady character.

as assistant Mr. Robert Smylie, who was ordained here in 1759, and died in this charge on the 31st of August, 1768, aged 35. The next minister was Mr. Alexander Marshall, who was ordained here by the Presbytery of Route, on the 18th of August, 1772. He died on the 10th of April, 1799, aged 50. In 1800 the congregation was annexed to the Presbytery of Ballymena, with which it remained long connected. The next minister was Mr. Benjamin Mitchell, who was ordained here by the Presbytery of Ballymena, on the 12th of November, 1800. Mr. Mitchell resigned the charge on the 9th of May, 1815, and died in the month of August following. He was succeeded by Mr. Robert Park, who was ordained here on the 18th of March, 1817. Becoming infirm, Mr. Park obtained as his assistant Mr. Alexander Patton, who was ordained here on the 5th of November, 1866. Mr. Park died on the 10th of May, 1876, after a ministry of 59 years, during 35 of which he had acted as clerk to the General Assembly. Mr. Patton, on receiving a call from the congregation of 1st Bangor, resigned this charge in 1879, and was succeeded by Mr. Nathaniel Ross, who was ordained here on the 25th of November of the same year. Mr. Ross resigned the charge on the 24th of April, 1882, and was succeeded by Mr. J. D. Osborne, who was ordained here on the 8th of November, 1882.*

BALLYNAHINCH 1st.

The first minister noticed in this parish was Mr. William Reid, ordained here by the Presbytery of Down, July 14th, 1696. His successor was Mr. Henry Livingston, son of Mr. Henry Livingston, minister of Drumbo.† He was ordained here April 16th, 1704, as assistant and successor to Mr. Reid, who died May 7th, 1708. The next minister was Mr. James M'Alpine, formerly of Killyleagh Castle, who was installed here March 20th, 1714. He died in this charge October 27th, 1732. His successor was Mr. Alexander Maclaine, son of Mr. Archibald Maclaine, of Markethill, and uncle to the

* There are now three congregations connected with the General Assembly in Ballymoney.

† Mr. Livingston was descended from the first Lord Livingston of Scotland ; and from him the late John Barnett, D.D., of Moneymore, was lineally descended.

celebrated Dr. Archibald Maclaine, the translator of Mosheim's Ecclesiastical History. Mr. Maclaine was ordained here by the Presbytery of Killyleagh, August 18th, 1735. A considerable party, amounting to about 120, were dissatisfied with this election, and applied by their Commissioners, Mr. Alexander Holmes and others, to be erected into a separate congregation; but this was refused by the Synod in 1736. Mr. Maclaine removed to Antrim in 1742. The next minister was Mr. John Strong, who was ordained by the Presbytery of Killyleagh, October 10th, 1744. Mr. Strong died August 10th, 1780, and was succeeded by Mr. John M'Clelland, ordained here by the Presbytery of Dromore, October 21st, 1783. Becoming infirm, his son, Mr. James M'Clelland, was ordained his assistant and successor August 25th, 1812. Mr. M'Clelland, senior, died March 5th, 1818, and his son resigned through ill health in 1829. In consequence of disputes respecting the choice of a minister, the congregation was put under the care of a committee of Synod in 1831; and by this committee Mr. John Shaw, formerly minister of Ballinderry, was installed here August 10th, 1831. Mr. Shaw died on the 29th of March, 1870, and was succeeded by Mr. John M'Ilveen, who was ordained here on the 27th of December of the same year. Mr. M'Ilveen, on his removal to 1st Lurgan, resigned this charge on the 25th of February, 1879; and was succeeded by Mr. John Boyd, who was ordained here on the 3rd of February, 1880.

BALLYNURE.

THERE was a congregation at Raloo in the neighbourhood of Ballynure, long before there was a congregation in Ballynure itself. The Presbytery in 1659 permitted the people of Raloo to choose a minister; but the Restoration which immediately followed, defeated this design for a time. At length in November, 1671, the year before the first grant of *Regium Donum* was made, the Presbytery was again applied to. The people now requested that Mr. Robert Kelso should be settled among them as their pastor, and that the people of Glynn should be added to their congregation. This latter point being refused by the Presbytery, the people agreed to support a minister themselves, and Mr. Kelso was ordained at Larne, on the 7th of May, 1673. Mr. Jo. Anderson of

Glenarm preached and presided on this occasion. The ordination was private, as at that time the ministers subjected themselves to heavy penalties by performing it. This also was the reason why it took place not at Raloo, but at Larne. In the June following, John Blair and Alexander Dunlop, elders, attended the Presbytery and in the name of the congregation publicly accepted Mr. Kelso as their minister. In April, 1674, however, after various ineffectual attempts to secure a sufficient maintenance for Mr. Kelso, the congregation acknowledged themselves unable to support a minister; and the Presbytery at his desire accordingly loosed Mr. Kelso from his charge. He was subsequently settled, first at Wicklow, and then at Enniskillen. No farther attempts were made for upwards of a century and a half to establish a congregation at Raloo. But in 1722 Mr. Andrew Lorimer and other commissioners presented a petition to the Synod of Ulster praying to have Ballynure erected into a separate congregation. The application was opposed on the part of Ballyclare; but was, notwithstanding, granted. Mr. Nevin and Mr. Michael Bruce protested against this decision. The final settlement of the separation was referred to the next Synod. The people then offered £30 yearly stipend to a minister, and stated that they had scruples to live under the non-subscribing minister at Ballyclare as one reason why they wished a separation. In 1747, David Archibald the commissioner from this congregation, represented to the Synod that as Mr. Clotworthy Brown had been transferred from Ballinderry to them, they think he may be continued their minister without being formally installed. The reason of this seems to have been that Mr. Brown had some scruples about subscribing the Westminster Confession of Faith. Another part of the congregation, by their commissioner, James Scott, represented it as the desire of a great number there, that Mr. Brown should be installed. The Synod decided that the Presbytery of Templepatrick should install Mr. Brown as soon as convenient, but in the following year the Presbytery reported that they had not installed Mr. Brown, he having joined the nonsubscribing Presbytery of Antrim, and having been installed by them. Mr. Brown was afterwards removed to Belfast as a minister of the first congregation where he died on the 19th of May, 1755. The next minister of Ballynure was Mr. William Rodgers, who had before been minister of the second congregation of

Holywood. Mr. Rodgers was installed here by the Presbytery of Templepatrick, December 10th, 1751. Mr. Rogers growing infirm, Mr. Adam Hill who had been ordained by the Presbytery of Route for America, was installed here on the 16th of August, 1785. Mr. Rogers died April 29th, 1786. Mr. Hill becoming infirm, Mr. James Whiteside M'Cay was ordained his assistant on the 21st of December, 1826. Mr. Hill died on the 21st of July, 1827, leaving a family; Mr. M'Cay died on the 15th of October, 1847; and on the 28th of March, 1848, Mr. Samuel Alexander Hamilton was ordained to this charge. Mr. Hamilton resigned the charge on the 1st of July, 1859; and emigrated to Australia. On the 26th of September of the same year, Mr. A. R. B. M'Cay, son of the former minister, was ordained to the charge. Mr. M'Cay resigned on the 2nd of May, 1865, and also emigrated to Australia;* and on the 31st of March, 1866, Mr. William Kerr was ordained to the pastoral charge.

BALLYRASHANE 1st.

A minister appears to have been settled here nearly a year before the death of Oliver Cromwell. We read of the ordination of Mr. Robert Hogsyard, or Hodgeheard, at Ballyrashane, in October, 1657. He was deposed for non-conformity in 1661, but nothing is known of his after history. He was succeeded by Mr. Thomas Harvey, who was licensed by the Presbytery of Antrim, and ordained to the charge of this congregation by the Presbytery of Route, towards the end of the year 1673. He retired to Scotland at the Revolution; but, in May, 1690, he signified his willingness to return to his flock, and probably did so. We find Mr. Thomas Elder ordained on the 5th of October, 1700. Mr. Elder demitted his charge in 1704, and removed to Scotland. He would appear to have afterwards settled at Kilmore, County Down. The next minister was Mr. Henry Neill, who was ordained here on the 25th of July, 1709. He died in this charge on the 10th of March, 1745. He was succeeded by Mr. Samuel Buys, who was ordained here on the 28th of October, 1746.

* Mr. M'Cay is now minister of Castlemaine, in Victoria. He acted for a number of years as Professor of Church History for the Australian Church; and has meanwhile distinguished himself as one of the ablest divines in the country.

He died in September, 1760, and was succeeded by Mr. John Logan, who was ordained here on the 24th of November, 1765. Becoming infirm, Mr. James Dunlop was ordained his assistant and successor in December, 1809. Mr. Logan died on the 10th of May, 1816, leaving a widow and family. Mr. Dunlop died on the 16th of November, 1830. He was succeeded by Mr. John Alexander, who was ordained here on the 20th of June, 1832. Mr. Alexander was the nephew of the Rev. James Elder, of Finvoy. Mr. Alexander died on the 16th of March, 1881. He had previously obtained leave for his congregation to choose an assistant and successor; and accordingly on the 28th of September, 1880, Mr. Charles W. Hunter had been ordained here.

BALLYRONEY.

THIS congregation was first organised in 1708. It had formerly been a section of Rathfriland congregation. The first minister was Mr. James Moor, who was ordained here on the 25th of August, 1709. Mr. Moor died in this charge on the 22nd of March, 1738. He was succeeded by Mr. Robert Thompson, who was ordained here by the Presbytery of Armagh on the 14th of May, 1782, as assistant to Mr. Moor. Mr. Thompson died on the 4th of September, 1743. The next minister was Mr. Samuel Thompson, who was ordained here on the 14th of March, 1749. Having become feeble in intellect, he resigned the charge. The next minister was Mr. Alexander Wilson, who was ordained here by the Presbytery of Dromore on the 20th of August, 1751. He died here on the 8th of May, 1782, leaving a widow and children. He was succeeded by Mr. William Fletcher, who was ordained here on the 3rd of June, 1783. He died in this charge on the 7th of May, 1824, leaving a widow and family. The next minister was Mr. Alexander Heron, formerly minister of Portadown, who was installed here on the 15th of August, 1826. Mr. Heron died on the 17th of November, 1865. He was succeeded by the Rev. William Wylie, who was ordained here on the 4th of May, 1866. On the 11th of September, 1879, Mr. Wylie resigned this charge, on his removal to 2nd Larne; and was succeeded by Mr. William Shepherd, who was installed here on the 29th of April, 1880.

BALLYSHANNON.

A congregation seems to have existed at an early period at Ballyshannon: but it was long associated with Raneny or Donegal, the minister preaching two Sabbaths in Raneny and one in Ballyshannon. This state of things continued until 1834, when Ballyshannon was erected into a separate congregation. The first minister was Mr. J. G. Murphy (now Dr. Murphy, of Assembly's College, Belfast), who was ordained here by the Presbytery of Raphoe on the 26th of October, 1836. In 1841 Mr. Murphy removed to Belfast, having been appointed Head Master of the Classical Department in the Royal Academical Institution. He was succeeded by Mr. Andrew Lowry, who was ordained here on the 16th of March, 1842.

BALLYWALTER 1st.

The first minister of Ballywalter was Mr. James Hamilton,* nephew to Lord Claneboye, who was ordained here in 1626. He was deposed by Leslie, Bishop of Down and Connor, in 1636, on which he removed to Scotland, and became minister, first at Dumfries, and latterly at Edinburgh, where he was again deposed in 1660, and died shortly after. Ballywalter continued vacant from 1636 to 1642, when Mr. James Baty, who had been chaplain to the Lord of Aird's regiment, was ordained to this charge by the Presbytery of the Scots army, Mr. Hamilton, their former minister, now sent over by the General Assembly, presiding on the occasion. Mr. Baty was imprisoned by Venables in June, 1650, and, shortly after, either died or fled to Scotland. He was succeeded by Mr. William Reid, who was deposed, in 1661, by the Bishop of Down. In 1688, Mr. John Goudy was ordained here. The charge then included Ballyhalbert and Greyabbey; and in 1710, the Presbytery of Down ordered a central meeting-house, for both places, to be built at Ballygin. The Synod confirmed this sentence, but gave the Presbytery liberty, on sufficient grounds, to erect a new congregation out of Ballywalter, Ballyhalbert, and Greyabbey. Mr. Goudy died in this charge, March 20th, 1733, aged 78 years. He was succeeded

* It may interest some of our readers to know that Mr. Hamilton, who was one of the most distinguished of the Fathers of the Irish Presbyterian Church, wore a gown in the pulpit.—*Reid's Hist.* I. 104.

by his son, Mr. Robert Goudy, ordained here, April 9th, 1734. Mr. Goudy joined the Presbytery of Antrim, and died, March 13th, 1761. At his death, the congregation returned to the care of the Bangor Presbytery, which ordained Mr. James Cochrane here, July 27th, 1762. He died in this charge, September 22nd, 1802, and was succeeded by Mr. Andrew Goudy, ordained on the 3rd Tuesday of December following. He died here December 8th, 1818, leaving a widow and family. In the end of the year 1819, the congregation called Mr. John Gibson; but, certain charges being preferred against him, his ordination was deferred; and, in 1820, the Synod of Ulster withdrew his license. This led to a schism in the parish, as the bulk of the people adhered to Mr. Gibson, who was ordained irregularly, and continued to preach here till his death, in May, 1861. In 1844, Mr. Gibson applied for admission to the General Assembly; and, as circumstances had arisen tending to invalidate the testimony on which he was condemned, he was, in that year, regularly ordained in Ballywalter, by a Commission appointed for the purpose. Mr. Gibson becoming infirm, Mr. Henry Gamble became his assistant. Mr. Gibson died on the 13th of May, 1861, and Mr. Gamble was ordained, shortly afterwards, his successor. On the withdrawal of Mr. Gibson from the Synod of Ulster, in 1820, a portion of the people left him; and, over this minority, Mr. John Templeton was ordained pastor in March, 1821. Mr. Templeton died in August, 1856, and was succeeded by Mr. David Hill M'Murtry, who was ordained here, on the 31st of March, 1857. Mr. M'Murtry resigned the congregation on the 1st of April, 1859; and on the 16th of August of the same year, Mr. Samuel Edgar Brown was ordained to the pastoral charge. In 1861, Mr. Brown removed to Athlone, and was succeeded by Mr. David Magill, LL.D., who was installed here on the 19th of February, 1862. Dr. Magill has recently retired from the discharge of the active duties of the ministry.

BALLYWALTER 2ND.

THE history of this congregation is, to a great extent given in the preceding article. Mr. Gamble* resigned this charge on

* Mr. Gamble died in the prime of life. His widow has since been distinguished as the munificent benefactress of the Assembly's College, Belfast, in which he was educated.

the 5th of September, 1865; and was succeeded by Mr. David M'Kee, who was installed here on the 6th of March, 1866. Mr. M'Kee resigned the charge on the 5th of January, 1869, having received a call from Dublin, and was succeeded by Mr. John Rogers who was ordained here on the 3rd of June, 1869.

BALLYWILLAN.

TRADITION reports that Gabriel Cornwall was one of the first ministers of this congregation. He preached in the parish church, and was ejected at the Restoration. He is mentioned by Livingstone as having been here in 1656. We read subsequently of the ordination of Mr. William Houston here in 1700. He died in this charge on the 6th of May, 1721. Meanwhile Mr. James Thompson was ordained here on the 5th of May, 1718, as assistant and successor. Mr. Thompson died on the 25th of January, 1747. He was succeeded by Mr. Hugh Gaston, who was ordained here on the 23rd of February, 1748. Mr. Gaston died here on the 15th of October, 1766. He is well-known as the author of a work first published in 1763, under the title of "A Scripture Account of the Faith and Practice of Christians, consisting of large collections of pertinent texts of Scripture upon the sundry articles of Revealed Religion." This very useful work has passed through various editions, and is commended by Hartwell Horne in his "Introduction to the Critical Study and knowledge of the Holy Scriptures." Mr. Gaston left a widow who died in 1823, having enjoyed the Widows' Fund of the Synod of Ulster no less than 57 years. He was succeeded as minister of Ballywillan, by Mr. John Abernethy, who was ordained here on the 15th of August, 1769. Mr. Abernethy removed to Templepatrick in August, 1774, and was succeeded in Ballywillan by Mr. Robert Thompson who was ordained here on the 23rd of April, 1779. Becoming infirm, Mr. James Huey was ordained here as his assistant and successor on the 1st of December, 1812. Mr. Thompson died on the 10th of July, 1815. Mr. Huey died on the 20th of January, 1862*; and on the 24th of June of the same year Mr. Matthew Woodburn was ordained to the pastoral charge.

* John Henry Huey, Esq., J.P., of Clonaven, Coleraine, is the son of this minister.

Mr. Woodburn died on the 28th of November, 1877; and was succeeded by Mr. Hugh Wells who was ordained here on the 6th of August, 1879.

BALTEAGH.

IN 1822 the inhabitants of this district applied to the Synod of Ulster to be erected into a congregation. They were permitted to build a meeting-house, and for some time the neighbouring ministers were appointed to supply them with preaching. In the following year they were erected into a congregation, and on the 16th November, 1824, Mr. Samuel Templeton was ordained as their first minister. They are at present connected with the Presbytery of Limavady. Mr. Templeton died on the 11th of September, 1866. He was succeeded by Mr. William D. Wallace, who was ordained to the pastoral charge on the 26th of April, 1868. Mr. Wallace resigned this charge on the 15th of January, 1872, and removed to 1st Ramelton. He was succeeded by Mr. Richard Dill Macky, who was ordained here on the 22nd of November, 1872. Mr. Macky resigned this charge on the 17th of November, 1883, on his removal to New South Wales. He has since returned, and resumed the charge of the congregation.

BANAGHER.

THIS congregation originally formed part of that of Cumber. It became a distinct charge about the year 1755, and its first minister was Mr. Jo. Law, who was ordained here on the 5th of July, 1756. He died in this charge in January, 1810, leaving a widow. The next minister, who was ordained in 1812, was Mr. James A. Johnston, known among his friends as "the lovely divine." He was a very handsome man, but not a deep theologian. He resigned the charge in May, 1831, and removed to Holywood, where he became minister of the congregation connected with the Presbytery of Antrim. He was succeeded in Banagher by Mr. Thomas Ellison, who was ordained here on the 5th of March, 1822. On the formation of the General Assembly, Banagher became connected with the Presbytery of Glendermot. Mr. Ellison died on the 6th of January, 1847, and was succeeded by Mr. R. L. Rogers, who was installed here on the 25th of November,

1847. Mr. Rogers died on the 15th of October, 1879, and was succeeded by Mr. W. J. D. Williamson, who was installed here on the 3rd of September, 1880.

BANBRIDGE 1ST.

BANBRIDGE was originally part of Magherally congregation, which was proposed to be divided in the year 1716. One part called *Seapatrick* was erected into a separate charge; and in the same year a meeting-house was build at Banbridge. This caused great divisions in Seapatrick and Magherally, all which were referred to the Synod in 1717, when it was determined that Mr. Young, the minister of Magherally, should preach alternately in the two congregations. This arrangement did not continue long. The people of Banbridge at length obtained a minister of their own, viz., Mr. Archibald Maclaine, son of Mr. Maclaine, of Markethill, who was ordained here, April 26th, 1720. He died in this charge, February 23rd, 1740. He was succeeded by Mr. Henry Jackson, who is said to have been nearly related to General Jackson, President of the United States. Mr. Jackson was ordained at Banbridge by the Presbytery of Armagh on the 8th of November, 1743. In 1772, it was reported to Synod that bequests to the amount of £130 had been made to the congregation of Banbridge, and that the interest was regularly paid to the minister. Mr. Jackson was grandfather to the late Rev. H. J. Dobbin, D.D., of Ballymena. On the 6th of January, 1790, Mr. Jackson resigned the charge of the congregation of Banbridge; and, on the same day, Mr. Nathaniel Shaw was ordained as his assistant and successor. Mr. Jackson died, February 26th, 1795, leaving a widow and family; and Mr. Shaw died, July 4th, 1812. The next minister was Mr. James Davis, who was ordained here March 23rd, 1814. Mr. Davis adhered to the New-Light party in the Arian controversy; and, in 1829, those who withdrew from his ministry were erected into a congregation by the Presbytery of Dromore; and, on the 22nd of June, 1830, Mr. Robert Anderson was ordained as their minister. Mr. Anderson died on the 29th of February, 1872, and was succeeded by Mr. John Sinclair Hamilton, who was installed here on the 3rd of July, 1872. Mr. Hamilton resigned this charge on the 14th of February, 1884, on his removal to

Dublin; and was succeeded by Mr. Thomas Boyd, formerly of Magheramason, who was installed here on the 7th of August of the same year.

BANGOR 1st.

In 1623, Mr. Robert Blair, who had been invited from Scotland by Lord Claneboy, came over to Bangor and was ordained to the ministry by Echlin, Bishop of Down, and some of the neighbouring pastors. He remained here till he was deposed in 1636, when he retired to Scotland and became minister successively of Ayr and St. Andrews.* After the rebellion of 1641, this congregation attracts particular notice, and we find a session ordained in it in 1642. It did not, however, obtain a minister until 1646, when Mr. Gilbert Ramsay came over from Scotland, recommended by Mr. Blair, and was ordained here. Mr. Ramsay suffered several imprisonments; was deposed in 1661; after the Restoration, his meeting-house was pulled down by Lady Clanbrasil in 1669; and he at length died, in August, 1670. Another minister from Scotland, Mr. Archibald Hamilton, who had been six years pastor of Wigton, was settled in Bangor in 1672. He retired to Scotland at the troubles in 1689, and died at Wigton in June, 1695. He was succeeded at Bangor by his grandson, Mr. Hamilton, whose ministry was only of one year's continuance. After, as it would appear, a long vacancy, Mr. William Biggar, a minister from Scotland, was installed here, March 1st, 1704. In March, 1728, Mr. Biggar resigned the charge, and removed to Scotland, where he became minister of a parish in Galloway. In 1730, the congregation was still vacant, and Robert Blackwood, Esq.,† appeared at the Synod, as its commissioner, seeking for supplies. In 1731 a call was given to Mr. Cochrane, minister of Kilraughts, but the Synod refused to sanction the removal. The next minister was Mr. James Mackay, who was ordained here November 15th, 1732. In 1747 the congregation was again vacant; and in 1748 the Synod agreed to permit the removal of Mr. Cochrane, of Kilraughts, to whom the people of Bangor had

* Mr. Blair was one of the most able and distinguished of the Fathers of the Irish Presbyterian Church. He was a gentleman by birth; and he acted for some time as chaplain to Charles I.

† This gentleman was the ancestor of Lord Dufferin.

renewed their call. Mr. Cochrane, who at this time was Clerk of the Synod, was accordingly installed here, December 6th, 1748. The congregation promised him £60 and twenty bolls of oats yearly. In 1758 Mr. Cochrane resigned his office as Clerk of the Synod; and, in consequence of his increasing infirmities, the congregation applied to the Synod, in 1760, for supplies. On this occasion Mr. Hugh Jackson appears as their commissioner. Their next minister was Mr. James Hull, formerly minister of Cookstown, who was installed here January 4th, 1763. Mr. Cochrane, now the senior minister, died June 2nd, 1765, leaving a widow and family. Mr. Hull becoming infirm, Mr. David Taggart was ordained his assistant, May 21st, 1793. Mr. Hull died March 30th, 1794, and Mr. Taggart was drowned at Bangor quay, March, 16th, 1808. He was succeeded by Mr. Hugh Woods, ordained November 15th, 1808. During his ministry, Second Bangor, Groomsport, Ballygilbert, Ballygrainey, and Conlig were erected within the bounds of his charge. In 1856 Mr. Woods retired from the discharge of the active duties of the ministry; and on the 24th of February, 1857, Mr. Joseph C. M'Cullagh was installed as his assistant and successor. Mr. Woods died on the 4th of April, 1869. Mr. M'Cullagh died on the 1st of December, 1878; and was succeeded by Mr. Alexander Patton, formerly of 1st Ballymoney, who was installed here on the 17th of June, 1879.

BANGOR 2ND.

THIS congregation was erected by a Committee of the Synod of Ulster, specially appointed in 1828. The meeting-house was erected some time afterwards. On the 5th of August, 1829, Mr. William Patteson was ordained to the ministry here by a committee of Synod. Mr. Patteson obtained leave for his congregation to choose an asssistant and successor in June, 1879; and on the 31st of July, of the same year, Mr. William Clarke was installed here. A new church, on a different site, is about to be erected for this congregation.

BELFAST CONGREGATIONS.

BALLYMACARRETT 1st.

IN the early part of the present century there was no place of worship whatever in Ballymacarrett. The population was comparatively small, and generally in very humble circumstances. About sixty years ago attention was drawn to its spiritual destitution, and various denominations commenced preaching in it. The Methodists erected a small chapel; the Episcopalians also erected a place of worship; and the Presbyterians likewise took steps to supply ordinances to those connected with their communion. The congregation of 1st Ballymacarrett was erected in 1835. The first minister was Mr. John Meneely, who was ordained here on the 20th of March, 1838. Mr. (now Dr.) Meneely long laboured here with much acceptance, and during his ministry the church was greatly enlarged and improved. Becoming infirm, Mr. William M'Kean, formerly minister of 2nd Raphoe, was installed as Dr. Meneely's assistant and successor on the 8th of December, 1881.*

DONEGALL STREET.

IN 1773 Mr. James Bryson, who had formerly been minister of Lisburn, was called to the charge of what was then known as the 2nd congregation of Belfast (now Unitarian). Some disagreement at length arose between Mr. Bryson and a number of his people; and in 1792 a new place of worship was erected in Donegall Street by the party adhering to him, of which he was recognized as the minister. Mr. Bryson died October 3rd, 1796, leaving a widow and family, and was succeeded by Mr. Robert Acheson, formerly minister of Glenarm, who was installed here June 20th, 1799. He died in this charge February 21st, 1824, leaving a widow and family. The next minister was Mr. George Bellis (afterwards D.D.), who was ordained here May 24th, 1825. In 1841 Mr. Bellis, on his appointment as missionary secretary for the General Assembly, resigned the charge of the congregation, and was succeeded by Mr. Isaac Nelson, formerly

* There are now three Presbyterian congregations in Ballymacarrett; and the erection of a fourth is contemplated.

minister of 1st Comber, who was installed here by the Presbytery of Belfast, on the 31st of March, 1842. Mr. Nelson having obtained leave to retire from the active duties of the Ministry, Mr. George Magill, formerly of 2nd Donagheady, was installed here on the 9th of December, 1880. The old church has since been taken down, and a new building on a different site is in course of erection.

FISHERWICK PLACE.

THIS congregation was erected at a *pro-re-nata* meeting of the Synod of Ulster specially convened in Moneymore, on the 31st of December, 1823. It may now seem strange that the erection of this congregation was keenly opposed on the ground that there was already a sufficient amount of church accommodation in Belfast. There were then only three or four orthodox Presbyterian Churches in the town, and one or two of these were very poorly attended. The commissioners for the new erection who attended the Synod were Dr. James Thompson, Professor of Mathematics in the Belfast Academical Institution, and father of the present celebrated Sir William Thompson; Alexander Mackey, Proprietor of the *Belfast News-Letter;* and Charles Thomson, uncle to Sir Thomas M'Clure, Bart. These gentlemen presented to the Synod a list of 162 intended seat-holders who engaged to pay an annual stipend of £213 15s 6d. The congregation was then put under the care of a Committee of Synod. Several years passed away before the house was ready for worship. There were at that time only a very few houses near the place on which it stands, as the town had not then commenced to move out in the direction of the Botanic Gardens. The ground on which the Church now stands was little better than a swamp; and after the foundations were laid they remained long without any superstructure. The house was at length opened for worship on the 23rd of September, 1827, by Dr. Chalmers. The preacher chose for his text on the occasion, James, i. 20, "The wrath of man worketh not the righteousness of God;" and, as the Arian controversy was then raging, many thought that the discourse was intended to moderate the strife of the disputants. After some disputing respecting the qualifications of those who should be permitted to vote for the first minister, the matter was finally arranged by the Synod in 1828. In the month of August of that year, a unanimous call was presented to the Rev. James Morgan (afterwards D.D.), then minister of Lisburn. Mr. Morgan accepted the call, and was installed here on the 4th of November, 1828. His ministry was a signal blessing, not only to the town of Belfast, but also to the whole Presbyterian Church of Ireland. He did much to create and foster a Missionary spirit; and under him the congregation of Fisherwick Place became a model to all the other churches of the Assembly. For many years Dr. Morgan was the Secretary of the Foreign Mission, of which he may be considered the father. He was by nature of an extremely delicate constitution, and yet he survived to old age. He was remarkably temperate in his mode of living, and systematic in all his proceedings. He died on the 5th of August, 1873; but meanwhile, in consequence of his increasing infirmities, his congregation had obtained leave to select an assistant and successor; and on the 15th of March, 1870, the Rev. Henry M. Williamson was installed in the pastoral charge.

FITZROY AVENUE.

In 1820, the Rev. John Edgar (afterwards D.D.) was ordained to the pastoral charge of a small Seceding congregation recently erected in Belfast. At the time of his ordination his little flock possessed no place of worship, and continued for a considerable period to meet and celebrate religious ordinances in a small building in a back lane in the neighbourhood of Waring Street. At length by dint of begging, not only in Belfast, but in England and Scotland, the young minister contrived to obtain funds for the erection of a very humble sanctuary. It was built in what had formerly been little better than a quagmire; and, on the day on which it was opened for public worship, those who repaired to it had to find their way along planks laid to prevent them from sinking into the mire. But its young pastor soon proved that he was no ordinary man; his zeal and eloquence began to attract more and more attention; and in 1829, when he commenced the Temperance Reformation, he had already acquired a high reputation. The little meeting-house at length proved insufficient for the accommodation of the increasing flock; and in 1836 a larger and more ornamental church was erected in its immediate vicinity. To this edifice the congregation was transferred; but the little original building was preserved as a mission house; a minister was put in charge of it; and gradually another congregation was collected. Several other congregations were subsequently organised in the same place—one hive, as it were, swarming off and permitting another to take possession. Meanwhile the Synod of Ulster and the Secession Synod became united: and in 1848, Dr. Edgar, now professor of Divinity for the General Assembly, resigned the pastoral charge. He was succeeded by the Rev. George Shaw, who was ordained on the 27th of June, 1849. Since that time a great change has taken place in the state of the town. Many buildings then occupied as dwelling-houses have been entirely devoted to business purposes: and a large portion of the population has been gradually removing to the suburbs. Thus it has been found necessary to erect new churches in what not many years ago were town parks. The second church erected by Dr. Edgar in Alfred Street was not long since sold to be converted into a large mercantile establishment; and in its stead one of the most beautiful ecclesiastical structures in the North of Ireland has been built for the use of Mr. Shaw's congregation in Fitzroy Avenue. The new church was opened for public worship in 1874. It has a handsome spire, and has connected with it ample accommodation in the way of school-rooms, committee-rooms, and lecture-room. The whole has cost upwards of £8,000.

MAY STREET.

THIS congregation was erected by the Presbytery of Belfast in 1829. The church was specially erected for the Rev. Henry Cooke, D.D. (afterwards LL.D.), formerly of Killileagh. He was installed here on the 24th November, 1829. Vast crowds attended his ministry when the church was opened; and sometimes the Sabbath collection, mostly in halfpence, amounted to £10. Throughout life he continued to be the most popular preacher in the Church. For the greater part of his ministry in Belfast he conducted three public services in May Street Church every Lord's Day. Dr. Cooke died at his house in Ormeau Road on the 13th of December, 1868, in the 81st year of his age and the 61st of his ministry. His remains were honoured by a public funeral—one of the most imposing demonstrations which has ever taken place in the town of

Belfast. It was attended by the members of the Corporation in their robes of office, by the members of the various public Boards, by the Professors of the Queen's College and of the Presbyterian College in official costume, and by a vast number of public officials from various parts of the country. As the procession passed through the streets every window was filled with spectators, and every place was thronged. He was buried in Balmoral Cemetery. Some time before his decease he was obliged, in consequence of declining health, to give up his pastoral charge; and on the 4th of March, 1868, Mr. John M'Intosh, who had formerly been minister of Connor, was installed here. On the 4th of January, 1881, Mr. M'Intosh, having accepted a call from the 2nd Presbyterian Church of Philadelphia, resigned the care of the congregation; and on the 31st of January, 1882, Mr. R. J. Lynd, formerly minister of Berry Street, was installed as pastor. The church, erected in 1829, and then considered one of the finest ecclesiastical buildings in Belfast, has since been much improved.

ROSEMARY STREET.

THE first minister in Belfast, after the restoration of Presbytery in 1642, was Mr. Anthony Shaw. A session was first erected here in 1645, and Mr. Shaw was shortly afterwards ordained. He was much persecuted by Ormond's party in 1649, and by the Republicans in 1650, so that he fled to Scotland shortly afterwards, and never returned. The next minister was Mr. William Keyes, who was settled here in 1660. Mr. Keyes had at one time also charge of Carrickfergus, but of this he was relieved in 1672, when the people of Belfast undertook to pay him an annual stipend of £60. In July of the same year, he was sent to supply the congregation of Bull-Alley in Dublin, where he continued till December, when they presented him with a call. Belfast, however, opposed his removal, sending in January, 1673, Mr. William Muir, and Michael and John Briggart, as their commissioners to the Presbytery; but the committee of all the Presbyteries in April confirmed his removal to Dublin. On this the congregation sent Mr. Anderson and Mr. Chalmers, as their commissioners to the Presbytery, to object once more against it, but the matter having been issued by the committee, the Presbytery would not interfere. In May, Mr. Keyes, himself applied to be permitted to remain here, stating "that Lady Donegall was dissatisfied at his removal, and likely to be prejudiced against the Presbytery on that account." At this time Lady Donegall appears to have been at least an occasional attendant on Presbyterian ordinances. Mr. Keyes was, however, obliged to remove to Dublin, and the Presbytery wrote vindicating their proceedings to Lady Donegall, and continued to supply the vacant congregation. In January, 1674, the Presbytery sent two of their members to wait on Lord and Lady Donegall to deal with them "for the people's liberty to choose whom they please, with the meeting's consent, according to principles owned by us." In the succeeding April, Messrs. Hall and Cunningham, the two brethren appointed to execute this commission, reported that they had conferred with the Countess of Donegall, who "promised she would be no hindrance to the settling of a godly minister in Belfast;" and, in the end of the same month, they obtained a favourable answer from Lord Donegall. In May, William Moore and Alexander Arthur, are their commissioners to the Presbytery, and on July 7th, they gave a call to Mr. Patrick Adair,* minister at Cairncastle, who, after the other Presbyteries had been consulted, was declared transported to Belfast, on October 13th, 1674. He remained in this charge till his death in the beginning of the year 1694. At the Synod in June, 1694, Mr. William Crawford, sovereign of Belfast, Mr. David Smith, burgess, and others, appeared as the commissioners from Belfast, requesting that Mr. John M'Bride, minister of Clare, should be transported to them, which was soon after granted, and he was accordingly installed here in October, 1694. In 1706 they called Mr. James Kirkpatrick, minister at Templepatrick, to become the assistant and successor of Mr. M'Bride, who was now absent in Scotland, but the Synod refused their request, though they granted supplies. Towards the end of the year 1706, Mr. Kirkpatrick was, however, settled in Belfast. In 1707, the Presbytery divided the congregation, and in 1708, Mr. Kirkpatrick took charge of the new erection. A committee of Synod met in Belfast, in September, 1708, to be present at the division of the congregation. The old congre-

* Mr. Adair was the author of a work long preserved in manuscript, and not long since published under the title of "Adair's Narrative." He was married to the daughter of Sir Robert Adair, the proprietor of the Ballymena estate, and the ancestor of Lord Waveney.

gation had complained of the conduct of the Presbytery in encouraging the division, and their commissioners to the Synod of 1708 were Mr. Andrew Maxwell, Mr. Henry Chads, and Mr. John Black, elders; with Edward Bryce, Esq., Dr. Peacock, Mr. Isaac Macartney, Mr. Robert Lennox, Mr. Richard Ashmore, Mr. Samuel Smith, Mr. John M'Munn, Mr. Gilbert Moore, and some others. In 1718, they called Mr. Abernethy, of Antrim, to be assistant and successor to Mr. M'Bride, but the Synod determined against his removal. Mr. M'Bride, died July 21st, 1718. They then called Mr. Fleming, minister of Lurgan, but the Synod in 1719 determined against his transportation. They at last obtained Mr. Samuel Haliday, jun., who was installed here July 28th, 1720. At this time lax views began to make their appearance in the Synod of Ulster; and the ministers of Rosemary Street identified themselves with the New-Light party. In consequence a large number of their hearers withdrew from their pastoral care, erected another place of worship in a tenement immediately adjoining; and called Mr. Charles Masterton, previously minister of Connor, to occupy the pulpit of their new meeting-house. Mr. Masterton was installed here towards the end of the year 1722. The commissioners of the congregation, Mr. Samuel Smith and Mr. Jo. Young complained to the Synod in 1724, of several grievances from the tardiness of the two other congregations to grant dismissions to people wishing to join them. Mr. Masterton was at the Synod of 1745, but he appears to have resigned shortly afterwards, as in 1746 the people applied to the Synod for supplies of preaching. In 1747 the Synod sanctioned the removal of Mr. William Laird from Ray to Belfast on the promise of £70 per annum during Mr. Masterton's life, and at his death £80 and an assistant minister supported, or £100 if Mr. Laird undertook the whole charge. Mr. Laird was accordingly installed here by the Presbytery of Bangor, on the 16th of September, 1747. Mr. Masterton died July 15th, 1750. Mr. Laird becoming infirm, Mr. Sinclair Kelburne, was ordained here by the Presbytery of Belfast on the 8th of February, 1780. Mr. Laird died on the 8th of December, 1791. He was the great-grandfather of Sir Thomas M'Clure, Bart. On the first Tuesday of November, 1799, Mr. Kelburne resigned this charge on account of the precarious state of his health and bodily infirmity; and was succeeded by Mr. Samuel

Hanna, formerly minister of Drumbo, who was installed here on the 11th of December, 1799. Mr. Kelburne died March 31st, 1802. Mr. (afterwards Dr.), Hanna in 1838 obtained leave for his congregation to choose an assistant and successor; and in 1840, Mr. (afterwards Dr.), Gibson was elected his assistant and successor. Dr. Gibson resigned this charge in 1847 on his appointment as Professor of Christian Ethics; and was succeeded by Mr. John Macnaughtan, formerly of Paisley, who was installed here on the 25th of October, 1849. Becoming infirm, Mr. Macnaughtan obtained as his assistant Mr. William Park, formerly minister of 1st Ballymena, who was installed here on the 2nd of September, 1873. Mr. Macnaughtan died on the 27th of May, 1884.

TOWNSEND STREET.

This church is connected with a new era in the History of Presbyterianism in Belfast. When its establishment was first contemplated the town did not reckon more than the fifth part of its present number of inhabitants; but it was increasing with wonderful rapidity, and the amount of church accommodation was quite inadequate. A large and commodious piece of ground, situate in the midst of the working class population, was kindly granted in perpetuity, at a merely nominal rent, by the Rev. John Brown, an excellent Episcopal minister, and Allen Brown, Esq.; and in the autumn of 1833, the foundation stone of the new edifice was laid by the then Marquis of Donegal. The services on the occasion were conducted by Drs. Hanna and Cooke, and Messrs. Bellis and Morgan. In the spring of 1835 the building was ready for the accommodation of worshippers, and it was then opened by the Rev. Dr. Norman M'Leod, of Campsie, father of the still more celebrated Dr. M'Leod, of Glasgow, whose death a few years ago was so much lamented. The collection at the opening service amounted to £130. On the 2nd of February, 1836, the Rev. Josias Wilson was installed as its first minister. Mr. Wilson laboured here for several years with great zeal and acceptance, and gathered around him a numerous congregation. On the 7th of October, 1844, Mr. Wilson resigned the charge, having received a call to River Terrace, London; and on the 29th of November of the same year, the Rev. John Weir, formerly of Newry, was inducted as minister. On the 6th of July, 1847, Mr. Weir resigned the charge, and removed to London; and on the 21st of September of the same year, the Rev. William Johnston (now D.D.), formerly minister of Berry Street congregation, was installed in Townsend Street. The congregation has flourished greatly under Dr. Johnston. Meanwhile, the structure erected in 1833 having exhibited various indications of decay, it was resolved to build on the old site a new and more commodious edifice. The present Presbyterian Church of Townsend Street is one of the best and most handsome in the Assembly. It is furnished with all the needful accompaniments of school-rooms, lecture hall, and other useful apartments. It cost upwards of £11,000, and was opened free of debt on Sabbath, the 15th October, 1878, by the Rev. W. F. Stevenson, D.D., Rathgar, and the Rev. Francis Petticrew, D.Lit., Faughanvale.

YORK STREET.

FIFTY years ago the population of Belfast was increasing with amazing rapidity; and the Rev. James Morgan, who shortly before had been installed as the first minister of Fisherwick Place, became deeply impressed with the importance of providing for the spiritual wants of the new inhabitants. But when he proposed to erect a Presbyterian church in York Street, many regarded the project with no great favour, thinking that there was already sufficient accommodation for all who were likely to attend on Sabbath ordinances. His own capacious meeting-house had been recently erected; the large Presbyterian church of May Street had been built soon afterwards; and the Presbyterian church of Townsend Street had been only lately opened. But the minister of Fisherwick Place persevered, and his efforts were at length crowned with success. Throughout he was much encouraged by Dr. Cooke, who was so well pleased with the result that he pleasantly suggested St. James', after the Christian name of its originator, as the proper designation for the new ecclesiastical structure. On the 11th of February, 1840, the Rev. David Hamilton, who had previously been minister of Connor, was installed as pastor, and for nearly twenty years he occupied the pulpit with much acceptance and efficiency. In the year of the great awakening (1859) he was unremitting in his exertions, and it was believed that his health was then undermined by excessive toil. He died of fever on the 13th of January, 1860. The vast multitude in attendance on his funeral attested the respect entertained for him by the whole community. He was succeeded as minister of York Street by Mr. David Hanson, who had previously been minister of Fahan, and who was installed here on the 20th of September, 1860. His ministry was short, as he died here in the prime of life on the 8th of January, 1865. By this time Mr. Thomas Hamilton, the eldest son of the first minister, was nearly ready for licence; and the congregation testified at once their deep respect for the father, and their high expectations in reference to the son, by electing the young licentiate to the vacant office. Mr. Thomas Hamilton was ordained here by the Presbytery of Belfast on the 22nd of August, 1865. He has recently signalised himself by carrying off a prize of £100 for an essay on the Sabbath from upwards of 240 competitors.

BELTURBET.

This place began to be supplied with preaching by the Synod of Ulster in 1709. About the same time the Synod also commenced preaching in Carrickmacross. On the 23rd of March, 1714, Mr. Robert Thompson was ordained as minister of Belturbet. But he did not long retain the charge in consequence of the insufficiency of his maintenance. He resigned it in 1721. The place now remained long without a minister. At length, in 1854, the Presbytery of Cavan reported to the Assembly that they had established a mission station in this town; and on the 28th of June of the same year they ordained Mr. Robert Jamieson to the pastoral charge. Having accepted a call from the Missionary Directors, Mr. Jamieson resigned the charge on the 8th of January, 1856, and subsequently proceeded to Canada. He was succeeded as minister of Belturbet by Mr. James Thompson, who was ordained here on the 27th of June, 1856.

BENBURB.

Benburb is classic ground. On the 5th of June, 1646, the Scottish forces, led on by Monro, here encountered the Irish Confederates under the famous Owen Roe O'Neill, and sustained a complete overthrow. Had O'Neill followed up his victory, he might have crushed the Scots in Ulster; but, as if given up to infatuation, he marched away southwards, and permitted the Covenanters to recruit their strength. Thus his triumph proved almost fruitless. There were Presbyterians in and around Benburb perhaps ever since the time of this memorable battle. A Mr. Walkinshaw appears to have been minister here shortly after the Restoration, but of him little is known. He was succeeded by Mr. Archibald Hamilton, son of Mr. James Hamilton, nephew of Lord Claneboy, and minister of Ballywalter. Mr. Hamilton settled at Benburb about 1670, and continued in this charge till 1672. He seems to have been very poorly supported; and in consequence, he removed to Armagh towards the close of 1672. He is said to have been succeeded by Mr. James Johnson, who died here. The next minister was Mr. John Boyd, who was ordained here by the Presbytery of Tyrone on the 17th of July, 1706. He died October 16th, 1712. He was succeeded by Mr. John Kennedy, who was ordained here on the 13th of July, 1714. Mr. Kennedy died in this charge on the 25th of June, 1761, at the age of 77. He was succeeded by Mr. Alexander Johnson, who was ordained here on the 23rd of May, 1763. He died August 9th, 1771, leaving neither widow nor family, and aged 52 years. He was succeeded by Mr. James Whiteside, jun., probably son of Mr. James Whiteside, sen., of Tobermore. He was ordained here on the 23rd of December, 1772. Becoming infirm, Mr. Joshua Willis was ordained his assistant on the 31st of March, 1815. Mr. Whiteside died on the 18th of May, 1821, leaving a widow and family. In March, 1822, Mr. Willis was suspended for one month for celebrating marriage irregularly. He was afterwards suspended and dis-annexed; and, after a long vacancy, Mr. James Fullarton was ordained here by a Committee of the Synod of Ulster, on the 2nd of December, 1836. In June following he resigned the charge, and emigrated to Australia. The next minister was Mr. Hugh Montgomery, who was ordained here on the 20th of June, 1838. Mr. Montgomery died on the 24th of December, 1873. He was succeeded by Mr. Gawn Malcom who was ordained here on the 26th of August, 1874. On the 11th of April, 1876, Mr. Malcom resigned this charge on his acceptance of a call from a congregation in England; and was succeeded by Mr. William Clements, formerly minister of Tartaraghan, who was installed here on the 21st of June, 1876.

BILLY or BUSHMILLS.

THE first minister of this congregation was Mr. Jeremiah O'Quin, a native Irishman, educated by Mr. Upton, of Templepatrick. Mr. O'Quin was settled here by the Presbytery in the year 1646. In consequence of refusing to join in the protest against the execution of Charles I., and for taking part with the Republicans and Independents, he was suspended by the Presbytery in April, 1649. He was subsequently restored. He was here in 1656, being mentioned by Livingstone among his acquaintances. He died on the last day of January, 1657. He was succeeded, as minister of Billy, by Mr. Gabriel Cornwall, who was here for perhaps twenty years. He seems to have been succeeded by Mr. Adam White, who was here in 1691. He had been minister of Ardstraw previously. He died minister of Billy on the 19th of December, 1708. The next minister was Mr. John Porter, who was ordained at Bushmills, on the 28th of July, 1713. He died in this charge on the 13th of June, 1738. On the death of Mr. Porter the people split into parties in favour of different candidates; and in 1742 their Commissioner, Mr. Adam Auld, supplicated the Synod of Ulster to grant them a new poll. Mr. John Logue was at length ordained on the 1st of July, 1746. At this time the people of Dunluce belonged to the congregation, but some years afterwards they were erected into a separate charge. In November, 1756, Mr. Logue removed to Buckna, of which he was the first minister. He was succeeded by Mr. Samuel Moore, who was eventually degraded. The next minister was Mr. Hugh Moore, who was ordained here on the 26th of September, 1779. In 1780 he removed to Usher's Quay, Dublin, and was succeeded by Mr. William Douglass, who was ordained here on the 1st of February, 1783. He died in this charge on the 29th of May, 1794, leaving a widow and family. The next minister was Mr. Daniel M'Kee, who was ordained here on the 22nd of November, 1796. On the 13th of June, 1820, he was set aside for drunkenness. He was succeeded in the charge by Mr. Hugh Hamill, who was ordained here on the 28th of November, 1820. Mr. Hamill died on the 31st of March, 1864; and on the 19th of November of the same year the Rev. James Boyle was ordained to the pastoral charge.

BOARDMILLS.

BOARDMILLS is one of the earliest of the congregations established by the Seceders in Ireland. Its first minister was Mr. Andrew Black, who was installed here on the 22nd of June, 1749. He had formerly been minister of Cumbernauld in Scotland. He was present at the formation of the first Burgher Presbytery constituted in Ireland, and was one of its members. This Presbytery was formed on the 24th of July, 1751. After a ministry of 33 years here, Mr. Black died at Boardmills on the 6th of July, 1782, in the 82nd year of his age. The next minister was Mr. Joseph Longmoore, who was ordained in 1784. After a ministry of 25 years he died on the 10th of October, 1809, and was succeeded by Mr. John Sturgeon, whose ministry was of thirty years' duration. He died on the 22nd December, 1840. Meanwhile Mr. George H. Shanks, who was ordained on the 13th of October, 1840, had been appointed his assistant and successor.

BOVEVA.

IT would appear that the first minister here was Mr. Hans Stewart, a licentiate of the Presbytery of Linlithgow. He seems to have been settled as minister of Boveva in 1701. He died on the 6th of May, 1737. He was succeeded by Mr. John Lyle, who was ordained here in 1738. He died in this charge on the 20th of May, 1765. The next minister was Mr. William Stewart, who was ordained here on the 18th of June, 1770. His ministry was of short duration. He was succeeded by Mr. Samuel Patton, who was ordained here by the Presbytery of Derry on the 20th of August, 1773. Mr. Patton removed in the following year to Moneyrea. He was succeeded by the Rev. Francis Gray, who was ordained here some time afterwards. He continued in this charge till his death on the 2nd of August, 1817. The next minister was Mr. Henry Kyd, who was ordained here on the 7th of June, 1818. Mr. Kyd was a man of singular piety, and displayed considerable ability as a writer. He died in this charge on the 4th of June, 1839. After a lengthened vacancy, Mr. Adam Magill was ordained to the pastoral charge on the 8th of March, 1843.

BRIGH.

The first minister of Brigh or Donaghendry, was Mr. Archibald Hamilton, who was settled here in 1630, and ejected in 1661. He died in 1674. His tombstone is in the churchyard there. He was succeeded by Mr. John Abernethy, the ejected minister of Aghaloo or Minterburn, who continued here about ten years and removed to Moneymore. He was succeeded by Mr. Alexander Osborne, who held this charge till January, 1688, when he was removed to Dublin. He was succeeded by Mr. Robert Hamilton in the end of the same year. In 1691 we find their commissioner, Mr. Richard Spier, supplicating the Synod that Mr. Hamilton may be permitted to remain with them, though they cannot give him above £20 per annum. It would appear that shortly afterwards he resigned the charge and removed to Bangor. The next minister was Mr. Thomas Kennedy, son of the minister of Carlan, who was ordained here on the 6th of November, 1700. In 1708 the people complained that they would be injured by a new erection at Coagh; but the Synod deemed them still sufficient to support a minister. Mr. Kennedy died in this charge on the 3rd of July, 1746. He was succeeded by Mr. John White, who was ordained here on the 23rd of July, 1747. He died on the 20th of October, 1787. The next minister was Mr. Thomas M'Kay, who was ordained here on the 1st of August, 1788. He died in this charge on the 19th of December, 1821, aged sixty-six. After much disputing, Mr. James Denham, afterwards D.D., was ordained here by a Synodical Committee on the 11th of July, 1826. Receiving a call to Derry, he resigned this charge on the 20th of April, 1837, and was succeeded by Mr. Samuel H. Elder, who was ordained here on the 1st of August, 1837. Mr. Elder died on the 11th of October, 1844; and was succeeded by Mr. John Maxwell, who was ordained here on the 30th of June, 1847. Mr. Maxwell died on the 29th of June, 1883; and was succeeded by Mr. John Huey Morton, who was ordained here on the 15th of January, 1884.

BROUGHSHANE 1st.

This congregation was originally called Braid, and had for its first minister the Rev. John Douglass, who was ordained here in August, 1655. He was succeeded by the Rev. Fulk

White, who was ordained July 6th, 1687. The congregation engaged to pay Mr. White a stipend of £20 in money and 16 bolls of corn yearly. This minister was well acquainted with Hebrew, and was in the habit of giving instruction in that language to candidates for the ministry. He died August 24th, 1716.* About two months prior to his decease, his son, Mr. James White, was ordained his assistant and successor. The Rev. James White was long an influential minister of the Synod of Ulster; and from him John White, Esq., of Whitehall, near Broughshane, late High-Sheriff of the County Antrim, is lineally descended. He died April 24th, 1761. He had become infirm long prior to his death; and, in consequence, on the 13th of January, 1756, the Rev. Alexander M'Mullan was ordained his assistant. Mr. M'Mullan removed to Cullybackey about two years afterwards, and was succeeded in Broughshane by the Rev. Charles Brown, who was ordained in October, 1759. From this minister the great merchant princes of the same name, of Liverpool and the United States of America, are collaterally descended. Mr. Brown died in September, 1810. In the May of the preceding year, the Rev. Robert Stewart was ordained his assistant and successor. At that time little attention was paid to the question of Sabbath sanctification; and even in cases where the election of a minister was strenuously contested, it was not unusual to take the poll of the congregation on the Lord's Day. When a candidate for the pastoral charge of Broughshane, Mr. Stewart encountered a vigorous opposition; and the voting, which commenced after public worship on Sunday, was continued till nine or ten o'clock at night. The Synod of Ulster at length saw the impropriety of permitting a poll to be taken on the day of sacred rest; and it is said that the Broughshane election terminated the history of this species of Sabbath desecration. Mr. Stewart early distinguished himself in the Synod, as an able debater, and in 1816 was chosen Moderator. He excelled in quick repartee, in clear discrimination, and in far-seeing sagacity. In 1827 he had a remarkable discussion with the Rev. B. M'Auley, Parish Priest of Ballymena, on the subject of the Papal Supremacy. This discussion, which took place in the courthouse of Ballymena, and which continued for three days, excited uncommon interest. Whilst it

* There is a graveyard attached to the 1st Presbyterian Church of Broughshane; and the first body buried in it is said to have been the remains of a soldier of King William III.

was going on, Mr. Stewart was occasionally to be seen looking into a chest of books which was beside him, and which he was obviously searching for authorities, when, at the same time, he was conducting a vigorous argument, and replying most effectively to some previous statements of his antagonist. In all intricate and important negociations he was usually employed by the Synod of Ulster. During the Arian controversy he exhibited great tact and coolness; and his speech in 1828, in support of the celebrated overtures, and in answer to Dr. Montgomery, was one of the happiest efforts of his eloquence. In 1843 he was elected Moderator of the General Assembly. He frequently visited London and Dublin, on deputations to Government. He died on the 26th of September, 1852, and his funeral was attended by an immense multitude. He was succeeded by Mr. Archibald Robinson, who was ordained here on the 23rd of August, 1853.

BUCKNA.

In the year 1756 the inhabitants of this place applied to the Synod of Ulster to be erected into a congregation. The application, though opposed on the part of the congregation of Broughshane, was granted. The first minister was Mr. John Logue, formerly of Billy or Bushmills, who was installed here on the 5th of November, 1756. He removed to America in 1772; and was succeeded by Mr. David Park, who was ordained here on the 26th of July, 1773. Becoming infirm, Mr. Richard Dill was ordained his assistant on the 13th of February, 1810. He resigned this charge on the 11th of February, 1812, and removed to Drumachose. Mr. Park died on the 10th of March, 1814, leaving a widow and family. The next minister was Mr. William M'Clintock Wray, who was ordained here on the 15th of November, 1815. Mr. Wray died on the 14th of November, 1848; and was succeeded by Mr. Samuel Hamilton, who was ordained here on the 5th of September, 1849. On the 29th of September, 1873, Mr. Hamilton retired from the discharge of the active duties of the ministry; and, on the 17th of March, 1874, Mr. John Huey was ordained as his successor.

BURT.

This congregation and Derry appear to have been originally a united charge. The first separate minister of Burt was Mr. William Hempton, a licentiate of the Presbytery of Dean, in Scotland, who was ordained here in September, 1673. Mr. Hempton appears to have returned to Scotland at the Revolution. His successor, Mr. Andrew Ferguson, who had been licensed in Scotland in 1689, came to Burt in 1690. Under him the congregation increased considerably, and in June, 1691, the Presbytery of Lagan required them to make an addition to the meeting-house. In 1695 Mr. Ferguson was called to Corboy or Longford; but the Synod decided that he should remain in Burt. In 1697 there was a dispute between Burt and Derry respecting their relative boundaries. In January, 1698, the Presbytery ordered " that the liberties of the city on that side the water wherein the city standeth should be the bounds of the congregation;" but Burt was dissatisfied with the decision, and appealed to the next meeting of Synod. When Mr. Ferguson became infirm, his son, Mr. Andrew Ferguson, jun., was appointed his successor. He was ordained by the Presbytery of Derry, February 16th, 1725. His father died on the 18th of July following. Mr. Andrew Ferguson, jun., was the great-grandfather of Sir R. A. Ferguson, Bart., at one time M.P. for the city of Derry. Becoming infirm, Mr. Hugh Brooke was ordained his assistant November 5th, 1783. Mr. Ferguson died January 30th, 1787. His funeral sermon, which was preached by the Rev. Andrew Alexander, of Urney, was subsequently published. In this discourse it is stated that "when he had numbered above eighty years, he discerned the same ardour in reading, conversing, and writing on various subjects for which he was distinguished at an earlier period;" and that "by Providence he was endowed with an ample fortune, which he enjoyed with moderation, and employed, as a man of virtue, in kind offices to his friends, in a decent hospitality, and acts of charity to the distressed." Mr. Brooke long ministered to the congregation of Burt, but at length becoming infirm, the Rev. Robert Gray, formerly minister of Dungiven, was installed his assistant on the 15th of October, 1833. Mr. Brooke* died on

---

* The Misses Brooke, the daughters of this minister, have distinguished themselves by their munificent contributions to the Irish Presbyterian Church.

the 17th of June, 1839. Mr. Gray died on the 19th of October, 1857; and was succeeded by Mr. H. P. Charlton, who was installed here on the 19th of October, 1858. Mr. Charlton resigned this charge on the 3rd of November, 1875, on his removal to Scotland; and was succeeded by Mr. William Clarke, who was installed here on the 27th of July, 1876. On his removal to 2nd Bangor, Mr. Clarke resigned this charge on the 28th of July, 1879; and was succeeded by Mr. Robert W. Hamilton, who was ordained here on the 30th of January, 1880. Mr. Hamilton has since removed to 2nd Lisburn.

CAIRNCASTLE.

PATRICK ADAIR* was ordained the first minister here, May 7th, 1646. The congregation was visited in March, 1674, and the following account returned:—"That they were considerably in arrear for every year of four, concluding at All Saints, 1672, and the year commencing at that and concluding at All Saints, 1673, not yet applotted; and no mention of this year current." In October, 1674, Mr. Adair was removed to Belfast, and we find Mr. John Campbell ordained here, May 2nd, 1677. He resided for a time in Belfast during the summer of 1685. In February, 1689, he retired on account of the approaching troubles to Scotland, and in April, 1690, there came a letter from Mr. George Meldrum and Mr. Verner, in the name of the Presbytery of Irwin, showing that Mr. Campbell had now a call from the parish of Newmills there. He returned, however, in the end of April. In March, 1691, Mr. Walter Campbell, of Walter-haughs, appeared a commissioner from Lowdon, in the Presbytery of Irwin, with a letter from the Earl of Lowdon, seeking the removal of Mr. Campbell thither. The Presbytery, however, resolved not to loose him from Cairncastle. In 1700 he asked advice of Synod, stating that he had an invitation from Largs and an offer from the Captain of Dunoon in that neighbourhood to settle all his estate upon him and his family in case he would settle near him at Largs. In the beginning of 1714 he ultimately removed to Scotland on this invitation. His successor was Mr. William Taylor, son of Mr. William Taylor, minister of Drumaul or Randalstown, who was ordained here by the Presbytery of

* The author of "Adair's Narrative."

Antrim on the 14th of June, 1715. He joined the non-subscribing Presbytery of Antrim in 1725; but at his death, in May, 1734, the congregation reverted to the Presbytery of Templepatrick, and by it Mr. John Lewson was ordained here on the 20th of December, 1738. Mr. Lewson becoming infirm, Mr. Thomas Alexander was ordained here as his assistant and successor on the 17th of December, 1793. Mr. Lewson died September 15th, 1802, leaving a family. In 1829 Mr. Alexander and a small part of the congregation seceded from the Synod of Ulster and held the meeting-house. The people adhering to the Synod gave a call to Mr. James Carmichael, who was ordained here on the 24th of May, 1832. Mr. Carmichael becoming infirm, obtained as his assistant and successor Mr. Samuel Edgar Stewart, who was ordained here on the 25th of July, 1871. Mr. Carmichael died on the 28th of July, 1873. Mr. Stewart resigned the pastoral charge on the 30th of October, 1882, on his removal to Carrickfergus; and was succeeded by Mr. John Christie, who was ordained here on the 2nd of October, 1883.

CARLAN.

THIS congregation was originally known by the name of Donoughmore (County Tyrone), and included in it the town of Dungannon, by which name also it was early distinguished. Its first minister was Mr. Thomas Kennedy. He was one of the Presbyterian worthies who lost their livings at the Restoration. He was deposed in 1661; but he settled at Carlan-bridge, where he continued in the exercise of his ministry. He was afterwards called Mr. Thomas Kennedy senior, to distinguish him from Mr. Thomas Kennedy junior, minister of Ballyclug or Brigh. At the Revolution he fled to Scotland. In September, 1691, the congregation applied to Synod to procure his return, offering "£19 per annum, and this year to plough and sow ten acres of land, if he will come over by May next, and they having not above a tenth-part of the land there yet planted, they are very hopeful, in a short time after his coming thither that their land may be planted and so his yearly maintenance be increased. They also promised him £5 towards building a dwelling-house." He returned in 1693, and continued here till his death in February, 1714. He died at the age of 80. At his death the congregation divided, and a part was erected into a separate congregation at Dungannon. Mr. Kennedy was succeeded at Donoughmore, or Carlan, by Mr. Robert Stuart, who was ordained here August 11th, 1720. He died in this charge, April 11th, 1746. He was succeeded by Mr. William Kennedy, who was ordained at Carlan, as it was now called, on the 2nd of April, 1754. Mr. Kennedy becoming infirm, Mr. Robert Stewart was ordained his assistant on the 9th October, 1798. Mr. Kennedy died April, 9th, 1801, leaving a family. Mr. Stewart died in 1812, leaving a family. The next minister was Mr. John Hogg, who was ordained here on the 31st of October, 1815. Mr. Hogg died on the 5th of December, 1846, having previously obtained leave to retire from the active duties of the ministry; and on the 29th September, 1846, Mr. Stewart Carse was ordained his successor.

CARLINGFORD.

CARLINGFORD and Dundalk originally formed a joint charge. The first minister was Mr. John Wilson, who was ordained here about 1700. In 1707, Dundalk was erected into a separate charge, and Mr. Wilson then became exclusively the minister of Carlingford. In 1729, Mr. Wilson emigrated to America. He was succeeded in Carlingford by Mr. Alexander Reed, who was ordained to the joint charge of Carlingford and Narrowwater on the 16th of November, 1731. He died in this charge on the 19th of November, 1737. The next minister was Mr. George Henry, who was ordained at Narrowwater by the Presbytery of Armagh on the 4th of October, 1743. He resigned these charges in May, 1764, and went to America. The next minister was Mr. Robert Dickson, who was ordained here on the 24th of November, 1765. He was elected Clerk to the Synod of Ulster in 1787. He died October 7th, 1804, leaving a family, and was succeeded by Mr. Samuel Arnold, who was ordained to the joint charge of Carlingford and Narrowwater on the 2nd September, 1805. In 1819, the Presbytery of Armagh informed the Synod that the persons now worshipping in Carlingford were so few, and the augmentation of their numbers so very improbable that Mr. Arnold's usefulness as a minister would be greater were he to discontinue his present practice of preaching there every sixth Sabbath, and devote his whole time to Narrowwater. The Synod partly sanctioned this arrangement; and in 1820, Mr. Arnold withdrew entirely from Carlingford. Carlingford, however, continued to be supplied with preaching till 1821, when it was erected into a separate congregation, and Mr. James Lunn was ordained here on the 31st of July of that year. Mr. Lunn joined the Remonstrants in 1829, and afterwards the Presbyterian interest in Carlingford became virtually defunct. But the cause there has recently revived. The Presbyterians of Carlingford have been formed into a congregation under the care of the Assembly, and on the 29th of March, 1869, Mr. William J. M'Cully was ordained to the pastoral charge of Omeath and Carlingford. A comfortable Church has since been erected in the town of Carlingford.

CARLOW.

This had once been a congregation under the Synod of Munster, but had become extinct about the year 1750. Preaching was revived in it early in 1818, and it was shortly afterwards erected into a congregation under the care of the Synod of Ulster and Presbytery of Dublin. Its first minister was Mr. James Morgan (afterwards D.D., of Belfast) who was ordained here on the 21st of June, 1820. He resigned this charge on the 19th of May, 1824, on his removal to Lisburn. The next minister was Mr. Edward Alexander, who was ordained June 23rd, 1825. He resigned the charge on the 5th of April, 1828, and was succeeded by Mr. William Blood, who was ordained on the 20th of March, 1830. Mr. Alexander died at Belfast in November, 1832; and Mr. Blood resigned the charge in August, 1835, and removed, first to England, and afterwards to America. The next minister was Mr. Warrand Carlile, who was ordained here on the 26th of May, 1837. Mr. Carlile resigned the charge on the 1st of November, 1842, and became a missionary to Jamaica. He was succeeded by Mr. David M'Taggart, who was ordained here on the 8th of March, 1843. Mr. M'Taggart resigned the charge on the 26th of June, 1848, and connected himself with the Established Church of Scotland; and, on the 1st of November following, Mr. John Powell, who had previously been minister of Bray, was installed as pastor. In 1855 Mr. Powell resigned the charge, and was succeeded by Mr. John Barnett, who was installed here on the 24th of June, 1856. Mr. Barnett resigned the charge on the 3rd of July, 1866, on his removal to Katesbridge, and was succeeded by Mr. R. S. Coffey, who was ordained here on the 10th of December, 1866. Mr. Coffey resigned this charge on the 18th of February, 1875, on his removal to Bandon; and was succeeded by Mr. George W. Neely, who was ordained here on the 7th of October, 1875. Mr. Neely resigned this charge on the 6th of November, 1878, having accepted a call from the congregation of Malin; and was succeeded by Mr. Neil S. Forsythe, who was installed here on the 20th of May, 1879.

CARNDONAGH.

THIS congregation, sometimes called Donagh, was pretty early settled. In May, 1695, the people called Mr. Robert Neilson, a probationer under the care of the Presbytery of Lagan, to be their minister. They were required to build a meeting-house, but not being found able to support a pastor, Mr. Neilson left them about 1698, without having been ordained. Mr. Neilson soon after settled at Kilraughts. In January, 1701, Mr. Thomas Harvey was ordained here as the minister. He died in this charge on the 24th of February, 1718. The next minister was Mr. Thomas Strawbridge, who was ordained here on the 3rd of October, 1721. Mr. Strawbridge died in this charge on the 2nd of April, 1762. The next minister appears to have been Mr. Samuel Patton, who was here in 1773. He was succeeded by Mr. Robert Scott, who was ordained here on the 22nd of November, 1777. Mr. Scott resigned this charge through bodily infirmity in 1801, and died October 1st, 1803, leaving a widow and family. After a long vacancy, Mr. Reuben Rogers was ordained here on the 27th September, 1808. Mr. Rogers becoming infirm, his son, Mr. Robert L. Rogers, was ordained as his assistant and successor on the 2nd of January, 1844. Mr. Reuben Rogers died on the 12th of February, 1846; and Mr. Robert L. Rogers resigned the pastoral charge on the 20th November, 1847, and was succeeded by Mr. Alexander Pinkerton, who was ordained here on the 28th of March, 1848. The Rev. Robert Morrison was, on the 16th December, 1884, ordained as his assistant and successor.

CARNMONEY.

THE first minister of this congregation of whom we have any account was Mr. James Shaw, who was ordained here in

May, 1657. He was deposed by Jeremy Taylor in 1661, but, notwithstanding, continued privately to officiate among the people. In September, 1672, he brought his servant, George Russell, before the Presbytery " for conferring with a spirit that was in the habit of troubling his dwelling-house," and, at the same meeting, asked the advice of the Presbytery about holding the communion in the parish. They advised him " to delay it a little till the confusion in the parish settle a little," and they also appointed a fast to be held there on September 17th, which was kept accordingly. Mr. Shaw, who never recovered the shock occasioned by these suspected evidences of witchcraft, died in December, 1672. In March, 1673, the congregation gave a unanimous call to his son, Mr. Patrick Shaw, who had been entered on trials in April, and was licensed in September, 1672. After passing his second trials he was ordained privately at Larne, November 12, 1673, Mr. Cunningham, of Ballycarry, preaching and presiding on the occasion. Mr. Shaw died in 1683. In August, 1684, the congregation gave a call to Mr. James Bruce, but he declined to accept it. Soon after, refusing the advice of the Presbytery relative to their settlement, two ministers were sent to remonstrate and to show them that " the Presbytery was troubled to see them so self-willed and disingenuous." In 1686 they gave a call to Mr. John Munro, an ordained Scottish minister at this time in Ireland, who accepted it and settled among them. In August, 1688, he received a call from his former congregation in Argyleshire, and in November, James Wylie, an elder, shows that " the rigid dealing of the landlords pursuing after rent occasions little done to Mr. Munro, and that in three years they are in arrear £48." The Presbytery, in consequence, threatened to permit Mr. Munro to return to Scotland. He continued, however, in Carnmoney until the troubles drove him out of the country in 1689, when he went to Scotland, and did not return. In January, 1690, Mr. George Lang, formerly minister of Newry, sojourning in this neighbourhood, undertook the supplying the congregation till he should be enabled to return to his former charge. Mr. Lang returned to Newry in May, 1692, when the congregation was again thrown vacant. The next minister was Mr. Andrew Crawford, son of Mr. Thomas Crawford, formerly minister of Donegore, who was ordained here about 1695. He died in this charge June 7, 1726. He was succeeded by Mr. John Thompson, who was ordained here by the Presbytery of Templepatrick, July 14th, 1731, and who died in this charge March 18th, 1764. He was succeeded by his nephew, Mr. John Thompson, who was ordained here by the Presbytery of Dromore, March 10th, 1767. Mr. Thompson, who was the grandfather of the Rev. W. M'Clure, of Londonderry, was long a leading minister of the Synod of Ulster. He possessed a remarkably vigorous mind united with great dignity of deportment, and, at a time when latitudinarian views were prevalent in the Synod of Ulster, was known as a decided Calvinist. Becoming infirm, Mr. William Craig was ordained his assistant, February 2nd, 1819. Mr. Craig removed to Dromara in December, 1823, and was succeeded by Mr. John Dill, who was ordained here May 10th, 1825. Mr. Thompson died March 23rd, 1828, in the 87th year of his age and the 62nd of his ministry. Mr. Dill died on the 19th of February, 1841; and was succeeded by Mr. David Wilson (now D.D.), who was ordained here on the 31st of January, 1844. On the 17th of December of the same year Mr. Wilson resigned this charge on his removal to Limerick; and was succeeded by Mr. Joseph Barkley, who was ordained here on the 28th of May, 1845. Mr. Barkley becoming infirm, obtained leave for the congregation to choose an assistant, and died on the 17th of November, 1880. He was succeeded by Mr. Hugh Waterworth, who was ordained here on the 29th of July, 1880.

CARRICKFERGUS 1st.

ABOUT 1620 Mr. Hubbard removed with his congregation from London to this place, where in died in 1623. After him Mr. James Glendinning resided here as a lecturer, but retired to Oldstone about 1625. On the arrival of the Scotch forces here, in 1642, Presbyterian worship was re-established and conducted regularly by their chaplains. The covenant was taken in the church in April, 1644—the Rev. James Weir presiding on the occasion. At length, in the end of the year 1646, Mr. John Greg became the fixed pastor. He was forced to fly from his charge in 1649, when Cromwell and the Regicides obtained the ascendency. The Rev. Timothy Taylor, an English Independent, held the parish under the Republican sway from 1650 till after the Restoration. In 1668 he removed to Dublin. The congregation remained vacant after his removal, but was supplied every other

Sabbath by Mr. Keyes, of Belfast. In December, 1671, Mr. Alexander Lees, their commissioner, supplicated the Presbytery that Mr. Keyes might be settled exclusively with them; but without success, as he was finally confirmed in Belfast in February, 1672.* In May, the Presbytery wrote to Scotland for Mr. Alexander Gordon, and the congregation sent a commissioner with the letter. But in November Mr. William Mayne appears before the Presbytery as commissioner, and declares there is no hope of obtaining Mr. Gordon. In March, 1673, Baptist Boyd was commissioner to the Presbytery, and in May the commissioners were Mr. Robert Dalway, and Mr. John Jowland, who expressed their anxiety for the settlement of a minister. In June the people succeeded in obtaining a hearing of Mr. Archibald Hamilton, formerly minister of Benburb, but now unsettled; and in July they presented him with an unanimous call; but, the Presbytery of Tyrone settling him in Armagh at this time, they were obliged to remain yet longer vacant. Mr. Robert Henry, a probationer, who had been licensed in June, is sent to preach here in October. In January, 1674, they presented him with a call; but at the same meeting the people of Glasslough, who had previously heard him, requested him to be sent back, which is refused; and he is enjoined to embrace the call from Carrickfergus. After second trials he is ordained in the neighbourhood of Ballyclare, at the house of Mr. John Crawford, on the 22nd of April, 1674. Mr. Thomas Hall, of Larne, preached on the occasion, from Matt. ii., 5, 6. The High Church party now rode rough-shod over the Presbyterians, maintaining that they violated the laws of the land by presuming to ordain ministers, and hence this ordination took place in a private dwelling many miles from Carrickfergus. In August, 1688, Mr. Henry had a call from Derry, presented by Mr. William Lennox and Mr. Robert Harvey, two gentlemen whose names soon afterwards acquired celebrity in connection with the siege of the maiden city. The call was further prosecuted in September, by Mr. Frederic Cunningham and Mr. Henry Long, from Derry, and opposed by Mr. John M'Gee, Mr. James M'Cullough, Mr. John Brown, and Mr. David Hood, from Carrickfergus. The result was that Mr. Henry was appointed to continue here. At the same meeting he had a call from Ayr, but the Presbytery would

* Belfast was then a small town; but it was early made a borough, and was represented in the Irish Parliament.

not entertain it. In February, 1689, Mr. Henry retired to Scotland, as Carrickfergus was in the hands of the partisans of King James, and the town suffered much during the Revolution. Mr. Henry returned to his congregation in November, but was again in Scotland during January and February, 1690. In March, 1691, Mr. William M'Cracken appeared as commissioner from Glenluce, in Galloway, seeking his removal there, but the Presbytery would not consent. The Synod, in September, 1691, sent him to supply the Capel Street congregation, in Dublin, for six weeks. In April, 1692, two calls were addressed to him, one from Glenluce, presented by Sir Charles Hay, and the other from Capel Street. Mr. John Brown, at that time one of the Sheriffs of Carrickfergus, Mr. William Dawson, and others, appeared as commissioners from the congregation opposing his removal; but the Synod decided that he should settle in Dublin. In 1693 the people gave a call to Mr. Joshua Fisher, but the Synod removed him to Donaghmore, County of Donegal. The next minister after Mr. Henry was Mr. Archibald Ross, who had been licensed by the Presbytery of Irwin, and who was ordained here in 1694. He is named as one of the trustees for the *Regium Donum* in the patent dated September, 1699. He died in the beginning of the year 1700. The next minister was Mr. Patrick Adair, who was ordained here December 9th, 1702. He died June 12th, 1717. This gentleman appears to have been related to the Adair family of Ballymena. His son, William Adair, Esq., acquired a considerable fortune, and died unmarried. By his last will he bequeathed £2,000 in consolidated three per cent. annuities, in trust to the Adair's of Ballymena, to go annually for the benefit of the poor freemen of Carrickfergus, and to be divided as the owner of the Ballymena estate for the time being may direct. Mr. Adair was succeeded by Mr. James Frazer, who was ordained here June 3rd, 1718. Even at this time the Presbyterians were considerably disturbed by the threats of the High Church party. They were particularly opposed in the license and ordination of ministers. In memoranda which he left behind him, Mr. Frazer relates that he was licensed to preach by the Presbytery of Armagh, in Lurgan, in March, 1710, between 11 and 12 o'clock at night, by Mr. Hutcheson, of Armagh; and that he was ordained as minister of Carrickfergus, in Captain John Davies' garden, by the Presbytery of Belfast. There was at this time an old meeting-house in

Carrickfergus, but a new one was erected very soon afterwards. The following account exhibits the quarterly payments of *Regium Donum* received by Mr. Frazer the year after his ordination :—

Jan. 6th, 1719, received my 1st quarter of "R.D".,					£1	19	10½
Mar. 12,	,,	,,	2nd	,,	,,	2	0	4
June 11,	,,	,,	3rd	,,	,,	2	0	7
Sept. 10,	,,	,,	4th	,,	,,	1	19	6½
			Additional *eodem die*,		0	16	6½
					£8	16	10½

Towards the close of Mr. Frazer's ministry, a committee of Presbytery appointed to compose certain differences existing in the congregation, reported that they " fully vindicated and acquitted Mr. Frazer of endeavouring to procure one seat more than another for Mr. Dalway," and for " receiving Mr. Dalway as a member of the congregation." Mr. Frazer died August, 1748, and was succeeded by Mr. David Fullarton, who, after a long vacancy, was ordained March 11th, 1756. At his ordination he subscribed the following formula,—" I believe the Westminster Confession of Faith contains a good system of the Christian doctrines, which I subscribe as the confession of my faith." In 1760, when Thurot appeared in Belfast Lough with three French frigates, Carrickfergus was taken, and Mr. Fullarton was sent to Belfast with a flag of truce and a letter to the Sovereign, or Mayor, in which the French Commodore threatened to burn the town, if not immediately furnished with a supply of provisions. The ministry of Mr. Fullarton in Carrickfergus was uncomfortable ; he was charged with indiscretion; and he at length resigned the congregation in 1767, and conformed to the Established Church. He was succeeded by Mr. William Blakely, who was ordained December 12th, 1770. He resigned in 1779, and was suspended *sine die*. In 1770 a petition was presented to the corporation from the Masters and Wardens of the Trades, requiring a grant of an old house in North Street, for the use of the Presbyterian minister, and it was ordered that a deed for ever be made to Marriot Dalway, Esq. (who in 1761 was elected M.P. for Carrickfergus), in trust for said minister for the time being, and that twenty guineas be given to Mr. Dalway towards building the same. In March, 1783, Mr. John Savage was ordained to the pastoral charge. He died December 19th, 1822. The next minister was Mr. James

Seaton Reid, formerly minister of Donegore, and afterwards D.D. and Professor of Ecclesiastical History in the University of Glasgow. In Dr. Reid's time the present church was erected. Having been appointed Professor of Ecclesiastical History in Belfast, he resigned this charge on the 6th of November, 1838, and was succeeded by the Rev. James White (son of the Rev. Patrick White, of Bailieborough), who was ordained here by the Presbytery of Templepatrick, on the 31st December, 1838. Dr. Reid died at Belmont, the seat of Lord Mackenzie, near Edinburgh, on the 26th of March, 1851, aged 52.

CASTLEBLAYNEY.

THE earliest notice we have of this congregation is in 1718, when the people applied to the Synod of Ulster for the hearing of a licentiate. They stated that they were able to pay £20 per annum stipend; and that Mr. Arthur Maxwell* of Drumbeg, in County Down, promised them £1 10s. a-year to assist them. At the same time Lord Blayney wrote to the Synod on their behalf, " setting forth his regard for the Protestant Dissenters in his country; that they want a meeting-house; that they were not able to build it; and that he is willing to assist them." They soon after obtained as their minister Mr. Samuel Hemphill, who was ordained here on the 24th of December, 1718. In 1729 he had a call to the 2nd congregation of Antrim; but the Synod continued him here. Lord Blayney wrote to the Synod praying Mr. Hemphill to be settled here. He died in this charge on the 28th of March, 1741. The next minister was Mr. James Gordon, who was ordained here on the 18th of January, 1744. In 1750 he was translated from this to Raphoe. He was succeeded by Mr. John Warnock, who was ordained here by the Presbytery of Cootehill in October, 1756. He was succeeded by Mr. John Davis, who was ordained here on the 13th of December, 1774. Becoming infirm, Mr. James Harpur was ordained his assistant and successor on the 11th of December, 1810. Mr. Davis died March 7th, 1818, leaving neither widow nor family. Mr. Harpur died on the 11th of December, 1838, leaving both widow and family. The next minister was the Rev. Thomas Boyd,

* This gentleman was a distinguished benefactor of the Irish Presbyterian Church.

formerly assistant minister of Magherally, who was installed here on the 21st of June, 1839. Mr. Boyd died on the 26th of November, 1863; and on the 13th of May, 1864, Mr. Joseph M'Askie was installed in the pastoral charge. Mr. M'Askie resigned this charge on the 4th of October, 1881; and was succeeded by Mr. Robert H. Smythe, who was installed here on the 27th of March, 1883.

CASTLEDAWSON.

THE first minister of this congregation of whom we have any account was Mr. John Tomb, who was ordained here about the year 1696. Prior to this time Maghera and Castledawson were united. Mr. Tomb continued in this charge till his death in February, 1718. He was succeeded by Mr. Hugh Wallace, who was installed here September 7, 1720. He had previously been minister of Loughgall, and the congregation of Castledawson now included Magherafelt. The latter place was erected into a separate congregation in 1738, and Mr. Wallace became the minister. Castledawson was thus left vacant, and it then obtained as minister Mr. Robert Henry, who was ordained here by the Presbytery of Route, June 7, 1743. He resigned this charge through age and infirmity October 28, 1798; and died November 1, 1802, leaving a family. He was succeeded by Mr. Solomon Brown,* brother to the Rev. John Brown, D.D., of Aghadoey, who was ordained on the 1st Tuesday of December, 1802. On the 24th of December, 1833, Mr. Brown resigned the charge through infirmity, and died November, 20, 1834. The next minister was Mr. James Glasgow, who was ordained here by the Presbytery of Magherafelt, October 6, 1835. At the first meeting of the General Assembly of the Presbyterian Church in Ireland Mr. Glasgow (now D.D.) was sent abroad as a missionary to India, and Castledawson became vacant. The next minister was Mr. John Radcliffe, who was ordained here on the 23rd of June, 1841. Mr. Radcliffe, having been appointed to a charge in the West Indies, resigned the congregation on the 15th of August, 1848; and was succeeded by Mr. Robert Gamble, who was ordained on the 1st of August, 1849, by the Presbytery of Magherafelt.

* Father of Dr. S. Browne, R.N., J.P., Belfast.

CASTLEDERG 1ST.

THE congregation of 1st Derg, or Castlederg, now belonging to the Presbytery of Donegal, was established about the year 1700. In July, 1699, Mr. Holmes, of Urney, signified to the Presbytery that there was a considerable prospect of a congregation being formed here, provided a part of his congregation and of Mr. Haliday's, at Ardstraw, were joined to the existing nucleus. There is reason to believe that the first minister was Mr. John Dunlop, who was ordained by the Presbytery of Convoy, September 15th, 1710, and died, November 29th, 1713. The next minister was Mr. Nehemiah Donaldson, ordained here, December 19th, 1716. Mr. Donaldson was the valued friend and pastor of the celebrated Mr. David Cairns, of Knockmany, one of the heroes of the siege of Derry; and Mr. Cairns, at his death, bequeathed to him a pledge of his affection.* Mr. Donaldson died, July 7th, 1747, and was succeeded by Mr. Hugh Young, who was ordained here, June 8th, 1748. In 1750, Mr. Young was called to be colleague to Mr. M'Collum, of Capel Street, Dublin; but expressing his sincere attachment to Derg, the Synod refused to require his removal. In 1772, it was reported to Synod that Hugh Edwards, Esq., had bequeathed to the congregation £10 yearly, for ever, a sum which is, we believe, still regularly paid to the minister. Mr. Young died in this charge in 1789, leaving a family. He was succeeded by Mr. James Henderson, who was ordained here, May 27th, 1791. Mr. Henderson was drowned, December 20th, 1818, leaving a widow and family; and was succeeded by Mr. James Adams, ordained here, September 27th, 1820. Mr. Adams died in this charge, May 22nd, 1837. In November, 1827, the congregation of Killeter was disannexed from that of Derg. In September, 1837, Mr. John Crockett, formerly of Killeter, was installed as successor to Mr. Adams. Mr. Crockett becoming infirm applied for an assistant, and died on the 11th of February, 1875; and was succeeded by Mr. James M'Cay, who was ordained here on the 20th of May, 1874.

* Mr. Cairns, who was long M.P. for Derry, died in May, 1722. He was married to Margaret Edwards. In 1743, Matthew Edwards, of the same family, was married to the daughter of Nehemiah Donaldson.

CASTLEREAGH.

This congregation was originally a joint charge, there being two congregations—one at Knock and another at Breda. The first minister of whom we have any account was Mr. Hugh Wilson, who, in 1661, was deposed by Bishop Taylor. Mr. Wilson continued to preach to his people as often as he had opportunity till 1690, when he removed to Scotland, and settled in the Presbytery of Wigton. His successor was Mr. James Montgomery. He died October 26th, 1710. He was succeeded by Mr. Francis Montgomery, who was ordained here April 27th, 1715. In 1741 he became infirm, and Mr. Samuel Alexander was ordained his assistant and successor by the Presbytery of Bangor, January 26th, 1742. Mr. Montgomery died in 1761. Mr. Alexander becoming infirm, Mr. Alexander Henry was ordained his assistant and successor, December 13th, 1774. Mr. Alexander died November 18th, 1787. Mr. Henry died July 14th, 1806. He was succeeded by Mr. Charles Grey, who was ordained March 3rd, 1807. On the 16th of March, 1814, he resigned this charge, and on the same day was suspended. He died February 14th, 1816. The next minister was Mr. Henry Haslett, who was ordained here September 24th, 1816. Mr. Haslett having retired from the active duties of the ministry, Dr. John James Given was installed as his assistant and successor, February 7th, 1854. Dr. Given, on his appointment to a professorship in Magee College, resigned this charge in June, 1870; and was succeeded by Mr. William Rogers, who was ordained here on the 3rd of August, 1871. Mr. Rogers (now LL.D.)* resigned the charge of this congregation in 1876 on his removal to Whitcabbey; and was succeeded by Mr. John B. Thomson, who was ordained here on the 13th of March, 1877.

CAVAN.

This congregation was erected in November, 1833. The first minister was Mr. James M'Clatchy, who was ordained here by the Presbytery of Monaghan on the 3rd of April, 1834. He died of consumption on the 21st of November,

* The great-grandfather of Dr. Rogers, who was minister of the Secession church of Cahans, was the first Professor of Divinity in Ireland appointed by the Secession Church.

1836, and was succeeded by Mr. Robert Fleming—who had been minister of the Seceding congregation at Bellaghy, in County Derry—but who had joined the Belfast Presbytery in 1836. He was installed here on the 5th of March, 1837. Mr. Fleming died on the 26th of March, 1851; and was succeeded by Mr. James Carson, who was ordained here on the 30th of June, 1851. On the 30th of July, 1879, Mr. Carson retired from the active duties of the ministry, and was succeeded by Mr. John Howard Murphy,* who was ordained here on the 27th of November of the same year. Mr. Carson died on the 21st of December, 1880.

CAVANALECK.

THIS congregation was at first called Aghalurcher or Five-mile-town. The first minister of whom we have any account is Mr. Josias Cornwall, who was ordained here by the Presbytery of Monaghan, May 21st, 1704. He was deposed for gross misconduct on his own confession, December 26th, 1728. In 1730 he came before the Synod, "confessed his sin, and made such professions of his repentance as were very satisfactory to the Synod." He was restored to the ministry by the Presbytery of Monaghan, October 4th, 1738, but never held a charge. The next minister was Mr. John Gibson, who was ordained here February 23rd, 1732. He removed to Keady in January, 1738. The next notice we have of this congregation is in the account of the ordination of Mr. Thomas Boyle, who was settled here May 21st, 1745. He died October 25th, 1780, leaving a family. He was succeeded by Mr. W. Johnson, who was ordained here by the Presbytery of Clogher, December 4th, 1781. Becoming infirm, the Rev. James Philips was ordained his assistant and successor May 19th, 1812. Mr. Johnson was afterwards suspended and finally degraded. Mr. Philips becoming infirm, Mr. John M'Michael was ordained his assistant and successor on the 29th of June, 1858. Mr. M'Michael having resigned the charge and emigrated to the colonies, Mr. David Greer was installed in this charge on the 29th of September, 1864. Mr. Philips died on the 21st of April, 1867. Mr. Greer died on the 17th of May, 1884, and was succeeded by Mr. James Melville Irwin, who was ordained here on the 14th of October of the same year.

* Son of Professor J. G. Murphy, D.D., LL.D., of Assembly's College, Belfast.

CLARE.

The first minister here of whom we have any account was Mr. John Macbride. He was here in 1679. In the year 1694 he was removed to Belfast, where he continued till his death. In 1697 Moses Cherry was ordained at Clare as his successor. He died in 1727. He was succeeded by his son, George Cherry, who had been ordained here as his father's assistant and successor on the 14th of December, 1725. Mr. Cherry died in this charge on the 17th of May, 1765, leaving a widow and children. He was succeeded by Mr. Samuel Livingston, who was ordained here on the 20th of August, 1765. He died minister of this congregation on the 26th of February, 1802, leaving a widow and family. After much disputing, Mr. Robert Adams was ordained here on the 22nd of June, 1807. In 1812 he was admonished and suspended one Lord's Day for neglect of his pastoral duty in not visiting the sick, and for transgressing the regulations of Synod respecting the celebration of marriage. This was the origin of much trouble in the congregation, as the people were very unwilling that Mr. Adams should return to the performance of pastoral duties among them. In 1816 it was at length agreed that the congregation should have liberty to choose a successor to Mr. Adams, on the understanding that Mr. Adams was to pay, out of the "*R.D.*", £30 per annum to such successor. Accordingly Mr. James Gardner was ordained here on the 28th of March, 1817. On the 9th June, 1824, he was set aside from the ministry for immorality. The next minister was Mr. John Bell, who was ordained here on the 21st December, 1824. Mr. Adams died about 1840. In 1876, in consequence of the increasing infirmity of Mr. Bell, leave was granted to his congregation to elect an assistant and successor, and on the 14th of November, 1877, Mr. David Wilson was ordained to the pastoral charge. Mr. Wilson, on his removal to Mourne, resigned this charge on the 5th of October, 1881; and was succeeded by Mr. Robert J. Whan, who was ordained here on the 28th of March, 1882.

CLOGHER or CARNTALL.

This congregation was originally known by the name of Clogher, and the earliest notice we have of it is in connection with an unsuccessful application of the people to the Synod of Ulster in September, 1691, for the continuance with them of Mr. Neill Gray, who was then about to be settled at Taughboyne or St. Johnstone. They promised to the Synod to make good to him £30 per annum. Their commissioners were Messrs. James Kennedy, William Cairns and William Ury. Mr. Neill Gray had been preaching to them for some time. He was succeeded by Mr. William Cornwall, who was ordained here about 1695. In 1717 he expressed his desire to demit the charge of the congregation, on account of the distance of his dwelling-house from the meeting-house, of his bodily indisposition, and of the great arrears due by the people. In 1718 he resigned this charge, purposing to go to America. He returned from New England, not long after his arrival there, and was settled at Taughboyne in 1722. The next minister was Mr. John Carlisle, who was ordained here on the 10th of January, 1722. He died in this charge May 22nd, 1748. He was succeeded by Mr. William M'Neill, who was ordained here May 22nd, 1754, by the Presbytery of Tyrone. In 1770 he was suspended, *sine die*, and the Synod in 1771 ordered that unless he satisfied the Presbytery of Tyrone as to the disposal of £20 bequeathed to the minister of Carntall, and of £20 bequeathed to the poor of said parish, he should be deposed. The next minister was Mr. Andrew Millar, who was ordained here June 15th, 1773. Becoming infirm, Mr. John Hanna was ordained his assistant and successor November 5th, 1829. Mr. Millar died on the 11th of February, 1831. Mr. Hanna died on the 7th of December, 1857. He was succeeded by Mr. James G. Robb, who was ordained here on the 24th of June, 1858. Mr. Robb (afterwards D.D.) resigned this charge on the 16th of March, 1874, on his removal to Toronto; and was succeeded by Mr. William H. Bailey, who was ordained here on the 18th of August, 1874.

CLONMEL.

In June, 1673, a letter from Colonel Sankey was laid before the Presbytery of Lagan, together with a call from certain people of Clonmel, to Mr. William Cock. He was accordingly ordained as their minister on the 25th of November, 1673. He was here in 1688. The congregation subsequently joined the Presbytery of Munster, and among its ministers was the Rev. William Campbell, D.D., so famous for his controversy with Dr. Woodward, Bishop of Cloyne. Dr. Campbell was a New Light minister, and notwithstanding his learning and ability, the congregation did not flourish under him. His successors were at least equally lax in their theology. In 1832 several families here applied to the Synod of Ulster for preaching, and soon afterwards a congregation was erected in the place. Their first elected minister was the Rev. M. Mitchell, formerly minister of the seceding congregation of Moneymore, but he died before his installation. The next minister elected was Mr. John Dill, who was ordained here on the 25th of May, 1836. Mr. Dill died on the 5th of August, 1868; and on the 30th of December of the same year Mr. H. H. Beattie (now LL.D.) was ordained as minister. On the 2nd of April, 1878, Dr. Beattie, having received an appointment as chaplain to the Forces, resigned this charge. On the 27th of June, 1878, the Rev. James Wilson was installed in the congregation of Clonmel as a joint-charge with Fethard.

CLONTIBRET 1st.

This congregation was erected in 1725. Their commissioner to the Synod in that year was George Meek. The first minister was Mr. William Sloan, who was ordained here by the Presbytery of Monaghan on the 3rd of April, 1728. He died in this charge on the 12th of June, 1732. He was succeeded by Mr. James Clarke, who was ordained here on the 26th May, 1736. He died in November, 1756. He was succeeded by Mr. James Kinnear, who was ordained here on the 25th of June, 1759. He died in this charge on the 21st of March, 1777. His successor was Mr. William M'Ferson, who was ordained by the Presbytery of Dromore on the 6th of May, 1778. He resigned the charge of the congregation on the 24th of August, 1789; and was succeeded by Mr. James Goudy, who was ordained here by the Presbytery of Monaghan on the 25th of March, 1790. He died on the 10th of September, 1826, leaving a widow and family. The next minister was Mr. Alexander Patterson, jun., son of the Rev. Alexander Patterson, of Magherally, who was ordained here by the Presbytery of Monaghan on the 3rd of July, 1827. On the 2nd of March, 1830, Mr. Patterson resigned this charge and removed to Ballymena. He was succeeded by Mr. John Arnold, who was ordained here on the 30th of

September, 1830. On July 3rd, 1835, Mr. Arnold resigned the charge and removed to Omagh. The next minister was Mr. James Buchanan Hamilton, a licentiate of the Church of Scotland, who was ordained here on the 1st of September, 1836. On the 3rd of October, 1843, Mr. Hamilton resigned the pastoral charge, having received a presentation to a parish in connection with the Established Church of Scotland; and on the 24th of June, 1845, Mr. Andrew Molyneux was ordained as pastor.

CLOUGH, Co. ANTRIM.

THIS congregation was early planted. The first minister was Mr. Andrew Rowan, who was originally from the neighbourhood of Glasgow, and who was ordained here about 1650. At the Restoration he was one of the few who conformed, and he was consequently admitted rector of Dunaghy, or Clough, by the Bishop of Down and Connor, on the 13th of September, 1661. This seems to have impeded the settlement of a Presbyterian minister here for some time. The next minister was Mr. Peter Orr, who was ordained to this charge in January, 1673. At the Revolution he fled to Scotland, but returned shortly afterwards, and remained here till his death, on the 27th of December, 1706. He was succeeded by Mr. Alexander Orr (probably his son), who was ordained here on the 20th December, 1709. His pastorate was short, as he died on the 1st of May, 1713. His successor was Mr. Thomas Cobham, who was ordained on the 12th of March, 1718. He died in this charge on the 3rd of February, 1732. He was succeeded by Mr. James M'Curdy, who was ordained here by the Presbytery of Coleraine on the 12th of August, 1735. He died in this charge on the 8th of January, 1758; and was succeeded by Mr. Joseph Douglass, who was ordained here on the 3rd of June, 1760. Mr. Douglass is said to have been a man of commanding presence; he was a captain of the Volunteers; and he sometimes preached in his military dress. His daughter Margaret—who is said to have been extremely beautiful—was married to Richard Bateson, Esq., of Londonderry, grandfather of Sir Robert Bateson, Bart., of Castruse, County of Donegal. Mr. Douglass resigned the charge of the congregation in consequence of age and infirmity on the 1st of November, 1795. The next minister was Mr. Thomas Kinnear, who was ordained here on the 23rd of June, 1801. He resigned the charge in December, 1804. Mr. Douglass died on the 18th of November, 1805. The next minister was Mr. John Hall, who was ordained here on the 17th of June, 1806. Becoming infirm, Mr. Hall retired from the discharge of the pastoral duties, and on the 14th of March, 1865,* Mr. James Rentoul was ordained his assistant and successor. Mr. Hall died on the 11th of January, 1866. Mr. Rentoul resigned this charge on the 14th of May, 1878, on his removal to 2nd Dromore; and was succeeded by Mr. S. E. Brown, formerly of Athlone, who was installed here on the 19th of November, 1878.

CLOUGH, Co. Down.

THE earliest notice of this congregation in the Synodical records is under the name of *Drumea*. Its first minister was Thomas Maxwell, who was here in 1687, and probably for some time before. He died in this charge on the 14th of July, 1705. He was succeeded by Mr. Hugh Ramsay, who was ordained here by the Presbytery of Down on the 7th of May, 1707, and who died on the 12th of November, 1720. The next minister was Mr. Hugh Williamson, who was ordained here by the same Presbytery on the 31st of July, 1722. He died in this charge March 3rd, 1748. He was succeeded by Mr. John Williamson (probably his son), who was ordained here by the Presbytery of Killileagh on the 4th of February, 1752, and who was a subscriber to the Westminster Confession of Faith. He was present at the Synod of 1766, but he is not afterwards noticed. The next minister was Mr. Robert Porter, who was ordained here on the 16th of June, 1773. Becoming infirm, Mr. William Campbell was ordained his assistant and successor on the 22nd September, 1813. Mr. Porter died on the 22nd of March, 1815. Mr. Campbell died on the 2nd of April, 1829. A dispute having occurred respecting the choice of a successor, and the Synod of Ulster having, in 1829, put the congregation under the care of a committee, a part of it seceded to the Presbytery of Antrim in July, 1829. The next minister was Mr. Francis Dill, formerly of Ray, County Donegal, who was installed here by the committee of Synod on the 3rd of November, 1829. The congregation was annexed by the Synod in 1830

* It thus appears that the ministry of Mr. Hall is one of the longest on record.

to the Presbytery of Dromore. About this time they commenced a suit for the recovery of the meeting-house, meanwhile occupied by the Arian party, and a decision was given in their favour by the Barons of the Exchequer in May, 1836. Mr. Dill becoming infirm, Mr. Edward Stuart was ordained his successor on the 3rd of February, 1842. Mr. Dill died on the 29th of January, 1848. Mr. Stuart having become infirm, Mr. Robert Scott was ordained as his assistant and successor on the 4th of July, 1883.

CLOUGHERNEY.

This congregation was erected off the 1st congregation of Omagh in 1720, and, with Pettigo, was under the ministry of Mr. Joseph Hemphill from 1721 till his death in 1747. It then became a separate charge under the name of *Termont*, and its first minister was Mr. James Scott, who was ordained here by the Presbytery of Strabane on the 16th of April, 1752. He was annexed to Clogher Presbytery in 1777, and was killed on the 2nd of January, 1780, leaving a widow. Mr. James Ker was ordained his successor by the Presbytery of Clogher on the 13th of February, 1781. He died in this charge on the 5th of June, 1823, leaving neither wife nor family, and was succeeded by Mr. Archibald Armstrong, who was ordained here on the 2nd of September, 1823. Mr. Armstrong died in September, 1849. He was succeeded by Mr. Joseph M'Caskie, who was ordained here on the 10th of September, 1850. On the 9th of April, 1864, Mr. M'Caskie resigned the charge of this congregation, having accepted a call to 1st Castleblayney. He was succeeded by Mr. Samuel Cochrane, who was ordained to the pastoral charge on the 27th of June, 1865.

COAGH.

The first notice we have of this congregation is in 1708, when the inhabitants about Coagh and Ballinderry complained to the Synod that the Presbytery of Tyrone had refused to erect them into a congregation, and join to them some from Moneymore and Ballyclug (now Brigh) congregations. The Presbytery was rebuked for this opposition; and in 1710 the whole matter, after many disputes, was satisfactorily adjusted, and Mr. David Thomb was ordained here on the 17th of October, 1711. He died in this charge on the

6th of October, 1726. He was succeeded by Mr. Hugh Sharp, who was ordained here on the 6th of June, 1732, after a vacancy of nearly six years. In 1751 the people applied to the Synod for supplies, Mr. Sharp having become infirm. He died on the 7th of February, 1753; and was succeeded by Mr. John M'Clelland, who was ordained here on the 9th of September, 1755. Mr. M'Clelland died in this charge on the 28th of August, 1798. The next minister was Mr. John Cowan, who was ordained here on the first Tuesday of May, 1801. Becoming infirm, he resigned the pastoral charge in 1835; and on the 5th of October of that year Mr. Edward M. Dill, M.D., was ordained his assistant and successor. Dr. Dill resigned this charge, and removed to Cork. He was succeeded by Mr. Robert Holmes, who was ordained here on the 29th November, 1839. Mr. Cowan died on the 26th of July, 1841. Mr. Holmes died on the 18th of September, 1881; and was succeeded by Mr. Alexander Coskery, who was ordained here on the 2nd of March, 1882.

COLERAINE, 1st.

The name of the first pastor of this congregation is unknown. On Easter Sunday, 1644, the Covenant was administered in the town by Messrs. Weir and Adair, ministers from Scotland, to the garrison and inhabitants, and was taken by Mr. Vesey, the minister. In 1668 and 1669, the congregation was vacant. Mr. Thomas Wylie, a Scotch minister, whose relatives lived in Coleraine, came over and supplied the place for three years, from 1670 to 1673, but declined settling in the charge. On his return to Scotland the people sent with him a blank call, dated June 25th, 1673, to be presented to such a person as he would recommend. He sent them over Mr. William Weir, who had been the minister of West Calder, in Scotland, and who had been brought prisoner to Edinburgh, on the 31st of July, 1673, for maintaining his Presbyterian principles. Mr. Weir continued in Coleraine from 1674 to 1687, when he returned to Scotland, where he died in the ministry at Linlithgow in 1695. In May, 1688, the congregation of Coleraine gave a call to Mr. Abernethy, of Moneymore, but partly in consequence of the unsettled state of the country, this minister did not remove there till 1691. The people promised him fuel, a dwelling-house, and £40 per annum stipend. Mr. Abernethy died in this charge November 14th, 1703. In 1705 the congregation wished to call Mr. Robert Gemmill from Scotland, but the Synod, not being satisfied with his testimonials, could not permit them. This created great and long-continued dissatisfaction in the congregation. The people at length agreed upon a call to Mr. Robert Higinbotham, who was ordained here, December 26th, 1710. In 1714 Mr. Higinbotham was rebuked before the Synod for refusing to marry Mrs. Martha Woods, of Four-loan-ends, in Belfast parish, and was allowed three months for fulfilling that contract, otherwise the Presbytery of Route were instructed to depose him. At the time of the disputes respecting subscription, he at first took the side of the non-subscribers, when a new erection was sanctioned in Coleraine, and he, in consequence, withdrew from the Synod; but in the year 1727 he returned, and professed his adherence to subscription and the Westminster Confession of Faith. He was now joined to the Presbytery of Derry, but the Sessions of Ballykelly and Boveva supplicated that he should be removed to another Presbytery, and he was joined to that of Templepatrick. He was afterwards connected with the Presbytery of Ballymena when it was formed in 1745. In 1761 he and his congregation supplicated to be put again into the Presbytery of Derry, and the Synod acceded to the application. Mr. Higinbotham becoming infirm, Mr. Arthur Kyle was ordained as his assistant September 23rd, 1761. Mr. Higinbotham died in 1770. On the 4th of June, 1799, Mr. Matthew Culbert was ordained as assistant to Mr. Kyle, who died in August, 1808. Mr. Culbert becoming blind, Mr. Andrew M'Caldin, formerly minister at Stratford, was installed here on the 20th of March, 1811. Mr. Culbert died January 30th, 1819. Mr. M'Caldin died on the 10th of July, 1844, and on the 6th of May, 1845, Mr. William Richey was ordained to the pastoral charge. It thus appears that Mr. Richey was the sixth minister of Coleraine since the time of the Revolution, and that the pastorate of Mr. Higinbotham extended over a period of about sixty years. Mr. Richey obtained as his assistant Mr. Robert W. Fleming, who was installed here on the 20th of November, 1860. Mr. Richey died on the 14th of October, 1867. Mr. Fleming retired from the active duties of the ministry some time previously, and died on the 23rd of July, 1882. He was succeeded by Mr. Francis Stuart Gardiner, who was ordained here on the 10th of May, 1882.

COLERAINE 2ND.

THIS congregation was erected in 1727, in consequence of the part taken by Mr. Higinbotham, the minister of the place, in the debates respecting subscription to the Westminster Confession of Faith. In December, 1727, Messrs. Hugh Bankhead, Robert Dunlop, and Isaac Tod appeared as commissioners at the Synod from this new erection. Their first minister was Mr. Charles Lynd, formerly minister of Fannet, who was installed here by the Presbytery of Route in the beginning of the year 1728. He died in this charge on the 21st of December, 1751. He was succeeded by Mr. John Simpson, who was ordained here on the 17th of October, 1753. He died in this charge on the 4th of March, 1795. The next minister was Mr. John Glasgow, who was ordained here on the 8th of March, 1796. He died on the 13th of July, 1801, and was succeeded by Mr. John Whiteside, who was ordained here on the last Tuesday of July, 1802. About the year 1840 a charge was brought against Mr. Whiteside, connected with the making of the will of Mr. Daniel Fulton, and a painful investigation followed. The result was that Mr. Whiteside retired from the discharge of the pastoral duties, and on the 10th of June, 1842, the Rev. Robert Knox was installed as his assistant and successor. Mr. Whiteside died on the 14th of April, 1843. Mr. Knox (afterwards Dr. Knox of Belfast), resigned the pastoral charge on the 27th of March, 1843; and on the 8th of August of the same year the Rev. Hugh Porter, formerly minister of 2nd Dunboe, was installed as the pastor of this congregation. Mr. Porter died on the 9th of June, 1847; and was succeeded by the Rev. James Alfred Canning, who had formerly been minister of Mourne, and who was installed here on the 11th of April, 1848. Mr. Canning died on the 9th of June, 1864; and on the 15th of March, 1865, the Rev. Robert Wallace was installed as the minister of this congregation.

COMBER 1ST.

THE first minister here was the Rev. James Gordon, who was ordained by the Presbytery of Down, about the year 1645. Mr. Gordon was deposed for nonconformity, in 1661, but afterwards conformed. He was succeeded by the Rev.

John Hamilton, who retired to Scotland, at the time of the troubles in 1689. Mr. Hamilton was subsequently appointed one of the ministers of Edinburgh. In 1687, and during the ministry of Mr. Hamilton, Mr. John Binning opened a philosophy school at Comber, where some candidates for the ministry received part of their education; but the scheme was interrupted by the revolution, and never resumed. Mr. Hamilton was succeeded by the Rev. Thomas Orr, who was ordained by the Presbytery of Down, in the year 1695. Mr. Orr continued in this charge till his death, in 1722. He was succeeded by the Rev. John Orr, probably his son, who was ordained here, January 6th, 1724. He joined the non-subscribing Presbytery of Antrim, and the meeting-house having been seized by those adhering to the Synod, in July, 1725, the congregation continuing to worship therein, obtained, as their minister, the Rev. Robert Cunningham, who was ordained here, by the Presbytery of Bangor, October 22nd, 1728. Becoming infirm, he demitted the charge in 1722, and died in February, 1776. He was succeeded by the Rev. William Henry, who had formerly been minister of the second congregation of Dromore. Mr. Henry was father of the Rev. Thomas Henry, minister of Randalstown, and grandfather of the late Rev. P. S. Henry, D.D., President of Queen's College, Belfast. Mr. Henry died June 19th, 1789, and was succeeded by the Rev. John M'Cance, who was ordained here, June 15th, 1790. Mr. M'Cance, becoming infirm, demitted the charge in 1837, and the Rev. Isaac Nelson * was ordained as his assistant, on the 27th August, 1838. In March, 1842, Mr. Nelson removed to Belfast, and on the 9th of May, 1843, the Rev. J. M. Killen (afterwards D.D.) was ordained to the pastoral charge. Mr. M'Cance died on the 4th of November, 1843. One of the Colville family granted for ever, at a small rent, to the congregation of Comber, the plot of ground on which the meeting-house and manse now stand. The grant was made before the time of the revolution. About half a century afterwards, the Colville property was purchased by the ancestor of the present Lord Londonderry. Dr. Killen died on the 3rd of September, 1879, and was succeeded by Mr. John M'Keown, who was ordained here on the 23rd of March, 1880. Mr. M'Keown has recently removed to Birmingham.

* Late M.P. for Mayo.

COMBER 2ND.

THIS congregation was erected in 1838, and its first minister was Mr. John Rogers, who was ordained here on the 27th of March, 1839. In 1869 Mr. (now Dr.) Rogers was elected Professor of Sacred Rhetoric in Assembly's College, Belfast. He was succeeded by the Rev. James Niblock, who was installed here on the 17th of June, 1873. Mr. Niblock, having accepted a call from a congregation in the Established Church of Scotland, resigned the charge in the summer of 1877, and was succeeded by Mr. David A. Taylor, who was ordained here on the 4th of December, 1877.

CONLIG.

THE congregation of 1st Bangor has been one of the most prolific in the General Assembly. Within the memory of many still living, it has given birth to no less than five other congregations, viz., Conlig, Ballygilbert, Ballygrainey, Groomsport, and 2nd Bangor. The late John Sinclair, Esq., of Belfast, father-in-law of the Rev. W. Fleming Stevenson, D.D., of Rathgar, was mainly instrumental in the establishment of the congregation of Conlig. Mr. Sinclair erected entirely at his own expense the handsome church in which the congregation now meets for worship. The district was then much more populous than it is at present, as the lead mines in the neighbourhood gave much employment. The first minister was Mr. Samuel Hamilton, who was ordained here on the 24th of February, 1846. Mr. Hamilton removed to 1st Saintfield in February, 1854, and was succeeded by Mr. S. J. Hanson, who was ordained here on the 22nd of August, 1854. Mr. Hanson removed to Kingstown in January, 1860, and was succeeded by Mr. William Craig, who was ordained here on the 4th of September, 1860. Mr. Craig died in 1872, and was succeeded by Mr. David Gordon, who was ordained here on the 7th of January, 1873. Mr. Gordon on his removal to New Zealand, resigned this charge on the 14th of February, 1884; and was succeeded here by Mr. Hugh Porter, who was ordained here on the 8th of October, 1884.

CONNOR.

THE first minister of this congregation was Mr. Robert

Dewart, who was put on trial, with a view of his settlement here, in March, 1658, and ordained soon after. In 1661, after the Restoration, he was deposed by Bishop Taylor, and thus his ministry here terminated. Mr. Thomas Gowan, formerly minister of Glasslough, supplied the congregation, without being fixed in the charge, from 1667 to 1671. On March 27th, 1672, Mr. David Cunningham was ordained minister. Having arrived from Scotland the year preceding, he was entered on trials by the Presbytery in August, 1671, and licensed in October. Such was the intolerance of the period that the ministers dare not venture on a public ordination at Connor. He was, in consequence, ordained privately at Cairncastle, Mr. Patrick Adair presiding. The Presbytery entered upon their records a declaration to the effect that "it was not convenient for him to preach at Connor for some time in their present circumstances." Mr. Cunningham accordingly went to Scotland, and returned in July, when the elders, in the presence of the Presbytery, and in the name of the congregation, received him as their minister. In February, 1674, Mr. John Blacklow appeared as the commissioner of the congregation before the Presbytery, and stated that "their kindness and dutifulness to their minister was considerable, tho' their quota came not altogether up to their expectation." In 1688, James Brown, on behalf of the congregation, stated to the Presbytery that they "would bestir themselves to get up arrears due to Mr. Cunningham, when victual came into their hands." About this time Mr. Cunningham, in consequence of declining health, expressed a wish to return to his native air in Scotland. The Presbytery gave him permission to do so; but he did not leave this country until March, 1689, when the troubles forced him to fly. In April, 1691, he again returned; and in June following the commissioner of the congregation, James Brown, promised that he should receive £30 in hand, and have security for £24, with from eight to twelve bolls of corn yearly. They also promised to repair his house. Mr. Cunningham died May 21st, 1697. He was succeeded by Mr. Robert Murdock, who was ordained December 6th, 1699. His ministry was short, as he died in June, 1702. The next minister was Mr. Charles Masterton, who appeared before the Synod in 1703, with his license from the Presbytery of Linlithgow, and who was ordained May 17th, 1704. Mr. Masterton was one of the most distinguished ministers of the Synod, and a staunch advocate of orthodoxy—then beginning to be attacked. In the month of February, 1723, he was removed to the congregation of Rosemary Street, Belfast. He was succeeded by Mr. Robert M'Master, who was ordained here by the Presbytery of Antrim, March 18th, 1724. In 1729 Mr. M'Master received a call from the congregation of Usher's Quay, Dublin. The congregation of Connor opposed his removal, and sent Messrs. James Dickie, William Harpur, and Samuel Blakely as their commissioners to the Synod, to protest against it; but the Synod deemed it expedient to permit him to go to Dublin. The congregation now remained a considerable time vacant; but at length, in August, 1733, Mr. Thomas Fowler was ordained here by the Presbytery of Templepatrick. His ministry was brief, as he died in June, 1736. The next minister, Mr. James Cochrane, was ordained by the Presbytery of Route, February 14th, 1738. He died December 19th, 1770, leaving a widow and family; and was succeeded by Mr. James Brown, who was ordained here February 27th, 1775. He demitted his charge here August 1st, 1788. The next minister was Mr. Henry Henry, who had previously been settled at Garvagh, and who was installed here December 9th, 1788. Becoming infirm, Mr. David Hamilton was ordained his assistant September 29th, 1829. Mr. Hamilton resigned this charge, and removed to York Street congregation, Belfast, in January, 1840. He was succeeded by Mr. John Hamilton Moore, who was ordained here 6th July, 1840. Mr. Henry died the November following. Mr. Moore (now D.D.)* on his removal to Belfast, in 1862, resigned this charge; and was succeeded by Mr. John S. M'Intosh, who was ordained here on the 5th of November, 1862. Mr. M'Intosh removed to Belfast, and resigned this charge in February, 1868; and was succeeded by Mr. Samuel Lyle, who was ordained here on the 29th of December, 1868. Mr. Lyle resigned the charge on the 1st of January, 1878, on his removal to Canada; and was succeeded by Mr. John C. Moore, who was installed here on the 28th of May of the same year. Mr. Moore resigned the charge on the 20th of August, 1883; and was succeeded by Mr. William Colvin, LL.D., who was installed here on the 28th of February, 1884.

* The great Ulster awakening of 1859 commenced in Connor congregation under the ministry of Mr. Moore.

CONVOY.

The parish of Raphoe formerly embraced that of Convoy, and the meeting-house was erected on the Montgomery estate at Convoy, though the minister was known in church records as the minister of Raphoe. There were a considerable number of Presbyterians in the district in the former half of the seventeenth century; and in April, 1644, the covenant was administered in the town of Raphoe to the whole regiment of Sir Robert Stewart, and a great multitude from the surrounding parishes, by the Revs. Messrs. Weir and Adair, ministers from Scotland. Two curates, named Leslie and Watson, opposed them, but without success. Mr. John Crookshanks appears to have been the first minister. He was succeeded by Mr. Samuel Haliday, who was ordained here in 1664, and who removed to Omagh in 1677. In February, 1678, Mr. James Alexander was ordained the minister. In February, 1691, the congregation paid to him £24 per annum of yearly salary, and twenty-four barrels of corn. He died November 17th, 1704. His successor was Mr. David Fairly. His son, Robert Fairly, was thrice mayor of the city of Derry, viz., in 1769, 1770, and 1782; and among his descendants are the Rev. William M'Clure, late senior minister of the first Presbyterian congregation of Derry, and his brother, Sir Thomas M'Clure, Bart., one of the original Trustees of the Belfast Presbyterian College. Mr. Fairly was licensed in 1708, and ordained to the charge of Convoy and Raphoe, March 21st, 1711. He was an excellent minister, and the traditions of the neighbourhood yet attest his integrity and piety. During his ministry the people of Raphoe were erected into a separate congregation; and in August, 1751, Mr. James Gordon, who had formerly been settled in Castleblayney, was installed to the pastoral charge. Mr. Fairly died January 7th, 1776, at a very advanced age. Mr. James Taylor was ordained August 28th, 1766, as his assistant and successor. The ministry of Mr. Taylor was also very extended; but, becoming infirm, Mr. John Wray was ordained his assistant and successor, March 13th, 1822. Mr. Taylor died on the 15th February, 1831, after a pastorate of 65 years. That of Mr. Fairly had been of the same length. Mr. Wray died March 6th, 1858. On the 23rd March, 1859, the Rev. Robert Beattie was ordained to the pastoral charge.

COOKSTOWN 1st.

THE first minister was Mr. John MacKenzie. He was ordained here in the summer of 1673. He was in the City of Derry during its famous siege, and published an account of it, in which he shows that George Walker was very much of a sham, that he would more than once have capitulated if he had been permitted, and that Colonel Adam Murray was the true hero who upheld the Protestant cause in its last refuge. The congregation of Cookstown was originally called *Derriloran*. In September, 1691, the people applied to the Synod for Mr. MacKenzie's continuance with them, though they could not promise him more than £15 per annum of stipend. The Synod recommended Moneymore, then vacant, to be joined with them. Whether this was done, does not clearly appear; but Mr. MacKenzie remained here till his death. He is said to have died in 1696, aged 49 years. The next minister was Mr. John M'Cleave, a licentiate of the Presbytery of Glasgow, who was ordained here on the 5th of February, 1701. He died in this charge on the 17th of June, 1749; and was succeeded by Mr. James Hall, who had been licensed in England, and had been received by the Synod in 1749. He was ordained to this charge on the 5th of August, 1752. In January, 1763, he removed to Bangor, and was succeeded by Mr. George Murray, who was ordained on the 10th of December, 1765. He died in this charge on the 8th of September, 1795, leaving a family.* The next minister was Mr. John Davison, who was ordained here on the 26th of September, 1797. In 1835, Mr. Davison resigned the pastoral charge; and, after many disputes, Mr. Alexander Fleming was ordained on the 28th of March, 1837, as assistant and successor to Mr. Davison. Meanwhile, a new congregation had been formed; and the first minister, Mr. John Knox Leslie, who had been ordained in August, 1834, as a Home Missionary, under the Synod of Ulster, was installed in the new charge on the 11th of November, 1835. On the 15th of April, 1846, Mr. Fleming resigned the charge of 1st Cookstown, having accepted a call to 1st Armagh; and on the 11th of August, 1846, Mr. Hamilton Brown Wilson (now D.D.,) was ordained to the pastorate. Mr. Davison died on the 22nd

---

* Formerly the Synod of Ulster very frequently held its annual meeting in Cookstown on account of its central position. The ministers and elders travelled to it mostly on horseback.

of November, 1847. The meeting-house was first placed in the old town of Cookstown, where it continued till 1701, when it was pulled down by the rector. Mrs. Margaret Stewart, of Killymoon, within three weeks, built a house, at her own expense, within the demesne, where the congregation worshipped till 1764. The present church is of recent erection.

COOTEHILL.

THIS congregation was erected off the congregation of Drum in 1718. Its first minister was Mr. Andrew Dean, who was ordained here on the 9th of October, 1721. He died in this charge in April, 1760, and was succeeded by Mr. Thomas Stewart, who was ordained here on the 22nd of April, 1766. Becoming infirm, Mr. John Johnston, was ordained here as his assistant and successor on the 2nd of February, 1808. Mr. (afterwards Dr.) Johnston, resigned this congregation on his removal to Tullylish a few years afterwards; and was succeeded by Mr. Robert Campbell, who was ordained here on the 8th of December, 1812. Mr. Stewart died on the 10th of December, 1816, leaving a family. On the 26th of February, 1828, the connection between the congregation and Mr. Campbell was dissolved by order of Synod; and on the same day Mr. James Bones was ordained to this charge. Mr. Campbell afterwards removed to America. Mr. Bones becoming infirm, his congregation obtained leave to choose an assistant, and Mr. John R. M'Cleery was ordained to the pastoral charge on the 27th of September, 1870. Mr. Bones died on the 23rd of August, 1884. Mr. M'Cleery, on his removal to 1st Dromara, resigned this congregation on the 23rd of August, 1880; and was succeeded by Mr. W. M. Henry, who was ordained here on the 7th of April, 1881.

CORBOY AND TULLY.

THIS congregation was originally known by the name of Longford. It was early planted, but its first minister, who was settled here about 1675, has not been ascertained. In 1697 Mr. John Mairs, of Loughbrickland, is transported thither, when we find him complaining of the greatness of his charge, "being at least ten miles over, and the two places for preaching, in each other Sabbath, being five miles distant." In 1706 the Synod loosed his relation to this people on account of "his intolerable grievances, his wife losing her health, his own craziness, and the greatness of the charge." He removed to Newtownards, and died there. Their next minister was Mr. William Hare, ordained here November 13th, 1708. He resigned the charge, and was installed in Enniskillen in 1720. Their next minister was Mr. James Bond, who was ordained here by the Presbytery of Longford, February 20th, 1723. In 1731 he was called to Armagh, but the Synod would not permit him to be removed. He was the grandfather of the late Willoughby Bond, Esq., of Fara, County Longford, an attached member of the Irish Presbyterian Church, who in his time was perhaps the largest landed proprietor connected with her communion. Mr. James Bond died, aged seventy years, on the 11th September, 1762. He was succeeded by Mr. Joseph Martin, who was ordained here November 19th, 1765. He died in this charge June 19th, 1767, aged thirty years. He was succeeded by Mr. William Fleming, formerly minister of Kingscourt, who was installed here in 1767, and died in this charge July 25th, 1784. He was succeeded by Mr. Robert Rodgers, formerly minister of Minterburn, who was installed March 9th, 1785. He died in March, 1791. The next minister was Mr. Joseph Osborne, who was ordained here March 16th, 1792. In May, 1799, he resigned the charge, and removed to Dungiven. The next minister was Mr. James Wilson, who was ordained March 5th, 1801. He died in September, 1816. He was succeeded by Mr. Thomas Kennedy, son of Mr. Kennedy, of Ballyjamesduff, who was ordained here May 17th, 1817. In 1839 he was suspended by the Synod—when he joined the Remonstrants; and was succeeded by Mr. John Henry, formerly minister of Drumbanagher, who was installed here by a committee of Synod, December 11th, 1839. On the 3rd of May, 1843, Mr. Henry resigned the charge and removed to Scotland. He was succeeded by Mr. John M'Cubbin, who was ordained on the 1st of November, 1843. Mr. M'Cubbin died in October, 1847, and the next minister was Mr. Robert W. Fleming, who was ordained here on the 17th of March, 1848. Mr. Fleming having received a call to Coleraine, demitted the charge of this congregation on the 15th of October, 1860; and on the 31st of December, 1860, Mr. Alexander Ferguson was installed as pastor. Mr. Ferguson, having received a call from Creggs and Roscommon, resigned this charge on the 15th of June, 1881; and was succeeded by Mr. William Burke, who was installed here on the 1st of November of the same year.

CORK—TRINITY CHURCH.

A PRESBYTERIAN congregation existed in Cork at an early period. In an account of a fund established in 1710 for the support of the Presbyterian interest in the South of Ireland, and published in 1815, we have the names of no less than thirteen ministers who had preached there in succession. It is further stated that, in 1718, when a sum of £800 per annum was added to the *Regium Donum*, the one-half fell to Presbyterian ministers in the South of Ireland, among whom was the minister of Cork. But New Light at length made its appearance in what was called the Southern Association, or the Presbytery of Munster, and in consequence evangelical religion languished and died. Upwards of fifty years ago Orthodox Presbyterianism again asserted its position in the city; a congregation was erected in it by the Synod of Ulster; and on the 11th of September, 1834, the Rev. Henry Wallace (now Professor Wallace, of Belfast Presbyterian College), was installed as the minister. In consequence of failing health, Mr. Wallace resigned this charge in the beginning of April, 1837. He was succeeded by Mr. Edward M. Dill, M.D., formerly minister of Coagh, who was installed here on the 26th of August, 1838. On the 21st of September, 1846, Dr. Dill resigned the charge, having accepted the office of General Itinerant Missionary Agent under the Directors of the Home Mission; and on the 13th of January, 1847, Mr. William Magill (now D.D.) was installed as minister. Dr. Magill retired from the active duties of the pastorate in 1884; and Mr. Samuel Law Wilson, late of Dungannon, was installed as his successor in December, 1884.

CORLEA.

IN 1816 a memorial was presented to the Synod of Ulster in the name of upwards of one hundred families residing in Ballytrain and its vicinity, promising £50 a year of Stipend to a minister, and praying to be erected into a congregation. The memorial was referred to the Presbytery of Monaghan. As they neglected to report to the next meeting of Synod, the business of the erection was meanwhile postponed. In the year 1823 the application was renewed and granted. The first minister was Mr. Matthew Adams, who was ordained here by the Presbytery of Monaghan on the 11th of May, 1824. The congregation obtained Regium Donum in 1827. In 1833 Mr. Adams was disannexed from the congregation by a committee of Synod; but, conducting himself improperly afterwards, he was eventually degraded. The next minister was Mr. John Parr, who was ordained here on the 24th of December, 1834. The congregation was, in 1835, entered on the minutes of the Synod as *Corlea*, instead of Ballytrain. Mr. Parr died on the 14th of February, 1876, and was succeeded by Mr. James M'Kee, who was ordained to the pastoral charge on the 19th of July, 1876. Mr. M'Kee resigned the charge on the 5th of February, 1878, having received a call from Lowtherstown; and was succeeded by Mr. James Knox, who was ordained here on the 23rd of July, 1878. Mr. Knox resigned the charge on the 21st of December, 1881, having accepted a call from Alt; and was succeeded by Mr. Alexander Milligan, formerly of Ballycolla, who was installed here on the 4th of April, 1882.

CREGGAN.

THE first notice we have of this congregation is the settlement of Mr. Alexander M'Comb, who was ordained here by the Presbytery of Killileagh on the 18th of April, 1733. He demitted this charge on the 5th of January, 1795, and died on the 3rd of June, 1797, leaving a widow and family. Meanwhile, Mr. Joseph Jackson was ordained his assistant on the 11th of June, 1795. Mr. Jackson's ministry was short, as he died on the 17th of January, 1801. The next minister was Mr. John Huey, who was ordained here on the 17th of August, 1802. On the 25th of April, 1809, the Presbytery dissolved the connection between the congregation and Mr. Huey, on account of his intemperance and other irregularities. He was succeeded by Mr. William Simpson Maclaine, who was ordained here on the 20th December, 1809. Mr. Huey was subsequently put under the care of the Presbytery of Tyrone, and died April 26th, 1820. In consequence of charges relating to certain money transactions, the Presbytery of Armagh, on the 1st of May, 1832, suspended Mr. Maclaine *sine die*, which sentence was confirmed by the Synod in June following. He died in December, 1835, leaving a family. He was succeeded by Mr. Daniel Gunn Brown, who was ordained by the Presbytery of Armagh on the 5th of March, 1833. On the 13th of May, 1835, the Presbytery dissolved the connection between Creggan and Newton-Hamilton, erected Creggan into a separate charge, and Mr. Brown continued in charge of Newton-Hamilton. The first minister of Creggan, as a separate congregation, was Mr. Thomas M'Williams, who was ordained here on the 27th of April, 1837. Mr. M'Williams becoming infirm, Mr. Thomas Croskery was ordained his assistant on the 17th of July, 1860. Mr. Croskery (now D.D.; and Professor of Theology in Magee College), resigned the charge on the 25th of February, 1863, on his removal to Clonakilty, and was succeeded by Mr. John Anderson, who was ordained here on the 1st of September, 1863. Mr. M'Williams died on the 16th of June of the same year. Mr. Anderson resigned this charge on the 6th of May, 1879, having accepted a call from Greyabbey; and was succeeded by Mr. Robert J. Smyth, who was installed here on the 26th of August, 1879. Mr. Smyth, having accepted a call from Tartaraghan, resigned this charge on the 6th of March, 1882; and was succeeded by Mr. Robert R. Drysdale, who was installed here on the 23rd of May, 1882.

CROAGHMORE.

THIS congregation was erected in 1828. The first minister was Mr. Robert J. Kennedy, who was ordained here by the Presbytery of Route, on the 23rd of February, 1830. Mr. Kennedy died in this charge on the 19th of August, 1851; and on the 17th of August, 1852, Mr. William Ritchie was ordained to the pastoral charge. Croaghmore is not far distant from the Giants' Causeway; and, in quarries there, stones of the same conformation as those at the Causeway may be seen.

CRUMLIN.

THE parent settlement whence this congregation proceeded was at Glenavy. At the erection of the congregation of Ballinderry, properly so called in 1713, Glenavy was much weakened; and, to effect a reparation, it was proposed, in 1715, that the meeting-house be removed to Crumlin, as Lower Kilmacaret, which only paid £8 per annum, would, in that case, pay £13 per annum. The first minister at this new place was Mr. Thomas Crawford, son of Mr. Crawford, of Carnmoney, who was ordained here by the Presbytery of Belfast on the 10th of June, 1724. He died, July 5th, 1782, leaving a widow and family; and was succeeded by Mr. John Gibson, who was ordained on the 18th of February, 1783. He died in this charge on the 18th of July, 1796, leaving a widow and family. Their next minister was Mr. Nat. Alexander,* who was ordained here, September 3rd, 1799. He separated from the Synod of Ulster in 1829. On the 6th of February, 1838, the Presbytery of Templepatrick erected the families in Crumlin who adhered to the Synod into a congregation; and the first minister was Mr. A. C. Canning, son of the minister of Malin, who was ordained here on the 9th of October, 1838.

CULLYBACKEY.

THE first notice we find of this congregation is in connection with the ordination of Mr. James M'Creight by the Presbytery of Route, on the 13th of December, 1730. He died in this charge on the 12th of March, 1757. He was succeeded by Mr. Alexander M'Mullan, who had been minister of Broughshane, and who removed here in 1758. Mr. M'Mullan demitted the charge in September, 1772, and removed to America. He was succeeded by Mr. Robert Christy, who was ordained here on the 17th of August, 1773. He died in this charge on the 1st of August, 1818; and was succeeded by Mr. William Cuthbertson, who was ordained here on the 22nd September, 1818. Mr. Cuthbertson having resigned the charge of the congregation, Mr. Hugh Hamilton was ordained on the 6th of May, 1832. Mr. Cuthbertson died on the 27th of March, 1836. Mr. Hamilton becoming infirm, Mr. George R. Buick was ordained on the 1st of February, 1868, as his assistant and successor. Mr. Hamilton died on the 31st of July, 1882.

CUMBER, Co. DERRY.

THIS congregation originally formed part of that of Glendermot, and there is reason to believe that the famous Colonel Adam Murray, the hero of the siege of Derry, was then con-

* Mr. Alexander had an Academy at Crumlin, which educated a large number of highly respectable pupils.

nected with it. It became a separate charge about 1717; and its first minister was Mr. Major Murray, who was ordained here on the 15th of April, 1718. He died in this charge in February, 1751. He was succeeded by Mr. Samuel Patton, who was ordained here on the 3rd of July, 1753. He died in this charge on the 30th of June, 1799, leaving a family. The next minister was Mr. James Allison, who was ordained here on the 14th of September, 1800. Mr. Allison died on the 13th of September, 1853; and on the 27th of December following, his son, the Rev. Samuel S. Allison, who had previously been minister of Donegore, was installed as his successor. On the 14th of November, 1867, Mr. Allison resigned the charge of Cumber, and returned to Donegore—where he appeared to be the only minister likely to please the congregation; and on the 5th of May, 1868, Mr. S. M. Dill, son of Professor Dill of Queen's College, Belfast, was ordained to the pastoral charge of Cumber. This congregation is commonly known as Lower Cumber, and is thus distinguished from another congregation in the same Presbytery of Glendermot, and which is called Upper Cumber. Mr. Dill, on his removal to 1st Ballymena, resigned this charge in May, 1874; and was succeeded by Mr. Hugh Morrison, who was ordained here on the 10th of November of the same year.

CUSHENDUN.

CUSHENDUN and Cushendall, two beautiful watering places in the glens of Antrim, had at an early date some Presbyterian settlers. In 1708 we find Mr. James Stuart minister at Cushendall. He had previously resigned the charge of the congregation of Macosquin. The place was not, however, sufficient to support a minister; and Mr. Stuart obtained special aid from a fund then at the disposal of the Synod of Ulster. He died here on the 22nd of March, 1719. For a long time afterwards there was no Presbyterian minister settled in this district; and those of our communion who resided there had to travel far when they wished to enjoy Presbyterian ordinances. At length a movement was made to revive the Presbyterian interest in this locality; and in November, 1848, the Presbytery of Ballymena, in conjunction with the Presbytery of Route, formed the Presbyterians of the Glens into a congregation. The site of the meeting-house led to much discussion; but, in the end, it was

arranged that it should be erected between Cushendall and
Cushendun. On the 23rd of October, 1849, Mr. Charles
Gillis was ordained here by the Presbytery of Ballymena.

DERVOCK.

THIS congregation was originally known by the name of
Derrykeichan. We find Mr. John Baird settled here in 1646.
The minister immediately before the Revolution was Mr.
Robert Stirling. In 1688 he fled to Scotland and officiated
at Stevenson till 1695, when he returned to Ireland, and died
in this charge in 1699. He was uncle to John Stirling, who
was Principal of Glasgow College in the early part of the
eighteenth century. He was succeeded as minister of Dervock
by his son, Thomas Stirling, who was ordained here June
22nd, 1703. He died in this charge on the 20th of November,
1718; and was succeeded by Mr. John Orr, who was ordained
here October 29th, 1723. Mr. Orr died December 5th, 1745.
The next minister was Mr. Joseph Douglass, who was
ordained here April 9th, 1751. Becoming infirm, he obtained
as his assistant Mr. Alexander Martin, who was ordained
here May 18th, 1790. Mr. Douglass died December 14th,
1799. Mr. Martin becoming infirm, obtained as his assistant
Mr. Joseph Bellis, who was ordained here September 11th,
1827. Mr. Martin died September 21st, 1838. Mr. Bellis
becoming infirm, obtained as his assistant Mr. Alexander
Field, who was ordained here on the 2nd of September, 1857.
Mr. Bellis died on the 31st of July, 1872.

DONAGHADEE 1ST.

THE first minister of whom we have any record here was
Mr. Nevin, who had previously been an Episcopalian, but
who became a Presbyterian in 1642. He was succeeded by
Mr. Andrew Stewart, son to Mr. A. Stewart, minister of
Donegore. He was ordained here about the year 1658. He
suffered many severe trials and persecutions, but died in this
charge, January 2nd, 1671. The next notice of this congregation does not occur till 1697, when we find the Presbytery
of Down stating to the Synod of Ulster, "that they used
their best endeavours to bring Mr. Henry Hamilton to
Donaghadee, but to none effect." It continued vacant till
this object was at last accomplished; and Mr. Hamilton, who

had been minister first of Falkland, and afterwards of Currie, was installed here in February, 1701. He was the son of the Rev. A. Hamilton, of Bangor. He died in this charge in August, 1730. The commissioner of the congregation to the Synod, in 1731, was Joseph Madowell, Esq. They had called Mr. M'Bride, of Ballymoney, and Lord Mount Alexander had written to the Presbytery of Route, requesting them to permit him to remove to Donaghadee; but the Synod appointed him to continue in Ballymoney. Their next minister was Mr. James Maxwell Stewart, ordained here, March 7th, 1733. He died in this charge, June 2nd, 1743; and was succeeded by Mr. William Warnock, ordained here by the Presbytery of Bangor, May 20th, 1747. He died, January 19th, 1768, leaving a widow and family; and was succeeded by Mr. John Adams, ordained by the Presbytery of Bangor, December 8th, 1772. He died, January 9th, 1779, leaving neither widow nor family. Their next minister was Mr. Alexander Goudy, ordained here, March 14th, 1780. His relation to this congregation was dissolved by the Presbytery, June 30th, 1791, and he emigrated to America. He was succeeded by Mr. James Knox, formerly minister at Drumbanagher, who was installed here, March 18th, 1794. On the 1st of May, 1798, Mr. Knox resigned this charge on account of mental infirmity. Their next minister was Mr. John Arnold, ordained here on the 11th of June, 1799. Mr. Knox died March 22nd, 1801; and Mr. Arnold died, August 10th, 1811, leaving a widow and family. Their next minister was Mr. William Skelly, ordained here, September 15th, 1812. In August, 1819, he was suspended *sine die* for alleged immorality, and the congregation declared vacant. The next minister was Mr. John M'Aulay, who was ordained here on the 4th of June, 1822. A part of the congregation still adhered to Mr. Skelly, and a second meeting-house was erected by them in Donaghadee. On the 10th of January, 1849, the Rev. W. J. Skelly, son of Mr. Skelly, was ordained by the Presbytery of Belfast to the pastoral charge of this congregation. In 1856, a commission of the General Assembly was appointed to reconsider the case of Mr. Skelly, sen. This commission agreed on the expediency of restoring him to the ministerial status. Some members protested against this finding; but before the case could come before the annual meeting of 1857, for final adjudication, Mr. Skelly died. Mr. M'Aulay becoming infirm, obtained as his assistant Mr. William Witherow, who was ordained here on the 3rd of March, 1874. Mr. M'Aulay died on the 27th of February, 1879. Mr. Witherow, on his removal to Killyleagh, resigned this charge on the 16th of March, 1882; and was succeeded by Mr. Samuel Walker, who was installed here on the 25th of July, 1882.

DONAGHADEE 2ND.

THE origin of this congregation is given in the account of 1st Donaghadee. It may be added that Mr. W. J. Skelly died on the 20th of July, 1875; and was succeeded by Mr. William Weir Hamilton (now LL.D.), who was ordained here on the 23rd of March, 1876.

DONAGHEADY 1ST.

THE first minister mentioned as connected with Donagheady is Mr. John Hamilton, who was ordained here in 1658. In 1688 he retired to Scotland, but he must soon have returned, as he was in Derry during the siege. He probably died shortly afterwards. The next minister was Mr. Thomas Winsley, who had been licensed by the Presbytery of Edinburgh, and had come to Ireland in 1698. He was ordained here by the Presbytery of Lagan on the 18th of January, 1699; he died October 28th, 1736. He was succeeded by Mr. William Armstrong, who was ordained here by the Presbytery of Strabane on the 21st of July, 1741. He died in this charge on the 17th of May, 1761; and was succeeded by Mr. James Turbit, who was ordained here on the 19th of June, 1764. He died June 14th, 1783, leaving a widow and family. The next minister was Mr. Hugh Hamil, ordained here on the 4th of March, 1784. He died December 7th, 1803, leaving a widow and family; and was succeeded by Mr. William M'Crea, ordained here December 13th, 1804. He died suddenly on the 17th of June, 1832, leaving neither widow nor family. The next minister was Mr. Samuel T. Wray, ordained here March 7th, 1833. Mr. Wray becoming infirm, obtained as his assistant Mr. John Roulstone, who was ordained here on the 19th of January, 1860. Mr. Wray died on the 16th of September, 1863.

DONAGHEADY 2ND.

THIS congregation originated in disputes relative to the appointment of a minister in the old congregation. The new congregation was annexed to the Presbytery of Letterkenny. Its first minister was Mr. Robert Wirling, formerly of Kilrea, who was installed here on the 13th of August, 1741. He died in this charge in April, 1765. Mr. John M'Mean had previously been ordained his assistant on the 15th of July, 1762. He was deposed in October, 1777; and was succeeded by Mr. John Holmes, who was ordained here on the 13th of April, 1779. Mr. Holmes, becoming infirm, resigned the charge in 1830; and was succeeded by Mr. Francis Porter, who was ordained here on the 28th of July, 1831. Mr. Holmes died on the 5th November of the same year. Mr. Porter died on the 22nd of November, 1872; and was succeeded by Mr. George Magill, formerly of Cork, who was installed here on the 23rd of April, 1874. Mr. Magill, on his removal to Belfast, resigned this charge on the 11th of November, 1880; and was succeeded by Mr. Robert Frizell, who was ordained here on the 19th of May, 1881.

DONEGAL.

THIS congregation was formerly called Raneny. We have no notices of it before the Revolution. In March, 1698, we find it presenting a call to Mr. Thomas Craighead, and promising to advance half a year's salary towards defraying the charge of transporting his family from Scotland. He accepted their call, and Mr. Alexander, of Raphoe, served the edict at Mountcharles. Mr. Craighead was ordained on the 6th July, 1698. He either died about 1714, or went to America, but there is no mention either of his death or removal in the Synod's records. He was succeeded by Mr. John Holmes, who had been received by the Synod from the Presbytery of Lanark in 1713, and was ordained here on the 27th September, 1715. He was called to Ardstraw in 1731, but the Synod decided that he should remain here. He removed to the 2nd congregation of Glendermot in April, 1744. Their next minister was Mr. Andrew Hamilton, who was ordained here on the 26th of December, 1744. He died in December, 1763, leaving a widow; and was succeeded by Mr. Robert Caldwell, who was ordained to the joint charges of Donegal, Mountcharles, and Beleek on the 16th of June, 1767. His call from these united congregations, dated 18th August, 1766, was in 1865 in possession of his very worthy grandson, Samuel Crawford, Esq., solicitor, Ballyshannon. Mr. Caldwell was married to the daughter of the Rev. Samuel Delap, minister of Letterkenny. Mr. Delap's wife, whose name was Sarah, was the daughter of the Rev. Robert Campbell, minister of Ray, who had fled from Scotland rather than take the oath of unqualified obedience to Charles II., and settled at Ray in 1671. Mr. Delap's direct ancestor four generations back, that is, in 1580, resided near Irvine in Ayrshire. Mr. Caldwell was succeeded in Donegal by Mr. William Houston, who was ordained here March 2nd, 1791. Becoming infirm, Mr. Samuel Thompson was ordained his assistant and successor on the 18th of March, 1824. Mr. Houston died on the 1st of June, 1831. In May, 1834, Ballyshannon was separated from Donegal, and erected into a distinct congregation. Mr. Thompson becoming infirm, the Rev. Archibald Lowry was installed as his assistant and successor on the 29th of August, 1861. Mr. Lowry died on the 12th of January, 1881; and was succeeded by Mr. William Waddell, who was ordained here on the 19th of October, 1881. Mr. Waddell, having accepted a call from Knappagh, resigned this charge in the spring of 1884. Early in the century a Seceding congregation was erected in the town, and Mr. William Niblock (afterwards D.D.), who was ordained the minister, collected the funds needed for building a church. Dr. Niblock died on the 23rd of July, 1868, and was succeeded by Mr. Robert Neilson, who was ordained here on the 30th of September of the same year. The two congregations meanwhile remained weak; and, on the resignation of Mr. Waddell, they agreed to amalgamate —Mr. Neilson undertaking to conduct an afternoon service for the convenience of the people of Raneny.

DONEGORE 1ST.

THE first minister of this congregation was Mr. Andrew Stewart. Several interesting particulars respecting him are to be found in the well-known book entitled, "Fleming's Fulfilling of the Scriptures." He commenced his ministry in this parish about the year 1627, and after seven years labour, died in September, 1634, aged 36. His tombstone is in Donegore church-yard, and his character is given by Livingstone in his "Memorable Characteristics." The next minister was Mr. Thomas Crawford, son-in-law to the preceding. He was settled here by the Presbytery on the 28th of August, 1655, the congregation having been destitute of a gospel ministry since the death of Mr. Stewart. He was deposed by Bishop Jeremy Taylor, and his tombstone in the church-yard relates that he died in December, 1670, aged 45. The next minister was Mr. William Shaw, ordained by the Presbytery of Antrim, in 1671, in a private manner, as prelatic persecution was then so severe that the ministers dare not venture on a public celebration. He demitted the charge in consequence of increasing infirmity, in 1687. There were then eight elders in the congregation. Mr. John Stormont and Mr. J. M'Keig appeared as commissioners to the Presbytery after the resignation of Mr. Shaw. His arrears were secured by Mr. Henry Shaw and Mr. Alexander Adair. In February, 1688, Mr. Crawford, Mr. Adair, and Mr. Henry Shaw, appeared at the Presbytery with a unanimous call to Mr. Francis Iredell, who had been entered on trials in May, 1683, and licensed in March following. He was ordained here June 19th, 1688, Mr. Anthony Kennedy, of Templepatrick, preaching and presiding. Mr. Shaw died the next month. In 1697, Mr. Iredell was ordered to remove to Armagh; but he refused compliance, and was, in consequence, rebuked by the Synod, though permitted to remain in Donegore. In December, 1699, he removed to Capel Street congregation, Dublin. Mr. Iredell was one of the most distinguished ministers of the Synod during his day. He was frequently in London on the public business of the Church, and, in 1715, in company with Mr. Upton, of Templepatrick,* he waited as a deputation from the Synod, on George I., after his arrival in England. On his return, Mr. Iredell reported that his Majesty received them very graciously, and appeared sensibly concerned when told of the grievances under which they laboured. His successor in this congregation was Mr. Alexander Brown, ordained here December 3rd, 1702. The ministry of Mr. Brown exceeded half a century. In 1754, the people applied to the Presbytery for supplies; and Mr. John Wright was ordained, April 15th, 1755, as assistant and successor to Mr. Brown. Mr. Wright was married to one of the Adairs of

* Ancestor of Lord Templetown. The Upton family remained connected with the Irish Presbyterian Church until their removal to England.

Loughmorne. Mr. Brown died, January 2nd, 1758. Mr. Wright becoming infirm, Mr. James Crawford Ledlie was ordained his assistant and successor, April 8th, 1806. Mr. Wright died, May 1st, 1807, and Mr. Ledlie (afterwards D.D.), resigned, May 10th, 1808, and removed to Larne. After much disputing, Mr. Henry Cooke, formerly minister of Dunean, was installed here, January 22nd, 1811. Mr. Cooke (afterwards D.D., LL.D), resigned this charge, July 6th, 1818, and removed to the congregation of Killyleagh. Their next minister was Mr. James Seaton Reid, ordained here, July 20th, 1819. Mr. Reid (afterwards D.D. and Professor of Church History in the University of Glasgow), resigned this charge, July 5th, 1823, and removed to Carrickfergus. He was succeeded by Mr. John Dogherty, who was ordained here, December 21st, 1824. Becoming intemperate, he was, in March, 1836, suspended from the exercise of his ministry by a committee of Synod, and subsequently suspended *sine die*. He died under melancholy circumstances, February 18th, 1837. After a protracted vacancy, the congregation chose Mr. Samuel S. Allison, son of the minister of Cumber, County Derry, who was ordained here, January 8th, 1839. In December, 1853, Mr. Allison resigned the charge of the congregation, on his removal to Cumber, County Derry, and was succeeded by Mr. William John Gillespie, who was ordained here on the 5th of December, 1854. Mr. Gillespie, on his removal to Australia, resigned this charge on the 7th of May, 1867; and was succeeded by Mr. S. S. Allison, who thus returned to his former charge. Mr. Allison, becoming infirm, withdrew from the active duties of the ministry in May, 1883; and was succeeded by Mr. Alexander M'Kinney, who was ordained here on the 4th of March, 1884. Mr. Allison died on the 19th of November, 1884.

DONOUGHMORE, Co. Down.

This congregation was erected off that of Newry in 1705 during the vacancy there caused by the death of Mr. Lang. The first minister was Mr. James Johnson, who was ordained by the Presbytery of Armagh on the 23rd of June, 1707. In the following year the Synod annexed Drumbanagher and the Glen to this new erection to enable it to maintain its minister. Mr. Johnson becoming infirm, Mr. James Richey was ordained here as his assistant on the 27th of June, 1763. Mr. Johnson died October 20th, 1765, leaving a widow and family. Mr. Richey died in this charge on the 7th of December, 1771, leaving a widow and family. He was succeeded by Mr. Joseph Hay, who was ordained here on the 9th of March, 1773. He died in this charge on the 15th of May, 1803, leaving a widow and family. The next minister was Mr. Moses Findlay, who was ordained here on the 4th September, 1804. In 1837 reports injurious to Mr. Findlay's reputation led to an investigation by the Presbytery, when he resigned the charge with all its emoluments. The next minister was Mr. Verner M. White, who was ordained here in 1840. Mr. White resigned the charge on the 5th of July, 1844, having accepted a call from Liverpool. He was succeeded by Mr. S. J. Moore, who was installed here on the 28th of October, 1845. Mr. Moore resigned the charge on the 20th of August, 1850, having accepted a call from Ballymena; and was succeeded by Mr. Patrick White, who was installed here on the 11th of March, 1851. Mr. White resigned the charge on the 26th of February, 1862; and was succeeded by Mr. John Elliott, who was installed here on the 29th of December, 1862. Mr. Elliott resigned the charge in 1875; and was succeeded by Mr. Henry M'Dowell, ordained here 18th January, 1876. Mr. M'Dowell retired from the discharge of active duty, on account of declining health, in July 1881; and was succeeded by Mr. Lawson Burnett, who was installed here on the 21st of December, 1881. Mr. M'Dowell died on the 25th of December, 1882.

DONOUGHMORE, Co. DONEGAL.

THE first minister of this congregation was Mr. Robert Craghead, who was settled here in 1658. After the Restoration, Mr. Craghead was deposed by Bishop Leslie. He became minister of Derry in 1690, and there distinguished himself in a controversy with Dr. King, bishop of the diocese. Mr. Craghead was succeeded in Donoughmore by Mr. Joshua Fisher, who was settled here in 1694. Mr. Fisher died March 11, 1706, and the following inscription on his tombstone in Donoughmore churchyard is still legible:—

> "The man whose dust under this stone doth ly
> Lov'd much the honour of his God on hy;
> Those that did ill he could not bear, therefore
> Th' abuse was great he suffered on that score."

Mr. Fisher was succeeded by Mr. Francis Laird, who was

ordained to the pastoral charge September 1st, 1709. Mr. Laird married the daughter of Captain Henderson, mentioned in the History of the Presbyterian Church in Ireland, (vol. iii., page 40, notes, second edition); and from this pair Sir Thomas M'Clure, D.L., Bart., is lineally descended. Captain Henderson, the father-in-law of Mr. Laird, was married to the sister of Sir Harry Cairns, baronet. Mr. Laird died June 7th, 1742; and was succeeded by Mr. Benjamin Holmes, who was ordained to the pastoral charge October 25th, 1744. Mr. Holmes died in February, 1798; and was succeeded by Mr. Samuel Dill (father of the Rev. S. M. Dill, D.D., of Magee College), who was ordained to the pastoral charge July 16th, 1799. Becoming infirm, Mr. Alexander Caldwell was ordained as his assistant on the 14th of August, 1844. Mr. Dill died in December, 1845. Mr. Caldwell removed to Australia in 1864; and was succeeded by Mr. Robert Smyth, who was ordained here on the 30th of March, 1865.

DOUGLASS.

This congregation separated from Clady, with which it had been previously connected, in 1831. The first minister was Mr. James Alexander, who was ordained here by the Presbytery of Letterkenny on the 3rd of November, 1831. Becoming infirm, Mr. Robert Dick was ordained as his assistant on the 12th of March, 1868. Mr. Alexander died sometime afterwards.

DOWNPATRICK.

The earliest minister of whom we have any account here was Mr. John Fleming. He was deposed in 1661 by Jeremy Taylor, Bishop of Down and Connor, for nonconformity; but we do not know what became of him afterwards. His successor was Mr. Archibald Young, who was ordained in June, 1673. He took refuge in Scotland at the Revolution, and in May, 1690, signified his willingness to return to his charge; but it seems probable he did not do so, as Mr. John Hutchinson was ordained here during the same year. Mr. Hutchinson was called to Armagh in 1694, but the Presbytery of Down did not permit him to remove at that time. He did so eventually in 1697. We find Mr. Thomas Jackson here in 1700; and he died in this charge on the 2nd of November, 1708. His successor was Mr. Thomas Nevin, who was ordained to this charge on the 20th of November, 1711. He joined the non-subscribing Presbytery of Antrim in 1725, and died here in March, 1744. The congregation was now under the care of a succession of ministers of suspected orthodoxy, among whom was Mr. William Nevin, who resigned the ministry, and became a physician. In 1791 Mr. James Neilson was ordained to this charge. Mr. Neilson died on the 28th of January, 1838. Meanwhile Mr. S. C. Nelson became the minister. In August, 1825, certain families in the town and neighbourhood applied to the Presbytery of Dromore, connected with the Synod of Ulster, for preaching, which was granted; and the Presbytery afterwards erected them into a congregation. About this time the pious Captain Hamilton Rowan * was governor of Downpatrick Jail, and he was mainly instrumental in promoting the establishment of the new erection. The first minister was Mr. William D. Stewart, who was ordained here on the 29th of March, 1827. He was a very acceptable and able minister, but his career was brief. He died here on the 21st of July, 1831. He was succeeded by Mr. James A. Canning, son of Mr. Canning, minister of Malin. He was ordained here by the Presbytery of Dromore on the 4th of September, 1832. Mr. Canning resigned this charge on the 1st of October, 1839, and removed to Mourne. He was succeeded by Mr. William White, formerly minister of Killyshandra, who was installed here on the 1st of November, 1839.

DROGHEDA.

IN 1708 the Presbyterians of Drogheda supplicated the Synod of Ulster for a supply of religious ordinances. The application was granted; and in 1710 the people gave a call to Mr. Hugh Henry, a licentiate of the Down Presbytery, who was ordained here by the Presbytery of Armagh on the 27th of March, 1711. Mr. Henry died in this charge on the 1st of August, 1744. At the meeting of the Synod in 1745 the people, at their own request, were transferred to the body known as "The Southern Association." What was called "the new light" was then making much progress in many Presbyterian congregations; and under its blighting in-

* Captain Rowan, who was nearly related to the present Lady Dufferin, gave influential support to Dr. Cooke throughout the Arian controversy.

fluence religion did not flourish in Drogheda. In the beginning of the present century Presbyterianism was all but extinguished in the place. About that time the Secession Church began to send preachers to it; and in 1822 the Rev. Josias Wilson, who had previously been minister of Tassagh, was installed in the charge of a newly-erected congregation. Mr. Wilson laboured here for years with great acceptance and success. In 1836 he was transferred to the newly-erected congregation of Townsend Street, Belfast; and was succeeded in Drogheda by Mr. Samuel Boyd. On the 4th of May, 1842, Mr. Boyd resigned the pastoral charge; and was succeeded by Mr. Thomas Logan, who was installed here on the 16th of August of the same year. Mr. Logan resigned the pastoral charge on the 29th of June, 1871. In consequence of increasing physical debility, Mr Logan, in 1865, had applied to the Assembly for leave to the congregation to choose an assistant; and on the 8th of November of that year Mr. A. R. Crawford (now LL.D.), was accordingly ordained to the pastoral charge.

DROMARA 1ST.

THIS congregation was originally a part of Dromore. In 1713 the Synod of Ulster erected it into a distinct congregation—annexing to it the townlands of Tullyniskey, Enoch, Girvachy, Fedoney, and Carnew, belonging to Magherally congregation; with those of Killalen, Leppoch, and the upper half of the townland of Ballykeel belonging to Dromore congregation. The first minister was Mr. John Campbell, who was ordained here by the Presbytery of Armagh, December 13th, 1715. He died in this charge June 25th, 1724; and was succeeded by Mr. John King, who had been licensed by the Presbytery of St. Andrews, in Scotland, and was received by the Synod in 1719. He was ordained here by the Presbytery of Armagh, December 14th, 1726. Mr. King died November 9th, 1762; and was succeeded by Mr. James Birch, who was ordained here by the Presbytery of Dromore, August 12th, 1764. Becoming infirm, his grandson, Mr. James Birch Black, was ordained his assistant and successor, July 30th, 1816. Mr. Birch died November 10th, 1820. On the 13th of May, 1823, Mr. Black was suspended *sine die* for drunkenness. Their next minister was Mr. William Craig, formerly minister of Carnmoney, who was installed here December 26th, 1823. Mr. Craig died on the 22nd of

December, 1871; and after his death the congregation was greatly disturbed by disputes respecting the choice of a successor. There was in the end a strong secession to the Reformed Presbyterians, who illegally took possession of the meeting-house, and held it until compelled by legal proceedings to give it up. After a lengthened vacancy, Mr. William Shepherd, formerly of 2nd Stewartstown, was installed here on the 23rd of September, 1874. Mr. Shepherd, having resigned this charge after a short incumbency, was succeeded by Mr. John R. M'Cleery, who was installed here on the 28th September, 1880. Mr. M'Cleery, on his removal to another charge, was succeeded by Mr. Edward Ekin, who was ordained here on the 28th of March, 1884.

DROMORE 1st.

It appears that the earliest minister of Dromore was Mr. Henry Hunter, who seems to have died shortly after the Restoration. Mr. William Leggat was next settled here. He was licensed by the Presbytery of Antrim in 1670, and was shortly afterwards ordained to the charge of this congregation. At the Revolution he retired for some time to Scotland; but in 1691 he returned here. He was Moderator of the Synod of Ulster in 1693, but absent from it in 1694. The congregation was vacant in 1697, but whether in consequence of the death of Mr. Leggat or his removal to Scotland, is not known. The next minister was Mr. Alexander Colville, who was ordained here in 1700. He died on the 1st of December, 1719. In 1724 the majority of the congregation, by their commissioners, Messrs. Robert Hamilton and Thomas Ingram, supplicated the Synod to be annexed to the Presbytery of Down; and a minority, by their commissioner, Mr. John Magill, supplicated to be continued with the Presbytery of Armagh. The Synod annexed them to Down. The subscription controversy had now commenced, and this congregation felt the effects of it. In 1724 Mr. Alexander Colville, son of the preceding minister—being refused ordination by the Presbytery, because he refused to subscribe the Westminster Confession of Faith—repaired to London, and was ordained there. He was afterwards irregularly installed in Dromore by the Synod of Munster. For this he was suspended by the Synod of Ulster in 1725, and many of the people withdrew from his ministry, and formed another congregation in Dromore. The first minister of this congregation was Mr. James Allen, who was ordained here by the Presbytery of Armagh on the 18th of May, 1726. He appears to have demitted this charge about 1752. He was succeeded by Mr. William Henry, who was ordained here on the 1st of May, 1753. Mr. Allen died on the 14th of January, 1764. Mr. Henry—who was grandfather of Dr. Henry, late President of Queen's College, Belfast—resigned this charge and removed to Comber, County Down, in 1776. He was succeeded by Mr. John Cochrane, who was ordained here by the Presbytery of Dromore on the 5th of May, 1777. He died September 8th, 1779, leaving neither widow nor family. He was succeeded by Mr. James Waddle, who was ordained here on the 3rd of August, 1784. He died in this charge on the 12th of July, 1815, leaving a widow and family; and was succeeded by Mr. James Collins, who was ordained here on the 17th of September, 1816. Becoming infirm, Mr. Collins obtained leave for the congregation to choose an assistant and successor; and on the 20th of January, 1857, Mr. Jackson Smyth was ordained here. Some time afterwards Mr. Smyth (now D.D.) resigned the pastoral charge, on his removal to Armagh; and on the 27th of March, 1860, Mr. James Kirker Strain was ordained to this charge. Mr. Collins died on the 19th of December, 1863.

DRUM 1st.

THIS congregation was originally called *Dartry*. In 1675 the Tyrone Presbytery asked advice about removing Mr. William Leggatt from Dartry, a statement from which it appears that the congregation was early settled. Its next minister was Mr. Hugh Kelso, who was ordained here on the 30th of March, 1704. He died February 7th, 1706. He was succeeded by Mr. Samuel M'Gaughey, who was ordained here on the 22nd September, 1708. In 1718 the congregation was divided, part of it being erected into a separate congregation at Cootehill. Mr. M'Gaughey (or Gachim) died October 12th, 1722. He was succeeded by Mr. Matthew Chalmers, who was ordained here in 1725. In 1729 Mr. Chalmers was removed by the Synod to Plunket Street congregation, Dublin. He was succeeded here by Mr. Alexander M'Kee, who was ordained here on the 16th of May, 1733. Mr. M'Kee was removed to Bailieborough in May, 1761. We have not been able to recover the name of the minister who next succeeded; but Mr. James Walker was ordained here on the 11th of December, 1786. He died in this charge on the 20th November, 1825, leaving neither widow nor family. Their next minister was Mr. William M'Ewen, who was ordained here on the 4th of October, 1826. On the 13th of May, 1849, Mr. M'Ewen resigned this charge and emigrated to America. He was succeeded by Mr. James D. Crawford, who was ordained here on the 27th September, 1849. Mr. Crawford resigned the charge on the 13th of February, 1866, on his removal to Hillhall; and was succeeded by Mr. James Steen, who was ordained on the 29th of June, 1866. Mr. Steen resigned this charge on his removal to Turlough, on the 13th of April, 1880; and the congregations of 1st and 2nd Drum were then amalgamated. On the 5th of May, 1881, Mr. Joseph M'Kinstry was installed as minister of the united charge. Mr. M'Kinstry, on his removal to Randalstown shortly afterwards, was succeeded by Mr. George Stuart Moorehead, who was ordained here on the 13th of December, 1883.

DRUMACHOSE.

This congregation originated in a dispute relative to the choice of a minister in Newtownlimavady in 1742. Many of the people were favourable to Mr. Areskine or Erskine; but his opponents obtained possession of the meeting-house, and induced the Presbytery of Antrim to ordain Mr. Joseph Osborne. Mr. Erskine's friends were now formed into the congregation of Drumachose, and he was ordained by the Presbytery of Derry on the 4th of May, 1742. Mr. Erskine's ministry was not comfortable. He was often in collision with his brethren, and he was charged with various irregularities. He demitted the charge in 1761, and was succeeded by Mr. Jacob Davis, who was ordained here by the Presbytery of Route on the 26th of April, 1763. He died December 30th, 1786, leaving a widow. The next minister was Mr. Daniel Blair, who was ordained here in the end of May, 1788. He died here on the 10th of February, 1811, leaving a widow and family; and was succeeded by Mr. Richard Dill, formerly minister of Buckna, who was installed here on the 10th of March, 1812. He resigned the charge January 28th, 1823, and removed to the adjoining congregation of Ballykelly. The next minister was Mr. John M'Laughlin, who was ordained here on the 28th of September, 1824. Mr. M'Laughlin, died suddenly on the 3rd of November, 1831; and was succeeded by Mr. George Steen, who was ordained by the Presbytery of Route on the 12th of March, 1833. Mr. Steen resigned the charge on the 31st of March, 1845, and removed to the lately erected congregation of 2nd Newtownlimavady; and on the 25th of November, 1845, Mr. Nathaniel M'Auley Brown (now D.D.), was ordained to the pastoral charge. According to the last return, the congregation consists of 206 families.

DRUMBANAGHER 1ST.

This congregation was originally a part of Newry congregation. At the erection of Donoughmore into a congregation, it formed a part of it, though the people were averse to the junction. The first notice we have of it as a separate charge is on the occasion of the ordination of Mr. Charles Heslem on the 22nd of July, 1740. Mr. Heslem's ministry was very short, as he died on the 27th of March, 1741. He was succeeded by Mr. Michael Henry, who was ordained here by the Presbytery of Killyleagh on the 20th of October, 1742. He died April 1st, 1789, leaving a widow and family. The next minister was Mr. James Knox, who was ordained here by the Presbytery of Killyleagh on the 29th of June, 1789. Mr. Knox removed to Donaghadee in February, 1794; and was succeeded by Mr. Alexander Patterson, who was ordained here on the 14th of June, 1796. Mr. Patterson resigned this charge in October, 1805, on his removal to Magherally. The next minister was Mr. James Black, who was ordained here on the 4th of March, 1806. In August, 1831, the Presbytery, by permission of Synod, authorised the congregation to choose an assistant and successor to Mr. Black; and accordingly Mr. John Irvine was ordained as his assistant and successor on the 8th of May, 1832. Mr. Irvine died at Clonmel, whilst there on the service of the Synod's Mission, on the 17th of April, 1835, and was succeeded in this charge by Mr. John Henry, who was ordained here on the 13th of October, 1835. Mr. Henry resigned this charge on the 26th of November, 1839, and removed to Corboy. The next minister was Mr. Robert R. Lindsay, who was ordained here on the 18th of August, 1840.

DRUMBO.

The earliest notice we have of this congregation is in 1655, when we find Mr. Henry Livingston ordained here. He was nephew to the famous John Livingston, of Killinchy. He continued in this charge till April, 1697, when he died, aged 66 years. His successor was Mr. Edward Bailly, who was ordained here shortly after, and who died June 23rd, 1703. The next minister was Mr. Thomas Gowan, ordained here March 29th, 1706. In 1716, he had an unanimous call from the English Presbyterian Church at Leyden, in Holland, which the Synod permitted him to accept. He was succeeded by Mr. Patrick Bruce, son of Mr. James Bruce, of Killyleagh, and brother of Mr. Michael Bruce, of Holywood. Mr. Patrick Bruce was ordained here on the 12th of June, 1717. Towards the close of the year 1728, he resigned this charge, and removed to Scotland, where he became minister of Killalan, in the Presbytery of Paisley, whence he subsequently returned to Killileagh. In 1729, the congregation of Drumbo was put under the care of the Presbytery of Bangor. In 1730, their commissioner, Captain Hamilton Maxwell, supplicated the Synod for supplies of probationers. Their next minister was Mr. Andrew Malcom, who was ordained here, November 27th, 1731. He died in this charge on the 2nd of March, 1763, and left a widow. He was succeeded by Mr. James Malcom, probably his son, who was ordained here on the 24th of December, 1764. In 1775, commissioners from the congregation reported to the Synod that Mr. Malcom had not been able to officiate for two years, and requesting to be declared vacant, which was granted. Their next minister was Mr. Hugh M'Kee, ordained here by the Presbytery of Belfast, September 25th, 1776. He demitted the charge in June, 1781. In 1792, Mr. Malcom having recovered, the people applied for his restoration to the ministry among them. The Synod appointed a committee to judge the case. They installed him in his charge towards the close of the same year; and the Synod approved of this proceeding. In May, 1794, in consequence of indisposition and infirmity, Mr. Malcom was again obliged to resign the pastoral charge. The next minister was Mr. Samuel Hanna,* who was licensed by the Presbytery of Ballymena in 1790, and ordained here on the first Tuesday of

* Afterwards D.D., and the first Professor of Divinity appointed by the Synod of Ulster.

August, 1795. He removed to Belfast in 1799, and was succeeded by Mr. James Riddle, who was ordained here on the 3rd of September, 1800. Mr. Malcom died October 3rd, 1805, leaving a widow and family. In 1825, Mr. Riddle was suspended for twelve months, and, in 1826, he was suspended *sine die*. The next minister was Mr. Campbell Blakely, who was ordained here by the Presbytery of Belfast, July 4th, 1827. Mr. Riddle died February 25th, 1828. Mr. Blakely becoming infirm, Mr. James M'Neill was ordained his assistant and successor on the 7th of May, 1867. Mr. Blakley died in December, 1872.

DRUMLOUGH.

In 1816 the inhabitants of this district supplicated the Synod of Ulster for supplies every Lord's Day. In 1817 they stated that the Presbytery of Dromore had supplied them with preaching one Sabbath in the month, and that they were able to support a minister. Their erection was, however, deferred for another year; but in 1818 they were at length recognised as a separate congregation in connection with the Presbytery of Dromore. The Presbytery received instructions not to ordain a minister until the debt due for the building of the meeting-house had been liquidated. The first minister was Mr. Samuel Crory, who was ordained here on the 23rd of March, 1819. In 1852, in consequence of certain charges preferred against him, Mr. Crory was set aside; and on the 2nd of July, 1855, Mr. John M'Clelland was ordained to the pastoral charge. Mr. Crory, who was subsequently restored, died on the 19th of May, 1861.

DRUMQUIN.

In 1792 Drumquin was separated from Castlederg and joined to Pettigo. Mr. Thomas Anderson was ordained the first minister of this joint-charge on the 21st of March, 1794. Becoming infirm, Mr. Samuel Armour was ordained his assistant on the 7th of December, 1812. Mr. Anderson died on the 27th of the same month, leaving a widow and family. In November, 1827, the congregation of Pettigo was disannexed from Drumquin and formed into a separate charge. Mr. Armour died on the 10th of March, 1844. He was succeeded by Mr. John Davison, who was ordained here on the 4th of June, 1845.

DUBLIN—MARY'S ABBEY—now RUTLAND SQUARE.

This congregation was at first known by the name of *Capel Street*. It originated in a division of the congregation of Bull-alley under Mr. William Jacque, who separated from that people, and bringing with him such as adhered to him, founded this new settlement in 1672. For this he was censured by the brethren in the North in the October of that year. He apologised to them for the step he had taken; and in May, 1673, "appeared before the Presbytery of Antrim, and gave satisfaction for his former irregularities in gathering a congregation after having been declared loosed from Bull-alley." He did not continue in this charge above ten years, when differences again arose between him and the people. He is mentioned in Renwick's Letters in 1683. A party went off in the middle of the year 1684, and founded another congregation at New-market. Mr. Jacque, however, continued in Capel Street. In March, 1691, he being valetudinary, their commissioner, Mr. Samuel Martin, applied to the Presbytery of Antrim—to which this congregation was annexed—to assist them in prosecuting a call to Mr. A. Hutchinson of Saintfield. This was granted, and Mr. Hutchinson was removed thither. He continued here, however, only till April, 1692, when, on account of his ill-health, he is loosed from this, and restored to his former charge in Saintfield. At the same time the Synod declared Capel Street to be "free of any relation to Mr. Jacque, he having never been fixed here by the Presbytery." Being thus free to choose a minister, their commissioners, Messrs. S. Martin, Thomas Bond, and Patrick Campbell, gave a call to Mr. Robert Henry, minister of Carrickfergus, in April, 1692; and, though his removal is opposed by Carrickfergus, he is transported hither in the end of that year. In June, 1698, they apply by their commissioners, Messrs. Patrick Campbell and Jo. Williamson, for leave to call a colleague to Mr. Henry —"he being now crazy." They soon after called Mr. Francis Iredell, minister of Donegore; and Mr. Henry dying in the beginning of the year 1699, the Synod in June of that year removed him to this charge—they promising him £100 per annum, and to defray the expenses of his transportation. The congregation increasing, the Synod sanctioned them in becoming a collegiate charge. They accordingly called Mr. John Milling, who, producing his license from London, and testimonials from Leyden—where he had been a minister—was installed here June 23rd, 1702. He died June 17th, 1705.* His successor, as colleague to Mr. Iredell, was Mr. Laughlin Campbell, minister in the Highland charge at Campbeltown in Kintyre, who was installed here by the Presbytery of Belfast on the 10th of September, 1707. He was not more than a year in this charge—as he died on the 6th of October, 1708. In 1709 their commissioners, James Kennedy, Esq., and Mr. Daniel Mills, commissioned by Alderman Bell and others, presented a call to Mr. Robert Craighead, jun., son of the minister of Derry. He accepted the call in preference to one from Derry; and he was accordingly ordained here as the third colleague to Mr. Iredell on the 11th of October, 1709. Mr. Craighead died in this charge on the 31st of July, 1738, aged fifty-four; and Mr. Iredell died on the 31st of January, 1739—so that the congregation was now altogether vacant. The first minister they obtained was Mr. James Smith, formerly minister at Newtownards—who was installed here on the 15th of February, 1740. In 1744 their commissioners, Col. Jo. Martin and Mr. Jo. Errving, supplicated the Synod to transport Mr. John Brown of Ballymena, but the application was refused. Mr. Smith died on the 23rd of February, 1745—Mr. Charles M'Collum, formerly minister of Loughbrickland, having been installed here a little before. His colleague was Mr. William Wight, who was ordained here August 9th, 1753. He became Professor of Church History in Glasgow in 1762, and afterwards, in 1778, Professor of Divinity in the same university. He died in 1783. Mr. M'Collum demitted his charge here in May, 1765; and Mr. William Knox succeeded him on the 21st of the same month. He was afterwards settled at Dunbo. Their next minister was Mr. John Beard, from the Isle of Man, who was installed here on the 11th of January, 1767. In 1777 the relation of Mr. Beard to this congregation was dissolved, and he was deposed from the ministry for several immoralities. He afterwards conformed to the Episcopal Establishment, and obtained the benefice of Cloughran. The next minister was Mr. Benjamin M'Dowell (afterwards D.D.), formerly minister of Ballykelly, who removed here in 1778. Mr. James Horner (also afterwards D.D.) was ordained here as co-pastor on the 4th of

* Mr. Milling is mentioned in "Steven's History of the Scottish Church, Rotterdam," p. 315, as minister of Leyden in 1696.

November, 1791. Dr. M'Dowell becoming infirm, Mr. James Carlisle (afterwards D.D.) was ordained his assistant on the 14th of May, 1813. Dr. M'Dowell died on the 13th September, 1824. Dr. Horner becoming infirm, Mr. W. B. Kirkpatrick (afterwards D.D.) was ordained his assistant and successor on the 29th of July, 1829.* Dr. Horner died in January, 1843, leaving Messrs. Carlisle and Kirkpatrick the two ministers of this charge. Dr. Carlisle, who had meanwhile retired to Birr to conduct missionary operations there, died in Dublin on the 31st of March, 1854. On the 8th of September, 1858, the Rev. John Hall, formerly minister of 1st Armagh (and afterwards D.D.), was installed here as colleague to Dr. Kirkpatrick. Soon afterwards, Alexander Findlater, Esq., J.P., erected at his own expense the splendid church of Rutland Square and presented it to the congregation. On Dr. Hall's removal to New York in 1867, he was succeeded by the Rev. David M'Kee, formerly of Ballywalter, who was installed here on the 8th of February, 1869. On the 27th of August, 1879, Mr. M'Kee resigned this charge on his removal to New Zealand; and on the 20th of January, 1880, the Rev. Andrew Charles Murphy, formerly minister of 1st Derry (and now D.Lit.), was installed here. On his removal to London, Dr. Murphy resigned the charge on the 22nd of August, 1883; and was succeeded by the Rev. J. S. Hamilton, formerly minister of 1st Banbridge, who was installed here on the 20th of March, 1884. Dr. Kirkpatrick died on the 23rd of September, 1882.

DUBLIN—USHER'S QUAY—NOW ORMOND QUAY.

THIS congregation originated in the year 1717. Mr. Arbuckle, who died in 1721, was the first minister. In 1721 their commissioners, Messrs. Bagnal, Newton, Lord, and Aickman, presented a call to Mr. William Gray of Taboin. The Synod ordered him to remove hither; but he was not installed until 1724. He demitted the charge in 1728, and returned to the North. Their next minister was Mr. Robert M'Master, from Connor, who was installed here in 1729.

* At this time the entrance to Mary's Abbey was, not from Capel Street, but by an inconvenient lane. An entrance direct from Capel Street was then purchased. In the reign of Henry VIII. the Irish Parliament met in Mary's Abbey.

The congregation increased so much that they found it necessary to take a colleague to Mr. M'Master. They obtained Mr. William M'Beath of Urney, who was installed here in 1745. Mr. M'Master died February 27th, 1754; and Mr. M'Beath died in the following year. The next minister was Mr. Thomas Vance of Ramelton, who was removed here in 1755. His colleague was Mr. Robert Nichol, who was ordained here on the 11th of September, 1760. He died in this charge in October, 1762. He was succeeded by Mr. James Caldwell, who was ordained here June 11th, 1763. Mr. Vance died June 1st, 1772. The congregation of Plunket Street now united with Usher's Quay under Mr. Caldwell; and in 1780 Mr. Hugh Moore, formerly minister of Billy, removed here as his colleague. He was installed by the Presbytery of Dublin on the 19th October of that year. Mr. Caldwell died on the 24th of May, 1783. He was succeeded by Mr. William Wilson, formerly minister of Magherafelt, who was installed here in 1785. He died on the 9th of June, 1807. He was succeeded by Mr. W. D. H. M'Ewen, who was ordained here on the 16th of March, 1808. He resigned this charge on the 30th of June, 1813; and was succeeded by Mr. Samuel Simson, who was ordained as colleague to Mr. Moore on the 23rd of May, 1815. Mr. Moore died on the 14th of December, 1824, leaving Mr. Simson in the sole charge of the congregation, in which he continued till the year 1835, when Mr. Richard Dill, formerly minister of Tandragee, was installed as his colleague on the 26th of August of that year. Mr. Simson died about 1846.* Mr. Dill died on the 8th of December, 1858; and was succeeded by the Rev. John James Black (now LL.D.), who was installed here on the 31st of May, 1859. During Mr. Dill's time a fine new church was built on Ormond Quay, when the congregation assumed its present designation. On his removal to Inverness, Dr. Black resigned this charge on the 21st of December, 1871; and was succeeded by the Rev. James Cargin, who was installed here on the 14th of January, 1873. On his removal to 1st Derry, Mr. Cargin resigned this charge on the 1st of December, 1880; and was succeeded by Mr. Samuel Prenter, who was installed here on the 13th of July, 1881.

* Mrs. Magee, who bequeathed legacies amounting to £60,000 for Presbyterian objects—including £20,000 for founding Magee College—was a member of Mr. Dill's congregation.

DUNBOE 1st.

THE first minister of Dunboe is said to have been Mr. Thomas Fulton, who was here in 1660. He appears to have been succeeded by Mr. Blair; but of his ministry nothing is now known with certainty. The next minister was Mr. John Wilson, who was here in 1684. He fled to Scotland in the troublous times which preceded the Revolution; and settled at Largs. The Presbytery of Irwin in 1691 supplicated for his removal from Dunboe, but the Synod of Ulster refused to accede to this proposal. He continued, notwithstanding, to remain in Scotland, and at length in 1697 the Synod yielded, and he was formally installed at Largs. After this a Mr. Woodside appears for some time to have ministered to the people. In October, 1719, Mr. Robert Knox was ordained to the ministry in this congregation. Mr. Knox died here on the 1st of April, 1746. The next minister was Mr. William Cochrane, who was ordained here on the 10th of May, 1748. In 1762 Mr. Cochrane resigned this charge, and conformed to the Established Church. He was succeeded by Mr. William Knox, who was installed here on the 18th of August, 1765. Mr. Knox had previously been minister of Mary's Abbey, Dublin. Mr. Knox died here on the 29th of August, 1801, and a stone inserted in a conspicuous position in the front wall of the place of worship still bears honourable testimony to the excellence of his character. His descendants, in good worldly circumstances, are still to be found in the neighbourhood of Coleraine; but with the exception of the family of the late Mr. Wark, of Castlerock, they no longer adhere to the Presbyterian Church. The next minister was Mr. Thomas Greer, who was ordained here on the 9th of March, 1802. Among his descendants are the Rev. Thomas Greer of Anahilt, and the late S. M. Greer, Esq., Recorder of Derry, and at one time M.P. for the county. Mr. Greer died on the 15th of December, 1812, and was succeeded by Mr. William Lyle, who was ordained here on the 7th of June, 1814. Mr. Lyle died on the 3rd April, 1867, and was succeeded by Mr. John Mark, who was ordained here on the 24th of July of the same year.

DUNDALK.

THIS congregation was established about 1706. The first

minister was Mr. John Wilson, who was ordained to the joint-charge of Dundalk and Carlingford about 1700. In 1706, Dundalk was permitted to become a distinct congregation, though the people could not pay to a minister above £15 per annum. Thirty pounds were added out of the General Fund of the Synod to enable the people to support a minister. Mr. Patrick Simpson was accordingly ordained here by the Presbytery of Armagh on the 30th of December, 1713. He resigned the charge in 1721, in consequence of insufficient maintenance, but was induced to resume it, and continue here some time longer. In 1725 he appears to have joined the Presbytery of Antrim, and he continued in connection with it till his death. The congregation then reverted to the Presbytery of Armagh, and by them Mr. Colin Lyndsay was ordained here on the 16th of August, 1779. His relation to this congregation was dissolved in 1785. The next minister was Mr. Andrew Bryson, who was ordained here on the 15th of August, 1786. He resigned this charge on the 22nd of June, 1796; and was succeeded by Mr. William Neilson (afterwards D.D.), who was ordained here on the 21st December, 1796. Mr. Bryson died in the month of March following. Dr. Neilson, who was one of the most distinguished linguists of his day, resigned this charge on the 23rd of July, 1818, and became Professor of Greek, Latin, and Hebrew in the Belfast Academical Institution. He died on the 27th of April, 1821. The next minister was Mr. David Davison, who was ordained here on the 2nd of March, 1819. He resigned this charge on the 6th of April, 1825, and removed to the congregation of Old Jewry, London. The next minister was Mr. William Cunningham, son of Mr. Cunningham, minister of St. Johnstone, County Donegal, who was ordained here on the 23rd of June, 1825. Mr. Cunningham was greatly beloved, but he was of a delicate constitution, and was not long able to perform the duties of the ministry. He died on the 15th of May, 1829. Meanwhile Mr. James Beattie had been ordained his assistant and successor on the 25th of November, 1828. Mr. Beattie died on the 28th of December, 1851; and was succeeded by Mr. W. M'Hinch, who was installed here on the 15th of June, 1852. Mr. M'Hinch died on the 7th of January, 1860; and was succeeded by Mr. Robert Black, who was installed here on the 26th of June of the same year. Mr. Black, having obtained leave for his congregation to choose an assistant and successor, Mr. John Macmillan was installed here on the 19th of May, 1880. Mr. Black died in the summer of 1885.

DUNDONALD.

THE first minister here was Mr. Thomas Peebles. He came from Scotland in 1642, as chaplain to Eglinton's regiment—at that time forming a part of the Scotch army that came over under Munroe. He was ordained at Dundonald, then including Holywood, in 1645; and was Clerk to the Presbytery during his life. He died after various vicissitudes in 1670. He was succeeded by Mr. Gilbert Kennedy, who was minister here in 1673. His tomb-stone is in the churchyard in this parish. He was succeeded by Mr. Thomas Cobham, who was ordained here in 1678. He fled to Scotland during the troubles, and was absent nearly five years. He was here in 1690, and died in charge of Holywood alone, on the 24th of June, 1706, Holywood being now separated from it, and Kirk, or Dun-donald having become a distinct charge. In 1704 the people of Dundonald applied to the Synod of Ulster to be erected into a separate congregation, promising, by their commissioner, Mr. John M'Kittrick, £20 per annum, with 20 bolls of oats, and engaging also to provide a farm. The application was granted. They were not able for some time to obtain a minister. At length Mr. James Stewart was installed here by the Presbytery of Belfast, May 24th, 1709. He died in this charge, March 3rd, 1748. He was succeeded by Mr. James Hamilton, who was ordained here, October 15th, 1754. He removed to Monaghan in the beginning of the year 1758. Their next minister was Mr. William Ray, who was ordained here June 16th, 1761. He demitted his charge in February, 1765, and sailed for North America in the following May. He was succeeded by Mr. Hugh Smith, who was ordained here by the Presbytery of Bangor, June 3rd, 1766. He died in this charge, February 11th, 1771. Their next minister was Mr. James Caldwell, who was ordained here 1st September, 1772. Becoming infirm, Mr. William Finlay was ordained his assistant and successor November 20th, 1810. Mr. Caldwell died October 2nd, 1814, leaving a widow. Mr. Finlay died in this charge June 14th, 1834, aged 47, leaving a widow. The next minister was Mr. William Graham, who was ordained here on the 18th of August, 1835. On the 1st of November, 1842, Mr. Graham (afterwards D.D.), having been appointed a Jewish Missionary, resigned the charge, and on the 30th of May, 1843, Mr. E. T. Martin was ordained to the pastoral charge. Mr. Martin, having obtained leave for his congregation to choose an assistant and successor, Mr. James Bingham, formerly of Bandon, was installed here on the 22nd of March, 1883.

DUNDROD.

IN 1827 the Presbytery of Templepatrick erected the inhabitants of this district into a separate congregation. The first minister was Mr. William Loughridge, who was ordained here on the 2nd of March, 1829. On the 6th of November, 1837, he was suspended *sine die*. He was succeeded by Mr. William Magill, who was ordained here on the 14th of January, 1840. On the 1st of February, 1876, Mr. Magill retired from the active duties of the ministry; and on the 16th of May of the same year Mr. John Clarke was ordained to the pastoral charge. On the 26th of June, 1879, Mr. Clarke resigned the care of the congregation, and on the 11th of March, 1880, Mr. Magill died. On the 22nd of June, 1880, Mr. John M'Connell was installed as minister. Mr. M'Connell resigned this charge on the 14th of February, 1884, having received an appointment from the Board of Missions to New South Wales; and was succeeded by Mr. Robert M'Bride, who was settled here in April of the same year.

DUNEAN.

THIS congregation and Grange originally constituted one charge. We find Mr. Joseph Hamilton minister here in 1670. In 1674 Mr. Wilson, who two years before had been ordained as minister of Randalstown, visited the place, and reported that " he found the preaching-house very inconvenient for the Grange, and yet the people of Dunean utterly unwilling to have a house accommodated to both places." Mr. Hamilton died in April, 1686. In June following, the people gave a call to Mr. Alexander M'Cracken, with bonds for £26 per annum of stipend; but he declined the charge, " particularly on the ground of the two meeting-houses to be here." In October, 1667, the people presented an unanimous call to Mr. James Scott, who had been entered on trials by the Presbytery in June, 1686, and licensed in February,

1687. Before his ordination the Presbytery sent a minister to "endeavour to get a central meeting-place convenient for all, as but few attend when there is preaching in the Grange;" but to this proposal the people in Grange would not agree. Mr. Scott was ordained June 19th, 1688, Mr. Munroe, of Carnmoney, preaching and presiding on the occasion. His text was 1 Tim. iv. and last verse. He continued here till his death, November 11th, 1710. In 1713 their commissioner, Major John Dobbin and others petitioned the Synod for assistance to support the Gospel among them, assigning as their reasons that several of their number had been removed by death, and that even before this they could not advance above £22 or £23 per annum. Their next minister was Mr. John Henderson, who was ordained here August 26th, 1713. He joined the Presbytery of Antrim in 1725, and died January, 1753. Mr. Robert Scott was ordained to the united congregations of Dunean and Grange on the 28th of June, 1762. Becoming infirm, Mr. Henry Cooke (afterwards D.D. and LL.D.), who had been licensed by the Presbytery in July, 1807, was ordained as his assistant November 10th, 1808. He resigned this charge on his removal to Donegore on the 13th of March, 1810. He was succeeded by Mr. Matthew Elder, who was ordained here June 21st, 1811. He resigned his charge here on the 7th of January, 1817, and on the 18th of May following was suspended *sine die*. He was succeeded by Mr. Archibald Hutchinson, who was ordained here November 10th, 1818. Mr. Scott died April 17th, 1813, after an incumbency of 51 years, leaving neither widow nor family. Mr. Hutchinson died on the 4th of December, 1843; and on the 27th of August, 1844, Mr. William Denham, who had formerly been minister of Bovedy, was installed in Dunean. Mr. Denham died on the 14th of July, 1883; and was succeeded by Mr. John J. M'Clure, who was ordained here on the 27th November, 1883.

DUNFANAGHY.

DUNFANAGHY and Kilmacrenan, in the County of Donegal, were long associated. The first minister in the joint charge would appear to have been Mr. Robert Drummond, son of Mr. Seth Drummond, of Ramelton. He was entered on trials by the Presbytery of Lagan in January, 1700, and licensed in May. He was ordained at Kilmacrenan on the 3rd of

November, 1702, and died on the 8th of June, 1712. The next notice we have of this joint charge is the ordination of Mr. James Cochran at Dunfanaghy, on the 20th of September, 1715. He removed hence and was installed in Greyabbey, County Down, in June, 1736. We have not been able to ascertain the name of his immediate successor; but Mr. David Allen was ordained here in August, 1775.* In May, 1778, he was suspended *sine die*, but was restored in 1779. The same year the people of Kilmacrenan prayed to be erected into a distinct charge. On this occasion it appeared that for some time there had been preaching only at Kilmacrenan. Mr. Allen died as minister of the joint charge on the 9th of January, 1812, and was succeeded by his son, Mr. John Allen, who was ordained here on the 12th of March, 1812. In 1829 these congregations were divided, and Kilmacrenan, with the Regium Donum, remained under the care of Mr. Allen. The first minister of Dunfanaghy in its separate state was Mr. David Reid, who was ordained by the Presbytery of Letterkenny on the 21st January, 1830. Becoming infirm, Mr. Reid, in 1849, obtained leave for his congregation to choose an assistant; and on the 19th of December of the same year Mr. Joseph Gallagher was ordained there. Mr. Reid died on the 11th of July, 1860. On the 22nd of June, 1869, Mr. Gallagher resigned the pastoral charge; and on the 4th of August of the same year Mr. William Kane was ordained his assistant and successor.

DUNGANNON, 1st.

THE congregation of Dungannon was also known, at an early period, by the name of Donoughmore. Its first minister was Mr. Thomas Kennedy, who was deposed for non-conformity at the Restoration, and who afterwards preached at Carlan Bridge. In February, 1673, the people of Dungannon were recommended by the Presbytery to adhere to their minister, Mr. George Keith, and to give him maintenance, otherwise it would be necessary for him to remove from them. Mr. Keith appears soon to have resigned the charge; and after the Revolution we find Mr. Thomas Kennedy, sen., ministering to the congregation, which was now joined with Carlan. On the death of Mr. Kennedy, aged 89, in 1714; Dungannon was erected

* About this time the family of Mr. Stewart of Ards was Presbyterian.

into a separate charge. In April, 1718, Mr. Nathaniel Cochrane was ordained the minister. He died here in March, 1735. A long vacancy seems to have now followed, as the next minister, Mr. Adam Duffin, was not ordained till October 10th, 1744. Mr. Duffin died in this charge September 14th, 1770, leaving a widow and family. From this gentleman Charles Duffin, Esq., J.P., of Belfast, is collaterally descended. Mr. Duffin was succeeded by Mr. Alexander Mercer, who was ordained here December 22nd, 1772. Mr. Mercer demitted the charge in 1776, and removed to the neighbourhood of Dublin. He was succeeded by Mr. William Stitt, formerly minister of Moira, who was installed here September 1st, 1777. About this time the Volunteers made their appearance; and on the 8th of September, 1783, one of the greatest political meetings ever held in Ulster assembled in the Presbyterian church of Dungannon. The Bishop of Derry and fifteen members of the Irish House of Commons were present on the occasion. On that day the Rev. Dr. Black, a distinguished minister, long connected with Derry, made a speech which electrified the auditory. During the course of the eighteenth century, the Synod of Ulster held its annual meeting no less than twenty-five times at Dungannon. Mr. Stitt died here September 1st, 1803, leaving a widow and family. The next minister was Mr. Thomas Waughope, who was ordained August 25th, 1804. He resigned the charge November 9th, 1805, and in the March following was suspended *sine die* by the Presbytery. He was succeeded by Mr. David Bennett, who was ordained June 7th, 1806. Mr. Bennett becoming infirm, Mr. Charles L. Morell was ordained as his assistant on the 16th of September, 1844. Mr. Bennett died on 8th March, 1847. Mr. Morell (now D.D.), at length obtained as his assistant Mr. S. L. Wilson, who was ordained here on the 8th of April, 1879. On receiving a call from Cork in October, 1884, Mr. Wilson resigned this charge; and was succeeded by Mr. David Wilson, formerly of Mourne, who was installed here in 1885.

DUNLUCE.

DUNLUCE was originally connected with Billy; but, on the settlement of Mr. John Logue there, a party in Dunluce appear to have been dissatisfied. At length in 1753 the people of Dunluce, by their commissioners, Messrs. Hugh Boylan and Robert Patterson, supplicated the Synod of

Ulster to erect them into a separate congregation, as they had built a new meeting-house; but this was not granted on the first application. They were, however, erected at the next annual Synod, and their first minister was Mr. John Cameron, who was ordained here on the 3rd of June, 1755. Mr. Cameron was a man of talent and literary attainments, as several of his remaining works still testify; but one of the Episcopalian ministers of the neighbourhood, with whom he was on habits of intimacy, seduced him into Unitarianism. In 1768 he was chosen Moderator of Synod. He died December 31st, 1799. He was succeeded by Mr. James Boyle, who was ordained here December 1st, 1801. In 1824 Mr. Boyle reported to Synod various donations and legacies left to this congregation, which are detailed in the minutes of that year. Mr. Boyle died November 13th, 1835. The next minister was Mr. William Oliver, who was ordained here September 20th, 1836. Mr. Oliver is the author of several well-known and highly valued publications. Becoming blind, Mr. Oliver obtained leave for his congregation to elect an assistant and successor; and, in consequence, Mr. James G. Kirkpatrick was ordained here on the 26th of September, 1865.

DUNMURRY.

This congregation was first erected between the years 1676 and 1683. In January, 1683, Mr. Alexander Glass was the ordained minister. In February, 1683, he retired to Scotland in consequence of the disturbed state of the country, and remained there. In June, 1694, the Synod of Ulster wrote to him, requesting him to return, but without success. The next minister was Mr. John Malcome, who had been minister of Lower Killead; but he removed here about 1699. He died in this charge May 17th, 1729. Mr. Malcome was a man of superior talent, and in the Non-Subscription controversy took a prominent part in support of the Westminster Confession of Faith. He was succeeded by Mr. John Moorehead, who was ordained here by the Presbytery of Templepatrick on the 17th of February, 1731. He died in this charge June 20th, 1768, leaving a widow and family; and was succeeded by Mr. James Stoupe, formerly minister at Enniskillen, who was installed here by the Presbytery of Bangor on the 3rd of June, 1772. He resigned the charge in May, 1780, and was succeeded by Mr. Robert Jackson, who was ordained here on the

11th of April, 1782. He died September 5th, 1788, leaving a widow and family. In 1790 we find the following entry in the minutes of the Synod of Ulster:—" Ordered that the Moderator write a letter to the Presbytery of Munster remonstrating against the conduct of Mr. Blair (of the Leap), a member of their Presbytery, for irregularly introducing a probationer to Dunmurry, and afterwards presiding in drawing up a call for him—Resolved, that we approve of the conduct of the Presbytery of Bangor respecting Dunmurry in deferring the ordination of Mr. Taggart in that place until the matter might come before this body." Mr. Taggart and the congregation annexed themselves to the Presbytery of Antrim; and on the 14th of May, 1805, his connection with this congregation was dissolved by them. The congregation reverted again to the Presbytery of Bangor in 1806 or 1807; and their next minister was Mr. Andrew George Malcom, who was ordained here on the 11th of March, 1807. He resigned this charge on the 11th of September, 1808, and removed to Newry. The next minister was Mr. Henry Montgomery (afterwards LL.D.), who was ordained September 14th, 1809. Dr. Montgomery was the great leader of the Arian party; and in 1829 he and many of the members of the congregation seceded from the Synod of Ulster, retaining possession of the Church, Manse, and other properties. A few years after this secession, the congregation of Malone, in the neighbourhood of Dunmurry, was erected by the Synod of Ulster; and on the 15th of February, 1837, Mr. Joseph Mackenzie was ordained the pastor. The congregation of Dunmurry was subsequently erected by the General Assembly; and on the 21st of November, 1860, Mr. Robert James Arnold was ordained pastor.

ENNISKILLEN.

The first minister of this congregation seems to have been Mr. James Tailzeur, or Taylor. He was here in 1677, and living within two miles of the town. He had come from the North of Scotland in 1675, recommended by Mr. Thomas Hogg, and in the month of September of that year was ordained to Monea, Enniskillen, and Derryvallen. He appears to have left this shortly after 1681. His successor was Mr. Robert Kelso. Mr. Kelso had been ordained at Raloo, in County Antrim, in May, 1673; but he demitted the charge in the following year, on account of the poverty of the people.

He then removed to Wicklow, where he was settled in 1675, and, after remaining a short time there, was called to Enniskillen. He was in this charge at the time of the Revolution, in 1688, and died shortly after. In 1690, the congregation was vacant. In November, 1695, the Presbytery of Lagan met at Ballindreat, and ordained Mr. John M'Guachin minister of Enniskillen and Magherabuy. In 1720, he complained to the Synod of his inadequate maintenance; and, though the congregation were willing to secure to him £32 per annum, he declared his inability to subsist on that stipend and do the duty of his congregation—some of his people being eight or ten miles distant from the meeting-house. The Synod, therefore, permitted him to resign the charge, and he was afterwards settled at Athy. He was succeeded by Mr. William Hair, who was installed here in the end of the year 1720. He had previously been minister at Corboy or Longford. He died in this charge, November 29th, 1745, and was succeeded by Mr. Thomas Plunkett, son of Mr. Plunkett, of Glasslough, who was ordained here December 14th, 1748. He was removed to Strand Street, Dublin, in January, 1769. He was the father of the late Lord Chancellor Plunkett, and grandfather of the present Archbishop of Dublin. The next minister of the congregation was Mr. James Stoupe, who was ordained here by the Presbytery of Monaghan, November 29th, 1769. In June, 1772, he removed to Dunmurry. Mr. Stoupe was succeeded by Mr. David Young. On the day appointed for his ordination, none of the Presbytery of Monaghan attended but one, who preached and performed all the duties, except the formal act of ordination by prayer and the imposition of hands. The Synod rebuked the Presbytery for their non-attendance, and ordered the ordination to take place in the August following. In 1773, it was reported to the Synod that Mrs. Cranston, near Enniskillen, had bequeathed £100 for the benefit of the minister there, that the money was in the hands of J. Armstrong, Esq., of Lisgool, the only surviving executor of her will, that the sum of £30, for the same purpose, was in the hands of the Rev. Mr. Plunkett, of Dublin, and that there was a third bequest of £5 per annum, by Mr. Cranston, secured on certain lands, but the advantage of which neither the present minister nor any of his predecessors had enjoyed, though a lawsuit was commenced for the recovery of it, as it could not be carried on for want of proper support. In 1775,

Mr. Young removed to Derry, and was succeeded by Mr. William Millar, who was ordained here by the Presbytery of Monaghan, January 13th, 1776. He removed to Killeshandra, May 7th, 1781, and was succeeded by Mr. Joseph Denham, who was ordained here, December 11th, 1781. Mr. Denham was father of the late Rev. Dr. Denham, of Derry, and grandfather of the late Rev. J. S. Denham, of 2nd Holywood. Mr. Denham also removed to Killeshandra, where he was settled in September, 1799, and was succeeded in Enniskillen by Mr. Christopher Josias Gamble, who was ordained here December 24th, 1799. He retired from the ministry in February, 1804. Their next minister was Mr. Ephraim Stevenson, who was ordained here July 10th, 1804. He resigned this charge in 1835; and on the 1st of March, 1836, Mr. Thomas Berkeley was ordained his assistant and successor. Mr. Berkeley died of fever, December 8th, 1836, leaving a widow. He was succeeded by Mr. A. C. M'Clatchy, who was ordained here, August 29th, 1837. Mr. M'Clatchy died on the 1st of March, 1882; and was succeeded by Mr. S. C. Mitchell, who was ordained here on the 25th of October, 1882.

ERVEY.

ERVEY and Carrickmaclim were originally united. They were known by the names of Breachy (or Banbreaky) and Kells. In 1700 the Presbytery of Tyrone was ordered to supply Breachy with preaching. In 1701 Kells was joined to it. In 1702 Mr. Hugh Grier was their commissioner to the Synod. On the 12th of May, 1703, Mr. John Lee, formerly minister of Glenarm, was installed here on condition of receiving £20 stipend for the first year, £25 for the second, £30 for the third; and to get out of the *Regium Donum* Fund £20 for the first, £15 for the second, and £10 for the third year. After the Presbytery and Synod had made many ineffectual attempts to secure his maintenance, he was at length, in July, 1710, loosed from this charge. He died October 29th, 1717. The next minister was Mr. William Patton, who was ordained here by the Presbytery of Longford on the 7th of December, 1721. In July, 1736, he removed to Lisburn; and was succeeded by Mr. David Hutchinson, who was ordained to this charge on the 20th of November, 1739. In 1744 he removed to Monaghan. The next minister was Mr. William Fleming, who was ordained here August

3rd, 1748. In 1767 he removed to Corboy ; and on the 22nd of June, 1768, Mr. William Moore was ordained here. Mr. Moore died on the 27th of June, 1811 ; and was succeeded by Mr. Robert Winning, who was ordained here on the 9th of June, 1812. Carrickmaclim was separated from Ervey in 1832, and Mr. Winning remained minister of Ervey. Towards the close of the year 1842, Mr. Winning conformed to Prelacy,* having obtained the promise of a living in the Established Church ; but his people declined to follow him. On the 22nd of June, 1843, Mr. James Armstrong was ordained to the pastoral charge. On the 28th of November, 1861, Mr. Armstrong resigned the pastoral care ; and on the 4th of June, 1863, Mr. John Wilson was ordained here.

FAHAN.

THIS congregation was formerly connected with Buncrana. The first minister of whom we have any account was Mr. Ninian Cochrane, who was ordained here on the 3rd of February, 1719. He demitted the charge in 1748, and was succeeded by Mr. Joseph Reagh, who was ordained here in August of that year. Mr. Cochrane died on the 21st of September, 1751. Mr. Reagh demitted the charge and emigrated to America in 1770. Mr. John Erwin was ordained here in September, 1777; but resigned the charge through bodily indisposition on the 22nd of February, 1796, and was succeeded by Mr. David Hamilton, who was ordained here on the 3rd of September, 1799. Mr. Erwin was deposed in 1801, for celebrating marriages irregularly. In October, 1834, the Presbytery dissolved the connection between Fahan and Buncrana ; and while the former continued under the care of Mr. Hamilton the latter was erected into a separate congregation. Mr. Hamilton died on the 31st of October, 1840 ; and was succeeded by Mr. John Macky, who was ordained here on the 7th of June, 1842. On the 5th of April, 1854, Mr. Macky resigned this charge, having been appointed by the directors of the Colonial Mission to go out to New Zealand. He was succeeded by Mr. David Hanson, who was installed here on the 12th of September, 1854. Mr. Hanson resigned the charge on the 23rd of August, 1860 ; and was succeeded by Mr. John Brown M'Bride, who was ordained on the 27th of December of the same year.

* He had been long before virtually in the pay of the Established Church as an agent of the Irish Society.

FANNET.

This congregation was known at first by the name of Clondevadock. It was originally associated with Ramullan. The first minister of the joint charge was Mr. Adam White. He was ordained here in 1654. In August, 1672, the congregation was found to be unable to support him. Major Alexander Stewart came as commissioner to the Presbytery, wishing him to be continued in the charge; but in September of that year the Presbytery released him from it. He afterwards settled at Ardstraw; and after the Revolution became minister of Billy, in County Antrim. Fannet continued to be only occasionally supplied for a length of time; but on the 25th of February, 1708, Mr. Charles Lynn was ordained the minister. In 1728, he removed to the 2nd congregation of Coleraine. He was succeeded in Fannet by Mr. John M'Gachin, who was ordained here by the Presbytery of Letterkenny on the 1st of April, 1730. He died in this charge in April, 1783, leaving a widow and family. The next minister was Mr. James Delap. He was ordained as Mr. M'Gachin's assistant on the 14th of November, 1782. He was suspended *sine die*, by the Presbytery on the 19th of November, 1806. The next minister was Mr. James Marshall, who was ordained on the 17th of February, 1808. Mr. Marshall died on the 1st of December, 1826, leaving a widow and family. He was succeeded by Mr. James Budd, who was ordained here on the 17th of October, 1827. On the 20th of April, 1837, Mr. Budd resigned this charge and removed to Clady. He was succeeded by Mr. Moses Houston, who was ordained here on the 21st of December, 1837. On the 10th of March, 1841, Mr. Houston resigned the charge of this congregation and removed to Letterkenny. In the same year Mr. Patrick Hay was ordained in Fannet. On the 15th of April, 1857, Mr. Hay resigned the pastoral charge. He was succeeded by Mr. James Keating, who was ordained here on the 17th of March, 1850.

FAUGHANVALE.

This was originally called the congregation of Muff. It formed part of Glendermot congregation in 1696. In 1730 the people presented a memorial praying to be speedily planted with a minister. Their first minister is said to have been Mr. James Smyth, who was ordained by the Presbytery of Strabane in 1732. He died here on the 13th of February, 1770. He was succeeded by Mr. Dunn, who was ordained here by the Presbytery of Derry, on the 18th of June, 1771. He was deposed by the same Presbytery on the 18th of May, 1784. The next minister was Mr. Henry Elder, who was ordained here on the 4th of February, 1786. He died in this charge on the 27th of July, 1817; and was succeeded by Mr. Marshall Moore, who was ordained here in the month of November, 1819. Mr. Moore died on the 14th of August, 1848; and on the 26th of March, 1850, Mr. Lowry E. Berkeley was ordained to the pastoral charge. On the 25th of August, 1858, Mr. Berkeley resigned this charge on his removal to Lurgan; and on the 17th of February, 1859, Mr. Francis Petticrew (now D.Lit.) was ordained to the pastorate.

FINTONA.

THIS congregation was first known by the name of Golan. Its first minister was Mr. Robert Coleheart. He was here in 1704, and died on the 26th of January, 1730. He was succeeded by Mr. Nathaniel Glasgow, who had been ordained to go to America on the 3rd of February, 1719, but who was installed here on the 5th of April, 1732. He had meanwhile been in another congregation, probably Ballyjamesduff. He died in this charge in April, 1743. The next minister was Mr. William Moorehead, who was ordained here by the Presbytery of Monaghan on the 26th of September, 1752. He died here September 15th, 1806. In 1834 Dromore was separated from Fintona. Meanwhile Mr. John Sampson had been ordained to the united charge on the 16th of September, 1808. In 1835 Mr. Sampson was required by the Synod to resign the pastoral charge. On the 4th of April, 1836, Mr. Robert Chambers was ordained his assistant. Meanwhile Mr. James Reid Dill was ordained as the minister of the separated congregation of Dromore on the 10th of November, 1835. A story has been often told to the effect that the Rev. Philip Skelton, when rector of Fintona, once preached in the Presbyterian meeting-house so much to the delight of the congregation that the people all joined the Established Church, and that Mr. Skelton paid to the minister ever afterwards £40 a-year, being the amount of his stipend, as a compensation for the loss of his income. But this is

J

obviously a misstatement. The same minister had the care of the congregation of Fintona during the whole time that Mr. Skelton was rector, as well as for many years after his removal, and there is documentary evidence that the stipend still amounted to £35. Mr. Chambers becoming infirm, Mr. George P. M'Kay was ordained here as his assistant and successor on the 17th February, 1874. Mr. Chambers died on the 29th of July, 1879.

FINVOY.

FINVOY congregation originated with a Captain Galland, one of Cromwell's officers, who had obtained part of the property of the M'Quillans in that parish. A portion of these lands was secured by a Colonel Hamilton, of the Dunnemana family, at Ballynegawey, in the parish of Finvoy, who also encouraged the settlement of a minister there. The first minister is said to have been Mr. Robert Henry, who was here about the time of the Revolution. He was succeeded by Mr. Robert Haltridge, who was ordained here by the Presbytery of Route in 1702. He died in this charge, December 22nd, 1727; and was succeeded by Mr. David Smylie, who was ordained here in 1734. He removed to Maghera in 1738. The next minister was Mr. Gideon Nelson, who was ordained here, November 9th, 1742. Becoming infirm, Mr. James Elder was ordained as his assistant and successor on the 13th of June, 1780. Mr. Nelson died on the 20th of November, 1783. Mr. Elder died on the 4th of November, 1843, in the 86th year of his age and the 64th of his ministry. He was long the father of the Synod of Ulster, and was noted for his steadfast orthodoxy. On the 8th of August, 1843, Mr. Andrew Todd was ordained as his assistant and successor.

GALWAY.

THE first pastor who ministered to this congregation was Mr. William Bigger of Limerick, who preached in 1698, and was imprisoned in consequence. Mr. Thomas Hooks was ordained in 1702. At that time the ministers of Dublin requested the Synod of Ulster to allow £10 towards his maintenance. This grant was not regularly paid, and Mr. Hooks removed to Dublin. The next minister was Mr. Nathaniel Orr, who was ordained here by the Presbytery of Down on the 2nd of December, 1707. He demitted this charge in 1710; and was succeeded by Mr. Alexander Hamilton, who was ordained here by the Presbytery of Monaghan on the 23rd of March, 1714. The people sent as commissioners to the Synod, after the resignation of Mr. Orr, Messrs. Evan Tyler, Jo. Dingwall, and Francis Montgomery. In 1722 Mr. Hamilton demitted the charge, there not being above eight or ten families belonging to the congregation, and these not able to pay the rent of the meeting-house.* The congregation was revived by the Synod of Ulster in 1833, and after having been supplied for some time by the Synods' Mission, Mr. Joseph Fisher was ordained here as fixed pastor on the 3rd of June, 1835. In February, 1845, Mr. Fisher resigned the pastoral charge and removed to England. On the 28th of January, 1846, Mr. William Adair was ordained to the pastoral charge. According to the last returns the congregation consists of 49 families, paying a stipend of £120. Mr. Adair becoming infirm, Dr. W. Ross Hamilton, formerly of Ballygawley, was installed here on the 2nd of April, 1872. Dr. Hamilton died on the 27th of July, 1873; and was succeeded by Mr. John C. Moore, who was installed here on the 21st of April, 1875. Mr. Moore, on his removal to Connor, resigned this charge on the 3rd of May, 1879; and was succeeded by Dr. J. G. Robb, who was installed here on the 4th of March of the same year. Mr. Adair died on the 13th of April, 1882. Dr. Robb died on the 8th of November, 1881; and was succeeded by Mr. John C. Clarke, who was installed here on the 4th of April, 1882.

GARVAGH 1st.

Mr. LAW was minister here in 1660. In 1671 he was connected with the Presbytery of Antrim; but he seems to have soon afterwards joined the Route Presbytery. In February, 1673, it was agreed by the several Presbyteries that Route may declare the congregation vacant, as Mr. Law had demitted the charge, and there was no hope of his returning to it. Mr. Robert Landish or Landess, who was ordained by the Route Presbytery in January, 1674, appears to have been his successor. Mr. Landish removed to Scotland at the Revolution. In 1691 the Synod wrote to him to return to his charge; but without effect; as he became minister of

* About this time a Roman Catholic bishop was set up in Galway. The people had before been under the care of a warden.

Blantyre. We hear nothing more of the congregation till 1700, when we find Mr. James Woodside minister here. He died or resigned in 1719. He was succeeded by Mr. Francis Ross, who was ordained here on the 7th of May, 1723. He died in this charge on the 4th of March, 1751. In 1756 the people gave a call to Mr. William Callender, minister of a new erection at Ardstraw. Mr. Callender accepted the call, and brought his credentials to the Presbytery; but on the day of his installation he did not appear, as he had meanwhile been induced to return to his former place. At length Mr. Robert Elder was ordained here in 1761. He died in this charge on the 18th of May, 1781. After much disputation, Mr. Brice Millar was ordained here on the 21st of December, 1784; but he soon afterwards went to America. He was succeeded by Mr. Henry Henry, who was ordained here on the 13th of May, 1788. Mr. Henry removed to Connor in the December following. He was succeeded by Mr. Gideon M'Mullan, who was ordained here in February, 1790. He died in February, 1793. The next minister was Mr. James Brown, who was ordained here on the 1st of December, 1795. Becoming infirm, he resigned the charge; and Mr. James Millar was ordained his assistant and successor on the 18th of February, 1840. Mr. Brown died on the 20th of May, 1850, in the 88th year of his age and the 55th of his ministry. Mr. Millar died on the 19th of November, 1859. He was succeeded by Mr. Thomas Davidson, who was ordained here on the 25th of September, 1860. Mr. Davidson died on the 2nd of August, 1865. He was succeeded by Mr. Thomas Madill (now LL.D), who was ordained here on the 21st of February, 1866.

GLASTRY.

This congregation was originally known as Ballyhalbert, and was annexed to Ballywalter. It was erected into a separate charge about 1720; and its first minister was Mr. John M'Murray, who was ordained here on the 28th of December, 1725. He died in this charge in 1750. He was succeeded by Mr. Thomas Scott, who was ordained here on the 14th of June, 1732. He died in April, 1770. He was succeeded by Mr. William Steel Dickson, who was ordained here by the Presbytery of Killyleagh on the 6th of March, 1771. He resigned this charge on the 1st of February, 1780, and removed to Portaferry. He was succeeded by Mr. James

Sinclair, who was ordained here by the Presbytery of Killyleagh on the 3rd of October, 1781. Mr. Sinclair having resigned the charge through age and infirmity, Mr. Alexander P. Goudy, son of the late Rev. Andrew Goudy, of Ballywalter, was ordained here on the 20th of September, 1832. Mr. Goudy resigned this charge in the Spring of 1833, and removed to Strabane. The next minister was Mr. John M'Roberts, who was ordained here on the 8th of June, 1834. Mr. M'Roberts died on the 17th of April, 1838; and was succeeded by Mr. Gilbert Jamieson, who was ordained here as assistant and successor to Mr. Sinclair on the 29th of January, 1839. Mr. Sinclair died on the 15th of June, 1841, aged 85. Mr. Jamieson having resigned the pastoral charge, Mr. Robert Workman was ordained as his successor on the 3rd of September, 1872. Mr. Jamieson died on the 29th of December, 1879.

GLENARM.

GLENARM is famous as the place where the celebrated Robert Blair landed on his arrival in Ireland before his settlement in Bangor. It is probable that there were some Scotch Presbyterians here at a very early period; but the first minister of whom we read, as located in it, is Mr. Alexander Gilbert, who was ordained in Glenarm on the 2nd of May, 1655. His continuance in the charge was very brief, as the place was vacant in January, 1656. Mr. James Fleming, who was ordained here in June, 1658, was ejected on the re-establishment of Prelacy in 1661; but he conformed to the Episcopal Church shortly afterwards. In July, 1671, the people presented a call to Mr. John Anderson, an ordained minister, who had fled from Scotland. He accepted the call with a reservation of liberty to return to Scotland when a door might be opened. In January, 1674, Mr. John Abernethy appeared as their commissioner before the Presbytery, and stated that the congregation paid Mr. Anderson £30 per annum—"the usual allowance to ministers in the country"—and that they were not much in arrear to him. In October, 1685, Mr. Anderson was removed to Antrim—his arrears on leaving Glenarm being upwards of £120. In July, 1686, the people presented a call to Mr. Hugh Crawford. Their commissioners on this occasion were Messrs. Henry Mitchell and Henry Dunn, who promised only £20 per annum. This call the Presbytery sent back, to be signed by

Mr. Donaldson, as being most forward for Mr. Crawford's settlement; and it is reported to the Presbytery in January, 1687, that Mr. John Donaldson and his eldest son had both subscribed it. The Donaldsons are said at that time to have been a family of note, and the remains of their castle were, until recently, pointed out in that locality. In February, 1688, Mr. Crawford went to Scotland—having been previously an ordained minister there—and about this time received a call from his former congregation in that kingdom. In September, 1688, the people presented a call to Mr. John Darragh—and Layd and Cushendall joined with Glenarm in this call—seeking preaching every fourth Sabbath from Mr. Darragh, as he had the Irish tongue.* The Presbytery appointed him to bring testimonials from Scotland and liberty from the Church there to settle in Ireland. In January, 1689, he accordingly produced testimonials from the Presbytery of Kintyre; but the troubles of the Revolution coming on, he retired to Scotland, and the congregation remained vacant. In April, 1691, the people gave a call to Mr. Peter Orr, of Clough, but the Presbytery of Route would not permit his removal. They at last obtained Mr. John Lee, who had been licensed by the Presbytery of Antrim in February, 1688, and who was ordained here in 1693. In 1703 he is declared transportable—that is, entitled to a removal—for what reason we do not know, but probably on account of inadequate maintenance. There was much difficulty in obtaining his arrears from Glenarm. They owed him £69, and the Synod required them to pay him £40 by instalments; but there was great altercation about the settlement of accounts. He removed to Kingscourt. The congregation did not obtain a minister till 1709, when Mr. James Creighton was ordained here on the 24th of May of that year. He died in this charge July 20th, 1731. He was succeeded by Mr. Thomas Brown, who was ordained here June 19th, 1732. On the night of November 17th, 1754, Mr. Brown, when turning to go over the bridge at Glenarm, fell into the river and was drowned, and his body was found next morning. He was succeeded by Mr. Thomas Reid, who was ordained here in March, 1756. He at length demitted the charge through infirmity, and Mr. Robert Acheson was ordained his assistant on the 17th of July, 1792. In June, 1799, he was removed to Donegall Street Congregation, Belfast. The next minister

* The Irish tongue is still spoken by many in this neighbourhood.

was Mr. Alexander Montgomery, who was ordained March 17th, 1801. Mr. Reid died February 25th, 1814, leaving neither widow nor family. At the time of the Unitarian Secession, in 1829, Mr. Montgomery and a part of the congregation left the Synod of Ulster and retained possession of the meeting-house. The congregation was soon after annexed to the Presbytery of Ballymena, and their next minister was Mr. Hugh Waddell, who was ordained here on the 24th of September, 1833. Mr. Waddell becoming infirm, Mr. James Scott was ordained here on the 28th of September, 1869. Mr. Waddell died on the 27th of August, 1873. Mr. Scott, on his removal to Banbridge, resigned this charge on the 21st of September, 1880; and was succeeded by Mr. Charles M. Cowden, who was installed here on the 19th of July, 1881.

GLENDERMOT 1ST.

THE first minister of Glendermot, then including Cumber and Faughanvale, was Mr. John Wooll or Will, who was ordained here in 1654. In 1679, he became infirm, and his session having substantiated against him several charges of unseemly carriage, he was advised by the Presbytery to resign, which he did accordingly. His successor was Mr. James Gordon, so well known in connection with the seige of Derry. He it was who advised the apprentice boys to shut the gates, and who afterwards urged Kirk to attempt the breaking of the boom. In the Presbytery book of that period Adam Murray is returned as the elder for Glendermot, and there is every reason to believe that he is the Colonel Adam Murray who was the true hero of the seige of Derry.* Mr. Gordon, as is well known, was on very intimate terms with him, and in co-operation with his minister, he took the bold stand which compelled Lundy to make his escape out of the city. Colonel Murray is interred in the graveyard of Glendermot. Mr. Gordon went to Scotland about the time of the Revolution, where he remained until immediately before the period of the breaking of the boom. In January, 1692, he demitted the charge of the congregation of Glendermot by letter addressed to the Presbytery of Lagan. He had for some time before been ministering to the congregation of Cardross in Scotland,

* A manuscript history of the Irish Presbyterian Church, by the celebrated Rev. Dr. Campbell, attests the Presbyterianism of Colonel Murray. Dr. Campbell had the best means of ascertaining the fact.

where he settled, and remained till his death. He was succeeded in Glendermot by Mr. John Harvey, who came from the Presbytery of Dumfries in May, 1695. He had previously been minister of New Abbey in Scotland. In December, 1695, the congregation supplicated the Presbytery for the settlement of Mr. Harvey, promising £40 per annum, and some corn, also to build him a dwelling-house and to keep up the aforesaid salary, though Cumber and Muff should fall off and not join with them. He was accordingly installed as minister in March, 1696. His son, Mr. David Harvey was ordained here by the Presbytery of Derry, as assistant and successor to his father, March 23rd, 1731. In 1737 he was removed to Derry; and his father died on the 20th of August, 1739. During the subsequent vacancy great dissensions prevailed in the congregation. At length Mr. William Hare was ordained here by the Presbytery of Derry, March 1st, 1743. He died in 1767, leaving a widow and family, and was succeeded by Mr. James Knox, who was ordained here May 1st, 1770. He demitted the charge in consequence of bodily infirmity in August, 1798. The next minister was Mr. William Monteith who was ordained here December 2nd, 1800. Mr. Knox died November 21st, 1813, leaving neither widow nor family. Mr. Monteith becoming infirm, Mr. Alexander Buchanan was ordained his assistant and successor on the 16th June, 1842. Mr. Monteith died on the 8th of February, 1849. Mr. Buchanan died on the 31st of October, 1871; and was succeeded by Mr. Thomas Thompson who was ordained here on the 16th of January, 1872.

GLENDERMOT 2ND.

This congregation was erected in 1743, and annexed for a time to the Presbytery of Route, which installed here Mr. John Holmes, formerly minister of Donegall, on the 19th of April, 1744. The congregation was subsequently annexed to the Presbytery of Letterkenny. Mr. Holmes died on the 15th of May, 1773, leaving no family, and was succeeded by Mr. Henry Miller, who was ordained here in May, 1776. Mr. Miller becoming infirm, Mr. Henry Carson was ordained his assistant and successor, March 12th, 1815. In April, 1820, Mr. Miller was suspended for the irregular celebration of marriage. He died January 1st, 1821, leaving a family. Mr. Carson becoming infirm, Mr. Marshall Moore* was

* He was son of the minister of Faughanvale.

ordained his assistant and successor on the 3rd of April, 1855. Mr. Moore died on the 4th of January, 1860; and on the 27th of September of the same year the Rev. Joseph Corkey (now LL.D.) was ordained his successor.

GLENNAN.

THIS congregation has been also known by the name of Glasslough. Its first minister was Mr. Thomas Gowan, who was born at Caldermuir, in Scotland, in 1631, and came to Ireland about 1650. When he settled here he was the only Protestant minister in the parish. He preached in the church and enjoyed the tithes. At the Restoration he was deposed, and he then removed to Antrim. The congregation now continued vacant and unplanted for some time. In 1673 the people called Mr. Robert Henry; but the Presbytery of Antrim settled him at Carrickfergus. Their commissioner on that occasion to the Presbytery of Antrim was Mr. Charles Caldwell. It does not appear that from this date they enjoyed a settled minister, but were united to the congregation of Kinnaird—now Minterburn. In 1713 the people petitioned the Synod to be erected into a distinct congregation. Their commissioners were Messrs. William Johnson of Tully, Henry Gillespie, James Widney, and John Stewart. Their desire was carried into effect, and sanctioned by the Synod in 1714, when it was stated that "all within the County of Monaghan towards Cur-bridge were to be members of this congregation," which was then indiscriminately called Treugh or Scarnagiroch. They soon after obtained a stated pastor, as Patrick Plunket was ordained here on the 11th of May, 1715. Mr. Plunket growing infirm, Mr. Samuel Kennedy was ordained here in October, 1757. Mr. Plunket died in 1760, and Mr. Kennedy also departed this life on the 7th of May, 1781. The next minister was Mr. John M'Curdy, who was ordained here on the 18th of October, 1783. Becoming infirm, Mr. William Smyth was ordained his assistant and successor on the 27th of November, 1820. Mr. M'Curdy died on the 19th of February, 1823. In 1846 Mr. Smyth applied for leave to his congregation to choose an assistant and successor; and on the 13th of May, 1847, Mr. James M. Field was ordained here. Mr. Field died on the 20th of January, 1855; and on the 28th of June, 1856, Mr. Robert Wallace, who had previously been minister of Scotstown, was installed in Glennan. Mr. Wallace resigned this charge on the 24th of September, 1861, having accepted a call from the congregation of Athy; and on the 28th of May, 1862, Mr. John Davidson was ordained to the pastoral charge.

GLENWHERRY.

As early as 1672 the inhabitants of Glenwherry applied to the Presbytery for preaching; but the country was then very sparsely inhabited, and it does not appear that they obtained any regular supply of ordinances. Shortly after that date, when Peden, the famous Scotch field preacher, was obliged to make his escape from Scotland, he found refuge in Glenwherry. The tradition is that he appeared in the country in the dress of a labouring man, and engaged himself to a farmer at a place still known as Shoptown, to thrash oats. His real character was soon discovered, for his constant prayerfulness did not escape the notice of the family, and he then confessed that he was the persecuted evangelist. He remained for some time in the country; and often preached to crowded audiences in private houses and in the open air. About the same time Willie Gilliland, the hero of Sir Samuel Ferguson's beautiful poem of that name, appeared in Glenwherry. He was a Scottish gentleman who was obliged to leave his native country about the time of the battle of Bothwell Bridge. He found shelter at the Collin, where Mr. Arthur Allen, an elder of the Presbyterian Church, and one of his descendants, now inherits a valuable estate. He had two sons, one of whom lived at Collin, and another at Tildarg, about two miles distant. From Willie Gilliland many respectable families in the North of Ireland are descended. Glenwherry long remained without a minister; some of the people attending worship at the Braid, some at Connor, and some at Ballyeaston; but at length in 1823 the inhabitants applied to the Synod of Ulster, and were erected into a separate congregation. Their first minister was Mr. John Montgomery, who was ordained here by the Presbytery of Ballymena on the 6th of September, 1825. Becoming infirm, Mr. Robert Jeffrey was ordained as his assistant on the 22nd of December, 1868. Mr. Montgomery died on the 22nd of July, 1869. Mr. Jeffrey resigned his charge of the congregation on the 23rd of January, 1873, and removed to Greyabbey. He was succeeded by Mr. James Morell, who was ordained here on the 3rd of March, 1874. Mr. Morell resigned this charge on the 1st of February, 1881, on his removal to Rathfriland; and was succeeded by Mr. Hamilton Moore, who was ordained here on the 1st of November, 1881.

GRANGE.

In the Grange, a district in the neighbourhood of Ballymena and Randalstown, the Quakers had one of their earliest settlements in Ireland. A Presbyterian congregation was also established here in the seventeenth century. It was originally associated with the congregation of Dunean. The two congregations had alternate supplies of preaching. This state of things was unsatisfactory; and a proposal was made that a meeting-house should be erected on some central spot, to which all could resort, and thus have public ordinances every Lord's day. But they could not agree to such a settlement. The following is one of several minutes relative to this subject:—"May 1st, 1688.—Mr. David Cunningham spoke to Mr. Dalway about the privilege of Grange, who declares that their privilege is of no weight to hinder their joining with Dunean in one meeting-place. On this, James Stuart, from Grange, declares they resolve to have a separate meeting-house, notwithstanding all that has been said. The meeting desired Mr. Elias Travers to speak to the Lord or Lady Massereene as to their mind on it." Again:—"As to the place of the meeting-house, they declare Dunean and Grange cannot be united, which is also the mind of my Lord Massereene, reported by Elias Travers; but both parties agree that both the meeting-houses be erected as near the march of Dunean and Grange as can be." Mr. Elias Travers, who is here mentioned, was chaplain to Lord Massereene. He was nephew to Lord Radnor, better known as Lord Roberts, who, in 1669, was Lord Lieutenant of Ireland. Mr. Travers could not conform to Prelacy, and became a Presbyterian minister. After the Revolution he settled in Dublin as minister of Cork Street congregation, and officiated there till his death in 1705. The Massereene family at this time took much interest in the affairs of the Presbyterian Church, and Lady Massereene seems to have been a Presbyterian. As the Massereene property was in the neighbourhood of Grange, we can well understand why Mr. Elias Travers, Lord Massereene's chaplain, and himself a Presbyterian minister, took so much trouble in endeavouring to arrange the site of the Grange meeting-house. Mr. Dalway, ancestor of Marriott Dalway, Esq., formerly M.P. for Carrickfergus, was a member of the Presbyterian Church. He was a man of influence in the county, and perhaps had some property in the district where the dispute was going on. The two congregations of Dunean and Grange remained united; but the association was found to be very inconvenient. In 1733 the people of Grange complained that Mr. Henderson, the minister of Dunean, had given up the charge of them. He had joined the Presbytery of Antrim in 1725. The Presbyterians of the district were now for a considerable time without a stated ministry. At length, on the 4th of June, 1745, Mr. Francis O'Bryan was ordained here. He demitted the charge in 1752, and died on the 30th of June, 1753. The congregation was again annexed to Dunean; and Mr. Robert Scott was ordained to the united charge on the 28th of June, 1762. Shortly after the death of Mr. Scott the union was again dissolved. In 1820 the people sought to be erected into a separate congregation; and the Presbytery of Ballymena was ordered to supply them with preaching. In the following year they were recognised by the Synod as a distinct charge. They then stated that they had their meeting-house in good order, and that they would engage to pay an annual stipend of £54. Their first minister in this separate state was Mr. Robert Rusk, who was ordained here on the 23rd of March, 1824. Mr. Rusk died here on the 25th of July, 1841. He was succeeded by Mr. Hall Stewart, who was ordained here on the 21st of July, 1842. Becoming infirm Mr. Stewart retired from the active duties of the ministry in August, 1881, and was succeeded by the Rev. Robert Erwin, formerly of Caledon, who was installed here on the 3rd January, 1882.

GREYABBEY.

THE earliest minister here was Mr. Fergus Alexander. He was imprisoned by Venables in 1650; but he had either left the country at the subsequent severities of the Republican party, or had died before 1660, as we do not find him then in the country. The people then joined the congregation of Ballywalter. In 1731 the people of Greyabbey, by their commissioners, Messrs. Rowan and Ferdinand Baillie, supplicated to be erected into a separate congregation, which was opposed by Ballywalter, and for a time deferred. It was ordered that Mr. Goudy, of Ballywalter, supply here every fourth Sabbath, they paying annually to him £7 10s., with meal and turf as usual. At the death of Mr. Goudy they were erected into a distinct congregation by the Synod in 1773, on their promise of £30 per annum and £10 worth of victual and turf. Captain Montgomery became security for this sum. Their first minister was Mr. James Cochran, formerly minister at Dunfanaghy, who was installed here June 9th, 1736. He died in this charge in the end of March, 1739; and was succeeded by Mr. Hugh Dickson, who was ordained here by the Presbytery of Bangor January 13th, 1742. Mr. Dickson died 18th May, 1771, leaving a widow and family; and was succeeded by Mr. Samuel Martin Stephenson, who was ordained here June 20th, 1774. He demitted this charge August 1st, 1785; and having obtained the degree of M.D., settled in Belfast as a physician, where he attained high distinction in his profession. He was the father of the late Dr. Stephenson, of Belfast. He was succeeded in Greyabbey by Mr. James Porter, who was ordained here July 31st, 1787. On the 2nd of July, 1798, Mr. Porter was executed on a rising ground in the immediate vicinity of his own house for his complicity in the rebellion. He was the only ordained minister connected with the Presbyterian Church in Ireland who suffered capitally at that time for treason. He wrote a famous pamphlet called "Billy Bluff and the Squire." Billy Bluff was Billy Lowry, a small farmer near Greyabbey, who was the bailiff of the estate; and the squire was Squire Montgomery of Greyabbey. The next minister was Mr. John Watson, who was ordained here September 3rd, 1799. In 1829 Mr. Watson and a part of the congregation seceded from the Synod of Ulster. The part of the congregation adhering to the Synod called Mr. David Jeffrey, who was ordained here September 13th, 1832. Mr. Jeffrey died on the 5th of December, 1872; and was succeeded by his son, the Rev. Robert Jeffrey, formerly of Glenwherry, who was installed here on the 4th of February, 1873. Mr. Jeffrey, on his removal to Bombay, resigned this charge on the 5th of November, 1878; and was succeeded by Mr. John Anderson, who was installed here on the 20th of May, 1879.

GROOMSPORT.

THE people of Groomsport were originally connected with the congregation of Bangor. Nearly fifty years ago a movement was made towards their erection into a congregation; but the lord of the soil strenuously opposed the measure, and refused to give any site for a place of worship. It so happened, however, that, in the very heart of the village, there was a tenement in perpetuity held by a Presbyterian willing to part with it on very reasonable terms; this was soon secured, and the congregation forthwith prospered. On the 18th of May, 1841, Mr. Isaac Mack was ordained as the first minister. Mr. Mack collected funds for the erection, not only of the church, but of the schools and other buildings connected with it. The people of Groomsport are indebted to Mr. William M'Murray, of London, for the very handsome balcony in front of the church, as well as for its clock and bell. Mr. Mack, who had a great taste for architecture, did much to improve the appearance of the village of Groomsport and its neighbourhood. He died on the 12th of July, 1877; and was succeeded by Mr. James Latimer,* who was installed here on the 2nd of April, 1878.

HILLSBOROUGH.

THIS congregation was erected by the Presbytery of Belfast in April, 1832, and its first minister was Mr. Henry Jackson Dobbin (afterwards D.D.), son of the Rev. H. Dobbin, of Lurgan. Mr. Dobbin was ordained here on the 18th of September, 1833. On the 30th of January, 1837, Mr. Dobbin resigned this charge and removed to 1st Ballymena. He was succeeded by Mr. Samuel Marcus Dill (afterwards D.D.), formerly minister of Magherally, who was installed here on the 3rd of October, 1837. On the 28th of September, 1853, Mr. Dill resigned this charge and removed to 1st Ballymena, as successor to Dr. Dobbin. He was succeeded in Hillsborough by Mr. Alexander Montgomery, who was ordained here on the 28th of March, 1854. On the 27th of August, 1854, Mr. Montgomery resigned this charge, having received a call to the congregation of Magherafelt. He was succeeded

* The congregation of Groomsport has recently been much indebted to Samuel Kingham, Esq., J.P., by whose encouragement and patronage a beautiful manse has been erected.

by Mr. Robert Templeton, who was installed here on the 27th of March, 1855. On the 9th of June, 1857, Mr. Templeton resigned this charge; and was succeeded by Mr. Galbraith H. Johnston, who was installed here on the 30th of September, 1857.

HILLTOWN.

THIS congregation was erected by the Presbytery of Dromore in 1826. The first minister was Mr. Edward Allen, who was ordained here on the 5th of June, 1827. His ministry soon came to a close, as he was set aside for immorality in the following year. The next minister was Mr. Robert Lockhart, who was ordained here on the 2nd of June, 1829. The congregation was still without the *Regium Donum*, and remained in this position for some time after the settlement of Mr. Lockhart. At length in 1831 it obtained the grant on what was then the 3rd class—that is, at the rate of £50 a-year, late Irish currency.

HOLYWOOD 1ST.

THE first minister here was Mr. Robert Cunningham. He had been chaplain to the Earl of Buccleugh's regiment in Holland, and was admitted to this charge by the Bishop of Down and Connor, November 9th, 1615. Mr. Cunningham was a man of eminent piety and great ministerial gifts. In 1636 he was deposed for nonconformity, when he fled to Scotland. He died the following year at Irvine, and his friend, the great Robert Blair, of Bangor, composed an epitaph in Latin verse, which was inscribed on his tombstone. After his deposition there was no minister here till after the Irish Rebellion of 1641. On April 8th, 1644, the Covenant was administered at Holywood by the Rev. William Adair, from Scotland, who preached and presided. An eldership or session had been ordained here in June, 1642. Holywood was united to Dundonald under the ministry of Peebles, Kennedy, and Cobham. Under the ministry of Cobham, in 1704, a separation took place, and Mr. Cobham died in the sole charge of Holywood June 24th, 1706. His successor was Mr. Michael Bruce, son of Mr. Bruce, of Killyleagh. He was ordained here October 10th, 1711. In 1715 he was called to Monaghan, but the Synod decided against his removal. The commissioners from Holywood on this occasion were Arthur Kennedy, Esq., Messrs. Jo. Kennedy, Jo. Hamilton, James Russel, and James Hamilton. In 1725 Mr. Bruce joined the Nonsubscribing Presbytery of Antrim. A schism soon afterwards took place in the congregation, some of them, with Mr. Bruce, separating from the Synod of Ulster, and retaining possession of the meeting-house; others remaining with the Synod, and erecting a new house of worship for themselves. Those who remained with the Synod were the poorer portion of the congregation. In 1729 they applied by their commissioner, Mr. Matthew Russel, to the Synod for assistance, having given a call to a probationer, and being able to advance only £17 per annum. Their first minister was Mr. William Smith, who was ordained here November 4th, 1729. He died in this charge October 1st, 1741; and was succeeded by Mr. William Rodgers, who was ordained here by the Presbytery of Bangor, November 20th, 1743. He removed to Ballynure in 1751. Their next minister was Mr. John King, who had been licensed by the Presbytery of Warrington, and received by the Synod in 1743. He was ordained here December 3rd, 1754. He died in this charge August 20th, 1777, leaving neither widow nor family; and was succeeded by Mr. Thomas Kennedy, formerly minister in America, who was installed by the Presbytery of Belfast August 4th, 1778. He died February 7th, 1788, leaving a widow and family. Their next minister was Mr. Joseph Harrison, who was ordained March 4th, 1788. He died February 12th, 1816, leaving a widow and family; and was succeeded by his son, Mr. William Harrison, who was ordained here March 19th, 1816. He died in this charge September 15th, 1824, leaving neither widow nor family. Their next minister was Mr. Henry Wallace, who was ordained here December 5th, 1826. Mr. Wallace (now Professor Wallace of the Assembly's College, Belfast) resigned this charge on the 6th of May, 1834, and removed to Cork. He was succeeded by Mr. William Blackwood, who was ordained here on the 17th of February, 1835. In February, 1844, Mr. Blackwood resigned the pastoral charge, and removed to England; and was succeeded by Mr. Henry Henderson, who was ordained here on the 25th of September, 1844. Mr. Henderson becoming infirm, Mr. Henry Halliday was ordained here on the 8th of January, 1878. Mr. Henderson died on the 7th of December, 1879.

INCH.

The Presbyterians of the island of Inch, near Derry, formerly belonged to Burt congregation, but their insular situation rendered it inconvenient and somewhat dangerous for them to attend public worship on the mainland with very great regularity. They were in consequence separated from Burt and formed into a distinct congregation by the Presbytery of Derry in 1831. Their first minister was Mr. Samuel Armour, who was ordained here on the 5th of March, 1833. Mr. Armour died on the 11th of June, 1853; and was succeeded by Mr. James Anderson, who had been ordained here by the Presbytery of Derry on the 23rd of September, 1852. According to the Minutes of the General Assembly this little congregation consists of twenty-two families.

ISLANDMAGEE 1st.

ISLANDMAGEE, a peninsula five or six miles long and one and a-half broad, on the eastern coast of the County of Antrim, has acquired a historical notoriety as the scene of a sad act of party retaliation. Towards the close of 1641, the Irish Romanists rose up in rebellion and massacred many thousands of the Protestants of Ulster. The butchery went on for upwards of two months, and, on the 3rd of January, 1642, a party of the insurgents murdered in cold blood about three score old men, women, and children, about a mile and a-half from Carrickfergus Castle. Some of the Protestants of the neighbourhood, irritated by these horrid cruelties, on the 9th of January, 1642, put to death about thirty Romanists in their own houses, or near them, in Islandmagee. The story that 3,000 Romanists were driven over the Gobbins there is a monstrous Popish fiction, invented long afterwards. At that time there was no Presbyterian minister in the district, for the Prelatic party, a few years before, had driven the Presbyterian ministers from their pulpits. About six years prior to this date, the Rev. Edward Brice, who had preached for twenty-three years to the people of Islandmagee and Ballycarry, had died, after having been sentenced to deposition by the Bishop of Down and Connor. The Presbyterians of Islandmagee now remained without a minister till 1647, when Mr. Henry Main was ordained among them. He was imprisoned by Venables in Carrickfergus in 1650. In 1651

K

we find him supplying a congregation within the bounds of the Presbytery of Paisley. In 1658 Mr. William Mill, from Aberdeen, was settled here, but, like others brought up in that part of Scotland, he was of unsteady principles, and he was one of the very few Presbyterian ministers in Ireland who conformed at the time of the Restoration. The next notice we have of this congregation is in 1671, when we find it supplied by Mr. John Haltridge, a probationer, who was ordained by the Presbytery of Antrim at Ballycarry on the 8th of May, 1672. It appears from Wodrow, that Mr. Haltridge had been previously chaplain to Sir William Cunningham, of Cunningham-head, in Scotland, and that he had been brought before the High Commission Court at Glasgow in 1664. He was then forbidden to preach by the Archbishop of Glasgow, and he, in consequence, came to Ireland. He continued in Islandmagee for twenty-five years, surviving the Revolution, and dying in 1697. His successor, Mr. Robert Sinclair was ordained here May 10th, 1704. He died in this charge January 5th, 1731; and was succeeded by Mr. Robert Leather, who was ordained here February 12th, 1733. He was deposed in 1740 for fornication. The next minister was Mr. George Heron, a licentiate of the Presbytery of Aberdeen, who was ordained here August 8th, 1747. He was translated from Islandmagee to a living in Scotland. He was succeeded by Mr. James Dunbar, who was ordained March 14th, 1758. Mr. Dunbar died in 1766, leaving a widow and family; and was succeeded by Mr. M'Aulay, who was ordained December 14th, 1769. He resigned ten years afterwards; and was succeeded by Mr. David Ker, who was ordained March 4th, 1783. Mr. Ker demitted the charge in 1788, and removed to America. He was succeeded by Mr. John Murphy, who was ordained here August 15th, 1789. Becoming infirm, Mr. William Campbell, a native of Killyleagh, was ordained his assistant and successor on the 14th of April, 1829.* Mr. Murphy died June 12th, 1842, in the 87th year of his age. Mr. Campbell died on the 17th of August, 1876; and was succeeded by Mr. David Steen, who was ordained here on the 14th of August, 1877.

* Soon after his ordination Mr. Campbell took with him one day from Belfast a bundle of young trees which he had purchased there; they were planted by him in the meeting-house green of which they are now distinguished ornaments.

KEADY 1st.

This congregation was established in the beginning of the eighteenth century. Its first minister was Mr. Thomas Milliken, or Mulligan, who was ordained here by the Presbytery of Armagh, December 17th, 1706. He died in January, 1734, and was succeeded by Mr. John Gibson, formerly minister of Cavanaleck, who was installed here January 13th, 1738. He demitted this charge in 1776. The people now gave a call to Mr. Robert Black, afterwards D.D. and minister of Derry, but he did not settle among them. Mr. Joseph Smyth was then ordained on the 15th of October, 1777. Mr. Gibson died September 25th, 1779, leaving neither widow nor family; and Mr. Smith died July 20th, 1795, leaving both a widow and family. The next minister was Mr. Henry M'Ilree, formerly minister of Vinecash, who was installed here by the Presbytery of Monaghan, March 8th, 1797. This installation was set aside by the Synod in 1798; but in 1800 it was ordered that he be again installed by the Presbytery of Monaghan; and the minority who opposed him were erected into a separate congregation. Mr. M'Ilree died November 8th, 1817. The next minister was Mr. Andrew Breakey, who was ordained here, August 10th, 1819. He resigned this charge on the 8th of March, 1831, and removed to Killyleagh. He was succeeded by Mr. Solomon Love, who was ordained December 28th, 1831. In 1836 Mr. Love was degraded. The next minister was Mr. H. W. Carson, now D.D., who was ordained here by the Presbytery of Armagh, September 12th, 1838.

KEADY 2nd

This congregation was erected in 1800, in consequence of disputes relative to the election of the minister of the 1st congregation. The first minister was Dr. William Steele Dickson, who was installed here March 4th, 1803. He had previously been minister of Portaferry. In 1812 he was suspended *ab officio* for refusing to retract the assertions contained in his famous "Narrative." Dr. Dickson was supposed to have been deeply implicated in the Rebellion of 1798. In 1815 the congregation reported that he had resigned the charge through infirmity. The congregation was then disannexed from the Presbytery of Tyrone and joined to that of Armagh. The next minister was Mr. Joseph Jenkins, who was ordained here March 20, 1816. Dr. Dickson was afterwards joined to the Presbytery of Bangor. and died December 27th, 1824. This congregation did not obtain *Regium Donum* till 1815. Mr. Jenkins becoming infirm, Mr. George Steen was ordained as his assistant and successor on the 9th of November, 1854. Mr. Jenkins died on the 30th of August, 1862.

KILLEAD.

THIS congregation appears to have grown out of an early settlement at Oldstone. Mr. James Glendinning removed to Oldstone in this parish about 1625, but continued only a short time, when he left the country. He was succeeded by Mr. Henry Colvert, who had been ordained by the Bishop of Raphoe, May 4th, 1629; was helper to Mr. Brice at Broadisland, and was admitted to the vicarage of Muckamore June 17th, 1630, on the presentation of Roger Langford, Esq. Being deposed by the Bishop of Down in 1636, he fled to Scotland, and being admitted minister at Paisley, in 1638, died in that charge. This congregation was, no doubt, early planted after the restoration of Presbyterianism, but the first notice we have of it is not till 1660, when we find Mr. Robert Hamilton minister here. He was deposed by the bishop in 1661, but he nevertheless continued to officiate among his people till his death in December, 1673. In February, 1674, Mr. Patrick Mortimer was their commissioner to the Presbytery. The following month they wrote to Mr. J. Frieland, in Scotland, to come over with a view to being settled here, with which he complied in May, and on July 7th they presented him with a call. In the end of the month, however, he returned to Scotland on a visit, and did not come back till January 7th, 1675, when he became constant supplier. In June their commissioners, Messrs. Alexander Gordon and Alexander Bellahill, promised to secure Mr. Frieland £30 per annum, 20 bolls of oats, and fuel, and he was ordained in the end of the year. In December, 1686, he proposed to have the parish divided, and a second minister settled. Accordingly in June, 1687, the parish gave a call to Mr. John Malcome to be the minister of Lower Killead, where he was ordained December 5th, 1687. Mr. Adair, of Ballyeaston, presided on the occasion, and preached from 2 Cor. ii. 16. Mr. Malcome removed to Dunmurry about 1699. Mr. Frieland died March 12th, 1716; and was succeeded by Mr. Robert Wirling, who was installed here May 16th, 1716. The division of this congregation into Upper and Lower was set aside in 1699, and the lower part, with Kilmakevit, was ordered to join with Glenavy; and Mr. Malcome removing at the same time to Dunmurry, the whole charge devolved on Mr. Frieland, and his successor Mr. Wirling. Mr. Wirling was deposed from the ministry in 1726, but for what offence the minutes do not specify. In 1730, however, having professed his repentance, and his resolution to carry more cautiously for the future, he was restored to the ministry, but was not suffered to preach in this congregation. The next minister was Mr. Hugh Scott, who was ordained here April 9th, 1733. He was present at the Synod in 1735, but removed in that year to the first congregation of Newtownards. He was succeeded by Mr. John M'Connell, who was ordained here May 3rd, 1737. He died June 8th, 1770, leaving neither widow nor family; and was succeeded by Mr. Andrew Hume, who was ordained here February 26th, 1772. He appears to have been deposed about the year 1783. Their next minister was Mr. Robert Orr, who was ordained here January 2nd, 1787. Becoming infirm, Mr. Joseph M'Kee was ordained to the charge September 5th, 1826. Mr. Orr died in Belfast on Sunday, the 13th of October, 1833, leaving a widow and family. Mr. M'Kee resigned the charge of the congregation in July, 1849, and died in 1856. Mr. Henry R. Mecredy was ordained to the charge in March, 1850.

KILLESHANDRA.

This congregation was at one time also called Croghan. In 1688 Mr. Samuel Kelso was minister here. At the Revolution he retired to Scotland, and probably never returned. The next minister was Mr. James Tate, who was ordained here by the Presbytery of Monaghan on the 10th of May, 1705. He died in this charge on the 17th of May, 1729. The next minister was Mr. James Hamilton, who was ordained here on the 23rd of February, 1732. He removed from this to Ballyjamesduff in the following year. He was succeeded by Mr. George Carson, who was ordained here on the 21st of May, 1735. In August, 1780, he resigned the charge through bodily infirmity; and was succeeded by Mr. William Millar, who had formerly been minister at Enniskillen, and who was installed here on the 7th of May, 1781. Mr. Carson died on the 10th of January, 1782. Mr. Millar resigned his charge here on the 1st of July, 1795; and was succeeded by Mr. Joseph Lawson, formerly minister at Lisluney, who was installed here on the 16th of June, 1796. He died in this charge on the 7th of February, 1799, leaving a widow and child. The next minister was Mr. Joseph Denham, formerly minister at Enniskillen, who was installed here in September, 1799. He was the father of the Rev. Dr. Denham of Londonderry. Mr. Denham died in this charge on the 21st of October, 1834; and was succeeded by Mr. William White, son of Mr. Patrick White, minister of Bailieborough. Mr. White was ordained here on the 29th of September, 1835. He resigned this charge on the 19th of October, 1839, and removed to Downpatrick. He was succeeded by Mr. William Sweeny, who had formerly been connected with the Covenanters, and who was installed here by the Presbytery of Monaghan on the 30th of March, 1841. Mr. Sweeny becoming infirm, Mr. William James Stronge was ordained as his assistant on the 31st of December, 1867. Mr. Sweeny died shortly afterwards. Mr. Stronge, on his removal to Churchtown, resigned this charge on the 29th of June, 1880; and was succeeded by Mr. John H. Whitsitt, who was ordained here on the 3rd of March, 1881.

KILLETER.

THIS congregation originally formed part of that of Derg. It was disannexed from it in November, 1827. The first minister was Mr. John Davis, who was ordained here by the Presbytery of Strabane on the 6th of February, 1828. Mr. Davis died on the 25th of February, 1832, leaving neither widow nor family. He was succeeded by Mr. Joseph Crockett, who was ordained here on the 20th of December, 1832. In August, 1837, Mr. Crockett resigned the charge and removed to Derg. He was succeeded by Mr. William Hamilton, who was ordained here by the Presbytery of Strabane on the 20th of February, 1838; but, this ordination having been effected in opposition to an appeal to the Synod, was declared irregular by the Synod in June, 1838, and Mr. Hamilton was consequently disannexed from the congregation. The next minister was Mr. Joseph Love, who was ordained here on the 26th of February, 1839. Mr. Love died on the 23rd of May, 1885; and on the 18th of August following, his son, the Rev. George C. Love, was installed here.

KILLINCHY.

THIS congregation was originally united to that of Killyleagh, under the ministry of Mr. Bole. Its first settled minister was Mr. John Livingston, who was ordained by the Bishop of Raphoe, and located here in August, 1630. After several vicissitudes, detailed in his Life, he ultimately fled to Scotland in the year 1637.* The congregation continued destitute of a regular ministry till 1657, when Mr. Livingston, now in Scotland, sent them over Mr. Michael Bruce, who was ordained in the parish church of Killinchy by the Presbytery in the autumn of the same year. At the Restoration he was deposed by the bishop, and fled to Scotland. After sustaining various hardships, both in Scotland and at London, he obtained permission to return to Killinchy in 1670. In the summer of that year the first meeting-house ever erected in the parish was built. In 1714 this house was thrown down and another erected on the same spot. At the troubles in 1689 Mr. Bruce again retreated to Scotland in spring; and becoming minister at Anworth, in Galloway, he died there in 1693, and lies buried in the church of that parish. He was succeeded by Mr. Archibald Hamilton, who removed from Armagh, and was installed here by the Presbytery of Down in March, 1693. He died at Belfast January 4th, 1699, and was buried at Bangor, where his tomb and epitaph are still to be seen. The next minister was Mr. James Reid, who was ordained here April 28th, 1702. He continued to be minister here for fifty-one years, and died in the beginning of June, 1753. Their next minister was Mr. Joseph Kinkead, who removed hither from Stranorlar in 1755; but owing to disputes between the people and the Presbytery of Killyleagh, his installation was a long time delayed. At length he was installed here by the Presbytery of Bangor April 28th, 1763. He died July 20th, 1782, leaving a widow and family. Their

* Mr. Livingston was one of the most awakening preachers of the age. The revival of the Kirk of Shots took place under a sermon he delivered.

next minister was Mr. George M'Ewen, ordained here by the Presbytery of Belfast March 11th, 1783. He died March 20th, 1795, leaving a widow and family; and was succeeded by Mr. Samuel Watson, who was ordained here in September, 1797. In August, 1835, Mr. Watson was suspended *sine die* for Arianism, whereupon he joined the Remonstrants; and was succeeded by Mr. David Anderson, who was ordained to this charge December 6th, 1836. Mr. Anderson died on the 25th of January, 1871; and was succeeded by Mr. David R. Moore, who was ordained here on the 2nd of April, 1872.

KILLYLEAGH 1st.

THE first minister of this congregation was Mr. John Bole He was blind. In 1639 he was imprisoned for refusing to take the "black oath," and dissuading his people from the same. The next minister was Mr. William Richardson, who was ordained here about the beginning of the year 1649. He died July 27th, 1670. He was succeeded by Mr. Alexander Ferguson, who had before, for twelve years, been minister of Sorbie, in Scotland. Mr. Ferguson settled at Killyleagh in 1670, and died there in 1684 in the 53rd year of his age. He was succeeded by Mr. James Bruce, son of Mr. Michael Bruce, of Killinchy, and ancestor of Sir Hervey Bruce, of Downhill. Mr. Bruce removed to Scotland at the Revolution, where he remained for some time, but returned in 1691. During the early part of his ministry here, the Hamilton family kept a chaplain in Killyleagh Castle, who was a member of the Presbytery of Down, and sat with it. His name was Patrick Peacock. It is said that he was married to a relative of the Hamilton family. In 1697 it is reported to the Synod of Ulster that a philosophy school, conducted by Mr. James M'Alpine, had been established at Killyleagh. It was designed to prepare young men going forward to the ministry with a philosophical education. Mr. James Bruce died February 17th, 1730; and was succeeded by his son, Mr. Patrick Bruce, who had previously been minister of Drumbo. Mr. Patrick Bruce was installed as minister of Killyleagh in the beginning of the year 1731, but died here April 9th, 1732. He was succeeded by Mr. Gilbert Kennedy, jun., who had been a short time minister of Lisburn, and was installed here in the beginning of the year 1733. In 1744 Mr. Kennedy removed to the 2nd congregation of Belfast, but still remained a member of the Synod of Ulster, though the congregation to which he was now transferred had been previously connected with the Presbytery of Antrim. Mr. Kennedy was succeeded in Killyleagh by Mr. William Dun, who was ordained May 29th, 1745. Mr. Dun removed to Cook Street Congregation, Dublin, in February, 1765. The next minister was Mr. Joseph Little, who was ordained to the pastoral charge November 18th, 1768. Mr. Little was a highly respectable scholar, and possessed of no small amount of talent. His influence was most beneficially exerted towards the end of the last century. He steadfastly opposed himself to the spread of revolutionary principles, so that the spirit of sedition which broke out into open rebellion in the year 1798 made comparatively little progress in the neighbourhood of Killyleagh. But his ministerial efficiency was greatly impaired by his eccentricities and his avarice. At the time of his demise he is said to have possessed property to the amount of £15,000 or £16,000. He died in July, 1813; and was succeeded by Mr. W. D. H. M'Ewen, who had formerly been minister of Usher's Quay, Dublin, and who was installed here August 17, 1813. Mr. M'Ewen removed to the 2nd congregation, Belfast, in 1817; and was succeeded by Mr. Henry Cooke (afterwards D.D., LL.D.), who had formerly been minister, first of Dunean, and afterwards of Donegore, and who was installed here September 8th, 1818. Shortly after his settlement at Killyleagh, Mr. Cooke distinguished himself as the assailant of Arianism; and in his efforts to free the Synod of Ulster from that heresy he was nobly supported by his elder, Captain Rowan. Mr. Cooke removed to Belfast in 1829; and was succeeded by Mr. Andrew Breakey, who had formerly been minister of 1st Keady, and who was installed here March 22nd, 1831. Mr. Breakey becoming infirm, Mr. William Witherow, formerly of Donaghadee, was installed here on the 5th of April, 1882. Mr. Breakey died on the 17th of November of the same year; and Mr. Witherow, on his removal to Westbourne Church, Ballymacarrett, resigned this charge on the 30th of January, 1883; and was succeeded by Mr. John R. M'Cleery, who was installed here on the 7th of August, 1883.

KILMORE.

THIS congregation was formed in 1713, when we find

Saintfield complaining of some townlands being taken from it and transferred to the new erection. The first minister was Mr. Thomas Elder, of whom we have the following notice in the Synod's minutes for 1715 :—"Down Presbytery reported that Mr. Thomas Elder, who was some time ago deposed from the office of the holy ministry by the General Assembly of the Kirk of Scotland, and he having represented his case to the Synod of Belfast, who, being well informed of his good deportment since he came into the bounds of that Synod, wrote a letter to the Assembly in his behalf, and that he went with said letter to the Assembly, who have now restored him to the office of the ministry." The act of the Assembly was accordingly read, and Mr. Elder acknowledged as a minister. He was installed in this charge on the 14th of June, 1716. He was present at the Synod in 1726, but he either died or left this charge soon after. He was succeeded by Mr. Samuel Fugie, or Fergie, who was ordained here by the Presbytery of Bangor on the 23rd of October, 1728. He died in this charge May 3rd, 1765, leaving a widow and family. He was succeeded by Mr. Moses Neilson, who was ordained here by the Presbytery of Killyleagh in 1767.* Becoming infirm, his son, Arthur Neilson was ordained his assistant and successor on the 13th of June, 1810. Dr. Moses Neilson died April 23rd, 1823, leaving a widow and family. In 1829 Mr. Arthur Neilson and this congregation seceded from the Synod of Ulster, but, at his death in 1831, the majority of the people returned to the Synod; and Mr. Moses Black was ordained here by the Presbytery of Belfast on the 2nd of April, 1833. The present place of worship was built mainly through the exertions of a single individual, the late worthy Mr. David K. Clarke. Mr. Black died on the 12th March, 1881; and was succeeded by Mr. Thomas Alexander, formerly of Courtrai, who was installed here on the 13th of September of the same year.

KILRAUGHTS 1st.

WE find Mr. Robert Nelson minister here in 1702. He appears to have been settled in the place some time before. In 1712 disputes commenced between Mr. Nelson and his

---

* The Neilsons were distinguished by their linguistic attainments, and did much to promote a knowledge of classical literature in the North of Ireland.

people, so that the Synod in the following year recommended his demission of the charge. He had been guilty of no immorality, but the Synod considered that his continuance here would not be for edification. The Synod required the people to pay an arrear of £60 due to him, and agreed that his *Regium Donum* should be continued. He died in May, 1721. He was succeeded by Mr. John Cochrane, who was ordained here on the 27th September, 1716. In 1731 he was called to Bangor; but the Synod decided that he should continue in Kilraughts. In 1748 the Synod, after a second application, permitted him to remove to Bangor. He was succeeded here by Mr. Robert Ewing, who was ordained on the 12th of June, 1751. He died on the 23rd September, 1786. The next minister was Mr. Matthew Elder, who was ordained to this charge in 1789. He died July 23rd, 1827, leaving a widow and family. Considerable disputes prevailed in this congregation after Mr. Elder's death. Mr. W. D. Killen (afterwards D.D.) obtained a call to the place; but a number of the people, absurdly suspecting him of Arianism, still remained dissatisfied. A second poll was taken at his request, when he was rejected after a close contest—145 voting for him and 74 against him. At length Mr. Thomas Leslie was ordained to this charge by a synodical committee on the 29th December, 1830. He resigned the charge on the 27th of January, 1835, and proceeded to Jamaica as a missionary under the Scottish Missionary Society. He died in Jamaica on the 18th August, 1835. The next minister was Mr. Robert Love, who was ordained here on the 21st of June, 1836. Mr. Love died on the 18th January, 1849; and was succeeded by Mr. Samuel Finlay, who was ordained here on the 12th of March, 1850.

KILREA 1st.

This congregation originally went by the name of Tamlagh. Mr. William Gilchrist was minister here for many years before the Revolution of 1688. He died in Derry during the siege. Tamlagh, Kilrea, and Bovidy formed one congregation. The charge was vacant for some time after the Revolution. In 1697 Mr. Matthew Clerk was ordained here. Mr. Clerk had served as an officer in the Protestant army during the civil commotions, and had received a wound at the siege of Derry. He was an excellent scholar; and, laying aside the military profession at the end of the wars, entered the Presbyterian ministry. He was thoroughly Calvinistic in his religious views, genial in his temper, and retained a good deal of the martial spirit as long as he lived. In 1729 he resigned the charge of the Kilrea congregation, and, though about seventy years of age, emigrated to America, where he became minister of the congregation of Londonderry. He died six years afterwards, January 25th, 1735, aged 76. He was succeeded in Kilrea by Mr. Robert Wirling, formerly minister of Killead, who was installed here in 1731. In 1741 the people complained to the Synod of their great weakness and inability to support a minister. In the same year Mr. Wirling removed to Donagheady. The next minister was Mr. Alexander Cumine, who was ordained here by the Presbytery of Route May 22nd, 1744. He died in this charge November 9th, 1748; and was succeeded by Mr. John Smith, who was ordained here October 31st, 1749. In 1779 the inhabitants of Bovidy prayed the Synod to be erected into a distinct congregation, having 226 heads of families in that quarter. This was opposed by Tamlagh, Kilrea, and Desert. The Synod directed Mr. Smith to divide his labours between the two places. A Seceding congregation was eventually erected at Bovidy. Mr. Smith died October 2nd, 1785. The next minister was Mr. Arthur M'Mahon, who was ordained here October 12th, 1789. Mr. M'Mahon was an excellent scholar, and had previously been tutor in the Londonderry family, which then was connected with the Presbyterian Church. From Mr. M'Mahon the great Lord Castlereagh, afterwards Premier of England, received his classical education. Mr. M'Mahon, in October, 1794, demitted the charge of the Kilrea congregation, and removed to Holywood. He subsequently became deeply implicated in the treasonable proceedings of the United Irishmen, and with difficulty escaped to France, where he is said to have entered the military service; and there is a tradition, we cannot say whether true or false, that he is the same individual who, as *General Mack*, acquired such distinguished reputation. He was succeeded at Kilrea by Mr. John Smyth, who was ordained here March 17th, 1795. In June, 1805, Mr. Smyth prayed the Synod to remove him from Route to Ballymena Presbytery, which was granted. Mr. Smyth died September 7th, 1821. He was succeeded by Mr. Hugh Walker Rodgers, who was ordained here April 12th, 1825. Mr. Rodgers was moderator of the Synod of Ulster in 1836. During his ministry the present excellent place of worship was built. Mr. Rodgers died in July, 1851; and was succeeded by his son, Mr. James Maxwell Rodgers, who was ordained 22nd June, 1853. Mr. Rodgers, on his removal to Derry, in March, 1869, resigned this charge; and was succeeded by Mr. James Heron, formerly of Muckamore, who was installed here on the 7th of May, 1869. On his removal to Knock in November, 1873, Mr. Heron was succeeded by Mr. James Stewart, who was installed here on the 27th of February, 1874.

KINGSTOWN.

This congregation was erected in 1827, and its first minister was Mr. William Freeland. He was ordained here on the 1st of June, 1828. In the year 1831 this congregation obtained *Regium Donum* on the 3rd class—that is, £50 late Irish currency. Mr. Freeland was disannexed from this charge in 1838, and afterwards installed in Ballygawley. He was succeeded by Mr. John Armstrong, who was ordained here on the 30th of June, 1840. At the Assembly of 1859, in consequence of the protracted ill-health of Mr. Armstrong, his congregation obtained leave to choose an assistant and successor; and on the 23rd of February, 1860, Mr. Samuel Jackson Hanson, formerly minister of Conlig, was installed here.

KIRKCUBBIN.

This congregation was originally part of Ballyhalbert or Glastry. In 1777 the people applied to the Synod to be erected into a congregation, but without success. Nevertheless they persisted, and gave a call to Mr. George Brydone, who was ordained to this charge by the Presbytery of Lauder, in Scotland. The Synod of Ulster in 1778 resented the interference of the Scottish Presbytery, and addressed a letter of remonstrance on the subject to the Moderator of the General Assembly. Mr. Brydone and his congregation were not received into connection with the Synod till 1783. He died here on the 6th of September, 1817, leaving neither widow nor family. He was succeeded by Mr. Alexander M'Ewen, who was ordained here on the 16th of October, 1817. Mr. M'Ewen becoming infirm, demitted the charge in 1837; and Mr. James Rowan was ordained to succeed him on the 30th of January, 1838. Mr. M'Ewen died on the 29th of January, 1839. In 1868 Mr. Rowan obtained leave for the congregation to choose an assistant and successor; and on the 1st of June, 1869, Mr. Samuel Hawthorne was ordained to the pastoral charge. Mr. Rowan died on the 5th of December, 1877.

KNOWHEAD.

THE earliest notice we have of this congregation is in connection with the ordination of Mr. Robert Huey. The congregation was then called Muff. Mr. Huey appears to have been the minister only for a short time. He was ordained February 10th, 1749; but shortly afterwards he resigned and went to America. He was succeeded by Mr. Stephen Brizzle, who was ordained here October 30th, 1776. He was deposed by the Presbytery of Derry on the 1st of February, 1780, and died at the advanced age of 92, on the 20th of January, 1831. The next minister was Mr. James Patton, who was ordained October 7th, 1783, and who died in this charge on the 24th of June, 1790. He was succeeded by Mr. Richard Dill, who was ordained here on the 9th of December, 1793. Mr. Dill becoming infirm, Mr. John M. Bleckley was ordained as his assistant on the 27th of June, 1848. Mr. Dill died on the 20th of November, 1850. On the 21st of October, 1856, Mr. Bleckley resigned the charge of the congregation and removed to Wicklow. On the 24th of March, 1857, Mr. John Camac was ordained to the pastoral charge.

LARNE 1ST.

THIS is one of the oldest Presbyterian congregations in Ireland. The first minister was Mr. George Dunbar, who had been minister at Ayr, in Scotland, and who settled here about 1620. He was deposed by the Bishop of Down and Connor in 1636, when he removed to Scotland, and died minister of Calder in 1638. On the fall of Prelacy, this congregation was speedily settled with a minister. Mr. Thomas Hall was ordained to this charge in 1646. He was subsequently obliged to make his escape to Scotland to avoid the persecution of the Republicans then in power, but returned to his people before 1660. He was deposed by Bishop Jeremy

Taylor immediately after the Restoration; but he continued privately to minister to his people amidst many outward discouragements. In March, 1674, Mr. Adair, the author of the celebrated Narrative of the early settlement of our Church in this country, visited Larne by appointment of Presbytery, and reported that "he found the people considerably in arrear with their minister, almost to the half of what was promised him, for these four years past." Mr. Hugh Porter, an elder, promised that they would be more punctual. Mr. Hall died in 1695, aged 75. Mr. William Leech was called to Larne in 1697; but his career here was short. He was succeeded by Mr. William Ogilvie, who was ordained here on the 5th of November, 1700. He died on the 12th of September, 1712. During the disputes which arose after his death the congregation was divided into two parts, which have ever since remained separate. One part chose Mr. James Hood as their minister, and subsequently joined the non-subscribing Presbytery of Antrim; the other chose for their minister Mr. Samuel Getty, who was ordained here on the same day as Mr. Hood—that is, on the 15th of June, 1715. Mr. Getty was the ancestor of John Getty, Esq., of Beechpark, Belfast, who lately bequeathed his large property to the Irish General Assembly. Mr. Getty died here on the 27th of February, 1724; and was succeeded by Mr. William Thompson, who was ordained here by the Presbytery of Templepatrick on the 7th of June, 1726. Mr. Thompson died in this charge on the 13th of May, 1763. He was succeeded by Mr. Isaac Cowan, who was ordained here on the 20th of August, 1765. He died on the 2nd of March, 1787, leaving a widow and family. The next minister was Mr. Robert Thompson, who was ordained here on the 9th of June, 1789. He died in this charge about the middle of August, 1814; and was succeeded by Mr. James Cochrane, who was ordained here on the 22nd of December, 1815. On the 7th of May following he was suspended by the Synod for immorality; but in 1817 he was restored. In 1823 he was again suspended, and finally on the 22nd of June, 1824, he was suspended *sine die*, and disannexed from the congregation. The next minister was Mr. Joseph Shaw, formerly minister of Portglenone, who was installed here on the 4th of January, 1825. He died in this charge, at the early age of 29, on the 13th of August, 1830. He was succeeded by Mr. Henry William Molyneux (afterwards D.D.), who was ordained here on the 9th of June, 1831. Dr. Molyneux died on the 23rd of August, 1871; and was succeeded by Mr. J. Brady Meek, who was installed here in the summer of 1872.

LETTERKENNY 1ST.

THE first minister here was Mr. William Semple, who was ordained in 1647, and died in this charge October 19th, 1674. The next minister was Mr. William Liston. About the time of the arrival of King William in Ireland, after the Revolution, some of the Presbyterians of the North of Ireland appear to have imagined that their system of ecclesiastical polity was about to be established by law in the country, as it had been in Scotland; and, in two or three places, they proceeded, rather prematurely, to take possession of the parish churches. Mr. Liston is said to have preached for two or three Lord's days in the Episcopal church of Letterkenny, and in some other Episcopal churches in the neighbourhood; but the Synod of Ulster, which met in Belfast July 3rd, 1690—only three days after the battle of the Boyne—required him not to repeat such conduct. He died in June, 1695. The next minister was Mr. Samuel Dunlop, who was ordained here August 13th, 1707. He died August 30th, 1762, leaving a widow; and was succeeded by Mr. Joseph Lyttle, who was ordained here April 20th, 1763. Becoming infirm, his nephew, Mr. Joseph Lyttle, jun., was ordained his assistant and successor May 31st, 1803. Mr. Lyttle, sen., died January 7th, 1805, leaving no family. Mr. Joseph Lyttle, *secundus*, becoming infirm, Mr. Moses Houston, who had been minister of Fannet, was installed his assistant and successor on the 6th of April, 1841. In 1847 Mr. Houston was set aside on a charge of immorality; and on the 27th December, 1848, the Rev. John Kinnear (now D.D.) was ordained to the pastoral charge. Mr. Lyttle died on the 19th December, 1852.

LIMAVADY 2ND.*

MR. DAVID WILSON was ordained here by the Presbytery of Route, August 18th, 1696. He died in this charge June 23rd, 1715. In 1718 William Connolly, Esq., wrote to

* What is now 1st Limavady was originally one of the earliest settlements of the Seceders in Ireland.

the Synod on behalf of Mr. John Hillhouse, a probationer, recommending him as the minister; but he went to America. At last they obtained as minister Mr. William Conyngham, who was ordained here February 3rd, 1720. He died in this charge 1740. After his death there was much contention in the congregation. Mr. Joseph Osborne was ordained here by the Presbytery of Antrim; but many of the people were dissatisfied, and refused to join his ministry. The malcontents were erected into the congregation of Drumachose, and Mr. Henry Areskine, or Erskine, was ordained as their minister by the Presbytery of Derry, May 4th, 1742. After living in a state of constant bickering with his co-presbyters, and being charged with several immoralities, he demitted his charge in October, 1761. He was succeeded by Mr. Jacob Davis, who was ordained here by the Presbytery of Route, April 26th, 1763. He died December 30th, 1786, leaving a widow. The next minister was Mr. Daniel Blair, who was ordained here in the end of May, 1788. He died on the 10th of February, 1811, leaving a widow and family; and was succeeded by Mr. Richard Dill, formerly minister of Buckna, who was installed here March 10th, 1812. He resigned this charge January 28th, 1823, and removed to the adjoining congregation of Ballykelly. Their next minister was Mr. John M'Laughlin, who was ordained here September 28th, 1824. Mr. M'Laughlin died suddenly on the 3rd of November, 1831, leaving neither widow nor family. He was succeeded by Mr. George Steen, who was ordained here by the Presbytery of Route on the 12th of March, 1833. In Mr. Steen's time a meeting-house was built in the town of Limavady, when he was called to the charge of the new congregation, resigning that of Drumachose. Becoming infirm, Mr. Steen obtained as his assistant the Rev. Robert Henry, who was installed here on the 30th of November, 1882.

LIMERICK.

It is probable that some members of the Church of Scotland settled in Limerick as early as the times of James I. or Charles I., but we have now no record to illustrate their history. The first minister of the congregation of whom we find mention was Mr. Squire, but of him we know nothing more than the name. Soon after the Revolution, the people rented the chapel of the old Augustinian Nunnery in Peter's Cell. (See History, Topography, and Antiquities of Limerick, II. 563). About that time the Rev. William Bigger was their minister. In 1698 Mr. Bigger was invited by some Presbyterians in Galway to preach occasionally and administer ordinances to them; but he was apprehended, brought before the Mayor, and committed to prison. He was soon liberated, but the case created much excitement. Mr. Bigger is said to have removed afterwards to Drogheda. He was succeeded by Mr. S. Smith, who was a high Calvinist. His successor was Dr. Labun, a minister probably of French extraction. He was succeeded by Mr. Wallace and Mr. Scawright. In 1776 the people erected a meeting-house in Peter Street, and built a house for the minister, at the expense of £500. Since the commencement of the present century the congregation has received an accession of numbers and wealth by the settlement of several Scotch merchants in the city, and since then the present commodious edifice of hewn stone in Glentworth Street has been built. Mr. Scawright was succeeded by Mr. John Pinkerton, who was followed by Mr. Dickie and Mr. Nelson. In January, 1837, Mr. M'Corkle, a licentiate of the Church of Scotland, was settled as the pastor. Mr. M'Corkle returned to Scotland; and, towards the close of the year 1844, Mr. David Wilson (now D.D.), who had previously been ordained at Carnmoney, removed to Limerick. The Presbytery of Munster, to which the congregation belonged, was at this time a separate body; but in 1854 it became incorporated with the Irish General Assembly. The Rev. Dr. Wilson, the present minister of Limerick, has been twice Moderator of the Assembly.

LISBURN 1ST.

THE first minister of this congregation cannot now be ascertained. At a meeting of Presbytery held at Ballyclare, on the 5th of April, 1687, Messrs. William Livingston and John M'Kneight appeared as commissioners from Lisburn, and "sought supply of ordained ministers in order to their being planted with a Gospel minister." In November following the people presented a call to Mr. Alexander M'Cracken, who had been licensed by the Presbytery in 1684, and who was ordained to the pastoral charge of the congregation on 3rd July, 1688. Mr. Patrick Adair, of Belfast, presided on the occasion, and preached from 1 Cor. iv. 1, 2. Mr. M'Cracken had the promise of £40 yearly of stipend. In 1707 the town of Lisburn was destroyed by a great fire, which consumed both the Episcopal church and the Presbyterian meeting-house. The fire broke out on Sunday, the 20th of April, a little before twelve o'clock. The meeting-house was rebuilt, at an expense of about £400. The edifice destroyed was valued at £500. Mr. M'Cracken had scruples about the oath of abjuration,* and was, in consequence of his refusal to take it, more than once brought into trouble. He was a loyal subject, and a staunch supporter of the house of Hanover; but he objected to some parts of the phraseology of the oath, and the High Church party most ungenerously took advantage of his scrupulosity to give him annoyance. He died in November, 1730; and was succeeded by Mr. Gilbert Kennedy, who was ordained to the pastoral charge June 7th, 1732. Mr. Kennedy soon afterwards removed to Killyleagh; and was succeeded as minister of Lisburn by Mr. William Patton, who had been minister of Ervey and Carrickmaclim, and who was installed here July 7th, 1736. During his ministry the Seceders made their appearance in the North of Ireland, and some of their earliest adherents had at one time belonged to the congregation over which he presided. Those who joined the new-comers eventually established the congregation of Hillhall. Mr. Patton removed to Plunket Street congregation, Dublin, in August, 1745; and was succeeded in Lisburn by Mr. Patrick Buchanan, who was ordained to the pastoral charge July 29th, 1747. Mr. Buchanan died in November, 1763; and was succeeded by Mr. James Bryson, who was ordained June 7th, 1764. Mr. Bryson removed to the 2nd congregation of Belfast in 1773; and was succeeded in Lisburn by Mr. George Kennedy, who was ordained February 15th, 1775. Mr. Kennedy's pastorate was short, as he died in April, 1779. He was succeeded by Mr. William Bruce, who was ordained here by the Presbytery of Bangor on the 4th of November, 1779. Mr. Bruce removed, first to Strand Street congregation, Dublin, and finally to the 1st congregation, Belfast. Dr. Bruce, when in Belfast, was president of the Academy, and a member of the Presbytery of Antrim. He was suc-

* The oath of abjuration was understood to imply that the Pretender was *not* the son of James II., so that, on this ground, many scrupled to take it.

ceeded in Lisburn by Mr. Andrew Craig, who had formerly been minister of Moira, and who was installed in Lisburn in 1783. Becoming infirm, Mr. James Morgan (afterwards Dr. Morgan), who had formerly been minister of Carlow, was installed as his assistant June 23rd, 1824. Mr. Morgan resigned the charge on receiving a call from Fisherwick Place congregation, Belfast; and was succeeded by Mr. Alexander Henderson, who was ordained on the 29th of June, 1829. Mr. Henderson, on receiving an appointment as military chaplain, resigned this charge on the 4th of December, 1855; and was succeeded by Mr. William Breakey, who was installed here on the 3rd of September, 1856. Mr. Breakey died on the 6th of April, 1872; and was succeeded by Mr. John L. Rentoul, who was ordained here on the 17th of October, 1872.

LISLOONEY.

THIS congregation was originally connected with Minterburn under the name of Kinnaird. It was erected into a separate charge in 1714; but it did not obtain a minister until some time afterwards. At length Mr. Samuel Irvine was ordained here by the Clogher Presbytery on the 1st of October, 1718. He died in this charge October 6th, 1729; and was succeeded by Mr. William Ambrose, who was ordained as minister of Kinnaird on the 2nd of August, 1732. He died in this charge on the 29th of December, 1765, leaving a family. He was succeeded by Mr. George Harris, who was ordained here on the 2nd of August, 1768. Mr. Harris died on the 15th of February, 1785; and was succeeded by Mr. James M'Adam, who was ordained on the 14th of March, 1787. He was deposed July 10th, 1788; and was succeeded by Mr. Joseph Lawson, who was ordained on the 15th of August, 1789. He removed to Killeshandra in June, 1796. Their next minister was Mr. James Gibson, who was ordained here on the 5th of August, 1801. In 1834 Mr. Gibson resigned the charge through infirmity; and was succeeded by Mr. Robert P. Borland, who was ordained on the 22nd of September, 1836. Mr. Gibson long survived his resignation, as he died in December, 1866. Mr. Borland died on the 26th of July, 1862. He was succeeded by Mr. James Carson, who was ordained here on the 24th of June, 1863. Mr. Carson resigned the charge of the congregation on the 20th of March, 1866, and removed to Waterford. The next minister, Mr. Edward F. Simpson, was ordained here on the 26th of September, 1866. Mr. Simpson, on his removal to Ballymena, was succeeded by Mr. Thomas Irvine, who was ordained here on the 31st of January, 1877.

LISSARA.

THE Seceders made their appearance in Ireland upwards of 140 years ago. In 1775 a small place of worship was erected at Lissara, and not long afterwards Mr. John Sturgeon was ordained by the Associate Seceding Presbytery of Down as minister of the united congregation of Lissara and Ballynahinch. Mr. Sturgeon remained pastor of Lissara and Ballynahinch till his death. About the time of his death these places were erected into separate charges, and early in the year 1796 Mr. John Reid was ordained as the Seceding minister of Lissara. Mr. Reid's pastorate here was short, amounting only to five years. He removed to Drumbanagher in 1801. He was succeeded by Mr. Denham, who was a medical practitioner as well as a preacher; and, in consequence of his intemperate habits, he was soon obliged to give up the ministry. He was succeeded by Mr. Joseph Lowry, who was ordained here on the 25th of April, 1809. His ministry in Lissara was long. He died here on the 21st of July, 1858, in the 82nd year of his age. Mr. Lowry gave instruction in classics at his own residence; and some of the present ministers of the General Assembly received their education from him. He was succeeded as minister of Lissara by Mr. John Gibson Thomson, who was ordained here on the 21st of December, 1858.

LONDONDERRY 1ST.

THE Presbyterians early obtained a settlement in Londonderry—but we know little of their state there immediately after the massacre of 1641. In May, 1644, the Covenant was solemnly administered in the Cathedral to great multitudes by Messrs. Weir and Adair from Scotland; and the sacrament was dispensed afterwards in the same place—the altar being removed. The first minister—whose name has not been ascertained—was soon subsequently settled here, and was deposed in 1661. Severe measures for a time were now employed to the great discomfort of Presbyterian ministers. We find the congregation vacant in 1670. Wodrow relates how they then called Mr. Alexander Moncrief, formerly minister of Scoonie, Fifeshire, but he declined the call. In January, 1672, they presented a call by their commissioners, Alderman Craigie and Mr. Reilly, to the Presbytery of Route, for Mr. Thomas Fulton, one of their ministers, but the Presbytery would not permit him to remove. In the end of the same year, however, they at last obtained a settled pastor in Mr. Robert Rule, formerly minister of Stirling, and brother of the celebrated Gilbert Rule. He continued unmolested in this charge till 1688, when he fled to Scotland and never returned. In September, 1688, they called Mr. Henry, of Carrickfergus, but he did not remove. Mr. Robert Craighead was now settled here. He was removed from Donaghmore in 1690. During his ministry the congregation revived greatly. We now find attending Presbytery as elders Aldermen H. Long, W. Smith, Lecky, Lennox, and Horace Kennedy. In 1696 they had a dispute with Burt about the boundaries of their congregations. The people of Elagh, Corquin, and Ballynegallagh refusing to join with Derry, the Presbytery determined the congregation to be limited by the liberties of the city on that side. Mr. Craighead growing infirm, the congregation called his son, Mr. Robert Craighead, in 1709—they promised £70 to the old man and £40 to the young—but the call was not accepted. They afterwards called Mr. James Bruce, of Killyleagh, but the Synod opposed the removal. Mr. Craighead, sen., died on the 22nd of August, 1711. In 1712 they called Mr. Abernethy, of Antrim, but this the Synod also opposed. They at length succeeded in obtaining Mr. James Blair, of Moira, who was installed here on the 2nd of June, 1713. He died January 21st, 1716. Being again vacant, they once more called Mr. Craighead, now of Capel Street, Dublin, but the Synod again prevented his removal. The next minister was Mr. Samuel Ross, who was ordained here on the 13th of February, 1718. He died in this charge on the 26th of October, 1736. At his death the congregation disputed respecting a successor, part being for Mr. David Harvey, minister of Glendermot, and Mr. Hair, a probationer, as colleague; and part complained that they were overlooked in this choice. The former sent to the Synod in 1737, as their commissioners, Messrs. Davis and

Cross—the latter, Messrs. Moore, Ewing, and Marshall; but, on a conference, both parties agreed to acquiesce in Mr. Harvey's call, " on condition that their right of electing a colleague to him should be preserved, and a maintenance of £40 per annum secured to such colleague." Mr. David Harvey was accordingly soon afterwards installed here; and in 1738 they supplicated for supply of probationers to assist their pastor. They soon obtained as colleague Mr. John Hood, who was ordained here on the 10th of June, 1742. Mr. Hood died June 21st, 1774, leaving a widow and family. They gave a call to Mr. Campbell, of Armagh, in November, 1774, but without effect. In 1775 Mr. David Young, formerly minister at Enniskillen, removed to this congregation. Mr. Harvey demitted his charge here in November, 1783; and Mr. Robert Black (afterwards D.D.), formerly minister at Dromore, was installed in his room,* as colleague to Mr. Young, on the 2nd Tuesday of January, 1784. Mr. Harvey died in April, 1794. In 1803 the Presbytery reported to the Synod that they had suspended Dr. Young *sine die.* He was succeeded by Mr. George Hay, who was ordained here as colleague to Dr. Black on the 18th of June, 1805. Dr. Black died, under melancholy circumstances, on the 4th of December, 1817, leaving a widow and family; and his place was filled by Mr. John Mitchell, formerly minister of Dungiven, who was installed here in August, 1819. On the 27th of August, 1823, Mr. Mitchell resigned; and was succeeded by Mr. William M'Clure, who was ordained here on the 1st of March, 1825, as colleague to Mr. Hay. Mr. Young died about May, 1827. Mr. Hay died June 10th, 1837; and was succeeded by the Rev. Henry Wallace, formerly of Cork, who was installed here on the 7th of September, 1837, as colleague to Mr. M'Clure. It was arranged that the collegiate charge should cease on the death or translation of either of these ministers. Mr. Wallace, on his appointment as Professor of Christian Ethics in Belfast Presbyterian College, resigned this charge on the 6th of November, 1867; and about the same time Mr. M'Clure asked leave for the congregation to choose an assistant and successor. On the 21st of May, 1857, Mr. Richard Smyth had meanwhile been installed as an assistant here; but, on

---

* Dr. Black, for many years, was the acknowledged leader of the Synod of Ulster. He was very lax in his theology; but he was gifted with commanding eloquence.

his appointment to a Professorship in Derry College, he resigned the charge on the 5th of September, 1865. On the 18th of March, 1869, Mr. Andrew C. Murphy was installed here. Mr. M'Clure died on the 22nd of February, 1874. On the 15th of December, 1879, Mr. Murphy resigned this charge on his removal to Dublin; and was succeeded by Mr. James Cargin, formerly of Dublin, who was installed here on the 27th of January, 1881.

LONDONDERRY 3RD.

THIS congregation was established in 1834, and its first minister was the Rev. James Denham, who had before been minister of Brigh. He was installed here on the 4th of May, 1837. Mr. Denham (afterwards D.D.) was one of the most acceptable ministers of his day; and under him the congregation greatly flourished. On the 18th of October, 1870, Dr. Denham resigned the pastoral charge, and died on the 18th of December, 1871. Meanwhile Mr. James Maxwell Rodgers, formerly minister of 1st Kilrea (and Moderator of the General Assembly in 1885), had been elected his assistant and successor, and was installed here on the 18th of March, 1869. This congregation is now one of the largest contributors to our Sustentation Fund—its donation for the past year (1885) amounting to £400.

LONGFORD.

THIS congregation was erected in 1833, and the first minister was Mr. Samuel M'Cutcheon, who was ordained here by the Presbytery of Monaghan on the 3rd of June, 1834. Mr. M'Cutcheon died on the 23rd of December, 1875; and was succeeded by Mr. Alexander Rentoul, who was installed here by the Athlone Presbytery on the 11th of May, 1877. On the 5th of April, 1881, Mr. Rentoul, on the eve of his removal to Dublin, resigned this charge; and was succeeded by Mr. Alfred H. Rentoul, who was ordained here on the 21st of May, 1882.

LOUGHBRICKLAND.

THE name of the first minister of this congregation cannot now be ascertained. It was vacant in August, 1687, and shortly afterwards Mr. John Mairs was ordained here. In June, 1697, he was removed to Longford. The next minister was Mr. George Lang, son of the minister of Newry, who was ordained here April 15th, 1701. Mr. Lang died May 29th, 1741. The next minister was Mr. Charles M'Collum, who was ordained here by the Presbytery of Dromore on the 6th of March, 1744. He removed to Capel Street, Dublin, in the end of the same year. The next minister was Mr. Timothy White, who had been minister at Ballyeaston, and who removed here in 1749. On the 12th of September of that year he was installed here by the Presbytery of Dromore. He died June 5th, 1756; and was succeeded by Mr. John Smith, who was ordained here on the 31st of October, 1757. He died May 27th, 1804, leaving a widow and family. The next minister was Mr. Hugh M'Alister, who was ordained here on the 11th of December, 1804. He died in this charge on the 10th of February, 1824, leaving neither widow nor family. The next minister was Mr. Robert Little, who was ordained here on the 28th of September, 1824. Mr. Little died on the 20th of January, 1841; and was succeeded by Mr. William Edmund Breakey, who was ordained here by the Presbytery of Banbridge on the 22nd of March, 1842. On the 4th of August, 1856, Mr. Breakey resigned the charge, and removed to Lisburn; and was succeeded by Mr. Robert Crawford, who was ordained here on the 31st of March, 1857. On the 11th of January, 1869, Mr. Crawford resigned the charge, and removed to Sinclair Seaman's Church, Belfast; and he was succeeded by Mr. Alexander Buchanan, who was ordained here on the 30th of March, 1869.

LOUGHGALL.

This congregation was established in the early part of the last century. In 1711 it applied to the Synod of Ulster for aid to enable it to support a minister, and £15 per annum was granted to it out of the General Fund. Mr. Hugh Wallace appears to have been the first minister. He was ordained here on the 10th of October, 1712. He resigned this charge and was installed in Castledawson in 1720. He was succeeded by Mr. James Orr, who was ordained here on the 30th of May, 1722. He died here on the 10th of April, 1755. The next minister was Mr. Robert Peebles, who was ordained here on the 26th of June, 1758. He died July

31st, 1761; and was succeeded by Mr. Moses Hogg, who was ordained here on the 25th of August, 1762. Mr. Hogg died here on the 23rd of November, 1802, leaving a widow and son. His son, Mr. Robert Hogg, succeeded him, and was ordained here on the 16th of March, 1803. He died in this charge on the 19th of January, 1830,* leaving neither widow nor family. The next minister was Mr. William Henry, who was ordained here on the 22nd of December, 1830. Mr. Henry died on the 20th of January, 1880. Mr. Henry had long before obtained an assistant in Mr. Edward Kimmit, who was installed here on the 19th of June, 1861. On the 25th of May, 1880, on his removal to Clonakilty, Mr. Kimmit resigned this charge; and was succeeded by Mr. William Smyth, formerly of Roscommon, who was installed here on the 11th of November, 1880.

LURGAN 1st.

THE earliest account we have of this congregation is in 1684, when we find it about to be planted. In 1686 Mr. Hugh Kirkpatrick was minister here. He retired to Scotland at the time of the Revolution, and became minister of a parish there. His successor was Mr. William Squire, who was settled here about 1694. In 1699 it is reported to the Synod that "he is wholly gone and continueth in England," so that the congregation was considered vacant. The next minister was Mr. James Fleming, who was ordained here by the Presbytery of Armagh, January 18th, 1704. It was still a very weak settlement, and in 1706 we find the sub-Synods of Belfast and Monaghan paying £20 to assist it in supporting a minister. In August, 1718, they obtained a lease of a plot of ground, on which they erected a meeting-house. In 1719, Mr. Fleming received a call from the 1st congregation of Belfast. His removal was opposed by his congregation, and their commissioners to the Synod were Miles Reilly, John M'Call, and others. Mr. Brownlow, the landlord, seems to have thought highly of Mr. Fleming—for he wrote a letter to the Moderator of the Synod, earnestly pleading for his continuance in Lurgan. The Synod resolved that he should not be removed; and, in a letter to Mr. Brownlow, thanked him for the kindness which he had shown to Mr. Fleming. This minister died in this charge August 16th, 1730. He

* Mr. Hogg was assistant astronomer in the Armagh Observatory.

was succeeded by Mr. John Menogh, formerly minister at Magherally, who was settled here in 1732. He died December 20th, 1771, leaving a widow and family, and was succeeded by Mr. Robert Rentoul, who had been ordained by a Scottish Presbytery in 1772, and who was installed by the Presbytery of Dromore, September 26th, 1773. He removed to Ballykelly in 1779, and was succeeded by Mr. William Magee, who was ordained here September 12th, 1780, and died July 9th, 1800. The widow of this minister inherited great wealth from brothers in India, and bequeathed, at her death in 1846, about £60,000 to the Irish Presbyterian Church, including £20,000 for the establishment of a Presbyterian College. Mr. Magee was succeeded in Lurgan by Mr. Hamilton Dobbin, formerly minister of Moira, who was installed here January 26th, 1802. Mr. Dobbin having become infirm, Mr. Thomas Millar was installed as his assistant and successor, on the 1st of October, 1844. Mr. Dobbin died on the 20th of October, 1851, and Mr. Millar was killed by a railway accident in May, 1858. Mr. Lowry E. Berkely, formerly minister of Faughanvale, was installed here on the 21st of September, 1858. On his appointment as convener of the Sustentation Fund in 1878, Mr. Berkely resigned this charge; and was succeeded by Mr. John M'Ilveen, formerly of Ballynahinch, who was installed here on the 19th of March, 1879. On his removal to Linen Hall Street congregation, Belfast, Mr. M'Ilveen resigned this charge; and was succeeded by Mr. Thomas M. Hamill, who was installed here on the 4th of March, 1884.

MACOSQUIN.

THERE was a settled minister here as early as 1670, but his name cannot now be exactly ascertained. Mr. John Laurie or Lowry, was minister here in 1688; and it would appear that he had three predecessors whose names were Boyd, Wilson, and Elliot. During the troubles of the Revolution Mr. Laurie retired to Scotland, and does not appear to have returned. In the meantime the people supplicated to be placed under the pastoral care of Mr. Boyd, of Aghadoey. This arrangement continued for some time; but they at length obtained the services of Mr. James Stuart, who had come from Scotland in 1701 as an ordained minister, and who was installed here by the Presbytery of Route on the 19th of August of that year. In March, 1706 he was suspended for various offences apparently proceeding from imprudence and ill temper: but the suspension was removed by the Synod following. The congregation, notwithstanding, remained dissatisfied; and in 1708 he demitted the charge and retired to Cushendall. He was succeeded by Mr. William Boyd, who was ordained here on the 31st of January, 1710. In 1725 he resigned this charge and removed to the old congregation of Taughboyne. His successor was Mr. John Thompson, who was ordained here on the 21st December, 1727. In early life Mr. Thompson obtained a commission in the army, but coming under deep religious impressions, he withdrew from the military profession and entered the Presbyterian ministry. His wife was the daughter of Stephen Ash, the descendant of Captain Thomas Ash, one of the heroes of the siege of Derry. Mr. Thompson died in this charge on the 7th of June, 1771, leaving a widow and family.* Mr. Thompson was succeeded by Mr. Robert Caldwell, who was ordained here September 1st, 1772, and demitted this charge in 1781. Mr. Caldwell was afterwards settled at Moville. The next minister was Mr. James M'Farlane, who was ordained here on the 1st of August, 1783. He died April 4th, 1816, leaving a widow and family, and was succeeded by Mr. John Patterson, who was ordained here on the 2nd September, 1817. On the 10th of September, 1822, he was suspended for intemperance. The next minister was Mr. Clarke Houston (afterwards D.D.), who was ordained here on the 30th of September, 1823. Dr. Houston died on the 23rd February, 1866, and was succeeded by Mr. Samuel Robinson, who was ordained here on the 28th of March, 1867. Mr. Robinson, having received a call from California, resigned this charge on the 1st of April, 1873; and was succeeded by Mr. John C. Huston, who was installed here on the 8th of July, 1873. Mr. Huston died on the 2nd of March, 1881; and was succeeded by Mr. Frederic Torrens, who was ordained here on the 8th of September, 1881.

MAGHERA.

IT would appear that Mr. James Kilpatrick officiated as minister of Maghera for upwards of twenty years prior to the Revolution. In 1690 the people were without a minister.

* The Rev. E. Thompson Martin, late of Dundonald, is one of his descendants.

We find them noticed in the following minute as supplicating for a pastor :—" Appeared from Maghera, Kilnonaghan, and several other places thereabout, Matthew Lorinan, James Garvan, Jo. Vernar, and Daniel Cairns, supplicating that, in consideration of their desolate condition as to the want of Gospel ordinances, and that they can give sufficient security for £25 per annum, being very hopeful it may grow to more after better planting, the four of whom will give security to the meeting of Tyrone for the same, they having already built a meeting-house, and they further promising here before the Synod to pay up to Mr. Abernethy whatever any of the said people shall be found due to him—that the Synod would be pleased to advise and concur with them as to their being planted with a minister." The Synod considering this affair and finding that Mr. James Ramsay had formerly a call from a part of the same people, and had passed all his trials upon the matter till something fell in that hindered his settlement, they then go on to appoint Mr. Ramsay to supply them for some Sabbaths in order to a call; Mr. Ramsay, however, refusing to settle there, the people called Mr. John Tomb of the Route Presbytery, who is advised to go, in the first place, to Scotland for laureation. This being done, he is settled here in 1696. He was succeeded by Mr. Archibald Boyd, who was ordained here by the Presbytery of Tyrone on the 28th of October, 1703. He was set aside in 1716. The next minister was Mr. James Dykes, who was ordained here on the 25th of May, 1720. He died in this charge on the 19th December, 1734. The people then gave a call to Mr. Robert Knox, a probationer under the care of the Presbytery of Route, but he died after having passed through second trials, previous to his ordination. The next minister was Mr. David Smylie, who had been ordained by the Presbytery of Route in Finvoy, and who removed here in the end of the year 1739. Mr. Smylié becoming infirm, Mr. John Glendy was ordained here by the Presbytery of Route in December, 1778. Mr. Smylie died August 1st, 1780, leaving a family. It was reported to the Synod in 1798 that " Mr. Glendy, being charged with seditious practices, was permitted by Colonel Leith to transport himself and property to America."* After much disputing Mr. Charles Kennedy was ordained here on the 29th

* Mr. Glendy subsequently became rather a distinguished minister in the Presbyterian Church of the United States. When minister of Maghera, Henry Cooke (afterwards D.D., LL.D.) was baptized by him.

of July, 1801. Mr. Kennedy becoming infirm, Mr. Smylie Robson was ordained his assistant and successor on the 16th of June, 1843. On the 20th of February of the following year Mr. Robson resigned the charge and became a missionary to the Jews. He was succeeded by Mr. Thomas Witherow, who was ordained here on the 1st of October, 1845. Mr. Kennedy died on the 8th of February, 1855. Mr. Witherow (now D.D.) having been appointed Professor of Church History in Magee College in 1865, resigned this charge, and was succeeded by Mr. Matthew Leitch, who was ordained to the pastoral charge on the 2nd of October, 1866. Mr. Leitch, on his appointment as Professor of Biblical Criticism in Belfast Presbyterian College in 1879, was succeeded by Mr. Robert H. F. Dickey, who was ordained here on the 26th of January, 1880.

MAGHERAFELT 1st.

THIS congregation originally formed part of Moneymore. There was an attempt made to have it erected into a separate charge as early as 1692. This, however, did not succeed. It was then annexed to Castledawson, and continued thus for many years. At length in 1737 Messrs. Robert Rainey and William Johnson appeared as Commissioners before the Synod, and stated that Magherafelt, being a large town in which there were 56 families of Dissenters, they ought to have a place of worship and not be obliged to travel two miles to Castledawson. The Synod of Ulster, however, still continued it in connexion with Castledawson; but allowed them half of the services of the minister of Castledawson. In 1738, however, differences between this congregation and that of Castledawson continued, and the Synod erected it into a separate charge, appointing Mr. Wallace, who had previously preached in Castledawson, as the minister, and adding 50 families to it which formerly belonged to Moneymore. This handing over of families from one congregation to another by Synodical authority would now be considered a very strange procedure. Mr. Wallace died in this charge on the 10th of March, 1761. He was succeeded by Mr. William Wilson, who was ordained here on the 19th of November, 1765. In 1785 he removed to Usher's Quay, Dublin. He was succeeded by Mr. George Dugald, who was ordained on the 30th of May, 1786. He died in this charge on the 9th of December, 1810, leaving a widow and family.

HISTORY OF CONGREGATIONS. 191

The next minister was Mr. James Wilson, who was ordained here on the 24th of September, 1813. Mr. Wilson died on the 10th of June, 1854. The next minister was Mr. Alexander Montgomery, who was installed here on the 20th of September, 1854.

MAGHERALLY.

THE first minister of this congregation was Mr. Andrew Maccormick. He was here in 1656, and was known to Livingston at that date. He was deposed in 1660, and, flying to Scotland, was killed at the battle of Pentland Hills in 1666. His successor was Mr. John Hunter. He was here in 1672, but fled to Scotland at the Revolution of 1688, and never returned. He was minister of Ayr and Alloway from 1690 to 1696. The next minister was Mr. James Heron, ordained here November 1st, 1693. He died in the beginning of the year 1699. His successor was Mr. Samuel Young, who was ordained by the Presbytery of Armagh, February 16th, 1704. He resigned the charge here and went to America in 1718. He was succeeded by Mr. John Menogh, who settled here about 1722. He removed to Lurgan in 1733. The next minister was Mr. James Moody, who was ordained here by the Presbytery of Armagh, May 28th, 1734. In 1740, Mr. Moody removed to Newry, and was succeeded by Mr. William Thompson, who was ordained here by the Presbytery of Armagh, October 20th, 1742, and died November 8th, 1756. The next minister was Mr. Isaac Patrick, who was ordained here June 22nd, 1758. Becoming infirm, Mr. Alexander Patterson, formerly minister of Drumbanagher, was installed as his assistant and successor, November 12th, 1805. Mr. Patrick died in October, 1814, leaving a widow and family. When Mr. Patterson became infirm, Mr. Samuel Marcus Dill (afterwards Professor of Divinity in Magee College) was ordained as his assistant on the 7th of April, 1835. Mr. Dill resigned this charge September 5th, 1837, and removed to Hillsborough. He was succeeded by Mr. Thomas Boyd, who was installed here by the Presbytery of Dromore, March 27th, 1839. Mr. Boyd resigned this charge June 3rd, 1839, and removed to Castleblayney. He was succeeded by Mr. James Thompson (formerly of Ballynahinch), who was installed here February 26, 1840. Mr. Patterson died 9th April, 1845. Mr. Thompson becoming infirm, Mr. J. D. Martin was ordained here on the 20th of March, 1883. Mr. Thompson died on the 27th of October of the same year.

MAGILLIGAN.

IN the year 1812 the inhabitants of this district supplicated to be erected by the Synod of Ulster into a separate congregation. This request was granted in the following year. The first minister was Mr. Samuel Butler, who was ordained here on the 15th of September, 1814.* Becoming infirm, his nephew, Mr. Hugh M'Intyre Butler, was ordained as his assistant and successor on the 16th of December, 1851. Mr. Butler, sen., died on the 9th of January, 1862.

MAGUIRESBRIDGE.

IN the year 1820 the inhabitants of this place belonging to the congregation of Enniskillen supplicated the Synod of Ulster to be erected into a distinct congregation, stating that they were seven miles from Enniskillen, and enjoyed divine service only every fifth Sabbath. The application was granted in 1821; the people engaged to pay a minister £59 per annum. The first minister was Mr. James M'Williams, who was ordained here on the 14th November, 1822. This congregation did not obtain *Regium Donum* until 1827. Mr. M'Williams died on the 20th of April, 1860; and was succeeded by Mr. Henry Cowan, who was ordained here on the 11th of September, 1860. On the 5th of October, 1865, Mr. Cowan resigned the charge of the congregation, having accepted a call from the congregation of Newbliss; and was succeeded by Mr. Samuel Huston Thompson, who was ordained here on the 29th of December, 1865. On the 6th of April, 1869, Mr. Thompson resigned the charge; and on the 20th July of the same year Mr. John H. Charleton was installed as the minister. Mr. Charlton resigned this charge on his removal to Clonduff in January, 1882; and was succeeded by Mr. John Sturgeon, formerly of Trenta, who was installed here on the 22nd of August, 1882.

MALIN.

THE earliest notice we have of this congregation is connected with the ordination of Mr. John Harvey, jun., on the 23rd of October, 1717. He died in this charge on the 7th of February, 1733. He was succeeded by Mr. John Montgomery,

* Mr. Butler published a volume of sermons.

who was installed here on the 8th of October, 1734. He appears to have resigned in 1737, though he continued a member of the Presbytery. Complaint was made in 1748 that he neither attended public worship nor the judicatories of the church. The Presbytery of Derry was ordered to enquire as to the grounds of this complaint, but Mr. Montgomery died on the 14th of March, 1749, and thus there appears to have been no investigation. Meanwhile Mr. David Walker was ordained towards the end of the year 1738. He continued here till his death, which occurred on the 21st of July, 1766. Another Mr. David Walker was ordained here on the 10th of October, 1768. He died in the end of May, 1782. The congregation was now for several years under the care of Mr. Scott of Donagh. At length, on the 23rd of March, 1798, Mr. James Canning was ordained to the pastoral charge. He died on the 13th of May, 1830. He was succeeded by his son Mr. John Canning who was ordained here on the 14th of March, 1832. Mr. Canning died on the 26th of November, 1877; and was succeeded by Mr. Joseph Thompson, who was ordained here on the 13th of June, 1878. On the 3rd of September, 1878, Mr. Thompson resigned this charge; and was succeeded by Mr. George W. Neely, who was installed here on the 20th of November of the same year. Mr. Neely resigned the charge on his appointment as a Missionary to New South Wales, in January, 1882; and was succeeded by Mr. Archibald Henderson, who was installed here on the 4th of April, 1882.

MARKETHILL 1st.

The first minister here of whom we have any account was Mr. Archibald Maclaine, who was installed here by the Presbytery of Armagh about 1700. He was the first Presbyterian minister in this country prosecuted by the Bishop's Court for celebrating marriage—though, as stated by Macbride in his work on the subject, he had episcopal ordination. He had previously been minister of Killbride in Arran. He was able to preach in Irish. He died in this charge on the 20th of July, 1734. After this the congregation divided. Those who adhered to the old meeting-house offered a stipend of £40 per annum and 20 bolls of oats—a boll being equal to six bushels. Those who adhered to the new meeting-house offered security for £30 and 15 bolls of oats. Both supplicated to be erected into distinct congregations, and their requests were granted. Mr. George Ferguson was ordained here on the 10th of March, 1741. Mr. Ferguson growing infirm, Mr. Samuel Sloan was ordained here June 18th, 1780, as his assistant and successor. Mr. Ferguson died on the 6th of June, 1782. Mr. Sloan died on the 25th of March, 1793; and was succeeded by Mr. William Charleton, who was ordained here on the 19th of March, 1794. On June 15th, 1808, the connection between Mr. Charleton and the congregation was dissolved by the Presbytery. The next minister was Mr. Paul Boreland, who was ordained here on the 26th September, 1809. Becoming prematurely infirm, Mr. John Fisher was ordained his assistant and successor on the 23rd of June, 1828. Mr. Boreland died on the 15th of July, 1831, leaving a widow and family. On the 25th of March, 1842, Mr. Fisher was suspended from the office of the ministry. He was succeeded as minister of Markethill by Mr. Alexander Goudy Ross,* who was ordained here on the 15th of June, 1843. Mr. Ross died on the 24th of February, 1858; and was succeeded by Mr. Hillis Kyle, who was ordained here on the 29th of September, 1858. Mr. Kyle died on the 24th of November, 1860. His successor was Mr. George Nesbitt, formerly minister of Tartaraghan, who was installed here on the 29th of May, 1861.

MILFORD.

This congregation was erected by the Presbytery of Letterkenny on the 15th of May, 1837. The first minister was Mr. Robert White, who was ordained on the 7th of December, 1837. Mr. White died on the 14th of January, 1873; and was succeeded by Mr. Hugh MacCulloch, who was ordained here on the 1st of October, 1873. Mr. MacCulloch, having accepted a call from Buncrana, resigned the pastoral charge on the 5th of January, 1881; and was succeeded by Mr. William James Young, who was ordained here on the 27th of July of the same year.

MILLISLE.

The early history of this congregation is buried in obscurity,

* Mr. Ross was the son of a respectable merchant in Monaghan, from whom he inherited a small estate.

and few records remain to throw light on the subject. We know, however, that Mr. Andrew Greer was ordained here by the Presbytery of Belfast on the 20th of May, 1771. Mr. Greer becoming infirm, Mr. John Walker was ordained his assistant and successor on the 13th of April, 1810. In 1814 Mr. Walker was deposed. The next minister was Mr. John Hanna, who was ordained here on the first Tuesday of May, 1815. Mr. Greer died on the 6th of April, 1819, leaving neither widow nor family. Becoming infirm, Mr. Hanna, in 1847, obtained leave for his congregation to choose an assistant and successor; and, on the 2nd of March, 1848, Mr. John M'Auley was ordained here. Mr. Hanna died on the 4th of January, 1850.

MINTERBURN.

This congregation being in the parish of Aghaloo, in Tyrone, was originally known by that name. The first minister was Mr. John Abernethy, who was ejected in 1661. He then removed to Brigh. He was succeeded by Mr. Joshua Fisher, who had been licensed by the Presbytery of Antrim in 1675, and who settled here shortly afterwards. He retired from this at the Revolution, supplied Ballymena for a time, and was finally settled at Donoughmore, near Raphoe. In September, 1691, we find the commissioner of this congregation, named Timothy Greer, supplicating for supplies at ten shillings a day till they obtained a minister. Mr. William Ambrose was ordained here by the Presbytery of Down in 1693. In 1714 this congregation was divided. Part went to form an erection at Teugh, or Glennan; part worshipped at Minterburn, whilst part continued at Kinnaird or Lisluney—the original settlement. Mr. Ambrose died towards the end of the year 1714. He was succeeded by Mr. Alexander Moor, who was ordained here on the 8th of October, 1716. He died on the 8th of July, 1724, and his tombstone is still said to be in Benburb churchyard. He appears to have been succeeded by Mr. William Ray, but some obscurity rests on this part of the history of the congregation. After this great disputes prevailed. In 1743 the result of a poll between two rival candidates, Messrs. Alexander Cumin and Adam Duffin, was reported to the Synod, but neither party succeeded. After much contention Mr. John Ker was at length ordained here by the Presbytery of Tyrone on the 9th of October, 1745. He died in this charge on the 11th of December, 1778. He was succeeded by Mr. Robert Rogers, who was ordained here on the 12th of November, 1782, and who removed to Corboy in March, 1785. The next minister was Mr. Hugh Boylan, who was ordained here on the 15th of November, 1785. He died here on the 9th of October, 1807, leaving a widow and family. He was succeeded by Mr. Andrew Shannon, who was ordained here on the 20th of December, 1808, and died on the 22nd of February, 1811. The next minister was Mr. Robert Cunningham, who was ordained here on the 24th of September, 1812. He died in this charge on the 29th of June, 1828; and was succeeded by Mr. James Collins, who was ordained here on the 26th of May, 1829. Mr. Collins died on the 23rd of December, 1849; and was succeeded by Mr. Alexander Gray, who was installed here on the 17th of December, 1850. Mr. Gray (now LL.D.) removed to Belfast in May, 1865; and was succeeded by Mr. Andrew James Wilson, who was ordained here on the 26th of September, 1865. On the 27th of September, 1883, Mr. Wilson resigned this charge on his removal to Malone; and was succeeded by Mr. Daniel Manderson, who was ordained here on the 8th of January, 1884.

MOIRA.

THIS is a congregation of ancient origin. It appears to have been in existence at the Revolution, but we do not know who was then the minister. It was vacant in April, 1692. The people then called Mr. Matthew Haltridge, minister at Ahoghill, but the Presbytery would not permit him to remove. Mr. Samuel Ferguson was ordained here towards the end of the year 1693. He died in this charge on the 21st November, 1703. In 1706 the people supplicated the Synod that, considering they were yet but a weak settlement, they would add to them some adjacent families then joined to Lisburn and Glenavy. They were still vacant in 1708. At last they obtained Mr. James Blair as their minister, and he was ordained here on the 17th of May, 1709. He was removed to Derry in June, 1713. His successor was Mr. Samuel Harpur, who was ordained here by the Presbytery of Belfast, on the 13th of March, 1717. In 1731 they supplicated the Synod that, as they were lately deprived of their meeting-house, assistance might be given them to build a new one. This was granted, and they were annexed to the Presbytery of Armagh. Mr.

Harpur joined the Presbytery of Antrim in 1726, and had probably died before this application to the Synod. The next minister was Mr. Thomas Creighton, who was ordained here by the Presbytery of Armagh on the 27th of May, 1734. In 1738 they built their meeting-house. Mr. Creighton died in this charge on the 29th of December, 1741. The Seceders now made their appearance in Ireland, and occupied the Moira meeting-house. This created much trouble. The congregation now remained long vacant on account of their poverty. The next minister was Mr. Joseph Mitchell, who was ordained here by the Presbytery of Bangor on the 29th of October, 1751. In 1752 the people complained that their meeting-house was seized by the Seceders, and that they had been at considerable expense in a law-suit for its recovery. In 1760 the Seceders still had the house, and the people again apply to the Synod for assistance. Mr. Mitchell died on the 5th of October, 1774, leaving a widow and children; and was succeeded by Mr. William Stitt, who was ordained here on the 10th of October, 1775. He removed to Dungannon in September, 1777; and was succeeded by Mr. Andrew Craig, who was ordained here on the 30th of June, 1778. He removed to Lisburn in 1783, and was succeeded by Mr. D. Trotter, who was ordained here on the 23rd of June, 1783. He removed to Summerhill; and was succeeded by Mr. George Dobbin, who was ordained here on the 1st of May, 1792. He died in this charge on the 21st of December, 1796, leaving a widow and family; and was succeeded by Mr. John Cochrane Wightman, who was ordained here on the 20th of March, 1798. In 1800 he removed to 1st Holywood; and was succeeded by Mr. Hamilton Dobbin, who was ordained here on the 10th of June, 1801. He removed to Lurgan in January, 1802. The next minister was Mr. John Mulligan, who was ordained here on the last Tuesday of November, 1802. Mr. Mulligan joined the Remonstrants in 1829, and died not long afterwards. The Seceders still kept up their interest in the place, and had established a congregation there, to which those who remained with the Synod of Ulster finally adhered. At the union in 1840 Mr. William Moffat was the minister, but not long afterwards he obtained as his assistant Mr. Robert Moorhead, who was ordained here on the 7th of November, 1843. Mr. Moorhead resigned the charge on the 23rd of September, 1844; and on the 2nd of April, 1845, Mr. Robert Scott Erwin was ordained here.

Mr. Erwin in a short time removed to Cargycreevy; and on the 2nd of January, 1850, Mr. Samuel Graham was ordained to the pastoral charge. Mr. Moffat died on the 25th of October, 1853.

MONAGHAN 1st.

THE first minister we find here is Mr. Robert Darragh. He appears to have been ordained about 1697. He had an unhappy career; and in 1712 he was degraded by the Synod for drunkenness and other irregular conduct. In 1715 the people called Mr. Michael Bruce of Holywood, and sent Messrs. Samuel Black, William Porter, John Gilmer, George Armstrong, James M'Conkey, and John Fee as their commissioners to the Synod to prosecute the call. The Synod decided that Mr. Bruce should remain in Holywood. The people at length obtained as their minister Mr. Thomas MacLaine, son of Mr. MacLaine of Markethill. He was ordained here March 19th, 1718. He died in this charge on the 11th of November, 1740. After his death the congregation was much distracted. In 1742 Messrs. Dacre Hamilton and John Porter were commissioners to the Synod. In 1744 Mr. David Hutchinson of Breaky was removed here; and in September, 1757, he was removed to Cork. He was succeeded in Monaghan by Mr. James Hamilton, formerly of Dundonald, who was installed here in 1758. He removed to Waterford in October, 1775. The next minister was Mr. Matthew Trumble, who was ordained here on the 24th of June, 1776. Becoming infirm, Mr. John Adams was ordained his assistant on the 3rd of February, 1818. On the 1st of August, 1820, Mr. Adams resigned his charge and removed to Strabane. Mr. Trumble died on the 28th of February, 1821. The next minister was Mr. John Bleckley,* who was ordained here on the 21st of February, 1821, a few days before the death of Mr. Trumble. Mr. Bleckley becoming infirm, Mr. J. A. Allison was ordained here on the 16th September, 1873. Mr. Bleckley died on the 1st of December, 1873.

MONEYMORE 1st.

THE first minister of whom we have any account in this congregation is Mr. John Abernethy, who accepted a call

---

* Mr. Bleckley taught an Academy in Monaghan. He was an excellent scholar, an eloquent preacher, and an influential minister.

from Moneymore in 1684, in preference to one which he had from Antrim. Mr. Abernethy had formerly been minister of Aghaloo, or Minterburn, in the Presbytery of Tyrone, and had been ejected after the Restoration of Charles II. He was then for some time minister of Brigh before his removal to Moneymore. He was the father of Mr. Abernethy, of Dublin, author of the celebrated sermons. At the Revolution, Mr. Abernethy, of Moneymore, had the honour of being sent by the Irish Presbyterian ministers to London, as one of their deputies, to wait on King William III. In September, 1691, he resigned the charge of Moneymore. The Presbyterians of Magherafelt and Moneymore had at one time been united under his ministry; but the people of Magherafelt meanwhile were formed into a separate congregation. When Mr. Abernethy resigned the charge, the people of Moneymore were recommended by the Presbytery to join with those of Cookstown, under the ministry of Mr. M'Kenzie. They were willing to agree to this arrangement; and, at the Synod held in April, 1692, they offered Mr. M'Kenzie £20 per annum, with Mr. Abernethy's farm and dwelling-house, provided they enjoyed "two parts of his labours;" but the proposal was not accepted. In 1697 Mr. Henry Crooks, son of Mr. Crooks, minister of Ballykelly, was settled in Moneymore. He demitted the charge in September, 1734. The next minister was Mr. Charles Caldwell, who was ordained here by the Presbytery of Tyrone May 16th, 1738. At the following Synod twenty-three families begged to be annexed to other congregations, as "they could not live under Mr. Caldwell's ministry." Mr. Caldwell died March 28th, 1780; and was succeeded by Mr. William Moore, who was ordained here May 14th, 1782. Mr. Moore becoming infirm, after much disputation Mr. John Barnett (afterwards D.D.) was ordained as his assistant and successor June 19th, 1827. Mr. Moore died May 27th, 1837, leaving neither widow nor family. Dr. Barnett becoming infirm, Mr. William M'Kean was ordained as his assistant on the 26th of March, 1872. Mr. M'Kean, on his removal to Raphoe, resigned this charge; and was succeeded by Mr. William Reid, who was installed here on the 18th of December, 1876. Dr. Barnett died on the 4th of January, 1880.

MONREAGH, Co. Donegal.

This congregation was originally known by the name of the parish in which it was—viz., *Taboin* or *Taughboyne*. It was early settled with Presbyterians. The Covenant was solemnly administered here by Messrs. Weir and Adair in the latter end of April, 1644. On that occasion an extraordinary concourse assembled here from fifteen miles round, and took the Covenant. The first minister, Mr. Robert Cunningham, who had been a Conformist, was settled in this place in 1645. In 1655 he was succeeded by Mr. John Hart. Mr. Hart was deposed in 1661 by Leslie, Bishop of Raphoe, and cast into prison with three other ministers in 1664. He remained in confinement for six years. In 1670 he was liberated, and he was here in 1685. He probably either died soon afterwards, or removed to Scotland at the breaking out of the troubles prior to the Revolution. In 1688 the people gave a call to Mr. Leggatt, of Dromore. The next minister was Mr. Neil Gray. He had been minister at Clogher, but removed from it at the troubles, and had taken up his abode at Taboin in the latter end of 1689. His former congregation applied to the Synod in 1691 for his restoration to them. The people of Taboin resisted, sending Messrs. Walter Patterson and James Marshall as their commissioners to the Synod. The subject was resumed at the Synod in 1692, Mr. John Bratton being commissioner from Taboin. It was finally settled that, because of his valetudinary state, he should be permitted to remain at Taboin. His health, however, continuing to decline, Mr. William Gray was ordained as his assistant and successor on the 18th of October, 1699. Mr. Neil Gray, however, did not die till March 3rd, 1715. Mr. William Gray was suspended by his Presbytery for having been married irregularly about four years before. He was required to acknowledge his sin before his congregation in presence of a minister sent thither for that purpose, and he fulfilled this requirement. In 1721 the congregation of Usher's Quay, Dublin, called him to be their minister. The call was opposed by the commissioners of the congregation of Taboin, who were Messrs. John M'Clintock, Jo. Moderell, and Robert Wilson; but the Synod determined in favour of his removal to Dublin. Soon after the congregation fell into disputes with the Presbytery of Derry, and divided among themselves. In 1723 a new erection was formed at

St. Johnston, Mr. William Gray, who had returned from Dublin, being the minister. The next minister of Monreagh was Mr. William Boyd, formerly minister at Macosquin, who was installed here on the 25th of April, 1725. The divisions between this and the new congregation still continued, and led to a *pro-re-nata* meeting of Synod in December, 1727, to consider the case. The commissioners from the Session here were Messrs. John M'Clintock, Tasker Keys, Walter Marshall, and Robert Wilson. Mr. Boyd was joined to the Presbytery of Route. The people now built a meeting-house at Monreagh, and secured to Mr. Boyd £40 per annum. He died May 2nd, 1772, leaving a family. The next minister was Mr. Pat Davison, from Scotland, who was installed here by the Presbytery of Route on the 9th of January, 1776. He was suspected as having a leaning to New Light doctrine, and having demitted the charge he returned to Scotland in October, 1786. He was succeeded by Mr. Moses Goorley, who was ordained here by the Presbytery of Derry on the 1st of November, 1787. He resigned this charge and went to America in August, 1794. After a long vacancy, Mr. Matthew Heron was ordained to the pastoral charge here on the 2nd of June, 1801. Mr. Heron becoming infirm, Mr. Andrew Long was ordained as his assistant and successor on the 24th of July, 1845. Mr. Heron died on the 27th of March, 1846. Mr. Long becoming infirm, Mr. James Latimer was ordained as his assistant and successor on the 21st of October, 1869. Mr. Long died soon afterwards. Mr. Latimer, having received a call from America, resigned this charge on the 24th of December, 1873; and on the 27th of May, 1874, Mr. William Thompson was ordained here. Mr. Thompson resigned this charge in November, 1882; and was succeeded by Mr. Hugh Cairns, who was ordained here on the 12th of April, 1883.

MOUNTMELLICK.

The origin of a Presbyterian Congregation here is not known, but it seems to have enjoyed occasional services from the ministers of Aughmacart and Ballybrittas, two considerable congregations in Queen's County, in the early part of the last century. At the close of the century, or about 1796, these congregations became extinct on the death of the ministers; and the large tracts of land held in fee for their use for one peppercorn a year not being looked after, were lost to the Presbyterian Church. Authentic documents show that there existed around Mountmellick as centre, congregations at Portarlington, Mountrath, Cullohill, Athy, The Leap, Rahue, and Edenderry, all having some landed property attached at a nominal rent, but from neglect passed into the hands of others. How these churches were broken up has not been clearly ascertained; but it is supposed the rebellion of 1798 caused the departure of many members, and as that was a period of general deadness in religion, internal decline had also its influence. In 1820 the Secession Synod established a mission in Mountmellick, and after supplying it for a time with licentiates, the people presented a call to the Rev. Thomas Clarke, who was ordained here by the Rev. David Stuart, D.D., Dublin; the Rev. Joseph Lowry, Lissara; and the Rev. John Coulter, Gilnahirk (a commission appointed by the Synod), on September 25th, 1829. Mr. Clarke laboured with great zeal and acceptance, until he resigned his charge in 1831, on receiving a call from Magherahamlet, County Down, where he ministered till his death, in June, 1861. After his resignation, the circumstances of Mountmellick were never so encouraging as to warrant the Synod in ordaining a successor; but, at considerable expense, they continued to supply the station with some of their ablest licentiates, amongst whom the names of Rentoul, Bell, and others, are still held in grateful recollection by the old members. Finally, the place was abandoned even as a mission station. In 1843 a highly-respectable family settled here from the north of Scotland, and some other Scotch people arrived not long afterwards. About this time the Rev. J. Edmonds, itinerant missionary of the General Assembly, visited the town, discovered the nucleus of a congregation, established a fortnightly service, and under his care a congregation was organised. On the 6th of August, 1846, the Rev. David Greer was ordained here by the Presbytery of Athone. Mr. Greer received a call to the Mariners' Church, Belfast, and resigned his charge of Mountmellick on the 7th August, 1849. Mr. Greer afterwards emigrated to America, in connection with the Colonial Mission. After some years he passed into the United States, and settled at Dickenson, Pennsylvania, near to which was fought the battle of Gettysburgh. After that terrible battle his church was for some weeks turned into an hospital. He then returned to Ireland,

and settled at Cavanaleck. After the departure of Mr. Greer from Mountmellick it was placed under the care of the Rev. Henry M'Manus, the Assembly's missionary to the Irish-speaking Roman Catholic population, who was then in infirm health, and the congregation was transferred from the Presbytery of Athlone to that of Dublin. In 1851, James Gibson, Esq.,[*] was appointed Chairman of Queen's County, and through his influence the congregation obtained the present site for their church and manse, having previously been without any church of their own. On the 6th September, 1853, Mr. M'Manus was installed pastor by the Presbytery of Dublin; on the same day, William Todd, Esq., Dublin, laid the foundation-stone of the new church; and on the 27th August, 1854, the edifice was opened for divine worship by Dr. Morgan of Belfast. Owing to ill health, Mr. M'Manus resigned the congregation on the 7th of April, 1858. He died in Dublin, 1864. A very interesting work appeared from his pen the year before his death, entitled "Sketches of the Irish Highlands." The congregation, after the resignation of Mr. M'Manus, presented a call to the Rev. Robert Harshaw, then assistant-minister at Mullingar, who was installed here on the 22nd of March, 1859.

MOUNTJOY.

The history of this congregation—formerly called Crossroads—is somewhat obscure. It had a minister upwards of a century ago, for it would appear that Mr. James Patton was settled here in 1775. Mr. James M'Clintock was ordained here at Cappagh on the 24th of May, 1791. Becoming infirm, Mr. John Hamilton was ordained as his assistant on the 6th of November, 1821. Mr. M'Clintock died in December, 1849. Mr. Hamilton resigned the active duties of the ministry, and was succeeded by Mr. John Gilmour, who was ordained here as his assistant on the 9th of September, 1862. Mr. Hamilton died on the 18th of June, 1874.

MOURNE.

The first minister of whom we read in connection with

---

[*] Mr. Gibson, who was for some time M.P. for Belfast, was a gentleman of distinguished zeal and piety. He frequently sat, as an elder, in the General Assembly.

this congregation was Mr. Charles Wallace. He was ordained here by the Presbytery of Down on the 21st July, 1696. After a ministry of forty years he died in this charge on the 12th of July, 1736. In 1739 a part of the congregation, assembling at the new meeting-house, supplicated to be erected into a distinct congregation. The place was now long vacant. At length Mr. Andrew Kennedy was ordained at Mourne by the Presbytery of Armagh on the 24th of February, 1741. His ministry was also of about forty years' duration. He died on the 9th of October, 1781, leaving a family only. The next minister was Mr. Moses Thompson, who was ordained here by the Presbytery of Dromore on the 22nd July, 1783. He died in this charge on the 21st of March, 1800, leaving a widow and child. He was succeeded by Mr. John M'Ilwaine, who was installed here on the 23rd of December, 1800. He died in this charge on the 16th of March, 1839. The next minister was Mr. James Alfred Canning, who was installed here on the 26th of November, 1839. On the 10th of March, 1848, Mr. Canning resigned the charge, having received a call from the 2nd congregation of Coleraine; and on the 6th of March, 1849, Mr. Samuel Mateer was ordained to the pastoral charge. Mr. Mateer becoming infirm, Mr. David Wilson was installed here on the 21st September, 1881. On his removal to Dungannon, Mr. Wilson resigned this charge; and was succeeded by Mr. William E. Campbell, who was ordained here on the 18th of September, 1885, but he died after preaching only a few Sabbaths. He was succeeded by the Rev. William M'Mordie, formerly of Tandragee, who was installed here on the 16th of March, 1886.

MOVILLE.

THE first notice we have of this congregation is on the occasion of the settlement of Mr. Thomas Harvey, jun., who was ordained here on the 26th of July, 1715. In 1718 he removed to Donagh. In 1720 the people gave a call to Mr. James Wallace, minister at Moywater or Killala, promising him as stipend £20 in money and oats by their commissioner, Mr. William Rankin. The Synod permitted him to accept the call, and he was installed here shortly afterwards. He died in this charge on the 21st of February, 1727. He was succeeded by Mr. Thomas Harvey, son of Mr. Harvey of Donagh. Mr. Harvey died here on the 13th of March, 1747.

The next minister was Mr. John Cochrane, who was ordained here on the 3rd of July, 1750. He demitted this charge on the 20th of April, 1754, and died on the 21st of June, 1762. The next minister was Mr. Henry M'Kinley, who was ordained here on the 4th of March, 1766. He was succeeded by Mr. Robert Caldwell, who had been minister at Macosquin, but who, through temporary aberration of mind, had been obliged to resign that charge in 1781. He was installed here on the 16th of November, 1784. Becoming infirm, Mr. William M'Clenaghan was ordained here as his assistant and successor on the 19th of December, 1820. Mr. Caldwell died in January, 1823, leaving a widow and family; and Mr. M'Clenaghan died in January, 1824, leaving neither widow nor family. The next minister was Mr. Hugh Mills, who was ordained here on the 22nd of June, 1824. He died here on the 21st of November, 1832, leaving neither widow nor family. He was succeeded by Mr. Andrew Clements, who was ordained here on the 26th of December, 1833. Becoming infirm, Mr. Clements in 1860 obtained leave for his congregation to choose an assistant and successor. On the 22nd of November, 1861, the Rev. John Bell was ordained to the pastoral charge. Mr. Clements died in the spring of 1867.

MULLINGAR.

In 1821 certain inhabitants of Mullingar and Tyrell's Pass supplicated the Synod of Ulster to be erected into a congregation, and promised to pay a stipend of £54 per annum. The congregation was accordingly organised, and the first minister was Mr. Alexander Gibson, who was ordained here on the 19th of March, 1823. Mr. Gibson was suspended from the ministry on the 8th of February, 1858. The next minister was Mr. R. H. Harshaw, who was ordained here by the Presbytery of Athlone on the 7th of December, 1858. Mr. Harshaw held this charge a very short time—as he resigned it on the 3rd of March, 1859, and removed to Mountmellick. Mr. Gibson died on the 12th of June, 1862; and on the 2nd of July of the same year Mr. Matthew Murphy, who had previously been ordained as a missionary for the district, was installed as the minister of this congregation.

NEWRY 1st.

WE have no account of any minister here before Mr. George Lang, who was in charge of the congregation in 1688. At the troubles he left Newry, and residing in the neighbourhood of Carnmoney in 1690 he undertook, with the consent of the Presbytery, to supply that congregation till he should have an opportunity of returning to his proper charge. He returned to Newry in May, 1692. In 1698 it is reported to the Synod that the meeting-house is now within a mile of that town, towards Narrow Water. Mr. Lang died on the 25th of January, 1702. His successor was Mr. Robert Rainey, who was ordained here on the 25th of June, 1706. He died in this charge on the 10th of September, 1736; and was succeeded by Mr. James Moody, minister of Magherally, who was settled here in 1740. Mr. Moody died in this charge on the 26th of May, 1779. He was succeeded by his son, Mr. Boyle Moody, who belonged to the Southern Association, and was installed here by the Presbytery of Armagh on the 11th of August, 1779. He died in this charge on the 5th of February, 1799. The next minister was Mr. John Thom, who was a native of Scotland, and a licentiate of the Presbytery of Aughterarder. He was ordained here on the 5th of August, 1800. His ministry was short, as he died here on the 18th of July, 1808, leaving a widow and family. He was succeeded by Mr. Andrew G. Malcom, formerly minister of Dunmurry, who was installed here on the 14th of March, 1809. In 1820 he received the honorary degree of D.D. He died January 12th, 1823, leaving a widow and family. The next minister was Mr. John Mitchell, formerly of Londonderry, who was installed here September 2nd, 1823. He was the father of Mr. John Mitchell of political notoriety. Mr. Mitchell at length avowed himself a Unitarian, and left the Synod of Ulster in 1829. He died on the 28th of February, 1840. In consequence of his theological views there was a considerable secession from his congregation; and another was formed in connection with the Synod of Ulster. Mr. James Shields was chosen minister, and was ordained here by the Presbytery of Dromore on the 20th of June, 1829. Mr. Shields resigned the charge of the congregation on the 28th of July, 1846, and left the ministry. He was succeeded by Mr. John Moran, who had for a short time been minister of

1st Ballibay, and who was installed here on the 16th of November, 1846. Mr. Moran resigned this charge on the 17th of March, 1862, on his removal to Belmont, near Belfast; and was succeeded by Mr. William Todd Martin, who was ordained here on the 19th of November, 1862. Mr. Martin resigned this charge on the 22nd of January, 1867, having accepted a call from Strean Church, Newtownards; and was succeeded by Mr. John H. Munro, who was ordained here on the 17th of December, 1867. Mr. Munro resigned this charge in the summer of 1873; and was succeeded by Mr. James C. Ferris, who was installed here on the 18th of February, 1874.

NEWTOWNARDS 1ST.

THIS congregation was early planted. The first minister appears to have been Mr. David Kennedy. He was deposed and fined by the High Commission Court in Dublin; but the sentence was reversed on the 14th of August, 1641. In 1642 an eldership or session was regularly ordained in this place, and Mr. John Maclellan was then the minister. He was not long here; and was succeeded by Mr. John Greg, who being obliged to make his escape from Carrickfergus, his former charge, settled here about 1650. He was deposed by Bishop Jeremy Taylor in 1661, but he nevertheless continued privately among his people till his death on the 20th of July, 1670. The next minister was Mr. Thomas Kennedy. He was here in 1688, but he must have been settled much earlier, for we find him a member of the Down Presbytery in November, 1671. A notice contained in the following minute of the Presbytery of Antrim suggests that Mr. Alex. Hutchinson officiated as minister of Newtownards about the time of the Revolution. The following is the minute:—November 4th, 1690—Appears from Newton, in the County of Down, Provost Corry (the ancestor of Sir J. P. Corry, Bart., M.P.), desiring this meeting to supply Newton four Sabbaths in Mr. Alex. Hutchinson's absence, then supplying Dublin." The next minister was Mr. John Smith, but the date of his ordination cannot now be ascertained. He died November 8th, 1704. The next minister was Mr. John Mairs, who was loosed from Longford in 1706, and settled here the following year. He died on the 25th of December, 1718. He was succeeded by his son, who was also John Mairs, and who was ordained here on the 10th of February,

1720. In 1725 he joined the Non-subscribing Presbytery of Antrim.* Meanwhile a number of the people appear to have become dissatisfied with his ministry, and in consequence, in 1723, they had become a congregation adhering to the Synod of Ulster. They do not seem, however, to have been able for a considerable time to maintain a minister. In 1726 Mr. James Moorhead appears to have been stationed here. He was succeeded by Mr. James Smith, who was ordained here by the Presbytery of Bangor on the 10th of April, 1739. Mr. Smith was removed to Capel Street, Dublin, in February, 1740; and was succeeded by Mr. James Huey, who was ordained here by the same Presbytery on the 6th of July, 1742. On the erection of the Presbytery of Belfast, this congregation was annexed to it. Mr. Huey becoming infirm, Mr. James Simson was ordained by the Presbytery of Belfast his assistant and successor on the 24th of August, 1790. Mr. Huey died on the 24th of October, 1794, leaving no family. Mr. Simson removed to America in May, 1799; and was succeeded by Mr. James M'Cullough, who was ordained here on the 20th of May, 1800. Becoming infirm, his son, Mr. Julius M'Cullough, was ordained here as his assistant and successor on the 28th of August, 1834. His father survived for several years. Mr. Julius M'Cullough having obtained leave for the congregation to choose an assistant and successor, Mr. Matthew M'Auley was ordained here on the 7th of November, 1865. Mr. Julius M'Cullough died on the 7th December, 1866. Mr. M'Auley resigned the pastoral charge on the 4th of February, 1879, having accepted a call from a congregation in the Presbytery of London; and on the 29th of July of the same year Mr. William Wright was ordained here.

NEWTOWNARDS 2ND.

THIS congregation was originally connected with the Antiburgher Seceders. Most of the individuals at first belonging to it resided about Conlig. The preaching commenced in the open air, as the people had not the accommodation of any large covered building. A temporary structure of a very humble description was provided; and, as it was within the bounds of the parish of Bangor, the con-

* This congregation still exists in connection with the Unitarian Body. The first Marquis of Londonderry, father of the celebrated Lord Castlereagh, was till his death a member of it.

gregation was in the beginning so called. Their first minister was Mr. James Martin. He was ordained at Conlig in 1753. In his time a house of worship was built in Newtownards. The date of its erection (1771) was on a stone above the south door; and the initials of the minister (J. M.) appeared on the tokens used when the Lord's Supper was dispensed. Mr. Martin appears to have preached in this meeting-house until about 1776, when he is said to have emigrated to America. He was succeeded by Mr. Francis Archibald, who was ordained here on the 5th of August, 1777. He continued in this charge till August, 1780, when he left the country. A long vacancy now occurred; but at length Mr. James Bigger was ordained pastor on the 13th of April, 1785. He was disannexed from this charge in 1797, the year before the rebellion, and he removed to North Britain. He was succeeded by Mr. James Gardner, who was ordained here on the 4th of November, 1801. Mr. Gardner was married to Magdalene Frazer, a lineal descendant of the celebrated Ralph Erskine, one of the founders of the Scottish Secession. Mr. Gardner died in January, 1812. The first four ministers of this congregation, viz., Messrs. Martin, Archibald, Bigger, and Gardner were all natives of Scotland. Mr. Gardner was succeeded by Mr. David Maxwell, who was installed here as pastor on the 23rd of September, 1812. He had been previously minister of Drumkeen, in County Monaghan. Mr. Maxwell died on the 11th October, 1859, and was succeeded by Mr. James Young, who was ordained here on the 26th of June, 1860.

NEWTOWNCROMMELIN.

This congregation was erected by the Presbytery of Ballymena in 1826. The first minister was Mr. Joseph Anderson, who was ordained here on the 8th of August of that year. The congregation obtained *Regium Donum* in 1831 in the 3rd class. In May, 1834, Mr. Anderson resigned the congregation and emigrated to America. He was succeeded by Mr. John Gemmil, a licentiate of the Church of Scotland, who was ordained here by the Presbytery of Connor on the 23rd of June, 1835. On the 18th of April, 1837, Mr. Gemmil resigned the charge, and became minister of Fairlie, near Largs, in Scotland. He was succeeded by Mr. Malcom Orr, who was ordained here by the Presbytery of Connor on the 28th of November, 1837. Mr. Orr died on the 8th of

December, 1876; and was succeeded by Mr. William J. Gilmore, who was ordained here on the 18th of December, 1877.

NEWTOWNHAMILTON.

THIS congregation was formerly connected with Creggan. The last minister of the united congregation was the Rev. Daniel Gunn Brown, who was ordained on the 5th of March. 1833.* After the separation, Mr. Brown remained minister of Newtownhamilton. Becoming infirm, he resigned this charge on the 1st of November, 1870. He had previously obtained as his assistant and successor Mr. John Kirkpatrick, who was ordained here on the 28th of May, 1868. On the 3rd of November, 1874, Mr. Kirkpatrick resigned this charge, having accepted a call from a congregation in the Presbytery of New York. On the 14th of December, 1875, Mr. Thomas Dysart was ordained to this charge.

NEWTOWNSTEWART 1ST.

LIVINGSTON in his "Memoirs" mentions, among his acquaintances in the ministry in Ireland, Mr. William Moorecraft of Newtownstewart, in the Presbytery of Lagan, in the year 1654. He was deposed in 1661, and probably soon after went to Scotland. For a long time the Presbyterians of Newtownstewart belonged to an adjoining congregation, and they had no place of worship in the town. In 1802 they supplicated the Synod of Ulster to be erected into a separate charge, and their request was soon afterwards granted. The first minister was Mr. John M'Farlan, who was ordained here by the Presbytery of Strabane on the 19th of December, 1804. In 1824 he was suspended for the irregular celebration of marriage and other misconduct. At length in 1825 leave was given to the congregation to elect another minister. Mr. Charles Adams was ordained to the pastoral charge on the 9th of August, 1827. On the 12th of May, 1830, Mr. M'Farlan was degraded for again celebrating marriage irregularly. On the 17th of August, 1842, Mr. Adams was suspended; and on the 29th of June, 1843, Mr. John M'Carter was ordained to the pastoral charge. Mr. M'Carter soon became unable to perform his ministerial

* Mr. Brown is (collaterally) descended from the Rev. James Kirkpatrick, the author of "Presbyterian Loyalty."

duties; and, in consequence, Mr. Robert C. Donnel was ordained as his assistant on the 28th of February, 1849. Mr. Donnel died very shortly after the Assembly of 1881. He was succeeded by Mr. William G. Black, who was ordained here on the 15th of March, 1882.

OMAGH 1ST.

MR. SAMUEL HALIDAY was minister here before the Revolution. He seems to have been here as early as 1664. He fled to Scotland in 1688, but returned in 1692. At his return he settled in Ardstraw, Omagh having declared its inability to support a minister, in which destitute state it continued till they obtained Mr. James Maxwell, who was ordained here November 8th, 1699. He died in this charge February 1st, 1750, aged 89 years; and was succeeded by Mr. Hugh Delap, who was ordained here by the Presbytery of Strabane June 5th, 1751. In the same year they apply to be annexed to the Presbytery of Letterkenny—as the Presbytery of Strabane had sent supplies to some malcontents who had resisted the settlement of Mr. Delap. Mr. Delap died June 12th, 1787; and was succeeded by Mr. Hugh Delap, probably his son, who was ordained here April 15th, 1790. On May 21st, 1805, he was degraded for immorality by the Presbytery. Their next minister was Mr. Samuel Cuthbertson, who was ordained here June 11th, 1806. Mr. Cuthbertson, being irregular in his conduct, was required to demit the charge by a committee of Synod appointed to visit the congregation; but was permitted to retain part of the *Regium Donum*. Mr. John Arnold, formerly minister of Clontibret, was installed as his assistant and successor July 15th, 1835. Mr. Arnold becoming infirm, Mr. James Maconaghie was installed here as his assistant on the 7th of April, 1875. Mr. Arnold died on the 22nd of July, 1881. Mr. Maconaghie, on receiving a call from Fortwilliam, Belfast, resigned this charge in the spring of 1886; and was succeeded here by the Rev. William Colquhoun, formerly of Ahoghill.

OMAGH 2ND.

THIS congregation originated in the dissatisfaction which existed at the time of the settlement of Mr. Hugh Delap as minister of the old congregation. In 1752, commissioners consisting of Mr. William Scott, Mr. James Nixon, and others, appeared before the Synod of Ulster, representing fifty families in the place, who prayed to be erected into a separate congregation. Their application was granted, and they were annexed to the Presbytery of Strabane. Their first minister was Mr. Robert Nelson, who was ordained here in July, 1754. He died in this charge on the 8th of April, 1801; and was succeeded by Mr. David Gilkey, who was ordained here on the 3rd of February, 1803. Mr. Gilkey, becoming infirm, retired from the ministry, and was succeeded by Mr. Josias Mitchell, who was ordained here on the 2nd of February, 1842. Mr. Gilkey died on the 15th of August, 1850. At the Assembly of 1879, Mr. Mitchell obtained leave for his congregation to choose an assistant and successor; and on the 16th of December of the same year Mr. Thomas M'Afee Hamill was ordained his assistant and successor. Mr. Mitchell died on the 22nd of July, 1882. On the 12th of February, 1884, Mr. Hamill resigned this charge on his removal to 1st Lurgan, and was succeeded by Mr. William Johnston, who was ordained here on the 30th of September following.

ORRITOR.

IN 1824 the inhabitants of the parish of Kildress, in County Tyrone, supplicated the Synod of Ulster for permission to be erected into a distinct charge. Their case was referred to the Presbytery of Tyrone, who sustained their claim. Mr. John G. Magowan, the first minister, was ordained here on the 26th of April, 1825. In 1831 the congregation obtained *Regium Donum* in the third class— that is, £50 yearly, late Irish currency. On the 1st of May, 1855, Mr. Magowan availed himself of permission, granted by the Assembly in 1848, for his congregation to choose an assistant and successor. On the 7th of May, 1856, Mr. William Wray was ordained to the pastoral charge; and Mr. Magowan died on the 19th of September, 1867.

PETTIGO.

WE find the congregation of Pettigo vacant in 1702. In 1704 it was proposed to be joined to Golan or Fintona. We hear nothing further of its state till the ordination of Mr. Joseph Hemphill by the Strabane Presbytery on the 12th of July, 1721. He held the joint charge of Pettigo and Clougherny. Mr. Hemphill died here in June, 1747. He was succeeded by Mr. James Ker, who was ordained to Pettigo alone on the 14th of April, 1752. He removed to Ahoghill in the following year. The congregation now seems to have remained for a considerable time in a languishing condition. About this period the Rev. Philip Skelton, one of the most remarkable men ever connected with the late Protestant Established Church, was rector of Pettigo; and the account which he gives represents the state of religion in the district as very deplorable. In 1792 Drumquin was separated from Derg and joined to Pettigo. In 1827 it was separated from Drumquin and formed into a distinct charge. Its first minister in this state was Mr. John Moore, who was ordained here by the Presbytery of Strabane on the 7th of February, 1828. Mr. Moore resigned this charge on the 12th of October, 1836, and removed to Glenelly. He was succeeded by Mr. William Fleming, who was ordained here on the 26th of March, 1837. Mr. Fleming died on the 5th of March, 1842; and was succeeded by Mr. Archibald Hunter, who was ordained here on the 29th of June of the same year. Mr. Hunter resigned the charge on the 4th of February, 1843; and was succeeded by Mr. Simon Nelson, who was ordained on the 27th of March, 1844. Mr. Nelson died on the 3rd of May, 1847; and was succeeded by Mr. John Donaldson, who was ordained here on the 29th of September, 1847.

PORTADOWN 1ST.

In 1821 the inhabitants of this town and its vicinity applied to the Synod of Ulster to be put under the care of the Presbytery of Dromore, and to be supplied with preaching every Lord's day. In the following year they were erected into a separate congregation, and their first minister was Mr. Alexander Heron, who was ordained here on the 12th of December, 1822. He resigned this charge in August, 1826, and removed to Ballyroney. Their next minister was Mr. William T. G. Dowlin, who was ordained here on the 1st of March, 1827. Mr. Dowlin died in this charge on the 7th of January, 1838; and was succeeded by Mr. Alexander Kerr, who was ordained here on the 21st of June, 1838. Mr.

Kerr resigned the charge on becoming a missionary to India;* and was succeeded by Mr. Leonard Dobbin Elliot, who was ordained here on the 17th of February, 1841. Becoming infirm, Mr. Elliot obtained as his assistant Mr. Robert Vint, who was ordained here on the 26th of January, 1875. On his removal to a congregation in England, Mr. Vint resigned this charge on the 26th of August, 1880; and was succeeded by Mr. W. J. Macaulay, who was installed here on the 20th of January, 1881. Mr. Elliot died on the 2nd of April of the same year.

PORTAFERRY.

THE first minister of this congregation was the Rev. John Drysdale. He had been chaplain to Lord Claneboy's regiment, and had remained in the country during the rebellion of 1641. He was soon after chosen minister of this charge, where he was ordained by Mr. Blair and the ministers of the army in July, 1642. In 1645 he was sent as a commissioner from the Presbytery to the General Assembly of Scotland, partly to obtain the opinion of that judicatory in some doubtful cases of discipline, and partly to procure an additional supply of ministers. In 1650 he was apprehended by a party of about eighty dragoons, by order of Colonel Venables, one of Cromwell's officers. Tradition says that this arrest was made during the time of divine service, and when he was preaching. Two of the gables of the church where it occurred, one of them ivy-mantled, still remain in Templecranny graveyard at Portaferry. At this period he was a prisoner in Belfast for sixteen days. In 1661 he and sixty other Presbyterian ministers, being almost the entire number then officiating in the province, were deposed and ejected from their benefices by the northern prelates. These ministers enjoyed the painful, though honourable, pre-eminence of being the first to suffer in the three kingdoms, after the Restoration of Charles II., for nonconformity. In 1663, Mr. Drysdale and six other ministers of Down were apprehended, and confined in Carlingford Castle, where they were treated with great harshness. They were charged with a share in a conspiracy, known as Blood's Plot, though some

* When the Irish General Assembly was formed in 1840, one of its first acts was the designation of two missionaries to the heathen. One of these was Mr. Kerr, who died soon afterwards; the other Mr. (now Dr.) Glasgow, is still living.

of them had never even heard of the affair until the time of their arrest, and though they were all quite innocent of any participation in it. After six weeks' confinement on this occasion, Mr. Drysdale was obliged to leave the country; and he retired for a time to Scotland. On his return he was not permitted to remain unmolested. In 1670 he and eleven others of the ministers of Down were summoned by Roger Boyle, Bishop of Down, to his court, and threatened with excommunication. The threat was only prevented from being carried into effect by the interference of Sir Arthur Forbes, who had influence with Primate Margetson. Such was the return made to the Presbyterian ministers for their firm adherence to the cause of royalty in the time of Oliver Cromwell. The next minister of Portaferry was the Rev. Arthur Strayton. At the Restoration he fled to Scotland, and never returned. His successor was the Rev. Samuel Shannon, who was ordained here early in 1697. Mr. Shannon continued long in this charge. A letter of his, and other documents to be found in "Kirkpatrick's Presbyterian Loyalty," show the virulence of the Irish Prelatical Church at that period. In 1739, Mr. Shannon having become infirm and unfit for duty, the congregation obtained leave from the Presbytery to choose an assistant and successor to him. He died June 26th, 1743. Meanwhile, the Rev. James Armstrong had been chosen as his assistant. He was ordained by the Presbytery of Killyleagh October 31st, 1739. His pastorate lasted forty years, his death having taken place October 23rd, 1779. His memory was long cherished with grateful affection. He was maternal grandfather of Dr. Robert Stephenson of Belfast, his daughter having been married to Mr. (afterwards Dr.) Stephenson, who was at one time minister of Greyabbey. The following is the inscription on his tombstone, which is to be found near the ivy-mantled gable of the old church in Templecranny graveyard:—

The Body of
the Rev. James Armstrong, A.M.,
lies here.
He discharged his duty
as a Pastor
with dignity and faithfulness, and
his life was an example
of fervent piety
and of sincere charity.
He died the 23rd October, 1779,
in the 70th year of his age.

In 1780 the Rev. William Steele Dickson (afterwards D.D.), who for nine years had been minister of the adjoining congregation of Ballyhalbert, now Glastry, was installed in Portaferry. Early in his ministry cock-fighting was an aristocratic as well as a vulgar amusement; and even the established clergy were, in many cases, quite ready to join in the sport. Dr. Dickson composed and preached a sermon on the subject, in which all the genteel and slang phrases of the occupation, which he had collected at different times from a servant who was quite an adept in the business, were most tellingly introduced. This discourse gave a death-blow to the practice among the more respectable classes of society—the sermon in manuscript having been extensively circulated and read. In June, 1798, Dr. Dickson was arrested on the eve of the Irish Rebellion, and for three years was kept a State prisoner at Fort George, in Scotland. The congregation was proclaimed vacant by the Presbytery of Bangor on the 28th of November, 1799; and the Rev. William Moreland was ordained to the charge on the 16th of June, 1800. Dr. Dickson, after his liberation from Fort George, obtained a call to the newly-erected congregation of 2nd Keady, which in 1815 he was obliged to resign from bodily infirmity. He died in Belfast December 27th, 1824. He left behind him several publications—viz.: "A Sermon on the Death of the Rev. James Armstrong," "A Treatise of Psalmody," "A Narrative of his Confinement and Exile," and a volume of sermons. In 1822 Mr. Moreland having become infirm, the congregation of Portaferry obtained liberty from the Synod of Ulster to choose an assistant and successor to him. He died October 23rd, 1825. Meanwhile the Rev. John Orr, A.M., was ordained by the Presbytery of Bangor on the 2nd of October, 1822. Becoming infirm, Mr. Orr obtained as his assistant Mr. Thomas E. Clouston, who was ordained here on the 5th of October, 1875. Mr. Orr died on the 4th of November, 1878. On his designation as a missionary to New South Wales, Mr. Clouston resigned this charge; and was succeeded by Mr. John Boyd, who was installed here on the 21st December, 1880. In 1841 the present handsome and unique church, rebuilt by the congregation, at an expense of upwards of £2,200, was opened for public worship. The congregational schoolhouse was erected in 1849 at the cost of £220.

PORTGLENONE 1st.

THE first notice we have of this congregation is in 1726, when the people made an application to the Synod of Ulster to be withdrawn from the Presbytery of Antrim and joined to that of Route. The application was granted. The people of Portglenone appear to have previously attended on the ministry of Mr. Shaw of Ahoghill; but, on his joining the Non-subscribing Presbytery of Antrim, they withdrew from him. Mr. John Hill was ordained as their minister on the 19th of December, 1727. He died in this charge on the 29th of July, 1759. Their next minister was Mr. Robert Kirkpatrick, who was ordained here on the 19th of August, 1762. The next minister was Mr. Alexander Spear, who was ordained here on the 23rd of February, 1773. Becoming infirm, Mr. Joseph Shaw was ordained as his assistant on the 10th of June, 1822. Mr. Shaw resigned this charge on the 23rd of December, 1824, and removed to Larne. He was succeeded by Mr. William Kennedy M'Kay, who was ordained here on the 7th of June, 1826. Mr. Spear died August 12th, 1835. Mr. M'Kay having obtained leave to resign, Mr. John Houston was ordained on the 19th of October, 1859, as his assistant. Mr. M'Kay died on the 15th of February, 1876.

PORTRUSH.

THIS congregation of the General Assembly was organised sometime in the spring of 1841,* and supplied with preaching by the Presbytery of Coleraine till the close of 1842. At this time a call was presented to the Rev. Jonathan Simpson, and on his acceptance of it, he preached his first sermon as their minister on Christmas Day, falling this year on Sabbath. He was installed on the Tuesday following (27th December, 1842), as their first pastor. Previously he had been ordained on 12th August, 1840, by a commission of the Presbytery of Dublin, in the then old church of Mary's Abbey. Having laboured a few months in the close of 1839 and the commencing months of 1840 in the Home Mission service, he was asked and urged by the Mission Board to accept ordination and remain at least a year. He visited all the counties of Leinster, Munster, and Connaught, and most of their leading

---

* The late Dr. John Brown, of Aghadoey, exerted himself much in the erection of the congregations of Portrush and Portstewart.

towns; and resigned this service in the close of 1841. His report to the Mission Board is published in the Minutes of the General Assembly for that year, pages 9, 10, 11. Of the thirty-three names appended to his call only three or four survive; and *not one of them is now in connection* with the congregation. They had then no church, and worshipped in the little Methodist chapel for nearly four years. Mr. Simpson left for the United States of America in June, 1843, and after an absence of about a year, in which he visited some part of twenty-two States of the Union and both Canadas, over fully 7,000 miles, he returned in the summer of 1844, having succeeded in raising about £1,150 (the original church, with enclosure, cost £1,263) for the erection of the first Presbyterian church of Portrush. In September of that year it was entered entirely free of debt. Very able services were conducted at the opening by the Rev. Dr. Walter M'Gilvray, then of Glasgow, and afterwards of Aberdeen. The famine in Ireland of 1846-47 made openings for the truth in districts before sealed. A deputation to the United States was decided on, to raise money to take advantage of these openings. Mr. Simpson, being successful in a private enterprise, was asked on this deputation, along with the Rev. E. M. Dill, M.D., and left for America again in November, 1848. Difficulties arising in the congregation of Portrush, Mr. Simpson saw there must be a manse; and obtained leave from the Mission Board to raise money for it when he finished their deputation work. Dr. Dill and he raised in about six months £5,400 sterling, which prepared the way years after for another deputation, consisting of the Rev. Drs. Edgar, Samuel M. Dill, and David Wilson, who succeeded in raising some £6,000. Mr. Simpson remained (after Dr. Dill's return) till the close of 1849, and raised over £600 more for Portrush manse. On Dr. Edward Dill's report to the General Assembly of 1849, the thanks of the Assembly were presented to him and Mr. Simpson. Portrush manse was built in 1850, and occupied by Mr. Simpson in May, 1851, also entirely free of debt. To complete the working machinery of the congregation a schoolhouse was necessary; and, after many difficulties, Mr. Simpson received from the late Wilson Kennedy, Esq., £150 sterling for that purpose; and, supplemented by a few friends, a schoolhouse, costing nearly £200, was erected and occupied in 1853, entirely free from debt. The marvellous

Revival of 1859 came on, and the church was so packed it was resolved to enlarge it. In the circumstances of the country, the Presbytery declined to allow Mr. Simpson to proceed to America to raise the money. In Scotland he obtained over £500; in Ireland nearly £500; and by a bazaar and collections other £500 were raised. The church was enlarged to double its former capacity at an expense of about £1,500, and entered again in 1861 entirely free of debt. The church property was held on a terminable lease of ninety years, and a small lot was thrown in on the rere by opening a new street. By waiting personally at Glenarm Castle on the Right Hon. the Earl of Antrim, Mr. Simpson obtained a grant of the additional lot, and a promise of a lease for ever on condition of erecting a teacher's house and a larger schoolroom at an expense of at least £600. Unable to fulfil the conditions in the time, the whole property was imperilled, when God, in His adorable providence, cut the gordian knot, and removed the difficulty. The second Council of the great Presbyterian Alliance was to meet in Philadelphia in October, 1880, and the minister of Portrush was appointed a delegate. When his name appeared in the paper, William Young, Esq., J.P., of Fenaghy, Ballymena, called on him (Mr. Simpson) and pressed him to go, offering £100 sterling subscription and other advantages. He was pressed into the service, and went again to America in October, 1880; and after the grand meetings of the Council closed, started the fourth tack of begging in the United States. And, thank God, and the noble Christian people of that great country, he succeeded in getting all that was needed. A loan was obtained from the Board of Works, and a teacher's house was built during his absence, and now all is complete at another additional sum of over £1,500, free of debt. The schoolroom and lecture-hall are admittedly the finest in the country, the stained glass window and reading-desk being presented by Mr. Young. Now the whole congregational property, costing over £5,500, where there was neither church, manse, or school, is all in beautiful order, and all free of debt—first-class teachers, first-rate schools, and overflowing congregations. Over all we inscribe: "*What hath God wrought?*" "*Not unto us, O Lord, not unto us, but unto Thy name give glory!*"

RAMELTON 1st.

THE first minister here was Mr. Thomas Drummond, who was ordained by the Presbytery of Lagan, in 1654. He was deposed by Leslie, bishop of Raphoe, in 1661, and was imprisoned in the castle of Lifford, where he remained for six years, or till 1670. Mr. Drummond was in this charge in 1681, but his subsequent history is not known. The congregation being without a minister, was afterwards joined to Letterkenny, under the ministry of Mr. W. Liston. In March, 1693, the people wrote, by advice of the Presbytery, to Scotland, for Mr. Seth Drummond, probably son of their former minister, and he appeared before the Presbytery, June 26th, 1696, with certificate of his license by the Presbytery of Edinburgh. He was ordained at Ramelton, December 16th, 1696, the people promising him £40, with 20 barrels of oats for the first year, hoping to do better afterwards, and promising to build him a dwelling-house—at this time there were six old elders remaining in the congregation. Mr. Drummond died in this charge, September 4th, 1740, and was succeeded by Mr. Thomas Vance, who was ordained here August 18th, 1747. In 1755 he was removed to the congregation of Usher's Quay, Dublin, and was succeeded here by Mr. William Burke, who was ordained July 25th, 1759. He died in this charge January 9th, 1803, leaving a widow and family. Their next minister was his son, Mr. William Burke, who was ordained here, June 20th, 1804, having been previously licensed by the Presbytery of Dublin. He resigned this charge, October 16th, 1805, and applying himself to the study of medicine, became M.D., and died at Dundrum, near Dublin, on the 4th of April, 1842, in the 64th year of his age. He was succeeded as minister of Ramelton by Mr. Edward Reid, who was ordained here December 8th, 1806. Mr. Reid was brother of the Rev. Dr. Reid, Professor of Ecclesiastical History in the University of Glasgow, and author of the History of the Presbyterian Church in Ireland. He was also father of Dr. James Seaton Reid, Professor of Materia Medica in Queen's College, Belfast. Mr. Reid died February 11th, 1838, and was succeeded by Mr. James Reid, who was ordained here September 13th, 1838. He had been previously connected with the Covenanting Church, and was not related to Mr. E. Reid. Mr. Reid resigned this charge on the 30th of August, 1860; and was succeeded by Mr. W. C. Robinson, who was ordained here on the 28th of August, 1861, and who resigned the charge on the 7th of March, 1862, on his removal to Ballykelly. He was succeeded by Mr. Joseph T. Mcgaw, who was ordained here on the 18th of September, 1862. On his appointment as a Professor in Magee College, Mr. Megaw resigned this charge on the 3rd of October, 1865; and was succeeded by Mr. R. S. Campbell, who was ordained here on the 30th of March, 1866. On the 15th of November, 1870, Mr. Campbell was set aside for misconduct; and on the 21st of February, 1872, the Rev. W. D. Wallace was installed as pastor.

RAMOAN.

THE first minister of this congregation was Mr. Daniel M'Neill. He was here in 1646, but was irregular in his conduct towards the Presbytery. At the Restoration he conformed, and was admitted vicar of Ramoan on the 12th of September, 1661. For a considerable time afterwards we hear of no minister in this district. At length, in 1700, Mr. Thomas Elder was ordained. He died in 1703. The next minister here was Mr. John Mairs, who was ordained by the Presbytery of Route May 24th, 1704. He died in this charge June 25th, 1723. The next minister was Mr. Samuel Dunlop, who had been minister at Athlone, and was settled here early in 1724. This charge he demitted in 1733, when he removed to Connaught. He was succeeded by Mr. Robert Brown, who was ordained here by the Presbytery of Route June 6th, 1738. He died in this charge May 18th, 1767; and was succeeded by Mr. William Lynd, who was ordained here June 11th, 1770. Becoming infirm, Mr. John Simms was ordained his assistant and successor July 28th, 1805. Mr. Lynd died in 1822. Mr. Simms becoming infirm, Mr. W. G. Boyd was ordained his assistant and successor on the 17th of November, 1853. Mr. Simms died on the 7th of January, 1866.

RANDALSTOWN 1ST.

THE earliest notice we find of this congregation is in February, 1655, when commissioners appeared from Drumaul praying the Presbytery, or Meeting of Antrim, to supply them with preaching. In October, 1655, Messrs. John Shaw and Hugh M'Atchison, commissioners, present a call to the Presbytery for Mr. John Couthart; and in December following, Messrs. James Duncan and John Parker, commissioners, present a bond from eleven in the parish, securing £50 a-year stipend, with a sufficient house, and fourteen acres of glebe, "convenient near to the church or preaching-house of the parish," which was, however, not yet built. In February, 1656, they state that they had "settled on the place where their preaching-house should be built, to wit, at the ironworks;" and on the 21st of May, 1656, Mr. John Couthart was ordained to this charge at Drumaul; and at this meeting "the parishioners of Drumaul were spoken to concerning building of their preaching-house, which they undertake to fall effectually about shortly, and would have been about it ere now, were it not for losing the season of the bark, they would not have liberty of wood." Mr. Couthart was here in 1658, but his subsequent history is unknown. In July, 1671, we find Mr. Richard Wilson supplying the place as probationer. He was ordained to this charge at Broughshane on June 5th, 1672. The Prelatic party then endeavoured to prevent Presbyterian ordinations, and threatened those concerned in them with heavy penalties, which accounts for the ordination taking place in comparative privacy, not at Randalstown, but many miles distant. Mr. Gowan, of Antrim, preached and presided at the ordination. Mr. Wilson died in June, 1685, having an arrear of £80 due him. In October following the people gave a call to his son, Mr. John Wilson; but the arrear due to his mother not being paid, and the people dividing with respect to himself in March, 1687, he returned the call, with permission of the Presbytery, " seeing that there were 200 persons for Mr. Wilson and about 120 dissenting, and that of the £80 due to Mrs. Wilson there were only £20 paid, and but £6 given to Mr. Wilson for his pains among them for the last two years." In November following, however, these differences being partly healed, they gave him a new call, and he was ordained here May 2nd, 1688, Mr. D. Cunningham, of Connor, preaching and presiding. At this time the congregation had two separate places of meeting; but, requiring a new house, the parties could not agree on a central position. In September following, however, they agreed to have it built three-quarters of a mile out of town, and that it should be forthwith erected. But disputes continuing among the people on this head, in November, 1690, Mr. Wilson wished to demit his charge, " because of the division about the meeting-house and other inconveniences which resulted from that." He continued in it, notwithstanding, till his death, which happened in the beginning of the year 1694. His successor was Mr. William Taylor, who was ordained here May 26th, 1697. Their payments to him were as irregular and scanty as to his predecessor. In 1718 his case became so urgent that the Presbytery of Antrim complained to the Synod that they had used all their diligence with the congregation to induce them to advance something to Mr. Taylor, but without success, though the people had no exceptions to make against him, but esteemed him much. He died in this charge in November, 1727. In 1732 the congregation divided respecting a call to Mr. William Henderson. The Presbytery of Templepatrick sustained the call, and the minority appealed to the Synod. On this occasion the commissioners from the majority were Colonel O'Hara, Clotworthy O'Neill, Esq., Mr. Henry M'Cullough, and Lieutenant Dobbin. The Synod sustained the call also, and Mr. Henderson was ordained here by the Presbytery of Templepatrick October 12th, 1732. He demitted his charge here in 1743; and was succeeded by Mr. James White, who was ordained here by the Presbytery of Ballymena April 28th, 1747. He died October 30th, 1781, leaving no family. He was succeeded by Mr. Thomas Henry, son of Mr. William Henry, minister of Comber, County Down. Mr. Thomas Henry,* who was ordained here June 19th, 1786, was father of the late Rev. P. S. Henry, D.D., President of Queen's College, Belfast. Becoming infirm, Mr. Henry resigned the charge of the congregation in 1823. In consequence of great disputes relative to the choice of his successor, the congregation was put under the care of a Committee of Synod, who ordained as his assistant and successor Mr. Archibald Jamieson, on the 11th of April, 1826. Mr. Henry died on the 30th of August, 1830; and Mr. Jamieson died on the 18th of March, 1835. After many disputes, the Rev. Alexander Crawford, who had been a member of the Associate Synod in Scotland and a missionary in India, was installed here by a Committee of Synod on the 3rd of January, 1837. Mr. Crawford died on the 4th of April, 1856. The Rev. James Brown Huston had been installed as his assistant and successor in February, 1856. Mr. Huston, on his removal

* Mr. Henry acted as a medical practitioner; and was commonly known as *Doctor* Henry.

to Aghadoey, resigned this charge on the 1st of December, 1874; and was succeeded by Mr. James E. Ferguson, who was ordained here on the 23rd of March, 1875.

RAPHOE 1st.

THIS congregation is one of the early Presbyterian settlements of Ulster. Old Bishop Knox, who was placed in the Episcopal See about the time of the Plantation of Ulster, encouraged Scotchmen to become tenants on the Episcopal lands; and thus it is that to this very day so many of the farmers in the parish are Presbyterians. The meeting-house was originally built at Convoy; and until about the middle of the last century, there was no Presbyterian place of worship at Raphoe. About that time Raphoe was erected into a separate congregation, and the old congregation was henceforth known by the name of Convoy. The first minister of the newly-erected congregation of Raphoe was Mr. James Gordon who had formerly been minister of Castleblayney, and who was installed here in the month of August, 1751. He died in this charge in 1785, and was succeeded by Mr. William Ramsay, who was ordained here on the 24th of August, 1786. Mr. Ramsay died on the 16th of April, 1827, and was succeeded by Mr. W. D. Killen (now D.D.), who was ordained here on the 11th of November, 1829. Shortly afterwards a series of misfortunes befel Episcopacy in Raphoe. One of the Episcopal clergy became demented, and another fled from the place on the evening of the Lord's Day to escape his creditors. On the morning of another Sabbath, the overheating of the flues set fire to the cathedral; and the building was so much injured that nearly a year elapsed before it was again fit for service. Meanwhile the Episcopalians had the use of the Presbyterian meeting-house. About the same time the bishopric was suppressed by Act of Parliament; and shortly afterwards the beautiful Episcopal palace, built by Bishop Leslie two hundred years before, was burnt to the ground. In 1841 Mr. Killen resigned the charge of this congregation on his appointment as Professor of Ecclesiastical History in Belfast; and he was succeeded by Mr. John Thomson, who was ordained here on the 19th of January, 1843. Shortly after the settlement of Mr. Thomson in this charge the second congregation was organised. The old place of worship, built fully a century before, had meanwhile become somewhat delapidated; and under the ministry of Mr. Thomson a new and handsome Presbyterian Church has been erected on the site of the former edifice. Mr. Thomson having become infirm, Mr. John A. Bain was ordained his assistant on the 12th of August, 1884.

RATHFRILAND 1st.

THE first minister of whom we have any account here was Mr. Alexander Gordon. He was in this charge in 1679, and continued in it after the Revolution. In 1708, the Presbytery of Armagh divided the congregation, one part to meet at Rathfriland, and the other to be formed into a new congregation at Ballyroney. Mr. Gordon died, February 11th, 1709, and was succeeded by Mr. Robert Gordon, who was ordained here March 27th, 1711, and died in this charge April 10th, 1762. He was succeeded by Mr. Samuel Barber, who was ordained here, May 3rd, 1763. He died in this charge, September 5th, 1811, leaving a widow and family. The next minister was Mr. John White, ordained here September 21st, 1813. He died here April 2nd, 1836; and was succeeded by Mr. William Rossborough, who was ordained here by the Presbytery of Newry, October 24th, 1837. Mr. Rossborough having received a call from the Free Church Congregation of East Campbell Street, Glasgow, resigned the charge of Rathfriland on the 13th of July, 1858, and was succeeded by the Rev. Henry Osborne, formerly minister of Granshaw, who was installed here on the 22nd of February, 1859. In the summer of 1862, Mr. Osborne removed to the congregation of Second Holywood. He was succeeded by Mr. James Wilson (now LL.D.), who was ordained here on the 29th September, 1863.

RAY 1st.

THIS parish was early settled with Presbyterians. In 1644 the Covenant was administered here to great multitudes. In 1647 Mr. Hugh Cunningham, who had in 1642 come over as chaplain to Glencairn's regiment, was settled here. He was deposed by the Bishop of Raphoe in 1661; but we are ignorant of what afterwards happened to him. Mr. Robert Campbell was settled minister here in 1671. We find him preaching in Burt on the 28th of February, 1678, and baptizing the infant daughter of Mr. Hempton, the minister there. Mr. Campbell fled to Scotland during the troubles connected with the Revolution, but afterwards returned to his charge in June, 1691, where he continued till his death, October 5th, 1722. He was succeeded by Mr. Patrick Vance, who was ordained here as assistant and successor to Mr. Campbell December 23rd, 1719. Mr. Vance died in this charge January 2nd, 1741. The next minister was Mr. William Laird, who was ordained here May 15th, 1744. Mr. Laird was son of the Rev. Francis Laird, minister of Donoughmore, near Strabane, and lineal ancestor of Sir Thomas M'Clure, Bart., Belmont, Belfast. Mr. Laird was removed from Ray to Rosemary Street congregation, Belfast, in 1747. In 1752 the congregation complained to the Synod of Ulster that the Seceders had seized their meeting-house, and that they had been at great expense in prosecuting a suit for its recovery.* In 1754 Mr. James Turretine was removed here from Tobermore, and installed on the 13th of June of that year. He died in this charge July 21st, 1764, leaving a widow and family. He was succeeded, after a long vacancy, by Mr. Francis Turretine—probably his son, for whom they had waited—who was ordained here January 18th, 1775. In 1778 he removed to Mountnorris; and was succeeded by Mr. Isaac Barr, who was soon after ordained here, and who removed to Killala in 1780. The congregation now continued vacant for many years. At length, on the 19th of November, 1795, Mr. Francis Dill was ordained to this charge by the Presbytery of Letterkenny. Mr. Dill and his congregation were subsequently annexed to the Presbytery of Route; but in 1825 they were re-annexed to the Presbytery of Letterkenny. On October 14th, 1829, Mr. Dill resigned this charge, and removed to Clough, Co. Down. He was succeeded by Mr. John Brown, jun., who was ordained here by the Presbytery of Letterkenny March 11th, 1830. Mr. Brown was brother to the celebrated poetess, Frances Brown. He died in this charge November 2nd, 1854; and was succeeded by Mr. Robert M'Morris, who was ordained here on the 14th of June, 1855.

* The house, when recovered, was quite too large for the congregation. A new church was built upwards of forty years ago.

RICHHILL.

This congregation continued united to Vinecash till 1823, after the resignation of Mr. Reid, the minister there. The people then applied to the Synod of Ulster to be erected into a separate congregation, and their request was granted. Their first minister was Mr. James Sinclair, who was ordained here on the 23rd of December, 1824. The congregation obtained *Regium Donum* in the third class, or £50 late Irish currency, about seven years afterwards. On the 3rd of May, 1836, Mr. Sinclair resigned this congregation, as well as the office of the ministry, and engaged in secular pursuits. The next minister was Mr. James Patterson, formerly minister of Gralla, near Rathfriland, belonging to the Scotch Seceders. He was installed here on the 1st of March, 1838. On the 7th of May, 1847, Mr. Patterson died of fever; and on the 16th of December of the same year Mr. Andrew M'Aldin was ordained to the pastoral charge.

SAINTFIELD 1st.

This congregation was originally called *Tannaghnive*. The first minister was Mr. Alexander Hutchinson, who was suspended by Bishop Jeremy Taylor in 1661. In 1690 he was removed to Capel Street, Dublin, where he continued till April, 1692, when his relation to that congregation was loosed on account of his ill health. At the Synod of 1691 there were commissioners from Saintfield—viz., Captain Gawin Hamilton, Messrs. Robert Ross, Robert Kyle, John Hamilton, and others, supplicating the return of Mr. Hutchinson, and the Synod of 1692 granted the application. He now continued here till his death in 1711. His successor was Mr. Archibald Dixon, who came from Scotland in 1705, and was received as a probationer, having been licensed by the Presbytery of Hamilton. He was ordained here by the Presbytery of Down April 19th, 1709, as assistant and successor to Mr. Hutchinson. In 1714 two townlands, called Munlagh and Tullygarvan, were taken from Comber and annexed to this congregation. Mr. Dixon died in this charge in March, 1739. He was succeeded by Mr. James Rainey, who was ordained by the Presbytery of Bangor March 8th, 1743. He died in this charge January 20th, 1745; and was succeeded by Mr. Richard Walker, who was ordained here

July 28th, 1747. He died in this charge January 20th, 1774; and was succeeded by Mr. Thomas Leslie Birch, who was ordained May 21st, 1776. He removed to America in November, 1798. Their next minister was Mr. Henry Simpson, who was ordained here December 10th, 1799. Mr. Birch died at his residence near Washington, Pennsylvania, on the 12th of April, 1828, aged 74 years. On the 23rd of May, 1843, Mr. James Wallace was ordained assistant and successor to Mr. Simpson. On the 2nd of September, 1846, Mr. Wallace resigned the charge of the congregation to become missionary to India; and on the 16th of December following the Rev. Robert M'Ewen was installed as Mr. Simpson's assistant. In June, 1853, Mr. M'Ewen was set aside and subsequently deposed; and on the 21st of February, 1854, the Rev. Samuel Hamilton, formerly minister of Conlig, was installed here. Mr. Simpson died on the 22nd October, 1849.

SCRIGGAN.

THIS congregation was erected off Boveva about 1773. The first minister was Mr. John Adams, who was ordained by the Presbytery of Derry on the 18th of May, 1774. He died in this charge on the 8th of June, 1789. He was succeeded by Mr. Robert Steel, who was ordained here on the first Tuesday of November, 1790. In 1798 it was reported to the Synod that "Mr. Steel had pleaded guilty to a charge of treason and rebellion before a court-martial; and his name was erased from the list of the Presbytery." He was succeeded by Mr. Joseph Osborne, formerly minister of Corboy, who was installed here on the 4th of June, 1799. He soon afterwards removed to Newtownards. The next minister was Mr. Andrew M'Caldin, who was ordained here on the 8th of March, 1803. In December, 1804, he removed to Stratford-on-Slaney, and he afterwards was settled in Coleraine. He was succeeded by Mr. John Mitchell, who was ordained here on the 19th of March, 1805. In August, 1819, he removed to Londonderry. The next minister was Mr. Robert Gray, who was ordained here on the 21st of December, 1819. He resigned this charge in 1833, and removed to Burt. The next minister was Mr. Joseph Gibson, who was ordained here on the 17th of June, 1834. In 1856 the Presbytery asked leave for the congregation to choose an assistant and successor; and on the 13th of May

Mr. William Reid Black was ordained to the pastoral charge. In May, 1864, Mr. Black was suspended; and Mr. Samuel Thomson was then ordained in his stead.

SPA, BALLYNAHINCH.

THE place now known as Spa, about two miles from Ballynahinch, has long been famous for its medicinal waters. Harris, in his book on County Down, written in 1744, thus speaks of it:—" Its virtues hitherto found out by experience appear to resemble those of other sulphureous waters, particularly in its great efficacy in scorbutic disorders, both by bathing in and drinking the waters, of which there happened a remarkable instance some years since of a Dissenting minister, who came to this well overrun with leprous-like eruptions on the skin, which had rendered his joints so rigid that he could neither hold his bridle nor feed himself. He returned home supple and clean after having drank the water and bathed in it a month." Every summer not a few, with a view to the improvement of their health, take up their abode for weeks together at the Spa; but for a long time invalids complained of its distance from a Presbyterian place of worship. Persons in delicate health, though desirous to attend regularly on ordinances, could not safely venture on a rainy Sabbath, or a sultry summer's day, to walk two Irish miles to the nearest sanctuary. The people in the immediate neighbourhood were not prepared to attempt the erection of a church, as they were not in affluent circumstances. At length a Christian gentleman, who was in the habit of visiting the Spa, solved the difficulty. The late Robert M'Quiston, Esq., of Belfast, offered to give £1,000 for the purpose.* A handsome Presbyterian church, built entirely at his own expense, and occupying a central position, now excites the admiration of every one who visits the locality. A manse for the residence of the minister—to which also Mr. M'Quiston most generously contributed—has recently been completed. The congregation has been recognised by the Assembly; and on the 5th of May, 1874, Mr. William Wilson was ordained to the pastoral charge. The church

* Mr. M'Quiston, who was a member of Linen Hall Street Presbyterian Church, Belfast, gave large donations to religious objects; and by his will devoted several thousands of pounds to the erection of a Presbyterian church in the neighbourhood of his own residence.

has proved a great blessing to the people of the neighbourhood; and its crowded appearance every Sabbath, especially during the summer months, attests how much it was required. Mr. Wilson, on his removal to Greenock, resigned this charge on the 2nd of July, 1879; and was succeeded by Mr. James Knowles, who was ordained here on the 30th of December of the same year.

STEWARTSTOWN 1st.

This congregation formed originally a part of Brigh. In 1788 a petition from 100 persons—twenty-three of whom formerly belonged to Brigh—was presented to the Synod of Ulster, stating that they were building a meeting-house in Stewartstown, and supplicating to be erected into a distinct congregation. The concession was not immediately made; but in 1789, when Mr. David Park appeared as commissioner, the request was granted. Their first minister was Mr. William Henry, who was ordained here on the 23rd of March, 1790. He resigned this charge on the 5th of January, 1791, and removed to Armagh. He was succeeded by Mr. James Adams, who was ordained on the 6th of December, 1791. Mr. Adams died here on the 26th of December, 1801, leaving a widow and family. The next minister was Mr. Moses Chambers, who was ordained on the 7th of September, 1802. Mr. Chambers died on the 20th of August, 1813, leaving a widow and family. He was succeeded by Mr. Robert Allen, who was ordained on the 7th of June, 1814. Mr. Allen, on his appointment as Superintendent of the Connaught Mission, resigned this charge; and on the 31st of July, 1849, Mr. Isaiah N. Harkness was ordained his successor. Mr. Allen died on the 1st of April, 1865. Mr. Harkness becoming infirm, Mr. J. A. Campbell, a licentiate of the Presbytery of Athlone, was ordained as his assistant and successor on the 20th of August, 1885. Mr. Harkness died on the 23rd of October following.

ST. JOHNSTONE.

This congregation originated in the divisive courses of Mr. William Gray, who had been minister of Taughboyne, and had removed to Usher's Quay, Dublin. Resigning Usher's Quay, he returned to the North, and erected a congregation in the village of St. Johnstone, near Derry, in an irregular manner. For this he was deposed. The people returned to the Synod of Ulster in 1731; and, after professing sorrow for their disorderly proceedings, were recognised as a congregation, and annexed to the Presbytery of Derry. In 1732 Mr. M'Clintock stated to the Synod that there were 160 families, who could pay £40 per annum to a minister. Their first minister was Mr. Thomas Bond, who was ordained here by the Presbytery of Derry August 20th, 1734. Mr. Bond died February 22nd, 1785. Mr. William Cunningham was ordained November 11th, 1783, as his assistant and successor. When Mr. Cunningham became infirm, Mr. Joseph M'Conaghy was ordained as his assistant and successor on the 12th of December, 1834. Mr. Cunningham died April 16th, 1836. Mr. M'Conaghy died on the 31st of December, 1875; and was succeeded by Mr. Francis Chambers, who was ordained here on the 7th of December, 1876.

STONEBRIDGE.

This congregation was at first known by the name of Clonis. Its first minister was Mr. Patrick Dunlop, who was here in 1700. He had previously supplied for a time the parish of Kirkowen in Scotland. In 1704 he demitted the charge of this congregation on account of bodily indisposition. He was succeeded by Mr. Alexander Fleming, who was ordained here on the 8th of May, 1706. He died in this charge on the 13th of October, 1750. The next minister was Mr. William Smith, who was ordained here by the Presbytery of Cootehill on the 26th of August, 1752. He died on the 7th of May, 1786. He was succeeded by Mr. James Whiteside, who was ordained here on the 5th of September, 1787. Mr. Whiteside died in this charge on the 20th of December, 1802, leaving a widow and family. The next minister was Mr. Archibald Meharg, who was ordained here on the 5th of June, 1804. On the 30th of November, 1819, the Presbytery of Monaghan suspended Mr. Meharg for various irregularities; and they subsequently dissolved the connection between him and the congregation. He was succeeded here by Mr. William White, who was ordained on the 18th of December, 1820. After a long pastorate, Mr. White retired in 1874 from the performance of the active duties of the ministry; and on the 19th of June of that year his son,

Mr. W. F. White, who had previously been minister of Westport, was installed as assistant and successor to his father. On the 25th of October, 1875, Mr. W. F. White resigned this charge on his appointment to the Mission Station of Lucan; and on the 2nd of November of the same year his father died. On the 11th of April, 1876, Mr. Moses Paul Kenny was ordained as minister of Stonebridge. Mr. Kenny died on the 2nd of July, 1880; and was succeeded by Mr. R. T. Megaw, who was ordained here on the 7th of December, 1880. Mr. Megaw, on his removal to Carrowdore, resigned this charge on the 12th of June, 1883; and was succeeded by Mr. James White, who was installed here on the 15th of July, 1884.

STRABANE 1ST.

THE first minister of Strabane on record is Mr. Robert Wilson, who was ordained here in 1659. He died in the city of Derry during the siege in 1689, having fled there for safety. His successor was Mr. William Holmes. He was born in Ireland, but had emigrated to New England, from which he returned in July, 1691, and having produced to the Presbytery of Lagan satisfactory testimonials, he was received by them, and having gone through second trials, was ordained December 21st, 1692. He was married to the daughter of Mr. Craighead, minister of Derry. In 1715 he demitted this charge, and again returned to New England. In 1716 the people applied to the Synod of Ulster for supplies, stating their reason for this step to be "that the place is of such consequence as to require particular regard." The application was granted, the congregation promising to pay each of the supplies ten shillings every Lord's day, and to bear their expenses while with them. They soon after obtained Mr. Victor Ferguson as their minister. He had been licensed by the Presbytery of Derry in 1713, and was ordained by the Presbytery of Convoy to this charge April 24th, 1717. The same year the Presbytery of Strabane was erected, of which consequently this congregation formed a part. Mr. Ferguson died in this charge May 15th, 1763, leaving a widow, but no family. He bequeathed a house and farm to his successors, which they still enjoy. Their next minister was Mr. William Crawford, who was ordained here February 6th, 1766. Mr. Crawford was great-great-grandson of Mr. Stewart, minister of Donegore, one of the fathers of the Presbyterian Church in Ireland. He wrote a "History of Ireland," and several other works. Mr. Crawford taught an academy in Strabane, one department of which was a species of collegiate institute, at which several ministers of the Synod of Ulster, and among the rest the late Rev. James Houston, of Ballindreat, received all their theological training. In October, 1798, Dr. Crawford resigned the charge of Strabane, and removed to Holywood. He was succeeded by Mr. William Dunlop, formerly minister at Badoney, who was installed here November 10th, 1798. Becoming infirm, Mr. John Adams, formerly minister of Monaghan, was installed here his assistant and successor August 31st, 1820. Mr. Dunlop died November 24th, 1821, leaving a widow and family. On the 30th of June, 1827, Mr. Adams resigned the charge of this congregation, and died December 17th, 1827. He was succeeded by Mr. William Mulligan, who was ordained here March 20th, 1828. Mr. Mulligan resigned the charge of this congregation on the 1st of August, 1832, having been appointed Professor of Mathematics in the Royal Belfast Institution. Their next minister was Mr. Alexander Porter Goudy, formerly minister of Glastry, who was installed here March 20th, 1833. Mr. Mulligan was drowned while bathing at Loughbrickland, on the 7th of August, 1834. Dr. Goudy, who possessed much influence in the General Assembly, and who was Moderator in 1857, died December 14th, 1858. One hundred ministers are said to have been present at his funeral. He was succeeded by Mr. James Gibson, who was ordained September 26th, 1859.* Mr. Gibson (now D.D.), on his removal to Perth, resigned this charge early in 1873; and was succeeded by Mr. John MacDermott, formerly of Armoy, who was installed here on the 11th of December of the same year. Mr. MacDermott, on his removal to Belmont, resigned this charge on the 3rd November, 1880; and was succeeded by Mr. John Irwin, who was ordained here on the 29th of September, 1881.

STRANORLAR 1st.

THE first account we have of this congregation is in connection with the ordination of Mr. Robert Wilson, who was

* The present excellent church was erected during the ministry of Mr. Gibson.

settled here on the 25th of June, 1709. In 1729 the people state that they are not able to pay above £9 per annum, and beg an increase of their allowance from the General Fund. The *Regium Donum*, then amounting only to £1,200 per annum, was handed over, in a lump sum, to certain ministers, as trustees for the rest; and some in poor frontier congregations obtained a larger share of it than those in more highly favoured districts. Mr. Wilson resigned this charge in 1727. In that year the Synod thought the congregation ought to be dissolved on account of its poverty. Mr. Wilson appears afterwards to have resumed the charge of the congregation, as he was here in 1735, but we do not know the date of his death. The next minister was Mr. Joseph Kinkead, who was ordained here September 4th, 1745. In 1755 he removed to Killinchy. After a long vacancy, Mr. Joseph Love was ordained here on the 16th of June, 1767. He died September 26th, 1807, leaving a family. He was succeeded by Mr. James Nelson, who was ordained here November 2nd, 1808. Becoming infirm, Mr. James Steele (afterwards D.D.) was ordained as his assistant and successor on the 8th of November, 1821. Mr. Nelson died in September, 1826, leaving neither widow nor family. Dr. Steele died on the 17th of June, 1859; and on the 28th of December following Mr. Hugh Clarke Graham was ordained to the pastoral charge. Mr. Graham having fallen into delicate health, Mr. William John Macaulay was ordained as his assistant on the 14th of October, 1874. Mr. Graham, on his subsequent appointment as a Professor in Magee College, resigned this charge on August 7th, 1878. Mr. Macaulay, on his removal to Portadown, resigned this charge on the 15th December, 1880; and was succeeded by Mr. James Curry, who was ordained here on the 11th of May, 1881.

TANDRAGEE.

THIS congregation was erected in 1825. Its first minister was Mr. Richard Dill, son of the Rev. Richard Dill, of Knowhead, who was ordained here on the 17th of December, 1829. In May, 1835, Mr. Dill resigned the charge of this congregation, and removed to Usher's Quay, Dublin. He was succeeded by Mr. James Bell, who was ordained here on the 3rd of December, 1835. Becoming infirm, Mr. William M'Mordie, formerly an Indian missionary, was installed as his assistant and successor on the 27th of September, 1882. Mr. M'Mordie, on his removal to Mourne, resigned this charge in the spring of 1886.

TEMPLEPATRICK.

THE first minister here was Mr. Josias Welsh, son of the celebrated John Welsh, minister of Ayr, and consequently grandson to John Knox, the great Scottish Reformer; as John Welsh was married to Elizabeth, the Reformer's third daughter. Mr. Josias Welsh was educated at Geneva; and on his return to his native country, was appointed Professor of Humanity in the University of Glasgow. He came over to Ireland in 1626, where he was ordained to the ministry by his kinsman Knox, Bishop of Raphoe, and settled at Templepatrick. The people of the country called him "The Cock of the Conscience," from his extraordinary awakening and rousing gift. He died of consumption in 1634. The people now remained destitute of a pastor till 1646, when Mr. Anthony Kennedy was ordained here by the Presbytery of Antrim on the 30th of October. Mr. Ferguson, of Antrim, preached and presided. There were present the Rev. Messrs. Adair, of Cairncastle; Buttle, of Ballymena; and Cunningham, of Broadisland. Mr. Kennedy was imprisoned by the Republican party, and deposed by Taylor, Bishop of Down and Connor. He nevertheless continued in the country, and preached to his people as he had opportunity. In 1688 he stated, in a memorial to the Presbytery, that "in consideration of his age and thereby of his infirmity and weakness of body, whereby he is disabled from any part of his ministerial work, except it be to preach now and then, as he is helped, and that he cannot catechise, visit families or sick when necessary, he now gives up the charge of his present flock, first to Christ, and then to his Presbytery, for their future supply." The Presbytery, however, did not accept his demission, and he continued in this charge till his death, which took place December 11th, 1697, when he had reached the age of 83. In the beginning of 1699 the people called Mr. James Kirkpatrick, son of Mr. H. Kirkpatrick, minister of Ballymoney, and he was ordained here in August, 1699. Mr. Kirkpatrick, who was the author of the well-known book called "Presbyterian Loyalty," removed to Belfast in 1706. In June, 1707, at the request of Mr. Upton, ancestor of the present Lord Templetown, the congregation was transferred from the Presbytery of Belfast to the Presbytery of Antrim. Mr. Upton was a zealous Presbyterian, and a staunch advocate of Orthodoxy. Mr. Kirkpatrick was succeeded in Templepatrick by Mr. William Livingston, who was ordained here March 30th, 1709. He resigned in 1755 from infirmity. Mr. Livingston was a zealous minister, a firm Calvinist, and a correspondent of the Scottish historian, Wodrow. In August, 1755, Mr. Robert White was ordained his assistant and successor. Mr. Livingston died September 1st, 1758. Mr. White died August 14th, 1772, leaving a widow, who was forty-two years on the Widows' Fund. The next minister was Mr. John Abernethy, formerly minister of Ballywillan, who was installed here August 12th, 1774. He resigned the charge January, 1796; and was succeeded by Mr. Robert Campbell, who was ordained December 20th, 1796. On the 4th of May, 1802, Mr. Abernethy was deposed from the ministerial office for celebrating marriages irregularly. Mr. Campbell, having seceded from the Synod of Ulster, with a part of the congregation, the remainder continued under the care of the Synod; and Mr. John Carson was ordained to the pastoral charge May 26th, 1831. Mr. Carson died on the 5th of August, 1859; and on the 27th of December of the same year the Rev. Hugh M'C. Hamilton was ordained to the pastoral charge of the congregation.

TOBERMORE.

An attempt was made in 1736 to induce the Synod of Ulster to erect a congregation here. As it was considered that the congregation of Maghera would thereby be seriously injured, the application was in the first instance unsuccessful. But it was renewed the year following; and the commissioners who urged it, and among whom were Messrs. Samuel Fulton and Alexander Black, made out such a strong case that the Synod agreed to sanction the erection. It was urged that some of the people were at least eight miles from Maghera. The boundaries of the new congregation were to be the Mayola River, from Newforge Bridge to Corrin Bridge. In 1743 nineteen families in Ballynahone, formerly belonging to Maghera, were annexed to this congregation, and the names of the heads of these families were John Bell, Thomas Jamieson, William M'Master, Jo. Laverty,

Roger Laverty, William Henderson, Jo. M'Allen, John Fulton, Jo. Paul, jun.; Widow Hunter, James Paul, Robert Paul, Samuel Young, James Young, Jo. Ewings, Robert Ewings, Andrew Ewings, James Phillips, and Samuel Neilly. They at last obtained for their minister Mr. James Turretine, who was ordained here by the Presbytery of Tyrone on the 5th of June, 1744. He demitted this charge in 1748, but again consented to become their minister, and was installed here by the Presbytery of Tyrone early in the year 1750. In 1754, however, he finally removed from this place, and settled in Ray. Their next minister was Mr. James Whiteside, who was ordained here on the 1st of August, 1757. He died on the 23rd of March, 1798, leaving a family; and was succeeded by Mr. Alexander Carson, who was ordained here on the 11th of December, 1798. In May, 1805, Mr. Carson withdrew from the Presbyterian Church, and joined the Baptists. Mr. Carson (afterwards D.D.) was a minister of great ability, and a distinguished controversial writer; but, notwithstanding, his new views have since made very little progress in the country. His withdrawal from the Presbyterian Church led to a long and expensive lawsuit relative to the property of the meeting-house; but the Synod eventually succeeded in securing possession of it. The next minister was Mr. William Brown, who was ordained here on the 20th of November, 1810. Mr. Brown died on the 19th of April, 1860; and he was succeeded by Mr. William Anderson, who was ordained here on the 29th of June of the same year. On the 1st of July, 1867, Mr. Anderson resigned this charge; and on the 30th of September of the same year Mr. James A. Robson was ordained to the ministry in this congregation. Mr. Robson died on the 27th of February, 1884; and was succeeded by Mr. Marcus Stevenson, who was ordained here on the 7th of May, 1884.

TULLAMORE, King's Co.

Birr, Parsonstown, was for many years the only Presbyterian church in King's County. Tullamore is the second. The first step to establish the Presbyterian cause in this the Assize town of the county was on 5th June, 1856, when Dr. James Coulter, an elder from Adelaide Road, Dublin, who had come to reside in Tullamore, and Mr. Oliver Dobbin, of the Bank of Ireland, appeared before the Athlone Presbytery at Corboy with a petition from twelve families, representing forty-eight individuals in and around Tullamore, praying to be organised into a congregation of the General Assembly, and offering at least £20 for the support of a minister. The prayer of the memorial was granted, a house in the town rented, two rooms made into one and fitted up for worship, and soon after supplies were sent them. On September 28th, 1856, they gave a unanimous call to Mr. Samuel Kelly, a licentiate of Bailieboro' Presbytery; and on 3rd December following Mr. Kelly was ordained the first minister of the congregation. After labouring here with acceptance, Mr. Kelly resigned the charge for an appointment to Australia on the Colonial Mission, and was designated on 22nd April, 1858, the Rev. W. M'Clure, Derry, giving a most impressive charge on the occasion. The next minister was Mr. James Duff Cuffey, a licentiate of Comber Presbytery, who was ordained here on 30th June, 1859; and at the meeting of Assembly the following week the congregation was transferred from the Presbytery of Athlone to that of Dublin. In less than two years Mr. Cuffey's health began to decline; he fell into consumption, and the congregation became greatly reduced. He died on 5th May, 1863, leaving a widow. The next minister was Mr. Andrew Burrowes, who was ordained here by the Presbytery of Dublin on 29th June, 1864. The congregation began to revive after his settlement. They felt the want of a suitable place of worship, and resolved to build a church. In 1865 they secured an admirable site at the head of the Main Street. The people subscribed liberally for their means, and were aided by friends throughout the country and some in Scotland. The late William Todd, Esq., Dublin, gave £60, and Dr. Edgar, Belfast, £250 out of a fund placed at his disposal for such purposes. A neat, commodious edifice was erected, and opened free of debt the following year, one of Dr. Edgar's last public acts being to preach the opening sermon. Mr. Burrowes having received a call to Waterford, resigned the pastorate of Tullamore on 16th July, 1868. The congregation unanimously chose Mr. Robert H. Smythe, a licentiate of Route Presbytery, for their minister, who was ordained here on 17th December, 1868. During Mr. Burrowes' ministry the congregation was steadily increasing, and after Mr. Smythe's induction it made still more rapid and healthy progress, so much so that the church had to be enlarged. A session room and a room for the Sabbath-school to meet in was built, and the church pewed and lighted with gas for evening services. Mr. Smythe also opened and sustained mission-stations in all the neighbouring towns and villages; and the congregation is represented in the printed report for 1874 as having raised for all purposes over £270. Dr. James Coulter, elder, died on 6th February, 1870. He was a staunch friend and supporter of the congregation from the beginning, and to him the congregation was indebted for wise counsel and generous aid. Mr. Smythe accepted a call from Carrowdore, Ards Presbytery, and resigned the charge of Tullamore on 11th June, 1879, to the great regret of all the congregation. It has been sneeringly said that a minister does not accept a call to another charge unless there is the inducement of a larger income, but Mr. Smythe's translation to Carrowdore is a striking exception. The congregation now called the Rev. David Mitchel, minister at Kilkenny, who was installed in Tullamore on 21st August, 1879, but he did not remain a year in the charge. Having accepted a call to Warrenpoint, he resigned Tullamore on 21st June, 1880. The congregation then called the Rev. William S. Frackelton, who had joined the Irish General Assembly in June from the United States of America. Mr. Frackelton was installed here on 19th November, 1880. Being appointed by the Board of Missions to the colony of New South Wales, Mr. Frackelton resigned this charge on the 2nd of September, 1884; and Mr. Henry Patterson Glenn, a licentiate of the Presbytery of Dublin, was ordained here on the 10th of December following.

TULLYLISH.

This congregation was also known by the name of Donacloney. The earliest notice of it is connected with the ordination of Mr. John Cunningham to the pastoral charge in the year 1670. He was here in 1688, when he retired to Scotland and never returned. The congregation continued vacant in 1697, and for some time after. The next minister was Mr. Gilbert Kennedy, who was ordained here by the Presbytery of Armagh March 23rd, 1704. He died in this charge July 8th, 1745. He was succeeded by Mr. Samuel Sims, who was installed at Tullylish by the Presbytery of Dromore November 4th, 1746. He had been formerly minister of Anahilt. He died in this charge October 14th,

1768, leaving a widow and family; and was succeeded by Mr. Samuel Morell, who was ordained here March 6th, 1770. He was shot by the Hearts of Oak March 6th, 1772, leaving neither widow nor family.* The next minister was Mr. John Sherrard, who was ordained here November 4th, 1774. Mr. Sherrard becoming infirm, Mr. John Johnston, formerly minister of Cootehill, was installed as his assistant and successor October 1st, 1811. Mr. Sherrard died June 18th, 1829, leaving a widow and family. Mr. Johnston (subsequently created D.D.) died on the 16th October, 1862. On the 2nd of December of the same year, Mr. James Cargin was ordained to the pastoral charge. On his removal to Dublin, Mr. Cargin resigned this charge on the 23rd of December, 1872; and was succeeded by Mr. John Morrison, who was ordained here on the 16th September, 1873.

URNEY AND SION.

THIS congregation is of ancient date. In 1654 Mr. James Wallace was ordained here. He died in this charge in November, 1674. His successor was Mr. David Brown, from the Presbytery of Stirling, who was ordained here in 1677. He fled to Derry in 1688, and died in the city during the siege. He was succeeded by Mr. William Holmes, who had been received by the Presbytery as a probationer on the 25th of June, 1695, and who was ordained to this charge on the 22nd of December, 1696. In 1697 he was suspended from the ministry on account of some "scandalous carriage" in the house of Mr. Rowat. He was appointed to appear before the Synod at Coleraine in February following; but having acknowledged his scandal before the Presbytery in January, his suspension was removed. He died in this charge in October, 1734. The next minister was Mr. William Macbeath, who was ordained here by the Presbytery of Strabane on the 22nd of December, 1737. He was removed to Usher's Quay, Dublin, in 1745. The next minister was Mr. Andrew Alexander, who was ordained here by the Presbytery of Letterkenny on the 31st of August, 1749. He died here April 30th, 1808, leaving a widow and family; and was succeeded by Mr. John Gillespie, who was ordained here on the

* A monument to the memory of Mr. Morell, erected by his friend, Sir Richard Johnston, Bart., is still to be seen in Tullylish Presbyterian church.

26th of January, 1809. He died here on the 28th of July, 1823, leaving neither widow nor family. The next minister was Mr. James Purss, who was ordained here on the 20th of May, 1824. He died on the 29th of August, 1836, leaving neither widow nor family. He was succeeded by Mr. John M'Conaghy, who was ordained here by the Presbytery of Strabane on the 14th of June, 1837. In 1881 it was reported to the Assembly that the Presbytery of Strabane had effected the union of the congregations of Urney and Sion ; and on the 11th of August of the same year the Presbytery installed the Rev. Matthew Neill, formerly a minister of the Reformed Presbyterian Church, in the congregation of Urney and Sion as colleague and successor to the Rev. John M'Conaghy.

VINECASH.

THE first minister of this congregation was Mr. Alexander Bruce, who was second son of Robert Bruce, Esq., of Kennet, in Clackmannan, who was lineally descended from King David Bruce. Mr. Bruce was minister of Kirkend, in Peebleshire from 1690 to 1695. He had supplied some congregation in the Presbytery of Down, in 1694, as his name appears in the roll of that Presbytery, at the Synod in that year. Mr. Bruce was married in 1677 to the daughter of Mr. James Cleland, surgeon in Edinburgh, by Isabel Kennedy, his wife, who was of the family of the Earl of Cassilis. Mr. Bruce's daughter, Rachel, was grandmother of the Rev. Dr. John Jamieson, of Edinburgh, author of the celebrated work on the Culdees, and various other well-known publications. Dr. Jamieson's sister was grandmother of Dr. Barnett, one of the munificent contributors to the Presbyterian Orphan Society. Mr. Bruce became minister of Vinecash, Co. Armagh, about 1697, and died in this charge April 16th, 1704. He was succeeded by Mr. William Mackay, who was ordained here by the Presbytery of Armagh, September 25th, 1707. Mr. Mackay died here November 14th, 1733. The next minister was Mr. William Dick, who was ordained February 12th, 1727, some years prior to the death of Mr. Mackay. Mr. Dick died in this charge December 23rd, 1740, and was succeeded by Mr. James Todd, who was ordained here July 22nd, 1747. Becoming very infirm, Mr. Henry M'Ilree was ordained here 30th August, 1791, as his assistant and successor. Mr. Todd died in January, 1795, leaving a widow and family. Mr. M'Ilree removed to the congregation of 1st Keady, in March, 1797. Their next minister was Mr. Wm. Reid, who was ordained to this charge May 24th, 1798. Mr. Reid died January 1st, 1824, leaving a widow. In the same year the Synod separated Richhill from this charge, so that Vinecash henceforth became a distinct congregation, and their first minister in this state was Mr. Thomas Dugal, who was ordained here November 29th, 1824. In June, 1837, Mr. Dugal resigned his charge and removed to Australia. He was succeeded by Mr. William Cromie, who was ordained here June 22nd, 1838. Mr. Cromie died on the 9th of March, 1876. He had previously obtained as his assistant Mr. Charles Cowden, who was ordained here on the 5th of October, 1874. Mr. Cowden, on his removal to Glenarm, resigned this charge on the 21st of June, 1881, and was succeeded by Mr. J. H. Forsythe, formerly of Culnady, who was installed here on the 25th of October of the same year.

WARRENPOINT.

UNTIL a late period this congregation was known as *Narrow-water*. About the time of the Revolution it was joined to Newry, and in 1697 it was put under the care of the Presbytery of Tyrone. But when Carlingford, which had formerly been joined to Dundalk, became a separate congregation : and when, in 1707, Mr. Wilson became the minister of Carlingford, Narrow-water was then associated with Carlingford, and placed under his joint charge. This arrangement did not give entire satisfaction. In 1712 the people of Narrow-water complained to the Synod that they had not the half of Mr. Wilson's labours, as had been originally determined. The Synod therefore ruled that, seeing Narrow-water pays the half of Mr. Wilson's maintenance, viz., £15 per annum and victual, it should have the half of his labours in summer, and one-third in winter. This congregation continued united with Carlingford till the year 1820, when Mr. Samuel Arnold, minister of the joint charge, was appointed by the Synod to labour exclusively here: and Carlingford became henceforth a separate congregation. During the Arian controversy, Mr. Arnold joined the New Light party, and withdrew from the Synod in 1829. The Orthodox party adhering to the Synod of Ulster now remained for some time without a minister: but at length on the 2nd June, 1833, the

Rev. Thomas Logan was ordained here by the Presbytery of Dromore. In 1842 Mr. Logan removed from Warrenpoint to Dundalk; and on the 27th of September, 1842, the Rev. John Martin was installed as his successor. Mr. Martin resigned this charge on the 28th of January, 1847, and on the 27th of July of the same year Mr. Isaac Patterson was ordained to the charge. On the 15th of November, 1875, Mr. Patterson resigned the charge of the congregation, and was succeeded by Mr. Andrew Halliday, who was ordained here on the 21st of September, 1876. Mr. Halliday, on his removal to England, resigned this charge on the 8th of March, 1880; and on the 7th July of the same year the Rev. David Mitchell was installed here.

WATERFORD.

PRESBYTERIANISM has long maintained an existence in Waterford. In the beginning of the year 1673 Mr. William Liston received a call from the congregation here. Our Church was then in very depressed circumstances in this country, and ordinations were performed with as little publicity as possible. On the 25th of November, 1673, Mr. Liston was ordained here in company with Mr. Cock, who had a call from the people of Clonmel. Mr. Liston did not remain long minister of Waterford, as, on account of his grievances here, he was disannexed from the charge in October, 1676. He was succeeded by Mr. Alexander Sinclair, who was ordained here in 1687. Mr. Sinclair resigned this charge in 1690, and removed to the congregation of Plunket Street, Dublin. The congregation was afterwards joined with the Southern Association, and remained long in that connexion. At length, in 1854, the Munster Presbytery was incorporated with the General Assembly; and the Rev. William M'Cance, who was then the minister of Waterford, became a member of the Supreme Judicatory of the Presbyterian Church in Ireland. Mr. M'Cance was the son of the Rev. John M'Cance, minister of 1st Comber, County Down. In October, 1864, Mr. M'Cance resigned the pastoral charge, and was succeeded by Mr. James Carson, who was installed here on the 29th of March, 1866. On the 27th of February, 1868, Mr. Carson resigned this charge, and was succeeded by Mr. Andrew Burrowes, formerly minister of Tullamore, who was installed here on the 12th of August, 1868. On the 8th of May,

1876, Mr. Burrowes resigned this charge, having received a call to labour as a missionary within the bounds of the Presbyterian Church of Canada, and was succeeded by Mr. John Hall, who was installed here on the 27th of July, 1876. Mr. M'Cance died, at an advanced age, in the Summer of 1882.

WHITEABBEY.

ABOUT fifty years ago there was no Presbyterian Church between Donegall Street Belfast and Carrickfergus.* A sermon might occasionally be preached in a school-house at Whitehouse, or in some other place along the Shore Road; but those who waited regularly on Sabbath ordinances were obliged to repair either to Belfast, Carnmoney, or Carrickfergus. At length a Presbyterian Church was erected at Whiteabbey; and on the 12th of November, 1833, the Rev. William Campbell was ordained as the first pastor. During the ministry of Mr. Campbell the congregation was but small, as many of the people of the district still adhered to the places of worship with which they had been previously connected. On the 15th of January, 1844, Mr. Campbell resigned the pastoral charge, having accepted a call from the congregation of Alexandria, in connection with the Free Church. He was succeeded by the Rev. John Lyle, who was ordained here on the 2nd of September, 1844. During Mr. Lyle's ministry the present manse was erected. He demitted the pastoral charge on the 14th of March, 1860, and was succeeded by the Rev. R. J. Lynd, who was ordained here on the 19th of September, 1861. Meanwhile the congregation increased much: and a considerable amount was expended on the enlargement of the church. Mr. Lynd resigned the charge of Whiteabbey on the 7th of January, 1874; and on the 27th of July, 1875, the Rev. John Armstrong, formerly minister of Academy Street Church, Belfast, was installed as the new pastor. After having preached in Whiteabbey only two Sabbaths, Mr. Armstrong, though in the bloom of youth, became suddenly so unwell that he could not continue his ministrations, and died on the 26th of December, 1875. He was succeeded by Mr. Wm. Rogers, LL.D., formerly of Castlereagh, who was installed here on the 16th of August, 1876.

* When King William III. arrived at Carrickfergus, shortly before the battle of the Boyne, he proceeded along the Shore Road to Belfast, and was met at Whitehouse, near Whiteabbey, by Duke Schomberg.

THE CONNAUGHT PRESBYTERY.

HISTORICAL FACTS RELATING TO THE CONGREGATIONS OF THE CONNAUGHT PRESBYTERY, FROM THE DATE OF THEIR FORMATION TILL APRIL, 1886.

☞ As most of the Congregations of the Connaught Presbytery have been erected in the present century, it has been thought right to furnish this separate account of them.

THIS Presbytery was organised on August 23rd, 1825, by the requisition of the Synod of Ulster, which met at Coleraine in June, 1825—viz.: "That the ministers and congregations of Sligo, Killala, Westport, Turlough, and Ballymote be erected into a Presbytery, and denominated the Connaught Presbytery." The ministers and elders met accordingly at Ballymote—Rev. Jacob Scott, Moderator. The other members were Revs. David Rodgers (Clerk), Robert Creighton, James Heron, and John Hamilton; with Messrs. Robert Orr and Samuel Henry, Sligo, ruling elders.

BALLINA.

BALLINA was originally a mission-station in connection with Killala congregation. In August, 1835, the Rev. David Rodgers, minister of Killala, was appointed by the Board of Missions to preach in Ballina on Sabbath evenings. His ministrations were blessed in retaining some valuable Presbyterians in connection with the Church, who otherwise would unavoidably have attached themselves to other denominations. During the nine years in which Mr. Rodgers supplied the Ballina station great changes took place in the population of that town; and his congregation felt the effects of the removal of many who had been steady attendants at his evening services. Afterwards there was an influx of Presbyterian settlers, which rendered the maintenance of a morning service desirable. The Rev. Archibald Lowry, afterwards minister of 1st Donegal, was accordingly appointed to take charge of the station. He preached his first sermon there on the 18th of August, 1844, and continued to officiate regularly till his removal to Roundstone, County Galway, in November, 1845. Mr. Lowry's work was twofold—first, to minister to the Presbyterians on the Sabbath and undertake their partial oversight; and, secondly, to act as itinerant agent in connection with the Irish schools, both of which duties he discharged with singular zeal and faithfulness. In November, 1845, the Rev. Thomas Armstrong, a licentiate of the Monaghan Presbytery, took charge of the Ballina Station, the Irish School and Roman Catholic Mission department having been specially assigned to the Rev. Mr. Brannigan. Having been erected into a congregation, the people presented a call to Mr. Armstrong, who was ordained the first minister of Ballina on 6th May, 1846. For some years public worship was maintained in a schoolroom; the inconvenience connected with this served to retard the progress of the congregation. A very suitable site having with difficulty been obtained, a church was built, and was formally opened for public worship by the Rev. Henry Cooke, D.D., LL.D., in July, 1851. A comfortable manse was also erected, and a schoolhouse, and subsequently an orphanage, in connection with the mission schools, under the superintendence of the Rev. Robert Allen, who for seventeen years was a regular member of the congregation, and materially assisted in its early struggles. The Rev. Robert Allen died on 1st April, 1865. The Rev. Thomas Armstrong, having been appointed his successor by the General Assembly, resigned the pastoral charge of Ballina on 8th April, 1868. Mr. Duff was ordained on the 30th of December, 1868; and on the 31st January, 1877, he removed to St. George's, Liverpool. The Rev. T. R. Cairns, formerly minister of Moy, was installed in the pastoral charge on the 24th October, 1877, and resigned on the 26th of August, 1879, on his appointment to the colonial field of New Zealand. The Rev. John Cairns was installed on the 29th of October of the same year.

BALLINGLEN.

In the year 1845 the Rev. Mr. Brannigan was appointed by the students of the General Assembly's Collegiate Classes in Belfast to take the oversight of the Irish Schools, and at the same time to act as itinerant missionary over a large tract of country. Before the end of 1846 twelve mission stations were formed. On the appointment of the Rev. Robert Allen to the superintendence of the Connaught Schools, Mr. Brannigan was directed to confine his labours more immediately to the Ballinglen district. From this station a memorial was presented to the General Assembly in 1848, signed by more than eighty persons, of whom a majority were originally Romanists, praying to be taken under the care of the Church. A commission having been appointed to inquire and report, the prayer of the memorial was granted, and Mr. Brannigan at once undertook the collection of the funds necessary for the building of the church, which was opened free of debt for divine service in 1850, by the Rev. Dr. Cooke, of Belfast. For a time the cause was well sustained, but emigration having set in, few of the original adherents remain, although at the census of 1861 over 150 registered themselves as Presbyterians. In November, 1864, both church and manse were burned down, but being insured, were rebuilt in 1865. Mr. Brannigan died in November, 1874, in the 29th year of his ministry and the 58th of his age. Mr. William Fearon was ordained January 26th, 1876, and resigned January 30th, 1879; and was succeeded by the Rev. James Wilkin, who was ordained on the 10th of April, 1879.

BALLYMOATE.

ABOUT the year 1760 a number of settlers from Ulster, with a few from Scotland, came to this district, with a view to the introduction of the linen manufacture. They were organized into a congregation, and ministered to successively by the Rev. Messrs. Nesbit, King, Caldwell, Scott, and Fleming. For many years the congregation flourished, but owing to emigration and other causes in 1850, when the present minister, the Rev. John Dewart, who was ordained here on the 9th of October of that year, entered upon the charge, it was greatly reduced. Since then a manse and offices have been erected, a church rebuilt, and a schoolhouse, with teachers' apartments, in 1865. The whole stands on a plot of ground, held by lease in perpetuity. In the face of many difficulties the congregational attendance is steady. The day-school is largely attended by Romanists, while there is reason to believe that the Lord's cause is making progress in the locality. Mr. Dewart becoming infirm, Mr. Joseph Northey, a licentiate of the Derry Presbytery, was ordained his assistant and successor on the 3rd March, 1886.

BOYLE.

THIS congregation is chiefly composed of Presbyterians from the North of Ireland. When the Rev. John Hall (now D.D., of New York), came as a missionary to Camlin, he preached fortnightly in the Wesleyan Chapel at Boyle. Mr. Hall having accepted a call from 1st Armagh, he was succeeded by the Rev. James Robinson, who commenced a Sabbath evening service in the courthouse, but changing the hour of service to mid-day, the use of the courthouse was withdrawn. The worshippers then rented a place for meeting, and in 1857 were organized into a congregation. Immediately after, in consequence of ill-health, Mr. Robinson left Boyle, when the Rev. Robert Alexander Caldwell succeeded to the pastorate in 1858. Mr. Robinson died on the 27th of June, 1858. A church and manse have been built, at a cost of £955, on a site kindly presented by Captain Robertson. The church was opened, almost clear of debt, for divine service in May, 1859. In October, 1863, Mr. Caldwell left for Australia; and was succeeded by the Rev. David M'Kee, who, after remaining about eighteen months, accepted a call to Ballywalter. Mr. John Watson, who was ordained on the 13th November, 1866, succeeded to the pastorate.

CASTLEBAR.

THE congregation of Castlebar thus originated. The Rev. Mr. Brown, upon his settlement in Turlough in 1854, commenced to preach in Castlebar, for a time in the courthouse, and afterwards in a schoolroom, every Sabbath evening. The building of a church was contemplated, but the impossibility of procuring a site retarded efforts in this direction for several years. When hope was on the brink of expiring, help came providentially from an unexpected quarter. Dr. Christie proposed, through his agent, Mr. John C. Lawrence, to dispose of his property in Charles Street, which was held by lease in perpetuity. The purchase was completed by the transfer of the lease to three trustees, of whom one was the late Rev. John Edgar, D.D., LL.D. Thus the property was acquired for the General Assembly in November, 1861. The purchase was for £300, of which Dr. Edgar paid £200. In November, 1863, the church was built, and opened for public worship by the apostle of temperance. The church of

Castlebar was made a joint-charge with Turlough by the General Assembly, and is now known by the name of "Turlough and Castlebar."

CLOGHER.

APPLICATION was made to our church in 1848 on behalf of a few neglected families in and about Clogher that they might be supplied with the means of grace. For three years preaching was continued every alternate Sabbath by the Rev. Messrs. Killen, Hall, and Dewart, each remaining for about twelve months. It was then proposed to be taken up by the students in connection with the General Assembly. To this they agreed; and at the close of the session of 1850-51 the Rev. John Barnett was appointed their first missionary to Clogher. Mr. Barnett remained till June, 1856, when he removed to Carlow. He was succeeded by the Rev. James Megaw, who left for Australia in April, 1858. The Rev. Samuel Johnston was appointed as the third missionary in June, 1858. The Rev. S. L. Harrison succeeded in January, 1873, and removed to Dromore West in March, 1878. Mr. James S. Smith was ordained as his successor in July, 1879. Miss Elizabeth Holmes, a lady of singular piety and zeal, to whose munificent encouragement the origin of the congregation must be traced, died on the 9th of June, 1877. Her remains are interred in the place to which her labours were so much devoted.

CREEVELEA.

IN January, 1832, a number of Scotch families came to settle at Drumkeeran, County Leitrim, with the intention of opening iron and coal mines. The Rev. James Heron, of Sligo, visited and occasionally preached to them on week days. A temporary place of worship was soon fitted up, and regular services conducted by members of the Presbytery. Mr. John Ashmore was appointed a constant supply, and after a short time was ordained on the 15th December, 1852. The church was maliciously burned down on the night of the first Sabbath of 1853, but was immediately rebuilt, and all went on satisfactorily for about four years, when the ironworks were abruptly suspended, and most of the Scotch families returned to their native land. At present there is a good church and comfortable manse. In addition to the charge of Creevelea, Mr. Ashmore conducts divine service in Manorhamilton, Dromahaire, and Collooney with great usefulness.

DROMORE WEST.

THIS congregation dates its origin from the year 1846. At that time the Rev. Mr. Brannigan commenced his labours in Connaught.* He gained an opening in this district for preaching. His early services were conducted in a private house, and the meetings were well attended both by Protestants and Romanists. In 1847 the use of a barn was kindly granted to him, where for a year he held a stated Sabbath service, with an encouraging congregation. This he continued until 1848, when the Rev. Matthew Kerr entered upon the field as stated missionary, and carried on the work which had been commenced with such marked success. In July, 1848, the heads of families attending the services forwarded a memorial to the General Assembly, praying that a church should be erected, and that the congregation might be permanently established. Through Mr. Kerr's instrumentality a commodious house was erected and opened for public worship in May, 1850. A flourishing day-school was conducted in it during the week. The first communion was observed in June, 1850. In 1857 a manse was erected, and in 1860 a new schoolroom. Through the indefatigable exertions of Mr. Kerr, all was left free of debt. In June, 1862, Mr. Kerr resigned. Mr. S. E. Wilson was ordained to the charge on the 5th April, 1864. On his resignation in October, 1872, the congregation again became vacant. The Rev. Thomas Armstrong was installed on the 28th of May, 1873, and resigned 10th November, 1875. Mr. D. S. K. Coulter was ordained here on the 17th of May, 1876, and resigned 15th January, 1878. The Rev. S. L. Harrison, who was installed here on the 6th of March, 1878, resigned on the 17th of May, 1883. The Rev. William Stuart was installed on the 5th of September, 1883.

HOLLYMOUNT.

DURING the years 1851, '52, and '53 some Scotch and

* Mr. Brannigan could preach in Irish. He was a convert from Romanism.

Northumbrian families settled in this neighbourhood. Others followed in 1856. In the spring of 1852 the Rev. John Hamilton, of Turlough, visited the colonists, and occasionally officiated among them. In 1853 Mrs. Lindsay, of Hollymount House, gave the use of a schoolroom in the village for divine service, and here they continued to worship till 1856, being supplied at first by the Presbytery, until, in August, 1853, Mr. James Love was ordained the first minister of the congregation. In the spring of 1862 he removed to Queensland; and in the month of June following, Mr. Samuel Wilson was ordained to the pastorate. In consequence of ill-health he removed to Australia in January, 1863. In the same month the Rev. Andrew Brown, of Turlough, received a call from the congregation, and was installed on the 17th of February, 1863. A church and manse were erected at a cost of £1200. The church was opened for public worship in 1856, with a debt still remaining of £350, which has since been entirely removed by the noble and persevering efforts of the congregation.

KILLALA.

KILLALA (Mullafary) was originally known by the name of Moywater, as the church then stood near the river Moy, about three miles from its present position. For a time it was connected with Sligo, under the ministry of the Rev. Samuel Henry, and became a separate charge about 1698. Its first settled minister was the Rev. James Pringle, who having demitted the pastorate of Ballindreat, in July, 1699, entered upon his labours in the beginning of June, 1700. Mr. Pringle died January 1st, 1707; and was succeeded by the Rev. James Wallace on the 25th of August, 1709. In June, 1720, he removed to Moville, County Donegal. A long vacancy followed. In 1733 Mr. William Wilson was ordained to this charge by the Presbytery of Letterkenny. In 1746 Sir Arthur Gore wrote a sympathetic letter to the Synod in reference to his melancholy situation. He died January 12th, 1781; and was succeeded by the Rev. Isaac Barr, formerly minister of Ray, County Donegal. About 1792 Mr. Barr resigned the charge; and in December, 1795, the Rev. Alexander Marshall, formerly minister of Turlough, was installed. Mr. Marshall died on February 28th, 1819; and Mr. David Rodgers was ordained on the 11th September, 1820. Mr. Rodgers becoming infirm, Mr. Hamilton Magee was chosen as his assistant, and ordained on the 8th of August, 1849. On the removal of Mr. Magee to the superintendence of the Roman Catholic Mission in Dublin, Mr. John Wilson was ordained here on the 14th of March, 1854. Mr. Rodgers died in June, 1859. Mr. Wilson, having been appointed missionary to Queensland, was succeeded by Mr John Wilson, who was ordained on the 31st December, 1862. Mr. Wilson having removed to Lecumpher, Presbytery of Tyrone, the Rev. George Clarke Love was installed as his successor on the 1st of April, 1885. Mr. Love demitted this charge on his removal to Killeter; and on the 3rd of February, 1886, Mr. Thomas Edwards, a Licentiate of Derry Presbytery, was ordained here.

NEWPORT.

THE first Presbyterian family settled in Newport in 1851. Others followed, and in a short time a small Scotch colony was formed into a congregation. They were first ministered to by the Rev. David Adair, of Westport, assisted during the summer of 1853 by Mr. Grant, a theological student of the Free Church of Scotland, who left in October of the same year. The Rev. George S. Keegan has been in charge of the station since October, 1853. He was ordained by the Connaught Presbytery in March, 1854; and in August, 1857, the people were organised into a congregation. For four years worship was held in the courthouse, kindly granted by Sir Richard A. O'Donnel. At last efforts were made; a church was built; and on the 3rd of June, 1857, it was opened by the late Rev. John Macnaughtan, of Belfast; and in April, 1864, was pronounced free of debt. For several years past many of the congregation have emigrated, and the numbers are thus greatly reduced; but those who remain have made praiseworthy efforts to sustain the Lord's cause. A beautiful manse has been lately erected, which, by the help of a generous public, is now nearly free of debt.

SLIGO.

THE Rev. Samuel Henry was the first minister of this congregation of whom there is any record. He was ordained to the joint-charge of Sligo and Moywater (Killala) by the Presbytery of Convoy in May, 1695.* In July, 1698, Moy-

* The ordination is said to have taken place at Monreagh, between St. Johnston and Derry.

water was separated from Sligo, which latter was still under Mr. Henry's care. In 1727 Mr. Henry resigned the pastorate of Sligo and settled at Abbeyfoile. He was succeeded by Mr. Luke Ash, son of Captain Ash,* one of the defenders of the city of Derry during its eventful siege in 1689. Mr. Ash was ordained to the pastoral charge of Sligo by the Presbytery of Letterkenny on the 9th of August, 1732. He died in Sligo in 1742; and was succeeded by Mr. Hugh Nesbit, who was ordained on the 5th of May, 1756. Ballymote congregation was joined to Sligo about 1760. Mr. Nesbit died in 1778; and was succeeded by Mr. Joseph King, who was ordained by the Presbytery of Clogher on the 4th of August, 1784. Mr. King demitted the pastorate of Sligo in 1797; and was succeeded by Mr. Booth Caldwell, who was ordained about the close of the same year. Mr. Caldwell was a man of prayer and devoted piety. He laboured successfully in Sligo till his death, which took place on the 24th October, 1810. The next minister was Mr. Jacob Scott, who was ordained on March 19th, 1811, to the joint-charge of Sligo and Ballymoate. In 1823 Mr. Scott was appointed by the Synod of Ulster to labour exclusively in Ballymoate. Sligo henceforth became a separate charge. Mr. James Heron was ordained to the pastorate of Sligo on the 18th March, 1824. The officiating ministers on the occasion the Rev. Messrs. Bleckley, of Monaghan; Cunningham, of Minterburn; and Kennedy, of Corboy. Mr. Heron becoming infirm, Mr. Moffatt Jackson, A.M., was ordained as his assistant and successor on the 11th of April, 1855. Mr. Heron died on the 28th of July, 1860.

TURLOUGH.

About the middle of the eighteenth century, Colonel Robert Fitzgerald, the proprietor of an estate here, signified his intention of letting his lands to northern tenants, whereupon several families, principally from the Counties of Down and Donegal, settled upon his property. These families found that, though settled in one of the most beautiful parts of Connaught, they had a great disadvantage in being deprived of the ordinary means of grace. A deputation

* Captain Ash was married to the daughter of Mr. Rainey, a rich Presbyterian of Magherafelt, who established an endowed school there, still in existence.

accordingly waited on Colonel Fitzgerald to ask his counsel and encouragement in the matter of obtaining for them a minister of their own persuasion. As the colonists consisted of Presbyterians and Episcopalians, each party wished a minister of their own denomination. The colonel said, as one minister would be sufficient for both, he would put it to the vote, and give his vote with the majority. On the vote being taken, it was found that the Presbyterians had the majority. A call was made out in favour of the Rev. Henry Henry. Mr. Henry, who removed to Connor, was succeeded by the Rev. Mr. Marshall, who resigned the charge in 1795. In the same year the Rev. Mr. Hall was called to be the minister, who continued until his death in 1824. The Rev. John Hamilton followed, continuing until his death in May, 1854. Mr. Andrew Brown was ordained in September, 1854. Mr. Brown resigned this charge in January, 1863. Mr. John Cairns was ordained in Turlough the same year. The Rev. John Cairns demitted the charge in September, 1879; and was succeeded by the Rev. James Steen in May, 1880.

WESTPORT.

In the year 1776 a considerable number of Presbyterians, encouraged by the Earl of Altamont, settled in the town and vicinity of Westport. In the absence of any Presbyterian service, some of these and their descendants became united with other denominations. The Rev. James Hall, of Turlough, occasionally visited, preached, baptised, and administered the Lord's Supper among them. This state of things being represented to the Presbyterian Committee of Dublin, the Rev. James Horner and Rev. John Birch were deputed in 1821 to make inquiry and report. On their return the Rev. Henry Cooke (afterwards of Killyleagh) was sent to officiate for a few Sabbaths. A room in the market-house was granted for public worship by George Clendinning, Esq. He was succeeded by the Revs. Messrs. Bleckley, Monaghan; Johnston, Tullylish; Gardiner, Clare; Crozier, licentiate; and Henry Dobbin, Lurgan. A memorial was presented by the Rev. James Horner to the Synod of Ulster, the result of which was the formation of the Presbyterians of Westport into a congregation, under the care of the Presbytery of Dublin. The congregation was supplied with ordinances by the Rev. Messrs. H. Kidd, James Steele, Thomas

Dougald, and Joseph Bellis; and, after an interval of some months, Mr. Robert Creighton, of the Presbytery of Tyrone, was ordained first pastor of the congregation by the Revs. J. Horner, James Morgan, of Carlow; and J. Hall, on the 23rd of December, 1823. The service was performed in the market-house, and was largely attended, the Marquis and Marchioness of Sligo being present. In 1830 the Marquis granted a site for a church and manse, the erection of which was soon after commenced. A lease of lives, renewable for ever, has been recently converted by the present Marquis into a fee-farm grant. Mr. Creighton died in 1834; and on the 4th of June, 1837, Mr. James Smith was ordained to the charge. In October, 1845, Mr. Smith accepted a call to Edgerton, Scotland. He was succeeded by Mr. David Adair, who was ordained on the 8th of May, 1846, and died of small-pox in 1854. On the 20th of June, 1855, Mr. Richard Smyth (afterwards D.D.) was ordained to the pastorate. Mr. Smyth accepted a call to 1st Londonderry in 1857. The same year Mr. John James Black was ordained on the 8th of September, and resigned the charge on the 3rd of May, 1859, having received a call to Ormond Quay Church, Dublin. The Rev. William White was installed to the pastorate on the 2nd of August, 1859. Mr. White having demitted the charge in June, 1874, Mr. Joseph M'Kinstry was ordained here on the 6th of January, 1875. He resigned in April, 1881; and Mr. Samuel G. Crawford, the present minister, was ordained on the 5th of October following.

BIOGRAPHICAL NOTICES.

THE FATHERS OF THE IRISH PRESBYTERIAN CHURCH.

Irish Presbyterians have reason to speak with the highest satisfaction of the men who laid the foundations of their church in Ulster. They were, in every sense, the excellent of the earth. Most of them had demonstrated their earnestness and self-denial by resigning situations in their native Scotland rather than violate their consciences; and they were distinguished by their high social position, as well as by their superior scholarship. Edward Brice, the first Presbyterian minister who removed from North Britain to take charge of a parish in the County of Antrim, was the brother of a Scottish laird, and had previously been a professor in the University of Edinburgh. Robert Blair, who became minister of Bangor, was a gentleman by birth, and a man of erudition. Josias Welsh, who settled at Templepatrick, was the great grandson of Lord Ochiltree, and had been a professor in the University of Glasgow. James Hamilton, the minister of Ballywalter, was an excellent scholar, and the nephew of Lord Clandeboye. Patrick Adair, who wrote the Narrative of the Irish Presbyterian Church, which has recently awakened so much interest, belonged to the influential family of the same name, one of whom is at present the proprietor of the estate of Ballymena. John Livingston, the minister of Killinchy, was a scion of the noble family of Livingston, so well known in the Scottish peerage; and was noted for his attainments in Latin, Greek, Hebrew, Arabic, French, Dutch, and other languages. The Episcopal writers who describe the early Presbyterian ministers of Ireland as a race of low fanatics evidently know nothing whatever of the matter. As a body they were in every respect immensely superior to the Episcopal clergy by whom they were surrounded; for these, by competent contemporary authorities, have been described generally as men of low birth, of no education, and of very little principle. Even Strafford speaks of them in the most contemptuous language.

WALTER TRAVERS, A PRESBYTERIAN,

THE FIRST REGULAR PROVOST OF TRINITY COLLEGE, DUBLIN.

It is a fact which should be generally known that Presbyterians were originally admitted to all the honours and emoluments of Dublin College. Walter Travers, the first regular Provost of the Irish University, was a Presbyterian minister. It cannot be said that his ecclesiastical peculiarities were unknown when he obtained this high literary appointment, for he had long before been distinguished as one of the most able and zealous of the English Non-conformists. He was so much opposed to any recognition of prelatical authority, that he passed over into Holland to obtain Presbyterian ordination. He was subsequently appointed lecturer at the Temple, a situation which he occupied for several years. At this time he came into collision with the celebrated author of the "Ecclesiastical Polity," commonly called by Episcopalians, "the judicious Hooker." Hooker, as Master of the Temple, preached in the forenoon—Travers, as lecturer, officiated in the afternoon. Fuller, himself an Episcopalian, thus speaks of their respective services: "Mr. Hooker's voice was low, stature little, gesture none at all—standing still in the pulpit, as if the posture of his body was the emblem of his mind, unmoveable in his opinions. Where his eye was left fixed at the beginning, it was found fixed at the end of his sermon. His sermons followed the inclination of his studies, and were, for the most part, on controversies and deep points of school divinity." Mr. Travers' utterance was graceful, gesture plausible, matter profitable, method plain, and his style carried in it ' a genius of grace' flowing from his sanctified heart. Some say that the congregation in the Temple ebbed in the forenoon, and flowed in the afternoon, and that the auditory of Mr. Travers was far the more numerous—the first cause of emulation betwixt them. But such as knew Mr. Hooker," adds Fuller in his own sly fashion, " knew him to be too wise to take exception at such trifles, the rather because the most judicious is always the least part in all auditories." These two preachers could not long act together harmoniously. Hooker was an abettor of Arminianism as well as a strenuous advocate of Prelacy, whilst Travers was a staunch Calvinist, and a most decided Presbyterian. It therefore frequently happened that the doctrine propounded from the pulpit in the morning was overturned in the afternoon, and as the two divines ranked among the most accomplished representatives of Conformity and Puritanism, the most eminent characters of the day took a deep interest in their controversies. Not only young law students, but such men as Sir Edward Coke, were to be seen earnestly listening to the sermons, and noting down the various arguments. As Travers was by far the more effective preacher, the high church party speedily took the alarm; for they considered that, were he to succeed in gaining over all the gentlemen of the legal profession to the cause of Presbyterianism, the stability of the existing hierarchy would be seriously endangered. The Archbishop of Canterbury accordingly interfered, and silenced the eloquent lecturer. As he was just entering the pulpit, on a particular occasion, to deliver the afternoon sermon, a low official appeared and served him with a notice to desist from preaching. He was in consequence obliged to announce abruptly that he had received such an order, and to dismiss the congregation. When Travers was thus under suspension by the Archbishop of Canterbury, his old friend, Adam Loftus, then Archbishop of Dublin, invited him to become Provost of the newly-erected Irish University. In accepting this appointment he was not obliged to conform to the Episcopal discipline, for the statutes of the University were originally so framed that its highest offices were open to evangelical Presbyterians. Travers presided over the College for a number of years, but the civil wars at length obliged him to leave the country. He died at an advanced age in England in rather limited circumstances. We think it right to add that Archbishop Ussher, the most illustrious scholar ever produced by Trinity College, Dublin, was educated under the care of a Presbyterian Provost. At an early period the Irish University was in fact regarded as a kind of asylum for learned Puritans; but, about forty years after its erection, high church influence succeeded in changing its constitution and in shutting out all, save Episcopalians, from its Provostship and Fellowships.

THE REV. SAMUEL HANNA, D.D.

This eminent minister of the Irish Presbyterian Church was born at Kellswater, Ballymena, in the year 1771. He was educated at the University of Glasgow, where he obtained the degree of A.M. in 1789; and in 1790 he was licensed as a preacher in connexion with the Synod of Ulster by the Presbytery of Ballymena. From his first appearance in the pulpit his ministrations were most acceptable. His voice was peculiarly sweet, and, at the same time so full and distinct that, without almost any effort, it could be heard throughout the largest building. The tone of his preaching was remarkably evangelical, and his prayers, into which he largely and most felicitously introduced the language of Scripture, breathed a spirit of unaffected piety. In 1794, he received a call from the congregation of Drumbo, near Belfast; but in consequence of some difficulties thrown in the way of his settlement, he was not ordained until the month of August of the following year. His reputation as a preacher continued steadily to advance; and on a vacancy occurring in the congregation of Rosemary Street, Belfast, in consequence of the resignation of the Rev. Sinclare Kelburn, he received a call from the people, and was installed in that church in the month of December, 1799. Dr. Hanna's settlement in Belfast was an event of great importance to the Presbyterian Church in Ulster. When he became pastor of Rosemary Street, the congregation was in a rather dilapidated condition; but under his popular and effective ministrations, it gradually revived. In all the religious movements which marked the early part of the present century, Dr. Hanna took a deep interest. He was a warm supporter of the Sunday School Society; and, so great was his zeal for the circulation of the Word of God, that he permitted a portion of his own dwelling-house to be occupied, for a considerable time, as a depository for Bibles and Testaments. In 1809 he reported to the Synod of Ulster, on the part of a committee with which he was connected, that he had received in the course of about twelve months, upwards of eleven hundred pounds for copies of the Scriptures, sold at a cheap rate, to the Presbyterian poor of the North of Ireland. When Missions began to attract public attention, they found an earnest advocate in Dr. Hanna, and it is a fact worthy to be recorded, that so early as 1811, he recommended the Synod of Ulster to support a mission to the Jews. In the following year, when the pious and eloquent Dr. Waugh, of London, appeared before the Synod, as a deputy from the London Missionary Society, Dr. Hanna espoused his cause, and ever afterwards proved a firm friend to that noble institution. At the annual meeting of the Synod in 1817, he was unanimously elected Professor of

Divinity and Church History. Many of the members of the Irish General Assembly, were trained for the ministry under his tuition. He lived to see a blessed change in the condition of Irish Presbyterianism. When he entered the ministry, Unitarianism occupied the high places of the Synod of Ulster, education was at a very low ebb, vital religion was almost extinguished, a missionary spirit was unknown, and infidelity was powerful and truculent. He left the church furnished with a staff of theological professors, firmly adhering to the Westminster Standards, united in one great body, with more than double the number of ministers and congregations, and supporting four or five great missionary schemes. When the Union was effected between the Synod of Ulster and the Secession Synod, he was unanimously chosen the first Moderator of the General Assembly of the Presbyterian Church in Ireland. He died in April, 1852, in the 82nd year of his age; and the immense concourse of mourners who followed his remains to the grave, evinced the deep respect with which he was regarded by the people among whom he had so long ministered.

JAMES SEATON REID, D.D.

THE REV. DR. REID, Professor of Ecclesiastical History in the University of Glasgow, and author of the "History of the Presbyterian Church in Ireland," died on Wednesday, the 26th of March, 1851, at Belmont, the seat of Lord Mackenzie, near Edinburgh, after an illness of about two months' duration. Dr. Reid was a native of Lurgan, and was born on the 19th of December, 1798, so that at the time of his death he was in the 53rd year of his age. He was the 21st child of his parents, Forrest and Mary Reid, and having been at an early period intended for the Presbyterian ministry, in connection with the Synod of Ulster, he went through the usual course of preparatory study in the University of Glasgow, and took the degree of A.M. in April, 1816. Having completed his theological education and obtained license, he received a call from the congregation of Donegore, where he was ordained on the 20th of July, 1819. Four years afterwards he received a unanimous call from the Presbyterian Church of Carrickfergus, where he was installed on the 19th of August, 1823. In the year 1827 he was unanimously chosen Moderator of the General Synod of

Ulster at its meeting in Strabane. The Arian controversy was then approaching its climax, and, in the responsible situation which he occupied, he displayed singular tact and judgment. In 1830 he was unanimously appointed Clerk of the Synod. In January, 1833, the University of Glasgow conferred upon him the honorary degree of Doctor of Divinity; and, about three years afterwards, he was elected a member of the Royal Irish Academy. In 1834 Dr. Reid gave to the public the first volume of his celebrated work, the "History of the Presbyterian Church in Ireland." The effect of this publication was most salutary. It was read with intense interest by the Irish Presbyterians, and it placed their Church before the empire in a position which it had never hitherto occupied. At the annual meeting of the Synod, in Derry, in June, 1834, the thanks of the body were voted to the author for his work, and measures were subsequently taken for extending its circulation. In the year following, the congregation of Carrickfergus presented to him a magnificent service of plate, valued at considerably more than £100. Dr. Reid's second volume was issued in June, 1837; and in the following month, at the meeting of the General Synod, he was appointed Professor of Ecclesiastical History, Church Government, and Pastoral Theology. This new chair having been soon afterwards permanently endowed by the Government, he resigned the charge of the congregation of Carrickfergus on the 6th of November, 1838, and subsequently fixed his residence at Belfast. On the 2nd of April, 1841, he was nominated by the Crown successor to Dr. Macturk as Professor of Ecclesiastical and Civil History in the University of Glasgow. On his removal to Glasgow, Dr. Reid still continued to manifest a deep interest in the prosperity of his native Church. During the agitation relative to Irish Presbyterian marriages he published a series of letters, displaying alike his powers of acute discrimination and his intimate acquaintance with the historical bearings of the controversy. In the midst of all his engagements in Glasgow, he found time to edit a reprint of Mosheim's Ecclesiastical History, to which he added a variety of valuable annotations. In the year 1849 he had occasion to repel an attack made upon his history by Dr. Elrington, of Trinity College, Dublin. At that time he published a number of letters in vindication of his statements; and, in the end, the substantial correctness of his narrative was admitted by Dr.

Elrington himself. His remains lie interred in the Sighthill Cemetery, in the neighbourhood of Glasgow. He left behind him a widow, six sons, and three daughters.

We are happy to be able to add that the Irish department of Dr. Reid's most valuable library was purchased by the General Assembly. It will thus be handed down in the Irish Presbyterian Church as a memorial of its historian. Many of the volumes are extremely rare, and not a few of them contain important manuscript notes, written by Dr. Reid himself. After his death, the Government, with a considerate kindness, which elicited universal commendation, settled a pension of £100 per annum upon his family. At his death, Dr. Reid left a considerable portion of an additional volume of the History of the Presbyterian Church in Ireland in a state ready for publication. He had also carefully revised the two volumes previously published.

THE REV. JAMES CARLILE, D.D.

On the 31st of March, 1854, the Rev. James Carlile, D.D., died at his residence in Dublin. His health had been for a considerable time declining, and his demise had been long anticipated. Dr. Carlile was a Christian of the highest type, and a minister of great ability and learning. His father was an eminent merchant of Paisley, and one of the magistrates of the town—so that his son enjoyed all the advantages of a superior education and of highly cultivated society. Dr. Carlile was settled as one of the ministers of Mary's Abbey, Dublin, in May, 1813. On several important occasions he distinguished himself in the Synod of Ulster by his talents as a debater. When the Irish National System of Education was established he was appointed one of the Commissioners, and to him the country is indebted for some of the best of the school-books issued by the Board. Late in life Dr. Carlile took charge of the Birr Mission, and for a considerable number of years acted as the pastor of the Birr congregation. He was remarkable for single-mindedness. He never seemed to consider his own interest or his own credit, and no matter what course he pursued in reference to any debated question, his brethren felt that he was entitled to their respect. He was an excellent linguist, and it is said that at an early period of his ministry he had read through the whole of the Old Testament in the original Hebrew. He has left behind several works of standard excellence. On his death-bed he exhibited singular serenity and cheerfulness. "Mark the perfect man, and behold the upright, for the end of that man is peace."

JOHN EDGAR, D.D., LL.D.

Dr. Edgar was born near Ballynahinch in the early part of the year 1798. His father, the Rev. Samuel Edgar, D.D., was minister of the Secession Church of that place, and also Professor of Divinity for the Secession Synod. When a student at the Belfast Academical Institution, John Edgar obtained distinguished honours, having carried off no less than four silver medals. On November 4th, 1820, he was ordained by the Seceding Presbytery of Down to the pastoral charge of the small congregation of Alfred Place, Belfast; and, in 1826, he succeeded his father as Professor of Divinity for the Secession Church. In 1829 he commenced the Temperance Reformation. His efforts to promote the establishment of temperance societies were prodigious. For this purpose he travelled, not only throughout the four provinces of Ireland, but also throughout Scotland and England. He published a vast number of tracts, sermons, and speeches on the subject. It has been calculated that the number of copies of his publications which have obtained circulation amount to upwards of a quarter of a million. He founded the Ulster Female Penitentiary, and rendered important service to almost all the benevolent institutions of Belfast. He resigned the pastoral charge of the congregation of Alfred Street in 1848, and, on the death of Dr. Hanna, became sole Professor of Systematic Divinity for the General Assembly. At the time of the famine in 1847, he raised a fund of many thousand pounds for the relief of the starving population of Connaught, and afterwards established many churches and schools in that province. In 1859 he visited America, in company with Messrs. Wilson and Dill, and returned home with £6,000 to assist in the evangelization of Ireland. He subsequently obtained contributions to the amount of £18,000 for the Church, Manse, and School Fund. He died in Dublin on the morning of the Sabbath, the 26th August, 1866.

THE REV. JAMES MORGAN, D.D.

Dr. Morgan was a native of Cookstown, where he was born on the 11th of June, 1799. His parents were pious and highly respectable. When very young he was brought under deep religious impressions, and he was thus led to turn his thoughts to the ministry as his future profession. During his attendance at College he was known to all his fellows as a student of whose eminent godliness there could be no doubt whatever. On the 21st of June, 1820—when barely twenty-one years of age—he was ordained by the Presbytery of Dublin as minister of Carlow. There had at one time been a Presbyterian congregation in that place, but it had become extinct about seventy years before. Under the young minister the newly-established church enjoyed great prosperity. When at Carlow, Mr. Morgan became acquainted with a goodly number of the most devoted of the clergy of the Established Church, and with them he enjoyed much pleasant and profitable fellowship. He took an interest in the great evangelical movements of the day, and did much to promote the progress of the Bible Society. At that time he also became acquainted with Dr. Doyle—the famous J. K. L., the Roman Catholic Bishop of Kildare and Leighlin—for whose character he ever afterwards entertained a sincere respect. About four years after his settlement at Carlow, Mr. Morgan removed to Lisburn, where he was installed on the 23rd of June, 1824. His ministry there produced a great impression. As a preacher he was singularly popular. His voice was excellent; his manner was grave and dignified; his expositions of Scripture were simple and practical; and all his addresses from the pulpit were remarkable for their evangelical unction. After remaining somewhat more than four years in Lisburn, he was removed to Belfast, where he was installed as minister of the newly-erected congregation of Fisherwick Place on the 4th of November, 1828. The capital of Ulster did not then contain the one-fourth part of its present population, and among all classes there was much indifference in regard to religion. The settlement of Mr. Morgan in it marks an era in its spiritual history. He declined to attend merely fashionable parties, where the evening was to be spent in card-playing or dancing. He gave all to understand that he was a minister of God; and that if they did not wish for his services in that capacity, they must dispense with his presence. Society, where his influence extended, began to assume a new tone; and wherever he spent an evening the conversation was good to the use of edifying, and religious exercises were never neglected. The large church of Fisherwick Place was soon filled by a congregation of attentive and devout worshippers. At that period the duty of spreading the Gospel had been greatly overlooked, and Mr. Morgan's first appeal to the congregation of Fisherwick Place, on behalf of the Home Mission of the Synod of Ulster, only elicited a contribution of £5. The Temperance movement originated the year after he became an inhabitant of Belfast; he joined ardently with Dr. Edgar in the cause; and he was one of the first subscribers to the Temperance Pledge. About the same time the Arians separated from the Synod of Ulster; a monthly magazine called *The Orthodox Presbyterian* was started in support of those adhering to the Westminster Standards; and Mr. Morgan long acted as the editor of this publication. The project of a union between the Secession Synod and the Synod of Ulster had Mr. Morgan's most cordial approval, and its consummation filled him with the highest satisfaction. The union was auspiciously inaugurated by the establishment of the Foreign Mission of the General Assembly. Mr. Morgan was appointed Secretary or Convener of the Committee in charge of this new enterprise. It was then considered by many a very bold undertaking when the United Church pledged itself to support two missionaries to the heathen; but from the first the congregation of Fisherwick Place entered heartily into the scheme, and stimulated many others to generosity by its large contributions. The number of missionaries was gradually increased; a large bequest from Mrs. Magee, of Dublin, rendered important service; and the Foreign Mission prospered greatly. Shortly after the union, the establishment of a Presbyterian College began to occupy the attention of the Church; and the minister of Fisherwick Place did perhaps more than any other single individual to raise the funds required for the erection of Assembly's College, Belfast. About this time he received the degree of D.D. from the University of Glasgow. Dr. Morgan acted systematically in all his proceedings; and thus it was that, with apparent ease, he could accomplish so much. When he acted as Moderator of the Assembly in 1846 the annual meeting of the supreme court of the Church was the shortest on record; for with admirable tact he managed to repress useless speechifying; the whole business was well done; but every one was kept to the point immediately under discussion, and no time was wasted. Dr. Morgan has left behind him various important publications. Among these may be mentioned his treatise on the Lord's Supper, his work on the Holy Spirit, and his exposition of the 1st Epistle of John. He possessed a truly catholic spirit, and cultivated a good understanding with ministers of other denominations. His constitution was never robust; and after a lingering illness, during which he enjoyed abundantly the peace of God, he died on the 5th of August, 1873, in the 75th year of his age.

THE REV. HENRY COOKE, D.D., LL.D.

Dr. Cooke was born in a cottage near Maghera on the 11th of May, 1788. As he grew up he enjoyed no superior advantages in the way of education. When a mere boy he entered Glasgow College; but, partly owing to his youth, and partly to his want of sufficient preparation, he was not specially distinguished as a student either in literature or science. It was not until nearly the close of his career at the Scottish University that some of the professors discovered indications of those extraordinary powers which afterwards attracted so much attention. When still very young he was ordained as assistant to the Rev. Robert Scott, the aged minister of Dunean, on the 10th of November, 1808. This appointment supplied him with a very slender maintenance —amounting, we believe, to about £30 per annum—and on the 13th of November, 1810, he resigned the situation. For a short time afterwards he resided as tutor in the family of the late Alexander Brown, Esq., of Kells, near Ballymena. During his residence there he greatly signalised himself by the ability he displayed when unexpectedly required to officiate on a Sacramental Sabbath. The congregation of Connor, to which Mr. Brown belonged, is, as many of our readers are aware, one of the largest in connection with the Presbyterian Church in Ireland. It then reckoned a thousand families, and the services on communion occasions were quite sufficient to task the energies of two or three ministers. At such times the Rev. Henry Henry, the worthy pastor, had usually two assistants. It so happened, however, that one of his helpers failed him; and when about to enter the pulpit on the morning of the Sacramental day, he received an intimation to the effect that the other, in consequence of an accident, was unable to attend. To add to the perplexity, when Mr. Henry had gone through the preparatory exercises, and when he was addressing the first table, he became unwell, and was, with difficulty, able to finish his address. What was now to be done? Six tables remained; the services of each commonly occupied half an hour; and even the presiding minister was laid aside. In this emergency the elders bethought themselves of the young preacher who was residing in the family of Mr. Brown, and who happened to be present. Mr. Cooke at once responded to their application for aid; and, greatly to the satisfaction of all who heard him, conducted all the rest of the service. He delivered six consecutive table addresses, equally varied and appropriate, to the astonishment and delight of his auditors. Shortly after his resignation of Dunean, Mr. Cooke received a call from the highly respectable congregation of Donegore, where he was installed as pastor on the 22nd of January, 1811. His fame now rapidly increased; he began to attract notice at the annual meetings of the Synod of Ulster; and his services were occasionally solicited, even by congregations in Belfast, on public occasions. When in Donegore he was permitted for some time to attend the University of Dublin, where he applied himself specially to the study of medicine. At this period he was in the habit of travelling every Saturday to Carlow, and of preaching on the Lord's day to a congregation recently collected in that place. Mr. Cooke was minister of Donegore upwards of seven years. He then removed to Killyleagh, where he was inducted into the pastoral charge on the 8th of September, 1818. Though in his third congregation he was still only thirty years of age. About this period he became acquainted with a gentleman from whose intercourse he derived much benefit, and whose rame should be mentioned with reverence by all leal-hearted members of the Presbyterian Church to the latest generations. Captain Sidney Hamilton Rowan, a scion of the noble house of Clandeboye and Clanbrassil, was then a member of the Killyleagh congregation, in which he acted as an elder with exemplary faithfulness. He exercised the happiest influence over the mind of the young minister. Mr. Cooke had, indeed, before professed the doctrines of the

Westminster Confession of Faith; but his principles were not matured; and he had not hitherto been known as a champion of Orthodoxy. A sermon which he published when in Donegore is tainted with the spirit of the prevailing moderatism. On his settlement in Killyleagh he applied himself earnestly to the study of the system of evangelical truth, and in 1821 appeared publicly as the assailant of Arianism. The Unitarians of England had become so confident that they employed one of their ministers, named Smithurst, to propagate their principles in the North of Ireland. When visiting Ulster their missionary did not overlook Killyleagh, as it was understood there were some who might be expected to sympathise with him in that neighbourhood. Mr. Cooke and his elder were present at the service; and, at the close, Captain Rowan stood up and said to the stranger, "These are not the doctrines our minister teaches, and here he is." Mr. Smithurst professed his readiness to enter forthwith into discussion; but Mr. Cooke, not yet much practised in debate, and in the presence of an adversary who came armed at all points, deemed it prudent to use a little caution. He said that as Mr. Smithurst had chosen his own time and manner of procedure, he would do the same—that he would, on an early day, before his own congregation, refute the statements advanced; and then, should the stranger wish to reply, he would be prepared to meet him in discussion. About this period Mr. Cooke is said to have shut himself up day after day in his own meetinghouse, as the most retired place to which he could resort, and to have studied with intense care the great doctrine of which he was henceforth to be so distinguished an advocate. In due time he more than fulfilled the pledge he had given to the Unitarian apostle. After having vindicated the Deity of Christ in his own pulpit, he followed Mr. Smithurst to Downpatrick, Saintfield, and other towns adjacent, where he replied to the discourses of the missionary in the hearing of large and attentive audiences. Discovering that he had an antagonist with whom he could not grapple, the Englishman soon found it expedient to return to his own country.' About this time the influence of the Arian party began to preponderate in the management of the Belfast Academical Institution. The election of the late Rev. William Bruce to the Professorship of Greek created much dissatisfaction; and soon afterwards the Arian controversy fairly commenced in the Synod of Ulster. Mr. Cooke was at once recognised as the leader of the Orthodox majority, and the discussions at the annual Synodical meetings awakened intense interest all over the province. The champion of Trinitarianism had to contend against no common antagonists, as the late Dr. Montgomery of Dunmurry, one of the most brilliant speakers of his day, backed by a considerable number of able supporters, formed the opposition. The exertions of Mr. Cooke at this time were prodigious. Whilst leading his party with consummate ability in the Church Courts, he was obliged to repel many assaults made on him in the newspapers. He encountered his adversaries on the platform, and assailed their principles in the pulpit. When the struggle was approaching a crisis, he itinerated throughout many parts of Ulster; preached more than once almost daily; roused ministers and people to a sense of the importance of the emergency; and thus prepared the way for the victory which he soon afterwards achieved. The announcement of his appearance in any locality was sure to attract a large audience. His magnificent voice, his noble elocution, his stirring eloquence, and his masterly expositions of his great theme produced an immense impression. The people felt that the Calvinism which they loved was illustrated by the genius of a true orator, and they hung with admiration on his lips. Immediately after the separation of the Arian party from the Synod of Ulster in 1829, Mr. Cooke removed from Killyleagh to Belfast, where he ministered nearly forty years. For a large portion of this period he conducted three services every Lord's day in May Street Church. We have heard it stated, on excellent authority, that on his first settlement in the capital of Ulster, the Sabbath collections, consisting almost exclusively of halfpence, amounted to £10 daily. All strangers who visited Belfast were sure to repair to May Street to hear the great Presbyterian preacher; and, until old age began to impair his energies, his popularity remained unabated. Even in his declining years the "old man eloquent" often electrified his audience by flashes of his youthful fire. About the time of his settlement in Belfast, Mr. Cooke received the degree of D.D. from Jefferson College, United States. Trinity College, Dublin, subsequently bestowed upon him the degree of LL.D. In 1824 he was Moderator of the Synod of Ulster. In 1841, the year after its formation, he was unanimously elected Moderator of the

General Assembly. In 1862 he was re-elected. In 1847 he
was chosen Professor of Sacred Rhetoric and Catechetics in
the Assembly's College, Belfast. In 1846 he was appointed
by Her Majesty's Government Distributor of the *Regium
Donum* for the Synod of Ulster. He held this office till his
death. Dr. Cooke has left behind him little that will give
posterity a true idea of his extraordinary powers, for he may
be pronounced one of the most gifted of Irishmen. The
Irish Presbyterian Church has possessed men of more
extensive learning; but she never, perhaps, had a minister of
such rare genius. His name will live in the history of this
country; and, on one memorable occasion, he attracted the
attention of the whole empire by the intrepidity with which
he rolled back the tide of the Repeal agitation. When the
late Daniel O'Connell appeared in Belfast to prosecute his
favourite scheme, Dr. Cooke challenged him to discuss
publicly the merits of the question; and when the great
demagogue shrunk from the encounter, he exposed himself
to intolerable derision. O'Connell soon found that the
atmosphere of the North did not suit him; and the hero of
so many monster meetings, who could wield at will the fierce
democracy in Leinster, Connaught, and Munster, was obliged
to take his departure from Belfast under the protection of a
strong escort of police and military. On another occasion,
when the late Rev. Dr. Ritchie of Edinburgh came to Belfast
to prosecute the agitation of the Voluntary question, and
when, supported by a number of Irish brethren who held his
views, he met Dr. Cooke in a public discussion, the May
Street minister single-handed was more than a match for all
his antagonists. It is well known that, before the challenge
was accepted, he had made no special preparation for the
debate; but, with the help of one or two literary friends, he
speedily marshalled his materials; and such was the
versatility of his talent, and so wonderful the quickness of
his apprehension, that he appeared on the arena as if armed
at all points. It was on emergencies of this kind that his
powers appeared to peculiar advantage, for his most brilliant
speeches were purely extempore. At such times wit and
irony, logic and declamation, imagination and passion, were
called simultaneously into play, and their combined effect
was irresistible. In 1829, when the late Dr. Montgomery
attacked him in a carefully prepared speech of three hours'
duration, Dr. Cooke replied impromptu. For two hours his

auditors listened to an outpouring of eloquence such as they had never heard before. Their enthusiasm rose as he advanced; they at length found it totally impossible to repress their feelings; and, towards the close, he was frequently interrupted by thunders of applause. On that decisive day Arianism received its death-blow in the supreme court of the Presbyterian Church in Ireland. The Irish Presbyterian Church is specially bound to honour the memory of Dr. Cooke. To him, under God, it has been mainly indebted for its deliverance from the incubus of Unitarianism. His life was devoted to the service of his Church, and in labours he was most abundant. His assiduity in attending Church Courts was very exemplary. Until he was bowed down by the infirmities of old age, he was to be seen early and late in his place in the Presbytery, the Synod, and the Assembly. His interest in the business never seemed to flag; and, in cases of difficulty, his brethren were often greatly indebted to him for sound advice. After an illness of several months' duration, he died on Sabbath, the 13th of December, 1868, in the eighty-first year of his age, and the sixty-first of his ministry. His remains were honoured by a public funeral. All classes and denominations joined in the demonstration of respect. His statue, standing in front of the Royal Academical Institution, is a life-like likeness of this great orator.

WILLIAM KIRK, ESQ.

Mr. Kirk was a native of Larne, in the County of Antrim. He was trained to the linen business by his maternal uncles, the Messrs. Millar, who carried on that branch of trade very extensively in the neighbourhood of Ballymena. His uncle, Captain William Millar, was a Justice of the Peace for the County Antrim, and possessed considerable landed property at a place called the Ross, not far from the village of Connor. At an early period of life Mr. Kirk removed to Armagh, where he acted for some time as agent for one of the Belfast banks. He subsequently settled at Keady, where he long most successfully carried on the linen business. Some years before his death he purchased the Keady estate, comprising about eleven thousand acres. This estate is in a highly improved condition. Some of the finest machinery in Ireland is erected on it. The post town of Keady has grown, within the last fifty or sixty years, from a poor village into a place of considerable size, with a thriving population. It was a pleasant sight to see Mr. Kirk on the Lord's day sitting in the Keady Presbyterian Church, like a patriarch, in the midst of his tenantry. In many other parts of Ulster the landlord frequents one place of worship and the tenantry another; but here the lord of the soil was not the less honoured because he met for worship with the farmers and cottiers on his estate. Mr. Kirk long acted as a Justice of the Peace, and a member of the Grand Jury of the County Armagh. He was also a Deputy-Lieutenant of the County. In 1868 he was returned a third time as M.P. for Newry. When he previously represented the borough he was universally regarded as one of the most able and intelligent of the members for Ireland.

JOHN GETTY, ESQ., BEECHPARK, BELFAST.

LARNE holds a distinguished place in the history of the Irish Presbyterian Church. From an early period it has enjoyed the services of eminent ministers; and some of the best lay friends of Presbytery have been found in its neighbourhood. The Shaws of Ballygally, whose grand old castle may still be seen by the traveller as he passes to Glenarm, once ranked amongst its most steadfast supporters. The Agnews of Kilwaughter Castle, in former days, were also attached to its communion. The late William Kirk, Esq.—so long M.P. for Newry, and so well known for his services to the Church of his fathers—was a native of Larne. Sir Edward Coey—now a household name among the Presbyterians of Down and Antrim—was born in the same locality. During the year 1874 the Irish Presbyterian Church was reminded in another way how much she owes to Larne. Mr. John Getty, who died in April, 1874, was born there. One of his ancestors was a minister of Larne; and to the last Mr. Getty cherished a strong attachment to the place of his nativity. For many years he carried on business in Belfast; he was universally respected as a merchant; and he at length acquired a considerable fortune. In early life he had been brought under deep religious impressions; and throughout a long career he sustained the character of an humble and consistent Christian. As he had no family—for he never married—his household wants were easily supplied;

and for many years he was in the habit of devoting the large residue of his annual income to benevolent and religious objects. His liberality was soon widely known; and very many were the applications for assistance he received from all quarters. Every good cause was sure to receive support from him. When he thought the claim deserved it, he did not hesitate to give £500 in a single donation. He was always well supplied with £5 and £10 notes; and he evidently took special pleasure in their distribution. His brother Robert—who was his partner in business, and who died unmarried several years before him—was a man of a kindred spirit. Both devoted their substance to the advancement of religion. Any one who looked into the countenance of the late Mr. John Getty might discover an illustration of the truth of the statement of Scripture that wisdom's ways are ways of pleasantness, and that all her paths are paths of peace. Though living almost in solitude, he was a cheerful and happy man. He had realised the comforts of religion. He will be known in all time to come as one of the largest benefactors of Irish Presbyterianism. By his will he bequeathed property in perpetuity worth £3,000 per annum to the General Assembly—chiefly for missionary purposes. He died at his residence at Beechpark, after an illness of some continuance, in the 78th year of his age.

JAMES KENNEDY, ESQ., J.P.

On the 12th of September, 1878, James Kennedy, Esq., of Rosetta, near Belfast, finished his mortal career. He had for many years held the commission of the peace for the two counties of Down and Antrim; and had long been well known as one of the most enterprising, intelligent, and prosperous citizens of the capital of Ulster. He had been brought up under the pastoral care of the late Dr. Hanna, of Rosemary Street Presbyterian Church; and in his later years he took pleasure in recounting the number of useful and distinguished fellow-citizens who in youth had enjoyed the pastoral instructions of that eminently evangelical minister. Mr. Kennedy was subsequently a member of May Street Presbyterian Church; and, though differing in political views from its gifted pastor, he greatly admired Dr. Cooke, because of his genius, his eloquence, his benevolence, and his Christian chivalry. In his declining years Mr. Kennedy was connected with the Presbyterian congregation of Newtownbreda. In the Assembly's College, Belfast, of which he was a trustee, he always evinced the deepest interest. He may be considered as the founder of the Students' Chambers; he again and again made contributions to the College Library; and the curious Japanese bell—with the tones of which the students are so familiar—is his gift. Mr. Kennedy was strongly attached, by intelligent conviction, to the doctrine and polity of the Presbyterian Church; and, when in company with persons of other denominations he found it necessary to repel attacks made upon it; he could defend it with singular tact, good temper, and ability. At the time of his death Mr. Kennedy had approached the mature age of three score and ten.

WILLIAM M'COMB, ESQ.

Mr. M'Comb was born at Coleraine on the 17th of August, 1793. His father was engaged in business in Londonderry, and as he had frequently occasion to visit the capital of Ulster in the way of trade, he became acquainted with Mr. Thomas O'Neill, a well-known Belfast merchant, who had a wholesale warehouse in Donegall Street. His son William was apprenticed to this gentleman; and he thus formed an intimacy with Sinclare Ramsey, a youth of kindred spirit, who was being trained in the same establishment. At this period infidel principles were propagated with zeal in the North of Ireland, and the disciples of Thom Paine had set up a school in Smithfield, where they disseminated their pernicious doctrines. The two young apprentices had the Christian courage to attempt to counteract this movement, and for some time conducted a Sabbath-school in the same locality. This was one of the earliest Sabbath-schools established in Belfast. Mr. M'Comb had a taste for teaching, and for years he conducted with great success the Brown Street Daily School. He took a deep interest in the Arian controversy, and with the view of giving increased circulation to a sound religious literature, he commenced his career in High Street, Belfast, in 1828, as a bookseller and publisher. Shortly afterwards a monthly periodical, under the title of "The Orthodox Presbyterian," was started by the leaders of the Synod of Ulster, for the purpose of expounding their views, and of defending themselves against the assaults of the Unitarians. The original editors were Dr. James Seaton

Reid, the Historian of the Irish Presbyterian Church; Dr. Cooke, and Dr. Morgan; but its management devolved chiefly on the minister of Fisherwick Place. Mr. M'Comb was the publisher; and, at a most critical period in the history of Irish Presbyterianism, this magazine rendered efficient service to the Orthodox cause. At a later period the subject of this notice commenced the *Presbyterian Almanac*,* with which his name is still associated. Mr. M'Comb cherished an enthusiastic admiration of Dr. Cooke, to whom he had a considerable resemblance in personal appearance; and in June, 1842, when the great Presbyterian leader— then the Moderator of the General Assembly—repaired to Carrickfergus to celebrate the bi-centenary of the erection of the first Irish Presbytery in that classic town, he was accompanied by the poet-laureate of the Church. On that occasion Mr. M'Comb was stirred up to compose one of the happiest of his metrical productions.† This bi-centenary poem called forth the special applause of Dr. Chalmers. At a much earlier date Mr. M'Comb had signalised himself in this department of literature. His "Dirge of O'Neill" appeared in 1817, and his "School of the Sabbath" in 1822. A few months previous to his retiring from business in 1864, he published, in a handsome volume, a complete edition of his poems. Some of them are very tender; some exhibit a fine appreciation of the beauties of nature; and all are evidently the production of a devout spirit. He took an active interest in the education of the dumb, the deaf, and the blind; and when an institution for their benefit was about to be established in Belfast, he wrote some beautiful verses, which awakened much public sympathy in favour of the movement. He was an ardent lover of flowers, and spent many pleasant hours in his garden attending to their cultivation. He died at his residence in Colin View Terrace, Belfast, in the eightieth year of his age, on the 13th of September, 1873. He left behind him a widow and an only daughter.

---

* The first issue was for the year 1840.

† "Two Hundred Years Ago."

THE REV. WILLIAM M'CLURE, DERRY.

This well-beloved and distinguished minister, who closed his mortal course on the 22nd February, 1874, was the son of William M'Clure, Esq., a highly respectable Belfast merchant. His mother was the daughter of the Rev. John Thomson, of Carnmoney, a man who in his day was one of the leading members of the Synod of Ulster. Until the year 1825, the Synod had no printed code of discipline; but Mr. Thomson was thoroughly acquainted with Church law; and, in cases of difficulty, his decision as to the course of procedure commanded general deference. Mr. M'Clure was licensed to preach the gospel by the Presbytery of Ballymena; and in 1825 he was ordained as one of the pastors of the Presbyterian Church of Derry, and as colleague to the Rev. George Hay. He had a very pleasing voice, and excellent delivery; and his discourses exhibited a pure taste and an evangelical spirit. He soon became known all over the church as a most kind-hearted, zealous, and upright minister. He was the very soul of hospitality, and a fine specimen of a Christian gentleman. For nearly thirty years he acted as Convener of the Colonial Mission of the General Assembly. To the young ministers who emigrated to the Colonies, he acted the part of a father; and his memory will be long cherished by many who are now settled at the ends of the earth. In the city of Derry he possessed much social influence. He was one of the authors of the "Plea of Presbytery;" and in 1847 he was chosen unanimously to the office of Moderator of the General Assembly. At the time of his death he was nearly 73 years of age. Sir Thomas M'Clure, Bart., of Belmont, Belfast, is his only surviving brother.

SYDNEY HAMILTON ROWAN, ESQ.

Captain Rowan was born in 1789. He was the son of Archibald Hamilton Rowan, Esq., who was the lord of the manor of Killyleagh, and who was connected with the noble houses of Dufferin, Bangor, and Roden. Mr. A. H. Rowan, though a nominal Presbyterian, held Unitarian views, and was implicated in the treasonable proceedings connected with the rebellion of 1798. His son in early life joined the army; and it was when in England on military duty that he was brought under deep religious impressions. After some time he gave up the life of an officer, and settled at Killyleagh. His eminent piety soon attracted attention, and he was chosen a ruling elder. He was in this position, when Mr. (afterwards Dr.) Cooke was chosen minister of the congregation; and his influence with the young pastor soon led to most important results. He had much to do with the commencement of the controversy which terminated in the removal of the Arian party from the Synod of Ulster. At a later period of his life he removed to Downpatrick, and he was mainly instrumental in establishing there the present congregation connected with the General Assembly. He was one of the first elders of the new congregation. He died at Downpatrick on Sabbath evening, the 14th of November, 1847, in the 58th year of his age. Dr. Cooke delivered the funeral address, of which the following is an extract:—" He was one whose example recommended the religion he professed. In him the rich and the poor, the learned and the ignorant—the young in their joyousness, and the aged in their sorrows—in him each read that religion was a reality. The example manifested itself especially in plans and works of benevolence. His was not a religion of many words. It lay more in the deep thoughts, the fixed purposes, the sympathetic feelings, and the untiring energies of well-doing. His heart was a heart of love. He sought and seized every opportunity of doing good. For the erection of schoolhouses and the organization of Sabbath and Daily Schools, his best exertions were put forth. Nor can I overlook his invaluable contributions to our schools and families in his admirable edition of the Shorter Catechism; a work which, however simple (for everything truly Scriptural is simple), will remain a monument of his profound knowledge of evangelical principles, and of his successful efforts for their propagation. Let me turn your attention to a kindred view of the character of our departed brother—his zeal and liberality in the cause of Christian missions. He was the founder of our Home Mission, which originated in the Synod of Ulster, and from which, as from a root which the Lord has blessed, has sprung up our Foreign Missions to the heathen and the Jews. Our Church Extension cause has also been deeply indebted to him—nor would it be difficult to point to several of our most hopeful settlements that, under divine providence, owe their existence entirely to his zeal and labours. When we think of his memory our sorrow must be mingled with joy—with sorrow because he is gone, but with joy for the graces with which God had endowed him, and the blessed and abiding work which he was called and enabled to effect. And the power by which, under God, all these things were done was the power of humble, unostentatious, ardent piety, which conducted to self-denial, self-restraint, and self-government: a piety which looked upon self, till self became as nothing: a piety which looked upon Christ till Christ became 'all in all.' One other feature in the character of our departed brother may not be omitted—his sterling, unswerving, indestructible friendship, of which so many are private witnesses, and of which a public evidence may be seen in his firm and unswerving attachment to the Presbyterian Church—the Church of his Fathers and of his Fatherland. Under repulsive agencies from within, and attractive agencies from without, he still adopted the motto of his noble ancestor,* 'I adhere to the Presbyterians.' We undervalue not the excellencies of any faithful Protestant Church; we heartily wish them all 'God speed;' but we glory in the memory of the man who laboured, prayed, and wrote for the purity and efficiency of our Zion."

WILLIAM TODD, ESQ., OF RATHGAR.

THIS gentleman died on the 12th September, 1881, at the advanced age of seventy-nine. He was a Scotchman by birth, but he was long resident in Ireland, and, as a merchant in Dublin, he acquired an ample fortune. Strongly attached to the Presbyterian Church, he contributed to its various schemes with princely generosity. The Assembly's College, Belfast, of which he was a trustee from the time of its erection, had a large share in his benefactions. Very recently he was one of the five contributors who gave £1,000 each to its Professorial Endowment Fund. The Magee College, Londonderry, also received from him a number of most generous gifts. For about forty years he acted as an elder of the Presbyterian Church, Adelaide Road, Dublin; and, notwithstanding his advanced age, he continued to a comparatively late date to attend regularly the weekly prayer meeting, as well as the noon-day and evening diets for worship on the Lord's Day. He died full of faith and hope.

* The first Lord Clandeboye.

Immediately before he ceased to breathe, his face became suddenly lit up as with heavenly radiance, and his eyes seemed to be gazing with delight on the opening glories of the better land.

MISS HAMILTON, OF MOUNT VERNON.

THE Irish Presbyterian Church has been adorned by many "honourable women," but it has seldom possessed so fine a specimen of female excellence as that presented by the late Miss Elizabeth Hamilton, of Mount Vernon, near Belfast. Though of the most gentle and unobtrusive disposition, the light of her piety could not remain concealed; and for upwards of thirty years she was known all over the North of Ireland as one of the most generous supporters of every Christian enterprise. She used to say that she would wish to have a stone in every new place of worship, and every new manse erected by the Assembly. She took the deepest interest in all the Missions of the Church: in the year of famine she exerted herself much for the relief of the suffering poor in Connaught; and she was one of the largest contributors towards the building of the Assembly's College. Miss Hamilton valued much the privilege of a gospel ministry; and was most exemplary in her attendance on Sabbath ordinances. She stimulated many to works of benevolence: and her name should be held in honour by the Irish Presbyterian Church to the latest generations. She knew from experience that it is "more blessed to give than to receive," and she never appeared to be so happy as when performing some act of munificence. This excellent lady died in peace at Mount Vernon, during the week of prayer, on the 6th of January, 1869.

JOHN SINCLAIR, ESQ., OF THE GROVE.

DURING the year 1856 Belfast lost one of her worthiest and most distinguished citizens. On the 17th day of January of that year John Sinclair, Esq., departed this life, aged 47. Mr. Sinclair was a man of few words, but his deeds were most eloquent. In his native town he introduced a new scale of giving for the cause of the Gospel. Every one admitted that he was endowed with superior intellect, and that he possessed mercantile genius of the highest order, so that his large donations at first created much astonishment. But others at length caught the infection of his generosity, and not a few began to wonder that they did not sooner see how pitiful had been their religious contributions. The Conlig Presbyterian Church was built almost entirely at his expense. Shortly before his death, Mr. Sinclair, with his partner, gave the princely subscription of £1,000 to the Church and Manse Fund of the General Assembly. It is an instructive fact, that this bountiful giver was an eminently prosperous merchant. "The Sinclair Seaman's Church" will long remain a memorial of the respect in which he was held by the community; for never before has Belfast erected such a noble and costly monument to any of her citizens. " He being dead yet speaketh;" and the sight of this edifice should be a sermon to every merchant who passes along our quays.

THE REV. JOHN THOMSON.

The Rev. John Thomson was born at Shilvodan, near Connor, in the county Antrim, on the 2nd January, 1741. He was educated at the University of Glasgow, where he entered the Logic class in 1760. He matriculated in 1761, and his name is thus entered in the Register of the University in his own hand writing.

"Johannes Thomson, filius natu secundus Caroli, Mercatoris in Comitatu de Antrim in Hibernia."

During this session he was a student of the Moral Philosophy class under the celebrated Adam Smith. He was licensed to preach the gospel by the Presbytery of Ballymena, and ordained as minister of Carnmoney, near Belfast, on the 10th of March, 1767, as successor to his uncle, also named John Thomson. He thus was placed at an early period of life in charge of one of the largest congregations in connexion with the General Synod of Ulster. In the discharge of his ministry he was distinguished by diligence and faithfulness. Never resting contented with the superficial performance of any duty, it was his great aim that everything should be done systematically and in the best and most efficient manner. His theology was the theology of the Reformation, and of the Westminster Confession of Faith. He expounded the doctrines and enforced the truths of the gospel, with a power and clearness that could not fail to command the attention, and enlighten the understanding. At a time when latitudinarian views were somewhat fashionable, and orthodoxy of sentiment was regarded in many quarters with coldness and contempt, he became, if possible, more decided and uncompromising than ever, in upholding the truth. He always firmly held, and boldly proclaimed the whole counsel of God. His preaching was at the same time eminently practical. He was careful to shew that Christianity did not consist in cold and barren orthodoxy, but in real spiritual life—the result of living faith in the Son of God. Much as he excelled as a preacher, he did not fail in the other departments of the ministry. No man was better fitted than he to guide the serious inquirer, to comfort the mourner, to reprove, rebuke, and exhort with all longsuffering and doctrine. Under his superintendence the system of the Presbyterian Church was fully carried out in the parish of Carnmoney. The congregation was divided into districts, over each of which an elder was placed, and the session were accustomed to hold frequent meetings, to consider the religious and spiritual condition of the people. Public baptism was never discontinued as in other places, and banns were proclaimed previous to the celebration of marriage. In addition to his pastoral visitations from house to house, Mr. Thomson was in the habit of assembling the members of his flock, in their respective districts, for special religious instruction. The writer of this can never forget some occasions of this kind, when in childhood he was permitted to be present. These scenes were deeply interesting. The people, old and young, rich and poor, often met under an humble roof. Their venerable pastor was received with every token of respect: at his approach their countenances filled with delight—in their hearts they welcomed him. After the offering of praise and prayer, and the reading of a portion of God's Word, the examination proceeded; and not the young merely, but all, of every age, were expected to answer. The Shorter Catechism—that admirable compend of theology—formed the basis of instruction. Thus were the doctrines of the gospel deeply and clearly impressed upon the mind. Thus did the faithful pastor take heed to all the flock committed to his care—thus did he warn every man, and teach every man, in all wisdom, that he might present every man perfect in Christ Jesus. Mr. Thomson took a very active part in the public affairs of the Church. He had studied with deep attention its constitution and laws, and was regarded as a high authority in all questions and cases of difficulty. In such cases he was almost always appealed to for his opinion, and that opinion seldom failed to decide the finding of the body. At the request of the General Synod of Ulster, he drew up and published an abstract of its laws and previous decisions, from its earliest records to the year 1800. He consequently held a very conspicuous place in the courts of the Church, especially in the Synod, where his addresses were always heard with the utmost attention and respect. For several years previous to his death, he had been senior member, or father of that reverend body. As a member of Church courts, he was eminently distinguished for the correctness of his views, the uprightness of his conduct, his unwillingness to swerve in the smallest degree from what he knew to be right, and his determination to enforce, without respect of persons, the most strict and rigid discipline. The training of candidates for the ministry, was a subject to which he directed much of his attention; and into all the arrangements that were calculated to promote their instruction, and prepare them for future usefulness, he entered with paternal solicitude. Though he had himself been a student of Glasgow college, and naturally attached to that ancient and honoured seminary of learning, he was one of the first to appreciate and advocate the importance of home education. His interest in the progress and training of the students of the Church, was manifested to the last by his invariable attendance on the public examinations, at the close of each collegiate session, at the Belfast Institution; and by the anxiety he evinced for the establishment of a theological faculty. At one its annual meetings in the beginning of this century, the Synod of Ulster appointed four of its ministers to take steps for the circulation of Bibles and Testaments among the people. Mr. Thomson was one of that number. This circumstance deserves to be noticed, not merely on account of the confidence reposed in the zeal and activity of these brethren, but because it is an evidence of the early interest taken by the Presbyterian Churches in Ireland, in the dissemination of the Scriptures, and proves that they had directed their energies to this all-important work. This Committee was subsequently dissolved in consequence of the formation of the Hibernian Bible Society and its branches in the North. Towards the close of his ministry he removed to Belfast, and became one of the guardians of several religious and benevolent institutions in that town. Mr. Thomson's services were invaluable. Economical in the application of public funds, yet most anxious to relieve the destitute and distressed, he guarded against every species of useless expenditure, with zeal, which never wearied, and circumspection which never relaxed. His marriage with Jane, eldest daughter of the Rev. William Laird, second minister of the congregation of Rosemary Street, Belfast, took place in November, 1770. His private life and character gave weight to his public instructions. His deportment was calm and dignified, yet kind and thoughtful. As a Christian bishop he was given to hospitality. Habitually cheerful and lively, delighting in the society of his relatives and literary friends, he rendered his domestic circle ever attractive and happy. Though firm and decided in his public conduct, no sternness marked his private walk and conversation. All unnecessary restraint was removed by the benignity and suavity of his manners. A kind husband, an affectionate parent, a steady friend, a faithful pastor, an undaunted witness for the faith as it is in Jesus—his whole life evinced the transforming influence of the gospel. Believing in Christ—rejoicing in Him as all his salvation, and all his desire, he calmly passed away, with a hope full of immortality, on the 23rd March, 1828, having entered on the sixty-second year of his ministry, and eighty-seventh of his life. He was interred in the parochial burying-ground of Carnmoney, and a simple monument now marks his resting-place. His funeral was attended by upwards of forty clergymen of various religious denominations. One sentiment of profound respect for the character of this venerable man pervaded the assembled multitude; and his remains were consigned to the tomb, amidst demonstrations of public respect and tears of private and personal affection. While he lived he was "an ensample to the flock." Being dead he is not forgotten. "The memory of the just is blessed."

THE REV. HENRY JACKSON DOBBIN, D.D.

THIS distinguished minister died at Ballymena on the 15th of April, 1853. His grandfather, the Rev. Henry Jackson, who was minister of Banbridge, is said to have been related to General Jackson, President of the United States of America. His father, the Rev. Hamilton Dobbin, was minister of Lurgan. Mr. Henry Jackson Dobbin was ordained to the pastoral charge of the congregation of Hillsborough by the Presbytery of Belfast on the 18th September, 1833. He soon distinguished himself in the courts of the Church by his gentlemanly bearing, his knowledge of the forms of ecclesiastical procedure, and his graceful and fluent elocution. In 1837 he removed to the congregation of First Ballymena, where he was installed on the 20th of June in that year. In 1848 Dr. Dobbin was chosen Moderator of the General Assembly. He was the youngest minister who has ever yet occupied that position; and yet he discharged its duties with a tact and dignity which elicited universal admiration. He possessed a fine taste and a highly-cultivated mind. His library, at his death, consisted of upwards of 2,000 volumes. Nearly forty ministers, including some who had travelled from a great distance, followed his remains to the grave. The immense concourse of individuals at his funeral, not a few of whom were in tears, attested the regard in which he was held by all classes of the community.

JAMES YOUNG, Esq., BALLYMENA.

In the beginning of the present century, Ballymena, though now a large and flourishing town, presented a not very attractive appearance. With three or four exceptions, the houses were all thatched; and a steep hill in Church Street, between the Market-house and Meeting-house Lane, was a formidable obstacle in the way of the old mail coach, as it moved forward on its course from Belfast to Londonderry. The parish church, standing in the middle of the present graveyard, was frequented by few worshippers; and the incumbent,—a quiet gentleman, and, after the fashion of the times, a Justice of the Peace—was not likely very much to disturb the thoughts of any of his auditors who might feel inclined to repose. The Meeting-house—for there was only one in the town—was a larger building; but it was in a state of naked simplicity, as it was without stove, ceiling, or flooring. An apartment adjoining, in which the elders met, was used on weekdays as a schoolhouse; and there a goodly number of the children of the place received the elements of education. The elders connected with the meeting-house were persons of more or less influence. One of them—Thomas Dickey—was the agent of the Ballymena estate: another, William Gihon, J.P., was one of the very few Presbyterian magistrates then in Ulster; another, Dr. Patrick, was the father-in-law of Mr. Brown, one of the merchant princes of the great American Republic; another John Killen—long the session clerk—was the father of Dr. Killen, President of Assembly's College, Belfast; and another, was William Young. Mr. Young was noted for his shrewdness and overflowing wit; and a venerable queue, which adorned his powdered head, marked him out in the congregation as one of the leaders of the people. He had four sons, one of whom, John, died before he had well reached manhood. The other three—James, William, and Robert—lived to advanced age. Robert, who recently passed away full of years, and high in the esteem of all who knew him, became an eminent linen merchant; and dispensed an ample fortune with a generous hand. William—the father of John Young, Esq., D.L., Galgorm Castle—was a skilful physician, who had large practice throughout the County Antrim. At a more advanced period of life he was manager of one of the Ballymena banks. He possessed a vigorous intellect; he could clothe his thoughts in most graceful diction; and, somewhat after the manner of the late Archbishop Whateley, he delighted, by putting questions and suggesting difficulties, to test the logical capacity of those with whom he engaged in conversation. James, who was the senior member of the family, was of a different temperament. He had few words, and was disposed to shrink from publicity. It was understood that the three brothers were in partnership in business. A stranger might have seen nothing very striking in his appearance; but those who knew him well were aware that he possessed great mercantile ability, and that to his sagacity and sound judgment the firm was very much indebted for the high commercial position which it eventually occupied. In early life James Young was brought under deep religious impressions. He was a great admirer of the late Dr. Cooke, the eloquent minister of May Street Church, Belfast; and he was wont to say that he had derived from him his first clear views of the way of salvation. During the Arian controversy Mr. Young took a decided stand on the side of orthodoxy; and he was one of those men who, like the late Captain Rowan, of Downpatrick, contributed to give a tone to public sentiment in the neighbourhoods with which they were connected. At that period the doctrine of many people in Ballymena was not well-defined. Dr. Cooke visited the place during the crisis of the Arian struggle, preached to a crowed congregation, and thus rendered important service to the Trinitarian cause. On this occasion he received a hearty welcome and hospitable entertainment at the house of Mr. James Young. Mr. Young was one of the founders of the Wellington Street Congregation of Ballymena. He saw that the town was greatly in want of church accommodation. A pew in the old meeting-house was considered a kind of freehold, and was sometimes sold at a high price. Many of the people found it impossible to obtain sittings. But when the formation of a new congregation was proposed, the erection of the building was dreaded as a most formidable undertaking. Mr. James Young at once put down his name for £30—then deemed an extraordinary contribution; and afterwards added largely to this subscription. The new congregation proved to be a great success; the Rev. Alexander Patterson was chosen as the first minister; the spacious edifice was soon filled in all its parts with attentive worshippers; and Mr. James Young was chosen by common consent as one of the first elders. He contributed much, by his social influence and weight of character, to the prosperity of the congregation. Missions were then in their infancy; but from the first he was a bountiful contributor to their support. His purse was open for the encouragement of every good design. When he found that, in the midst of his mercantile engagements, he could not perform the duties of an elder so efficiently as he desired, he employed a pious Scripture reader, and paid him a handsome salary, to visit his district of the congregation. In the early part of 1847—the year of famine—Mr. Patterson, his minister, fell a victim to the prevailing fever. Mr. Young, who had been his steady and generous friend, sincerely deplored his removal. In a few weeks afterwards he was himself numbered with the dead. He died, as he had lived, in peace; and left behind a most fragrant memory. Long will the people of Ballymena remember the humble Christian walk, the large-heartedness, and the look of benevolence which beamed from the countenance of Mr. James Young. Our readers will be gratified to hear that

William Young, Esq., J.P., of Fenaghy, one of the elders of our Church, is the son of the gentleman of whom we have supplied this brief notice. Mr. William Young is the author of the paper on "Systematic and Proportionate Giving as the Secret of Successful Church Finance," which has obtained such extensive circulation, and rendered such service to our Sustentation Fund. Infidels may scoff; but no one who respects the statements of Scripture will despise the blessing of being descended from a godly parent. There is assuredly truth in the declaration of the Psalmist: "The children of thy servants shall continue, and their seed shall be established before thee."

SIGNIFICATION OF NAMES OF PLACES,

COMPILED CHIEFLY FROM DR. JOYCE'S "ORIGIN AND HISTORY OF IRISH NAMES OF PLACES."

Aghadoey—Duffy's field.
Anaghlone—marsh of the meadow.
Anahilt—the doe's marsh.
Ardglass—the green height.
Ardstraw—the height of (or near) the river bank.
Armagh—Macha's height.
Armoy—the eastern plain.
Athlone—the ford of Loan. Loan was a man's name, formerly common.
Aughnacloy—the field of the stone.
Badoney—the tent of the church.
Ballina—the ford mouth of the wood.
Ballinderry—the town of the *derry* or oakwood.
Ballindreat—the town of the bridge.
Ballinglen—the town of the glen.
Ballybay—the ford mouth of the birch.
Ballycarry—the town of the weir.
Ballycastle—the town of the castle.
Ballyclare—the town of the plain.
Ballygowan—the town of the smiths.
Ballygrainey—the sunny town.
Ballymena the middle town.
Ballymoney—the town of the shrubbery.
Ballymoate—the town of the moat.
Ballynahinch—the town of the island.

Ballynure—the town of the yew.
Ballyshannon—the mouth of Shannagh's ford. Shannagh or Seanach was a man's name in common use.
Ballywillan—the town of the mill.
Belfast—the ford of the sandbank, referring to a sandbank across the mouth of the Lagan.
Benburb—the proud peak.
Billy—the ancient tree.
Boveva—Maev's hut.
Brigh—a hill.
Broughshane—the border of John or Shane.
Carlingford—the fiord or bay of the deceitful pool. referring to a whirlpool existing there.
Carlow—the quadruple lake. There is a tradition that the Barrow anciently formed four lakes.
Carrickfergus—Fergus's rock.
Castlebar—Barry's castle.
Castlereagh—the grey castle.
Cavan—a hollow.
Cavanaleck—the hill of the flagstone.
Clare—a board.
Clogher—stony.
Clones—Eos's meadow.
Clontibret—the meadow of the spring.
Clough—the stone or stone building.
Coleraine—the ferny corner. It is said to have been formerly covered with ferns.

SIGNIFICATION OF NAMES OF PLACES.

Comber—the confluence, or the place where two rivers meet.
Conlig—the stone of the hounds.
Connor—the oakwood of the wild dogs.
Convoy—the plain of the hounds.
Cork—the swampy place.
Corlea—a grey round hill.
Creggan—rocky land.
Crumlin—the curved glen.
Cushendun—the foot of the river Dun.
Cushendall—the foot of the river Dall.
Derry—an oakwood.
Donaghadee—the Church of loss.
Donagheady—the church of Keedy or Caidoc. Caidoc is said to have been a companion of Columbanus.
Donegal—the fortress of the foreigners.
Donegore—the fortress of the O'Curras.
Donoughmore—the great church. It is said that Christian worship was established at a very early period at all places with the prefix *Donagh* or *Donough*.
Douglass—the black stream.
Drogheda—the bridge of the ford.
Dromore—a great ridge.
Drum—a ridge.
Drumbo—the cow's ridge.
Drumquin—Con's ridge.
Dublin—the black pool.
Dunboe—the fortress of the cow.
Dundalk—the fort of Delga, a chieftain who is said to have built a fortress near this place.
Dundonald—Donall's fortress.
Duneane—the fortress of the two birds.
Dunfanaghy—Finncha's fort.
Dungannon—Geanan's fort.

Dunluce—a strong fort.
Dunmurry—Murray's fort.
Enniskillen—Cethleen's island. Cethleen or Kehlen is said to have been the wife of a celebrated pirate chieftain.
Fahan—little.
Faunet—the sloping ground.
Fintona—the fair-coloured field.
Finvoy—the white or bright plain.
Garvagh—rough land.
Glennan—a little glen.
Glenwherry—the glen of the cauldron or deep whirlpool.
Gransha—a grange.
Hillsborough—so called from being the residence of the *Hill's*, or Downshire family.
Inch or Inish—an island.
Keady—a hillock.
Killinchy—the Church of the island.
Letterkenny—the hill-slope of the O'Kannanans, a powerful tribe.
Lisburn—the burned fort.
Loughbrickland—the lake of Bricrenn, an old Ulster chieftain.
Lurgan—a long low ridge.
Macosquin—the plain of Cosgran, a man's name.
Maghera—the little plain.
Monaghan—the little shrubbery.
Moneymore—the great shrubbery.
Mountmellick—the boggy land of the marsh.
Mourne or Mor-rin—the great hill.
Moville—the plain of the ancient tree.
Newry—the yew tree.
Portadown—the landing-place of the fortress.
Portrush—the landing-place of the peninsula.

s

Ramoan—Modan's fort.
Raphoe—the fort of the huts.
Rathfriland—Freelan's rath.
Ray—the fort.
Sion—the fairy mount.
Sligo—the shelly river.
Strabane—the fair or white river-holm.
Stranorlar—the river bank of the floor.
Tandragee—the backside to the wind.
Tobermore—a great well.
Tullamore—a great hill.
Tully—a little hill.
Tullylish—the hill of the fort.
Turlough—a lake which dries up in summer.
Urney—the oratory or prayer-house.

PUBLICATIONS SOLD BY JAMES CLEELAND,
26 ARTHUR STREET, BELFAST.

THE PLEA OF PRESBYTERY in behalf of the Ordination, Government, Discipline, and Worship of the Christian Church, as opposed to the Unscriptural character and claims of Prelacy. By Ministers of the General Synod of Ulster. Third Edition. 2s.

CATECHISM ON THE GOVERNMENT AND DISCIPLINE OF THE PRESBYTERIAN CHURCH. Tenth Edition. Forth-ninth Thousand. Price 1d., or 7s. per 100.

THE SHORTER CATECHISM, with Scriptural Proofs, Explanations of Words and Phrases, and Additional Questions. Compiled by S. Hamilton Rowan, Elder of the Presbyterian Church, Downpatrick. Price 1½d., or 8s. 4d. per 100.

THE SHORTER CATECHISM, with Short and Easy Questions and Answers, to which is added the Systematic Verse Book, containing Proofs for Scripture Doctrines. Price ½d., or 3s. per 100.

THE VOLUNTARIES IN BELFAST: Report of the Discussion on Civil Establishments of Religion, held in Belfast, between the Rev. J. Ritchie, D.D., Edinburgh, and the Rev. H. Cooke, D.D., LL.D., Belfast. Fourth Edition. Tenth Thousand. 8vo. Price 1s.

THE REPEALER REPULSED.—The Repeal Invasion of Ulster; Dr. Cooke's Challenge; and the Great Conservative Demonstration in Belfast. With appropriate Poetical and Pictorial Illustrations. Price 2s.

AUTHENTIC REPORT OF THE SPEECH OF THE REV. HENRY COOKE, in reply to the Rev. Henry Montgomery, at Cookstown, July, 1828. Price 3d.

BRIEF HINTS ON THE LORD'S SUPPER, for the use of Young Persons. By the Rev. Dr. Morgan. Price 1d., or 7s. per 100.

TRIAL OF ANTICHRIST for High Treason against the Son of God. Price 4d.

THE UNITARIAN MARTYR. A defence of John Calvin in the case of Michael Servetus. By the Rev. W. D. Killen, D.D., Second Edition, with a Reply to the Rev. John Scott Porter's Letter. Price 4d.

KILLINCHY, OR THE DAYS OF LIVINGSTON. A Tale of the Ulster Presbyterians. By the Author of "Our Scottish Forefathers." Price 1s.

LIFE OF ROBERT BLAIR, Minister of the Gospel sometime at Bangor, Co. Down. Price 8d.

www.ingramcontent.com/pod-product-compliance
Lightning Source LLC
Chambersburg PA
CBHW021623250426
43672CB00037B/1382